get writing

Sentences and Paragraphs

First Canadian Edition

Mark Connelly
Milwaukee Area Technical College

Melanie Rubens
Seneca College

Heather McAfee
George Brown College

Peter C. Miller
Seneca College

THOMSON
NELSON

Australia   Canada   Mexico   Singapore   Spain   United Kingdom   United States

THOMSON

NELSON

**Get Writing: Sentences and Paragraphs,
First Canadian Edition**
Authors:
Mark Connelly, Melanie Rubens, Heather McAfee, and Peter C. Miller

**Associate Vice President,
Editorial Director:**
Evelyn Veitch

**Editor-in-Chief,
Higher Education:**
Anne Williams

Director of Development:
Lenore Spence

Marketing Manager:
Sandra Green

Developmental Editor:
Beth Lariviere

**Executive Director,
Content and Media
Production:**
Renate McCloy

**Director, Content and Media
Production:**
Susan Calvert

**Senior Content Production
Manager:**
Julie van Veen

**Production
Service:**
International Typesetting
and Composition

Copy Editor:
Cathy Witlox

Proofreader:
Debra Gates

Indexer:
Edwin Durbin

Production Manager:
Cathy Deak

**Production
Coordinator:**
Ferial Suleman

Design Director:
Ken Phipps

**Interior Design
Modifications:**
Andrew Adams

Cover Design:
Faith Design

Compositor:
International Typesetting
and Composition

**Photo/Permissions
Researcher:**
Lynn McIntyre

Printer:
Edwards Brothers

**Library and Archives Canada
Cataloguing in Publication**

Get writing: sentences and
paragraphs / Mark Connelly . . .
[et al.].—1st Canadian ed.

Includes index.

ISBN-13: 978-0-17-625163-5

ISBN-10: 0-17-625163-4

1. English language—Sentences.
2. English language—Paragraphs.
3. English language—Rhetoric.
I. Connelly, Mark, 1951–

PE1441.G48 2006   808'.042
C2006-905582-3

Brief Contents

Contents

PART 2   DEVELOPING PARAGRAPHS   27

Chapter 3   Developing Topic Sentences and Controlling Ideas   29

Chapter 4   Supporting Topic Sentences with Details   45

Chapter 14   Writing Sentences   212

Chapter 15   Avoiding Fragments   229

Chapter 16   Building Sentences Using Coordination and Subordination   242

Chapter 17   Repairing Run-ons and Comma Splices   260

Chapter 18   Correcting Misplaced and Dangling Modifiers   276

Chapter 19   Understanding Parallelism   291

PART 4   UNDERSTANDING GRAMMAR   303

Chapter 20   Subject–Verb Agreement   305

Chapter 26   Using Other Marks of Punctuation   411

Chapter 27   Using Capitalization   428

Preface

The Goals of *Get Writing*

Get Writing helps students acquire skills and develop confidence as writers by engaging them in their own writing. *Get Writing* assumes that students have things to say about their goals, families, jobs, schools, personal interests, and the world around them. Throughout the book students are given opportunities to express themselves on a range of topics and to then examine and improve their words, sentences, and paragraphs. Above all, *Get Writing* connects critical thinking (what students are trying to say about a topic) with grammar and mechanics (what they have written about the topic).

Approach

Get Writing guides students to improve their writing by asking two questions.

1. **What are you trying to say?**
   Why did you choose this topic?
   What do you want readers to know about it?
   What details are important?
   What is the best way to organize your ideas?

2. **What have you written?**
   Are your words effective?
   Do your sentences clearly express what you wanted to say?
   Can readers follow your train of thought?
   What mechanical errors detract from your message?

Get Writing is designed to serve a variety of students, including recent high school graduates, working adults returning to school, and those for whom English is a second language. Writing exercises and sample paragraphs cover a range of interests—sports, history, politics, science, the media, popular culture, minority issues, and world events.

Get Writing does not teach writing in isolation. It assists students with the writing tasks they will encounter in other courses and in their jobs. Writing assignments ask students to comment on their progress in school, identify challenges, and consider strategies for improving their writing skills, study habits, and time management.

Focus on Writing

Get Writing offers students a variety of writing opportunities.

What Are You Trying to Say?/What Have You Written? Chapters begin by asking students to express their thoughts in sentences and paragraphs on a range of topics. After writing a draft, they are asked to examine what they have written. By examining their word choices, use of details, and critical thinking skills, they learn to improve their writing and to link what they are studying with their own work.

Responding to Images Visual prompts open and close chapters, encouraging students to use critical thinking to write about images that depict jobs, family, school life, and social issues. Photos are often paired to encourage analysis and comparison.

Critical Thinking Students are prompted to write about personal experiences and world issues ranging from economic and political issues to favourite television shows.

Real World Writing Throughout *Get Writing,* students write, revise, and edit documents they will encounter beyond the classroom: announcements, e-mail, résumés, and letters.

Working Together Collaborative writing and editing exercises demonstrate the value of peer review and provide practice working in groups.

Organization

Get Writing consists of five parts, which can be taught in different sequences to meet the needs of instructors.

Part 1: Getting Started introduces students to the importance of writing and provides strategies for succeeding in writing courses. The writing process, from prewriting to final editing, is explained in practical steps.

Part 2: Developing Paragraphs shows students how to build paragraphs by creating clear topic sentences supported by details. Chapters cover five patterns of development: description, narration, example, comparison and contrast, and cause and effect.

Unlike other textbooks, *Get Writing* integrates student and professional readings into each chapter.

Exam Skills demonstrate how students use different patterns of development to answer essay questions.

Student Paragraphs illustrate how students use a particular pattern of development to build paragraphs for personal essays, school assignments, and examinations.

Putting Paragraphs Together show how separate paragraphs work together to create a short essay.

Short professional essays demonstrate how writers use patterns of development. Readings include pieces by Douglas Coupland, Olive Johnson, Suzanne Britt, and Stephen King.

Part 3: Writing Sentences explains the parts of sentences and how they work together to express thoughts. Students are given practical tips for detecting and repairing common sentence errors.

What Do You Know? opens most chapters, offering a short quiz with answers so students can test themselves to see how much they know about each unit.

Sequenced exercises direct students to identify and repair individual sentences, then detect and repair errors in context.

Writing exercises guide students to develop their own sentences and paragraphs, then to identify and correct errors in their writing.

What Have You Learned? concludes each chapter, offering a short quiz with answers so students can test themselves, identifying areas that need review.

Points to Remember end each chapter, providing main points for quick review and easy reference.

Parts 4 and 5: Understanding Grammar and Using Punctuation and Mechanics demonstrate that grammar is not a set of arbitrary rules but a tool to express ideas and prevent confusion. *Get Writing* connects grammar with critical thinking, so students understand that decisions about sentence structure depend on what they are trying to say. As in Part 3, these chapters open and close with self-graded quizzes. Visual writing prompts, critical thinking exercises, and What Are You Trying to Say?/What Have You Written? offer students a variety of writing opportunities to connect what they learn about grammar with what they write. Cumulative exercises contain errors based on lessons in previous chapters, providing students with realistic editing and revising challenges.

Other Features

The **Handbook** summarizes rules and guidelines for easy reference.

Writing at Work offers practical advice on the most common writing tasks students face outside the classroom—writing e-mail, letters, and résumés.

Writing on the Web guides students to use the Internet to locate online writing resources.

ESL boxes provide help with specific writing problems encountered by students still mastering English.

New Chapter 10 Developing Paragraphs Using Persuasion.

Expanded Business Writing and **MLA/APA Guidelines** for writing for the "real world" outside the classroom.

Canadian examples and references.

Ancillaries

The *Instructor's Manual/Test Bank* is an inclusive supplement. The *Instructor's Manual* section includes a variety of teaching aids, including directions on how to use the integrated features of *Get Writing,* such as the Working Together group activities, visual writing prompts, Critical Thinking assignments, and What Are You Trying to Say?/What Have You Written? assignments. The manual also discusses how to incorporate the professional and student model paragraphs in class and provides additional writing assignments, collaborative activities, and teaching tips for every chapter. The *Instructor's Manual* offers additional ESL information for many chapters as well as suggestions for teaching to various learning styles.

The *Test Bank* consists of testing items: one test for each writing chapter and three tests—one diagnostic test and two mastery tests. These tests are a combination of generative testing items, which ask students to write their own sentences within guided parameters, and objective questions that cover the skills and concepts presented in the textbook.

Acknowledgments

From Heather McAfee

This book has truly been a collaborative effort. My special thanks go to Rod Banister, executive editor, for getting the project off the ground and Anne Williams, executive editor, for pulling it all together and making it a reality. I would also like to thank developmental editor Beth Lariviere for her incredible support and enthusiasm. Thanks also to Lenore Spence, Director of Development, Higher Education; Mike Thompson, Acquisitions Editor; and Colleen Shea, Developmental Editor, for their valuable assistance. Thanks to the talented Thomson Nelson production and marketing team: Julie van Veen, Senior Content Production Manager; Sandra Green, Marketing Manager; and Ralph Courtney, Senior Technology Solutions Manager; and Cathy Witlox, copy editor. Finally, my warm thanks go to my fellow writers, Peter Miller and Melanie Rubens.

Get Writing: Sentences and Paragraphs benefited greatly from the many reviewers who took the time to read the text-in-progress and to make comments and suggestions for its improvement:

Susan Adams – Sheridan College
Anita Agar – Sheridan College
Barbara Graham – St. Clair College
Kathleen Moran – Conestoga College
James Papple – Brock University
Gail Rees – Canadore College

From Melanie Rubens

Dedicated in loving memory to John Rubens . . . A special thanks to Frances and Gaye for their creative input and commentaries. I would also like to thank the Nelson team, especially Beth Lariviere, for their support of this project.

Part 1

Getting Started

Why Write?

GET WRITING

How do you write? Do you make plans first or just start writing? Do you consider how readers will respond to your ideas? Does what you write express what you are trying to say?

Write three or four sentences describing your method of writing and how you would like to improve it.

You probably did not enroll in college to study writing. Most of us think of writers as people who write for a living—novelists, reporters, biographers, and screenwriters. However, writing is an important part of almost anyone's job.

Thinking of your future career, you probably imagine yourself in action—a nurse treating patients, a police officer fighting crime, a marketer creating advertisements or a contractor walking through a construction site. All these professionals are writers. They may not publish books or articles, but they depend on writing to achieve their goals. Nurses and police officers record their daily actions and observations in charts and reports that may become evidence in court. Marketers and contractors write letters, marketing or design plans, proposals, and streams of e-mail to architects, suppliers, clients, and inspectors. Whatever field you enter, your success will depend on your ability to communicate ideas in writing.

GET WRITING

WRITING ACTIVITY

Describe your future career. What job do you want after graduation? In what situations do people in that field write to others?

_____

_____

_____

_____

_____

_____

_____

_____

_____

_____

_____

_____

_____

_____

_____

_____

Read what you have written and list the most important ways writing will shape your future.

_____

_____

_____

GOALS OF THIS BOOK

Get Writing has been created to

- increase your awareness of the importance of writing
- improve your knowledge of the writing process
- increase your understanding of sentences and paragraphs
- help you overcome common writing problems
- prepare you for writing challenges in college and in your future career

Using *Get Writing*

At first glance any textbook can be intimidating. Look through *Get Writing* to become comfortable with it. Mark useful passages with bookmarks or Post-It™ notes for quick reference. Remember to use *Get Writing* as a resource not only in English courses, but in any writing you do in or out of school.

WORKING TOGETHER

Discuss writing with three or four other students and ask them to list problems and questions they have—from getting started writing to using commas. List your own top five problems:

1. _____

2. _____

3. _____

4. _____

5. _____

Look at the table of contents and index in *Get Writing* to locate pages that address these problems.

NOTE

You will be asked to reflect back on your writing as you work through this textbook. We suggest that you keep all of your assignments and exercises in a portfolio or duotang.

What Is Good Writing?

Many students are uncertain about what is considered "good writing." Comments by teachers and professors can be confusing and contradictory. Furthermore, what is considered "good writing" in high school is often unacceptable in college. English teachers urge you to use colourful words and creative language to express yourself, while business and technical instructors insist that you avoid personal insights and use standard terminology. Writing that is effective in one situation is inappropriate in another.

The Writing Context

Although spelling, capitalization, and punctuation have standard rules, many elements of what makes writing "good" are shaped by the context. Writing does not take place in a vacuum. Writing occurs in a context shaped by four things:

1. the writer's goal
2. the readers' needs, expectations, beliefs, and knowledge
3. the situation, discipline, occupation, or event in which the writing takes place
4. the nature of the document

Context explains why a newspaper article about a plane crash differs from a government accident report or a lawyer's letter to an injured passenger. Written in simple language and printed in narrow columns for quick skimming, a newspaper article summarizes events for general readers. A government report written by engineers might run to hundreds of pages and contain technical terms most people would not understand. A lawyer writing to victims would use persuasive language to urge them to take legal action.

When you write, ask yourself four key questions about context:

What Is Your Goal?

Are you writing to share an idea, complete an assignment, answer a question, or apply for a job? Do you want readers to change their minds or take action?

Who Is the Reader?

Who are you writing to—a single person or a group? Is your reader likely to agree or disagree with your ideas? What information do you have to include to convince readers to accept your views?

What Is the Discipline or Situation?

Each discipline, profession, business, or community has unique traditions, standards, expectations, values, and culture. Humanities professors encourage students to present individual interpretations of novels, films, or paintings. Science instructors, however, expect students to follow rigid rules of objective research and avoid personal comments. An advertising agency depends on creativity, whereas an accounting firm demands accuracy. One city council might stress industrial development, whereas another values historical preservation. The writing situation greatly shapes the way you present ideas and format the document.

What Is Expected in the Document?

When you write, make sure your message matches the nature of the document. Don't expect people to read a ten-page e-mail or assume a professor will accept a two-page term paper.

WRITING ACTIVITY

A group of high school students are suspended for sharing prescription cold pills during a recent flu epidemic. Although no money changed hands and students followed the recommended dosage, they violated the school's zero tolerance policy on drug use.

Briefly describe the context of the following documents:

A suspended student explaining in an Instant Message to an online friend what happened:

the writer's goal _____

the reader _____

the discipline _____

the document _____

A parent's e-mail to the school board demanding her daughter be readmitted to school:

the writer's goal _____

the reader _____

the discipline _____

the document _____

A newspaper editorial supporting or criticizing the principal's actions:

the writer's goal _____

the reader _____

the discipline _____

the document _____

The school board's statement to local, provincial, and national media that have requested information about the incident:

the writer's goal _____

the reader _____

the discipline _____

the document _____

To learn more about writing contexts, look at websites, newspapers, and magazines. Notice how the style of articles in *Cosmopolitan, People,* and *Chatelaine* differs from that of *Maclean's, Newsweek,* and *The Economist.*

STRATEGIES FOR SUCCEEDING IN WRITING COURSES

1. *Review your syllabus and textbooks carefully.* Make sure you know the policies for missed classes, late papers, and incompletes. Note due dates on your calendar.
2. *As soon as possible, read descriptions of all assignments listed in the syllabus.* Reviewing assignments in advance allows you to think ahead and make notes for upcoming papers.
3. *Make sure you fully know what your instructor expects in each assignment.* Study your syllabus, sample papers, and handouts for guidance. If you have any questions about an upcoming paper, ask your instructor.
4. *Locate support services.* Many colleges have computer labs, tutoring facilities, and writing centres to assist students.
5. *Talk to other students about writing.* Bounce ideas off other students. Ask them to comment on your choice of topic, main idea, or support. Share rough drafts with others.
6. *Experiment by writing at different times and places.* If you are new on campus, you may find some places easier to work in than others. The casual atmosphere of a student lounge may be a better writing environment than a computer lab or the library. You may find it easier to write early in the morning or after working out.
7. *If you don't already write on a computer, learn.* Most colleges offer short courses in word processing. Once you graduate you will be expected to work on a computer. Though a bit cumbersome at first, writing on a computer makes your job as a student much easier.
8. *Read your papers aloud before turning them in.* The fastest and easiest way to edit papers is to read them aloud. It is easier to "hear" than "see" missing and misspelled words, awkward phrases, fragments, and illogical statements.
9. *Keep copies of all assignments.*
10. *Study returned papers, especially ones with poor grades.* When you get an F or D on an assignment, you might want to throw it away or bury it under some books. Although they are painful to look at, these papers hold the key to success. Note the instructor's comments and suggestions. List mechanical errors and note sections in *Get Writing* that can help you overcome these problems in future assignments.
11. *Never copy or use the work of others in your writing without informing your readers.*
12. *Write as often as you can.* Writing, like anything else, takes practice. Keep a journal or an online blog, e-mail friends, and take notes in class. Record your thoughts while you watch television. Any kind of writing will help you get used to thinking in sentences and paragraphs.

 GET THINKING AND WRITING

CRITICAL THINKING

Describe your writing experiences in high school or in a recent job. What assignments were the most difficult? What comments did teachers make about your writing? What letters or reports gave you the most trouble at work?

Read your comments and identify the most important ideas you discovered. Summarize your most important point in one sentence:

_____

_____

_____

What two or three things do you want to change about your writing?

1. _____

2. _____

3. _____

WHAT HAVE YOU WRITTEN?

Read your comments aloud. What changes would you make if you had to turn it in for a grade?

- Are there sentences that are off topic and should be deleted?
- Could you add more details and examples?
- Could you choose more effective words?
- Would a teacher or other readers understand your main point?

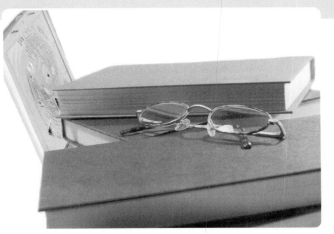

GET WRITING

What challenges do you face this semester? Review your syllabi and course outlines for upcoming assignments. Write three or four sentences describing the biggest challenge you face this semester. How can you increase your chances of success? Do you need to organize your time better? Do some assignments require outside help?

WRITING ON THE WEB

Exploring Writing Resources Online

The Internet contains a constantly expanding variety of resources for student writers: dictionaries, encyclopedias, grammar exercises, databases, library catalogues, editing tips, and research strategies.

1. Review your library's electronic databases, links, and search engines. Locate online dictionaries and encyclopedias that can assist you with upcoming assignments.
2. Using a search engine such as AltaVista, Yahoo!, or Google, enter key words such as *prewriting, proofreading, narration, capitalization, thesis statement, comma exercises, editing strategies,* and other terms that appear throughout the book, the index, or your course syllabus. In addition to providing formal databases, many schools and instructors have constructed online tutorials that can help you improve your writing, overcome grammar problems, and help in specific assignments.
3. If you write papers that make use of outside resources, the Internet is a valuable tool in the creation of a works cited list (a list of books, periodicals, etc. referenced in your paper). Using one of the above search engines, type in keywords such as *APA* or *MLA*—whichever referencing style your professor requests you use.
4. Check out your library's website for tools for automatically creating works cited lists. If there isn't a scheduled library visit in your class this term, visit the library in person; ask the staff about information sessions. A short session will provide you with valuable information about resources, research techniques, and referencing.

POINT TO REMEMBER

1. Writing is important not only in college or university but in any career you enter.
2. Writing takes place in a context formed by the writer's goal, the reader, the discipline or situation, and the nature of the document.
3. You can improve your writing by studying past efforts.
4. Writing improves with practice. Write as often as you can.

2

The Writing Process

GET WRITING

Where do you get your ideas? Are you a careful consumer of information? Do you ask yourself questions before you write?

Write a short statement explaining why it is important to think before simply repeating what you see and hear.

This book concentrates on the building blocks of writing—words, sentences, and paragraphs. To fully understand them, however, you need to see how they work together to create whole documents—essays, letters, and e-mails. You have to get the big picture.

This chapter explains the writing process: how to select a topic, explore ideas, organize details, and create a document that expresses what you want to say. Experienced writers work in many different ways, but most follow a step-by-step method to save time and improve their writing. Follow these steps in your first writing assignments, then feel free to make changes to create your own composing style, a way of writing that works with the way you think and the task you face.

THE WRITING PROCESS

Step 1	Prewrite: Use critical thinking to explore ideas.
Step 2	Plan: Establish context, develop a thesis, and outline ideas.
Step 3	Write: Get your ideas on paper.
Step 4	Cool: Put your writing aside.
Step 5	Revise: Review and rewrite your paper.
Step 6	Edit: Check the final version for mechanical errors.

POINT TO REMEMBER

You can improve your writing by asking yourself two questions:

What am I trying to say?

What have I written?

Although writing can be broken into separate stages, it is often a *recursive,* or repeated, process. Writers don't always work in fixed steps but write, revise, and edit as they go along. They may edit and polish the first paragraph before starting the rest of the paper. On another assignment, they may write the conclusion first. Writing on a computer allows you to move between writing and editing, adding in new ideas and fixing errors as you work.

Step 1: Prewrite

It is part of the business of the writer . . . to examine attitudes, to go beneath the surface, to tap the source.
JAMES BALDWIN

To be a successful writer, you need to see things with a "writer's eye." Good writers are not passive. They don't simply repeat what they have heard or seen on television, and they don't just jot down everything they "feel." Good writers use *critical thinking.* They observe their subject closely, ask questions, collect facts, test commonly held beliefs, and avoid making snap decisions. Good writing is never "about" a topic—it has a purpose and makes a point. A good paper shares more than facts and dates, first impressions, or immediate reactions. Good writing goes beyond the obvious to explore ideas and events, to analyze people and ideas.

STRATEGIES FOR INCREASING CRITICAL THINKING

1. *Study subjects carefully—don't rely on first impressions or make snap judgments.* If your car is stolen and your neighbour's house is broken into, you may quickly assume that crime is increasing in your community. However, until you study police reports, you really only know that you are one of two victims. It could be that crime is actually dropping but that you and your neighbour happen to fall into the shrinking pool of victims.

2. *Distinguish between facts and opinions.* Don't mistake people's opinions, attitudes, or feelings as facts. Opinions express a point of view. They can be valid—but they are not evidence. You can factually report that your sister sleeps until ten, doesn't make her bed, and won't look for a summer job. However, calling her "lazy" states an opinion, not a fact.

3. *Don't rely on limited evidence.* Isolated events and personal experiences may be interesting but lack the authority of extensive objective research. The fact that your great-grandfather smoked three packs of cigarettes a day and lived past ninety does not prove that tobacco is harmless.

4. *Avoid basing judgments on weak comparisons.* No two situations are ever identical. Because a policy works in Japan does not mean it will work in Canada. Strategies that work in a prairie election might not be effective in an election elsewhere in the country. Comparisons can be compelling arguments but only if supported by facts.

5. *Don't confuse a time relationship with cause and effect.* Events take place over time. If you develop headaches after a car crash, you might assume they were caused by the accident. However, the headaches could be caused by lack of sleep or a food allergy and have nothing to do with your recent accident.

6. *Judge ideas, not personalities.* Don't be impressed by celebrity endorsements or reject an idea because the person supporting it is controversial. Judge ideas on their own merits. Unpopular people often have good ideas, and popular people can be wrong.

7. *Avoid making absolute statements.* If you make absolute statements such as "all politicians are corrupt" or "people always regret buying a used car," your argument can be dismissed if a reader can provide a single exception.

8. *Examine quotations and statistics offered as support.* People often try to influence us by offering quotations by famous people or impressive statistics. However, until you know the full context of someone's statement or the origin of the statistics, they have little value. Statistics may be based on biased research and easily distorted. Even accurate numbers can be misinterpreted.

9. *Above all, think before you write.*

TIPS FOR BRAINSTORMING

1. **Focus brainstorming by keeping the final paper in mind.** Review the assignment instructions.
2. **Use full sentences to write out important ideas you may forget.**
3. **Use key words for a quick Internet search.** Glancing at a list of websites may stimulate new ideas.
4. **Think of the list as a funnel leading from broad subjects to defined topics.** Avoid creating a list of random ideas.

Prewriting Techniques

Prewriting puts critical thinking into action. Experiment with one or all of these methods to see which helps you the most.

Brainstorming lists ideas. A student brainstorming for an upcoming psychology paper starts with the title of a chapter in a textbook, then lists ideas to discover a topic:

TIPS FOR FREEWRITING

1. **Use freewriting for personal essays and open-topic assignments.** Freewriting allows you to explore your existing knowledge and beliefs. This method, however, may not help you respond to highly structured assignments or develop business documents.

2. **Use a question to focus freewriting.** Asking yourself "Why do kids drop out of school?" is a better starting point than a general idea of "writing a paper about public schools."

3. **Don't feel obligated to write in complete sentences.** Making lists or jotting down key words can save time.

4. **Save your freewriting for future assignments.**

5. **Highlight important ideas by underlining or circling them.**

- "Depressive Disorders"
- Depression
- Effects of depression
- Suicide
- SAD—Seasonal Affective Disorder
- Postpartum depression
- Postpartum depression and child neglect/abuse/murder (Toronto case)
- Topic: *Postpartum depression as basis for insanity plea*

In **freewriting,** you record your thoughts, feelings, attitudes, and impressions by writing as quickly as possible. When you freewrite, you are not trying to create a rough draft but discover ideas. Many students find that writing one idea triggers another. Freewriting is like talking into a tape recorder to capture everything you know about a topic. When you freewrite, don't stop to check spelling, think about writing in complete sentences, or worry about going off topic. Remember, you are not writing an essay but exploring ideas.

To freewrite, sit with a blank page or computer screen and write as fast as you can about a topic:

> Last week was a big campus demonstration against oil and gas companies on east coast of Canada. Students left the demonstration in gas guzzling SUVS. Problem of the envioment is that consumers dont want to change their lifestyles. People don't want oil drilling or refineries or oil tankers damaging the environment but they want to drive big cars, have big air-condition houses, power boats, lawnmowers, and they want all that energy cheap. People want to blame the government and corporate leaders for global warming and pollution. But can we save the envronment without making sacrifices. Driving small cars, living in smaller houses. Paying $1.50 a litre for gas like Europe. . . . Using less electricity. Buying less and recycling more and consuming less. We want some kind of magic solution, its like people who want to be slim and attractive but not have to diet or exercise. Or people who want the money and prestige of being doctors and lawyers but don't want to study or work hard. Maybe TV with it's instant solutions where every problem is solved in sixty minutes is to blame for our immature attitudes toward everything in society today.

The paragraph is filled with confusing sentences and spelling errors. It trails off into a series of unrelated observations. However, the student has identified the heart of a good paper—people's unrealistic desire to save the environment without changing their lifestyle.

Asking questions about a topic can identify your existing knowledge, reveal terms or ideas that need to be defined, and indicate what research might have to be conducted. Asking questions is a good way of putting critical thinking into action because questions leave room for doubt and further reflection. A student planning to describe her first apartment can improve her paper by asking questions:

> Why did I choose this topic?
> Why did I think of describing my apartment and not my car or favourite restaurant?
> What did it mean to me?
> What made it significant to me?
> What is the most important thing I want people to know about it?

TIPS FOR ASKING QUESTIONS

1. **Keep the assignment in mind as you pose questions.**

2. **Avoid questions that call for simple yes or no answers.** Use questions that ask "why?" or "how?"

3. **Remember that the goal of asking questions is to identify a topic and prompt critical thinking.**

What do I remember most about that apartment?

How do I feel about it now?

Was it a good or bad place to live?

How did my apartment help me grow as a person?

What problems did I have?

Would I want to move back?

What is the best/worst thing that happened to me there?

How did that apartment change my life? Did I learn any lessons from it?

Questions like these can spark insights and help the student write an interesting description that does more than list details about rooms and furniture.

Clustering (also called **diagramming, mapping,** and **webbing**) uses markers like circles, columns, boxes, and arrows to discover and organize ideas. If you are visually minded, this method may be easier to use than freewriting or asking questions. It can be very useful if you are writing about group of topics or comparing two subjects.

Here a student explores the influence of television on children:

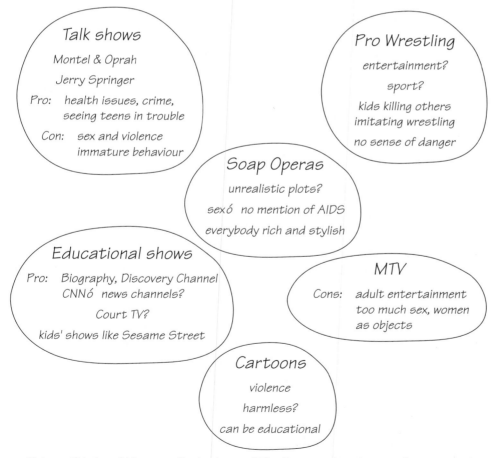

TV and Children

Talk shows
Montel & Oprah
Jerry Springer
Pro: health issues, crime, seeing teens in trouble
Con: sex and violence immature behaviour

Pro Wrestling
entertainment?
sport?
kids killing others imitating wrestling
no sense of danger

Soap Operas
unrealistic plots?
sex6 no mention of AIDS
everybody rich and stylish

Educational shows
Pro: Biography, Discovery Channel CNN6 news channels?
Court TV?
kids' shows like Sesame Street

MTV
Cons: adult entertainment too much sex, women as objects

Cartoons
violence
harmless?
can be educational

> **TIPS FOR CLUSTERING**
> 1. **Clustering is helpful when you have complex or conflicting ideas.** You can group related items and place pro and con items in separate columns.
> 2. **Keep the artwork simple.** Don't spend too much time on the appearance of your notes. Remember, you are not creating a visual aid for a formal presentation, just a rough diagram.

Points: TV gives kids unrealistic views of life. Soap and rock stars have casual sex but no one gets AIDS. TV cops and wrestlers engage in fights but never end up in wheelchairs. Maybe the solution is for parents to comment as they watch or get kids to see more responsible and realistic news and educational programs.

By mapping out ideas and balancing positive and negative aspects of television, the student has been able to focus on a main topic.

POINTS TO REMEMBER

1. The goal of prewriting is to explore ideas, develop a topic, and organize points—not write a rough draft.
2. Don't feel obligated to use a single prewriting technique—blend as many methods as you need.
3. Save prewriting notes. Ideas that may not be appropriate for one assignment could be useful for future papers.
4. Keep prewriting simple. Elaborate notes may be difficult to follow.

GET WRITING

WRITING ACTIVITY

Select one of the topics below or from the list on pages 459–460 and prewrite for ten minutes. You may use one or more techniques. If you have an upcoming assignment in any of your classes, use this opportunity to get started.

Topics

financial aid	talk show hosts	stem cell research
your worst job	qualities of a good parent	Ecstasy
campus daycare	singles bars	downloading music
your first car	favourite celebrity	campus fashion

Step 2: Plan

Moving from Topic to Thesis

Narrowing Your Topic

Once you develop a topic through prewriting, you may have to narrow it to a subject you can handle. There is little new you can say about crime in five hundred words, but you could write something interesting about the youth Criminal Justice Act, racial profiling, or DNA evidence.

Developing a Thesis

While the Youth Criminal Justice Act, racial profiling, and DNA evidence are all interesting topics, each must be narrowed from a topic into a thesis, or main point. For example, if you want to write about lie detectors, you might concentrate on their scientific reliability, moral implications, or influence on juries. As you think and write about your topic, you should develop a controlling idea or point of view—this will be your thesis. A good paper is not "about" a subject; it is centred around a thesis that makes a statement or expresses an opinion. The thesis states your opinion or explains your intent, what you want your readers to know:

Topic	lie detectors
Narrowed topic	scientific accuracy of polygraph examinations
Controlling idea	admissibility into courtrooms
Thesis	*Polygraph examinations should be admitted in court only when judges carefully explain to juries that lie detectors are not 100 percent accurate.*

Topic	my hometown
Narrowed topic	housing pattern in my hometown
Controlling idea	housing pattern's effect on young people growing up
Thesis	*The sprawling subdivisions of my hometown isolated young people from friends, school activities, and jobs, making them prone to loneliness and drug abuse.*

POINT TO REMEMBER

Don't confuse a *thesis* with a narrowed topic. A thesis does more than focus the subject of a paper. It is a debatable point or statement—it has to express an opinion.

WORKING TOGETHER

Select one of the general topics below or from the previous exercise and develop a narrowed topic, a controlling idea, and a thesis. When you are finished, share your work with other students. Make sure each person in the group develops a thesis and not just a narrowed topic.

General Topics

student housing	NHL and MLB salaries	reality television
sexual harassment	campus jobs	school loans
computer viruses	minimum wage	poverty
online dating	immigration laws	terrorism
used cars	annoying customers	police officers

General topic: _____

Narrowed topic: _____

Controlling idea: _____

_____

Thesis: _____

_____

Organizing Support

Once you have developed a thesis, you are ready to organize the paper, outlining the introduction, body, and conclusion. A few minutes of careful thought at the start of the process can save you time later on. In planning your paper, consider your goal, your reader, the discipline, and the nature of the paper.

Your goal	What do you want the paper to accomplish? What details, facts, or observations do you need to support your thesis?
Your reader	What information do your readers need? What support will they find most convincing?

Do readers have any biases or misconceptions you must address?

The discipline   Will your paper follow the standards used in this discipline or profession?

The paper   What is the appropriate format for this paper?

Creating an Outline

An outline does not have to be elaborate or use Roman numerals and capital letters. Even a rough sketch can organize ideas and save time. Your plan works like a road map to guide your writing—listing your paper's beginning, middle, and end. However, it is subject to change. New thoughts will come to mind, and you may expand or narrow your paper as you write.

The type of outline you develop depends on your topic. In planning a narrative, a simple timeline can organize ideas. In other papers, a more complex plan can serve to balance conflicting ideas, organize complicated evidence, or place confusing events in a logical order. Most outlines cover three basic parts of a document: introduction, body, and conclusion.

Introduction   grabs attention
announces the topic
addresses reader concerns
prepares readers for what follows

Body   organizes supporting details in a logical pattern

Conclusion   ends with a brief summary, a final thought or observation, question, call for action, or prediction

POINT TO REMEMBER

You can place your thesis at the beginning, middle, or end of the paper. If your audience is opposed to your opinion, you may wish to present facts or tell a story before expressing your point of view.

GET WRITING

WRITING ACTIVITY

Develop an outline for a topic and thesis you created in the previous exercise. Or you may use this opportunity to organize your next assignment.

Topic: _____

Introduction: _____

_____

Body: _____

_____

_____

_____

Conclusion: _____

Step 3: Write

After reviewing your plan, write as much as you can. Your goal is not to produce a final draft but to get your ideas on paper. Don't feel obligated to write in complete sentences—to save time, list ideas. Don't worry about spelling or grammar at this point. If you stop to look up a word in a dictionary, you will break your train of thought. Instead, highlight errors for future reference as you write:

> *Last year _____ people (get figures from Globe and Mail article) lost their most valuable possession—there ? identity. Computer hackers got their social insurance #'s, bank account, even passwords and empited their checking accounts, billed their credit cards, took out loans, bought cars, even used there ID's to post bale. According to (get the author's name) it can take two to three years for a victum to get there (?) records straight. In the meantime these people will have loans denied, be harassed by creditors, and find that most law enforement authorities are of little help.*

WRITING ACTIVITY

GET WRITING

Write a draft of the paper you planned in the previous exercise or for an upcoming assignment.

Step 4: Cool

This is an easy—but important—step. After you finish writing, put your work aside and let it "cool." When you complete a draft, your first thought might be to quickly go over your work. Because your ideas are fresh in your mind, it is difficult to be objective about what you have produced on paper. Set the work aside. Take a walk, do an errand, or study another assignment. Then return to your work. For example, if you have an e-mail to send today, try to write a draft in the morning, then set it aside so you can read and revise it in the afternoon.

Step 5: Revise

Revising means "to see again." It means much more than simply correcting spelling mistakes and adding missing details.

Revising Checklist
1. Print a copy of your draft. You may find revising on a computer difficult because the screen prevents you from seeing the whole paper.
2. Review your assignment and your goal. Does your draft meet the requirements and express what you want to say?

3. Examine the thesis—is it clearly expressed? Should it be located in another part of the essay for better effect?
4. Does the introduction gain readers' attention and prepare them for the body of the essay?
5. Does the body present enough details to support your thesis? Is the information clearly organized? Can readers follow your train of thought?
6. Are there any lapses in critical thinking? Should you present additional evidence or restate your opinions?
7. Are there missing details needed to support your thesis? Are there unrelated ideas that should be deleted?
8. Does the conclusion leave readers with a fact, comment, or question they will remember, or does it only repeat the introduction?

Having revised your work, you are ready to write additional drafts. Your work may need only minor changes. In other instances, it is easier to start a new version using a different approach.

Using Peer Review

Teachers often convince students that getting help with assignments is cheating. However, it is not cheating to have other people read your work, make suggestions, and answer questions you ask them. You should not let others *write* the paper for you, but you can benefit from hearing their criticisms and suggestions.

PEER REVIEW GUIDELINES

1. Make sure reviewers understand the writing task. They will find the writing hard to evaluate if they don't know who is supposed to read it or what it has to accomplish. Explain your assignment and any instructor's directions before showing people your writing.
2. Let the writing speak for itself. Don't coach people by telling them what you are trying to say. Explain the assignment, then let people read your draft so they can objectively examine the words on the page. After hearing their initial comments, you might explain what you want to say, then ask if they think you accomplish your goals.
3. Ask specific questions. If you just ask, "Is this any good?" or "What do you think?" you may get only vague responses. Instead, ask readers if they understand your thesis, if the introduction is clear, if you present enough details, if your arguments make sense.
4. Encourage readers to be critical. Too often friends and other students want to be polite and positive and may be reluctant to sound negative.
5. When reviewing other people's writing, be objective and make constructive criticisms. Don't just point out errors. Try to suggest changes, but be careful not to make the changes.

REVISING ACTIVITY

Revise the draft you have written. You may wish to share your work with other students and ask them to suggest ways of improving it.

Step 6: Edit

The final step in the writing process is editing the final form of the document. In editing, you want to make sure you not only correct spelling and capitalization errors but eliminate wordy phrases and rewrite confusing or weak sentences.

Editing Checklist

1. Read your paper aloud. It is often easier to "hear" than "see" errors such as misspelled or missing words, awkward phrases, clumsy sentences, and fragments. (See Chapters 15 and 28.)
2. Make sure your sentence structure is appropriate to the type of document. An e-mail should be written in short, easy-to-read sentences. A long essay or research paper, however, can include long and complex sentences. (See Chapter 14.)
3. Delete wordy phrases, such as "at this point in time" for "now" or "blue in colour" for "blue." (See Chapter 13.)
4. Make sure your final document meets the required format. Should it be single or double spaced? Do you need documentation such as parenthetical citations and a works cited page?

EDITING ACTIVITY

Edit the paper you have written and revised. Share your paper with other students. Refer to the index or table of contents of this book to find help with grammar problems.

AVOID PLAGIARISM

Never copy or use the work of others in your writing without informing your readers. Plagiarism is cheating. Faced with a tough assignment, you may be tempted to download an article from the Internet, copy a friend's paper, or take paragraphs from a magazine to put into your paper. Students caught copying papers are often flunked or expelled. If you use an outside source like a website or magazine, just changing a few words does not make your writing original. You can quote important statements or use statistics and facts if you tell readers where they came from. You don't always need detailed footnotes to prove you are not stealing. Just make sure you mention sources as you use them:

> *The Public Health Agency of Canada* recently reported that the West Nile virus made more than 1,300 Canadians ill in 2003 alone; the virus will continue to thrive in Canada unless people take active measures to control mosquito breeding sites around their homes and cottages.

Use quotation marks when you copy word for word what someone has said or written:

In his review of Margaret Atwood's novel *Oryx and Crake,* Thomas M. Disch warns us that

> "*Oryx and Crake* showcases a nightmare version of the present era of globalization on a globe coming apart at its ecological seams, with temperatures rising, species vanishing into extinction, cities sinking into

(continued)

the ocean, and a conscienceless technological elite trying to engineer the survival of their own eroding advantages. It is a scathing (because bang-on) portrait of the way we live now."

Also, as demonstrated above, indent and single space quotations that are longer than two lines. Quotations of such length should be kept to a minimum and can be expressed in your own words. Expressing someone else's idea in your own words is called *paraphrasing*. Mention the author when you paraphrase his or her ideas.

According to Thomas M. Disch, in *Oryx and Crake*, Margaret Atwood presents a future world that is crumbling in every imaginable way: out-of-control globalization, species eradication, and desiccated cities. The images he creates make us feel uncomfortable because they awaken realistic fears.

Plagiarism also includes using another student's work *with or without his or her permission* unless you credit the work as belonging to someone else. Having another student highlight areas of your writing that are problematic is a great editing tool; however, be careful about sharing your work with others. If parts or all of that work is submitted by another student (without due credit), this is plagiarism, and you will both be held equally responsible.

DOCUMENTATION

You will use one of two types of documentation. The MLA (Modern Language Association) style of documentation is used for research papers and many business reports. The APA (American Psychological Association) style of documentation is used in fields such as criminology, economics, nursing, social work, sociology, as well as some business disciplines.

MLA Style

When you use the MLA style to indicate the use of someone else's words or ideas within a paper, you must include the author's last name and the page number in parentheses directly after the quote or idea. This is called a *parenthetical citation* or an *in-text citation*. The parenthetical citation allows the reader to easily find the complete details of the work in the works cited list at the end of your paper.

Sample In-Text Citations:

As a result of the oil boom in the 1970s, the Saudi Arabian capital of Riyadh's population has grown from fewer than 100,000 inhabitants to over four and a half million (Viviano 16).

"Memory loss can start as early as age thirty" (Roizen 79).

According to Mathew Ingram, a team of scientists from Edinburgh University in Scotland has found a way to move objects "uphill against the force of gravity by manipulating the molecules of the hill" (Ingram).

(continued)

Sample Works Cited List for the Above Citations:

Ingram, Mathew. "Pushing Water Uphill." *Globe and Mail.com* 15 June 2005. 27 June 2005 <http://www.theglobeandmail.com/servlet/ story/RTGAM.20040622. geekwatchjun04/BNStory/Technology/? query=June+15%2C+2005>.

Roizen, Michael F., and Mehmet C. Oz. *You: The Owner's Manual.* New York: Harper Collins Publishers, 2005.

Viviano, Frank. "Saudi Arabia on Edge." *National Geographic* Oct. 2003: 2-41.

APA Style

When you quote someone or use another's ideas within a paper, the APA style requires that you place the author's last name, the year that the work was published, and the page reference in parentheses. As in the MLA style, this is called a *parenthetical citation* or an *in-text citation*. The full details of this citation must appear in the references list at the end of the paper.

Sample In-Text Citations:

As Freeman (2002, p. 896) puts it, analysts must recognize that "the 'strength' of inflation-averse parties in the country to which one pegs is a key element of the decision to fix one's own exchange rate."

To restore the confidence of financial markets, a fixed exchange rate was necessary to reestablish a more stable macroeconomic environment of Canadian business (Muirhead, 1999, pp. 195-6).

Our choice was influenced by our previous analysis of twenty years of questions on Canadian surveys about trade (Mendelsohn and Wolfe, 2001).

Sample References Entries for the Above Citations:

Freeman, J. R. (2002). Competing commitments. *International Organization,* 56(4), 889-910.

Mendelsohn, M. & Wolfe, R. (2001). Probing the aftermath of Seattle: Canadian public opinion on international trade, 1980-2000. *International Journal,* 56, 234-260.

Muirhead, B. (1999). Why Canada needs a flexible exchange rate. In D. Salvatore, J. Dean & T. Willett (Eds.), *The dollarization debate.* Oxford: Oxford University Press.

CRITICAL THINKING

GET THINKING
AND WRITING

How effectively do our leaders inform us? Do you feel that prime ministers, members of parliament, councillors, and mayors speak honestly and directly to the public? Do they provide valid reasons for their actions? Write a short paragraph stating your view about how a particular leader or political figures in general communicate to us.

GET WRITING

What skills does it take to present ideas to others? Why is it important to consider how others will evaluate a message? How can writing make a good impression on others? In three or four sentences state what you believe are the most important things for making writing effective.

WRITING ON THE WEB

1. Using a search engine like AltaVista, Yahoo!, or Google, enter terms such as *writing process, writing strategies, prewriting techniques, revising papers, improving college writing,* and *proofreading skills* to locate sites that might assist you in this course.

In the next few weeks, notice the language and level of formality you use in your e-mail to friends. You probably use short forms and Instant Messenger language, which is okay *only* when writing to friends and family. When writing any form of professional or academic communication (e-mail to business contacts, professors, teachers, government offices, etc.), however, it is important to use appropriate language and a friendly yet professional tone.

- Do not use slang or Instant Messenger language that may not be understood by those outside of your own peer group. *LOL* and *OMG* may make perfect sense to you but may not make sense to your professor or supervisor. Not only is it frustrating for the reader but using such language within a professional e-mail will send the message that this person/correspondence is unimportant to you—a bad move if you are hoping to set up a meeting, ask for help, or apply for a job.
- Always maintain an appropriate level of formality in professional e-mail. *Wuz up?* or *Howdy* are not appropriate unless writing to friends or family.

Reread all professional e-mail before hitting the send button. Revise and edit messages, ensuring that information is accurate, your intent/request is clear, and your grammar and spelling correct.

POINTS TO REMEMBER

1. Writing is a process—it does not occur in a single burst of inspiration.
2. Good writing has a purpose, a *thesis* or controlling idea. It is not a collection of random thoughts, first impressions, or feelings. Good writing reflects *critical thinking*—close observation, research, and analysis.
3. Prewriting techniques help explore ideas. Brainstorming, freewriting, and asking questions can identify topics, uncover new ideas, narrow a topic, and develop a thesis.
4. Outlines, whether formal or informal, organize ideas and identify missing information or unnecessary details.
5. First drafts serve to get ideas on paper—they are not expected to be flawless.
6. Reading papers out loud while revising and editing can help you detect missing details, awkward sentences, misspelled words, and grammar errors.
7. Avoid plagiarism. Never use the work of others without informing readers.

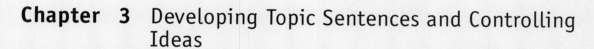

Part 2

Developing Paragraphs

3

Developing Topic Sentences and Controlling Ideas

GET WRITING

What do you consider success? What kind of career do you want? Are money and status important to you?

Write a short description of the job you would like to have in ten years.

29

What Is a Paragraph?

Paragraphs are the building blocks of anything you write. They play important roles in expressing your ideas and helping readers follow your train of thought.

> A paragraph is a group of related sentences that express a main idea.

Written without paragraphs, even a short paper can be hard to read:

```
                   Only Diabetes
I am not much of an athlete. I hate sports. I never
work out. But every October I take part in the annual
Run for Diabetes. I do it to help my sister. Ann was
a bright, funny, energetic fourteen-year-old until
diabetes changed her life. When she lost weight,
became tired, and collapsed on her way home from
school, I was afraid she had leukemia. Ann was diag-
nosed with diabetes, and I was relieved. It was only
diabetes. I thought all she would have to do was give
up candy and take a few shots to be OK. But diabetes
is far more devastating than most people realize.
Insulin keeps diabetics alive, but it is no cure.
Diabetes remains a leading cause of death. It is also
a leading cause of blindness. Diabetics can develop
ulcers and infections that require amputation. Ann
had to do more than give up candy. She must test her
blood six times a day, take painful injections, and
monitor everything she eats and drinks. Twice she has
gone into diabetic shock and been rushed by para-
medics to the emergency room. Ann's physical, emo-
tional, and social life has been radically changed by
a disease too many people think is easily managed. I
have seen a bright, fun-filled kid become a sombre and
often depressed girl who faces early heart disease
and failing eyesight. More research is needed to find
better treatments and maybe even a cure. This October
I will be running for Ann. Maybe you should join me.
```

The same paper written in paragraphs is easier to understand. Paragraphs highlight main ideas and the writer's train of thought. Each paragraph serves a specific purpose.

```
                   Only Diabetes
     I am not much of an athlete. I hate sports. I
never work out. But every October I take part in the
annual Run for Diabetes. I do it to help my sister.
Ann was a bright, funny, energetic fourteen-year-old
until diabetes changed her life. When she lost weight,
```

introduction

became tired, and collapsed on her way home from school, I was afraid she had leukemia. Ann was diagnosed with diabetes, and I was relieved. It was only diabetes. I thought all she would have to do was give up candy and take a few shots to be OK.

But diabetes is far more devastating than most people realize. Insulin keeps diabetics alive, but it is no cure. Diabetes remains a leading cause of death. It is also a leading cause of blindness. Diabetics can develop ulcers and infections that require amputation. Ann had to do more than give up candy. She must test her blood six times a day, take painful injections, and monitor everything she eats and drinks. Twice she has gone into diabetic shock and been rushed by paramedics to the emergency room.

transition and support

Ann's physical, emotional, and social life has been radically changed by a disease too many people think is easily managed. I have seen a bright, fun-filled kid become a sombre and often depressed girl who faces early heart disease and failing eyesight. More research is needed to find better treatments and maybe even a cure. This October I will be running for Ann. Maybe you should join me.

transition and conclusion

Paragraphs play key roles in organization:

- Paragraphs serve as building blocks.
- Paragraphs generally develop a single main idea expressed in a *topic sentence.*
- Paragraph breaks signal transitions, moving readers from one main idea to another.
- Like chapters in a book, paragraph breaks provide pauses, allowing readers to digest ideas before moving to new material.
- Paragraph breaks in dialogue indicate shifts between speakers.

WHAT DO YOU KNOW?

Answer each question about paragraphs True or False.

1. _____ Paragraphs organize ideas.

2. _____ Paragraphs make essays easier to read.

3. _____ Paragraphs must consist of at least five sentences.

4. _____ Long essays about complex topics must have long paragraphs.

5. _____ Introductions and conclusions should always be placed in separate paragraphs.

Answers appear on the following page.

GET|THINKING|
AND REVISING

WHAT ARE YOU TRYING TO SAY?

Write about one of the following topics:

- Compare your attitudes about music, jobs, or money with those of your parents.
- Explain your plans for this semester.
- Summarize the plot of your favourite book or movie.
- Describe your worst job interview, day at work, or school experience.
- Give your reasons for the success or failure of a sports team.
- Explain the need for better daycare, more parking, or improved tutoring at your school.

_____

_____

_____

ANSWERS TO WHAT DO YOU KNOW? ON PAGE 31:
1. true, 2. true, 3. false (paragraphs can be of any length), 4. false (complex essays often have short paragraphs to show transition or dramatize an idea), 5. false (short essays may not require whole paragraphs to introduce or end an essay)

_____

_____

_____

_____

_____

_____

_____

_____

_____

_____

_____

_____

_____

WHAT HAVE YOU WRITTEN?

Read your text carefully. Is it well organized? Did you use more than one paragraph? If you wrote a single paragraph, would breaks make your comments easier to follow? Are there short, choppy paragraphs that could be combined to join related ideas?

Topic Sentences and Controlling Ideas

Most paragraphs contain a **topic sentence** that states what the paragraph is about and conveys a **controlling idea** that expresses a main point or opinion. The other sentences in the paragraph relate to the topic sentence, supporting it with facts, details, comments, and observations. Topic sentences often open paragraphs to introduce the main idea and indicate the support to follow:

The Queen's Quay Inn is the best site for the alumni fund-raiser. Located on the water, the hotel ballroom and patio offer guests a sweeping view of the harbour. Unlike the major hotels downtown, the Queen's Quay Inn has free parking. Since most alumni will arrive from out of town, the harbour location will spare guests from having to contend with downtown traffic and the current construction on College Street. People flying in can take the hotel shuttle van from the airport, saving them the cost of renting cars or taking taxis.

But topic sentences can appear anywhere in a paragraph:

The neighbourhood youth centre has been in operation for almost thirty years but only recently began offering girls' basketball. Almost fifty girls now spend Saturdays and two weekday afternoons running and drilling in the gym. But the girls learn a lot more than athletics. Their coach, Judy Sanchez, has become a source of insight, support, and guidance many girls are missing at home or school. Judy talks to her players frankly about school, boys, fashion, dieting, and sex. She answers questions honestly and maintains a sense of humour that often does more to change a teenager's mind than threats or lectures. She encourages girls to stay in school, delay sexual activity, and make plans for college and careers. *Judy Sanchez is a role model who helps confused girls become thinking women.*

Topic sentences serve key roles in a paragraph:

- Topic sentences tell readers what the paragraph is about.
- Topic sentences make a general statement supported by the rest of the paragraph.
- Topic sentences indicate the kind of detail readers should expect in the paragraph.
- Topic sentences signal shifts in the writer's train of thought.
- Topic sentences dramatize a writer's main points, making writing easier to read and remember.

EXERCISE 1 Identifying Topic Sentences in Paragraphs

Underline the topic sentences in each paragraph.

1   Home is where the heart is. There's no place like it. I love my home with a ferocity totally out of proportion to its appearance or location. I love dumb things about it: the hot-water heater, the plastic rack you drain dishes in, the roof over my head, which occasionally leaks. And yet it is precisely those dumb things that make it what it is—a place

of certainty, stability, predictability, privacy, for me and for my family. It is where I live. What more can you say about a place than that? That is everything.

ANNA QUINDLEN, "HOMELESS"

2   The computer hacker is not a social animal. He struggles with small talk and has difficulty communicating with technically uninformed people, and his introversion confines him to a tightly knit circle of friends. Arriving unescorted at a party, he will drift about making perfunctory conversation before gravitating to the basement (or garage) to happily chat away in technobabble with two or three like-minded people. At the party's breakup, he will offer genuine thanks to the host, not so much for the Chivas, but for the chance to meet a fellow developer of self-propagating autonomous computer programs. A sporadic user of alcohol, the computer hacker breaks his prolonged dry spells with feverish bouts of whisky drinking with other hackers, who invariably spend the evening contriving a plot to destabilize the currency market.

JONATHAN RITTER, "THE WORLD VIEW OF THE COMPUTER HACKER"

3   The word *trade* was first recorded in 1546 to distinguish a "skilled handicraft" from a profession, business, or unskilled occupation. In Europe, there is a centuries-long tradition of tradespeople as vital, highly respected members of the community. First there was farming, then crafts or trades. Until recently, many British tradesmen went to work in a shirt and tie. There is a legend that the masters didn't even bother to change, so careful were they, so good at their craft that not even a small splash of mud could escape their skilled hand.

KATE BRAID, "A PLEA FOR THE PHYSICAL"

4   William Gibson has been recognized with numerous awards for his work on science fiction novels that portray a possible computer future just over the horizon. His fantasies are so realistic, so consistent with the present course of events, that inventors have developed some of the concepts and machines he describes because they make such sense as consistent moves "forward" from where we now stand with technology. Gibson describes a world far from Batula's, where the population spend much of their lives artificially stimulated by drugs and "slim-stims," virtual realities so real that people see no need to go to the trouble of immersing themselves in the real, messy, physical world itself.

KATE BRAID, "A PLEA FOR THE PHYSICAL"

READING TOPIC SENTENCES

No doubt by this point in the semester you have read textbooks in this and other courses. If you have underlined or highlighted as you studied, look at your textbooks.

1. Examine the sentences you highlighted. How many of them are topic sentences? Do they state a controlling idea supported by the rest of paragraph?
2. Skim through a few pages in your textbooks. How important are topic sentences in communicating ideas? Would it be harder to read and remember information if authors did not use topic sentences?

As you read, notice how writers use topic sentences to emphasize important ideas.

Writing Topic Sentences

To be effective, topic sentences have to be clearly and precisely worded. An abstract or general statement might express a controlling idea but give little direction to the paragraph. The more defined a topic sentence is, the easier it is for readers to grasp what you are trying to say.

EXERCISE 2 Topic Sentences and Controlling Ideas

Select the best topic sentence in each group.

1. a. _____ Halifax is the largest city in Nova Scotia.
   b. _____ I spent my freshman year in Halifax.
   c. _____ I loved going to college in Halifax.
   d. _____ My first semester in Halifax taught me lessons that shaped the rest of my life.

2. a. _____ Terrorism is a problem in our lives today.
   b. _____ Terrorism threatens to destroy the profitability of domestic airlines.
   c. _____ Terrorists have threatened the airlines.
   d. _____ The airlines face a major problem with terrorism.

3. a. _____ Car insurance should be mandatory in this province.
   b. _____ Last year over 15,000 uninsured drivers were involved in accidents.
   c. _____ My cousin was hit by a drunk driver who had no insurance.
   d. _____ Uninsured drivers pose a threat.

4. a. _____ Cyberstalking, which takes advantage of the anonymity of the Internet, has ruined lives, destroyed reputations, and led to at least six deaths.
   b. _____ Cyberstalking is a new kind of crime.
   c. _____ People have used the Internet to post threatening messages, spread rumours, or send counterfeit e-mails.
   d. _____ A disgruntled student sent official-looking e-mails identifying his teacher as a registered sex offender to dozens of citizens and government agencies.

5. a. _____ My high school football coach taught me discipline.
   b. _____ Playing basketball taught me the importance of teamwork.
   c. _____ I played on a tennis team that toured six states.
   d. _____ High school sports helped me make friends, learn the importance of teamwork, and appreciate the need for discipline.

EXERCISE 3 Developing Topic Sentences

Write a topic sentence for each subject, inventing details or opinions to express a controlling idea.

EX: Subject   **Binge drinking**

Topic sentence   *Binge drinking introduces students to a life-threatening set of habits.*

1. Subject Your favourite sports team

   Topic sentence _____

   _____

2. Subject Balancing work and school

   Topic sentence _____

   _____

3. Subject Teenagers and AIDS

   Topic sentence _____

   _____

4. Subject Shopping online

   Topic sentence _____

   _____

5. Subject High school gossip

   Topic sentence _____

   _____

Paragraphs without Topic Sentences

Some paragraphs may not have a topic sentence you can underline. But all have a controlling idea, a main point:

> The following morning the mayor and Red Cross officials, accompanied by a news crew, examined the damage left by Hurricane Hugo. More than a dozen beach homes had been swept out to sea, leaving only bent pilings. A quarter-mile section of the boardwalk, Margate's main street, was shattered. The beach was covered with shingles from nearby houses, toppled lifeguard towers, and thousands of cans and bottles blown from recycling bins. Wrecked sailboats were stacked like firewood alongside the main pier. The Margate Inn, a century-old bed and breakfast hotel popular with New York tourists, was ripped off its foundation and listed to one side like a sinking ocean liner.

The details about the storm are so clear that they can stand alone and do not need a topic sentence such as "Hurricane Hugo devastated Margate."

POINT TO REMEMBER

A paragraph may not have a topic sentence, but it must have unity and purpose. All the ideas in a paragraph should relate to a clear point readers will easily understand. *All paragraphs should have a controlling idea.*

EXERCISE 4 Identifying Controlling Ideas and Creating Topic Sentences

Read each paragraph and describe in your own words its controlling idea—its main idea. Then supply a possible topic sentence.

1   [When I was young], trips with Dad in the plane often felt like torture, but with hindsight I can see them as an exotic and charmed way to have spent a part of my youth. When I was around thirteen, my father flew my younger brother and me in the Twin Otter up to the Yukon. First, we overnighted in Whitehorse, a city of diesel fumes, hamburgers, beige dusty roads and people getting really *really* drunk at the local bars. The Klondike fulfills many expectations. The next day we headed off into Kluane (*kloo-awn-ay*) National Park—a place I never even knew existed, but to fly over it was to apprehend God or the next world or something altogether richer than the suburbs of home. Glaciers drape like mink over feldspar ridges like broken backs, and the twenty-four-hour midnight sun somehow burns paler and whiter than the sun in the south—and the horizon seems to come from a bigger planet. To see a wild landscape like this is to crack open your soul and see larger landscapes inside yourself. Or so I believe. Raw nature must be preserved, so that we never forget the grandeur it can inspire.

DOUGLAS COUPLAND, "THE YUKON"

Controlling idea: _____

_____

Possible topic sentence: _____

_____

2   The dabblers are the occasional users who go to the Net for several hours a week, usually to look up something specific, such as a Web site for a video game company or references to the Olympics for their son's school project. They might send an e-mail or two to friends across the country, explore tourist attractions in Florida, order concert tickets, or print out next week's train schedule. They might look up a site recommended by a co-worker, check a postal code, find a recipe, read a book review, or learn how to make a perfect martini. In other words, dabblers approach their computers with a particular task in mind. Once the task is accomplished, they log off and do something else. They see the Net as a tool, not a necessity. You know you're a dabbler if you'd rather watch TV, talk on the phone with a friend, or meet your sister for dinner than spend time in a chat room.

EVA TIHANYI, "CAUGHT IN THE NET"

Controlling idea: _____

_____

Possible topic sentence: _____

_____

3   At eight o'clock in the evening the house-doors will be locked. The children are having supper. The shops are shut. The electric-sign is switched on over the night-bell of the little hotel on the corner, where you can hire a room by the hour. And soon the whistling will begin. Young men are calling their girls. Standing down there in the cold, they whistle up at the lighted windows of warm rooms where the beds are already turned down for the night. They want to be let in. Their signals echo down the deep

hollow street, lascivious and private and sad. Because of the whistling, I do not care to stay here in the evenings. It reminds me that I am in a foreign city, alone, far from home. Sometimes I determine not to listen to it, pick up a book, try to read. But soon a call is sure to sound, so piercing, so insistent, so despairingly human, that at last I have to get up and peep through the slats of the Venetian blind to make quite sure that it is not—as I know very well it could not possibly be—for me.

CHRISTOPHER ISHERWOOD, "BERLIN DIARY"

Controlling idea: _____

_____

Possible topic sentence: _____

_____

4   Al Smith rolled heavy barrels of fish in and out of the market, put the fish on ice, cleaned them and wrapped them. He worked from four o'clock in the morning until five in the afternoon, except on Friday. On Friday, he started work at three. Returning home at night tired and dirty and reeking of fish, he scrubbed off the odor and went downstairs to the store. But in the 1890's twelve dollars a week was almost enough to support a mother and a sister. He stayed at the market for four years. Then, to increase his pay to fifteen dollars, he became a laborer, carrying heavy pipes at a pump works. It wasn't until 1896, when he was twenty-two years old, that he got his first political job.

ROBERT CARO, THE POWERBROKER

Controlling idea: _____

_____

Possible topic sentence: _____

_____

Revising Paragraphs

Even when you have an outline with clearly stated topic sentences, you may have difficulty making paragraph breaks as you write the first draft. New ideas will come to you as you write. Out of habit, you may produce a draft without paragraph breaks. In reading over paragraphs, look at your notes. What are your main ideas? Paragraphs should isolate main points and demonstrate transitions.

WORKING TOGETHER

Working with a group of students, read over this student essay and indicate where you would make paragraph breaks. What breaks will make the essay easier to read?

Television addiction is a compulsive disorder that affects the health and social development of many children. Although some experts dispute the accuracy of using the term *addiction* to describe excessive TV viewing, observers like Marie Winn insist the term applies. Like other addictive substances, television lets people blot out the real world and passively absorb rather than think or act. And like smokers or drinkers who want to quit, addicted TV viewers find it difficult to break the habit. Today television threatens the health of our children, who too often consume fattening junk food while they view television. Coming home from school, they watch cartoons, talk shows, soap operas, or the myriad of cable offerings. Instead of playing games or engaging in sports, they spend their free hours viewing television. Obesity is becoming a serious problem for adolescents, and many doctors confirm that excessive television watching plays a key role in promoting overeating and inactivity. In addition, excessive TV viewing has detrimental effects on a child's social development. The child who isolates himself or herself to watch TV does not interact with others by talking or playing games. He or she may feel more connected to sitcom families and soap opera characters than to brothers and sisters. Too often "family time" consists of people watching television together. Isolated and lonely children fall into a vicious circle of passive viewing rather than interacting with other people or exploring the world outside. Parents, accustomed to protecting children from the dangers of the outside world—crime, drugs, bad companions—often fail to see the damage TV poses.

_____

_____

_____

_____

_____

_____

_____

_____

_____

_____

_____

_____

_____

_____

_____

_____

_____

_____

_____

_____

_____

_____

In trying to get your thoughts on paper, you may find yourself listing ideas in two- or three-sentence paragraphs. In revising, identify your controlling ideas and organize supporting details to create fully developed paragraphs.

EXERCISE 5 Revising Paragraphs

Examine this draft of a student essay. Identify its main ideas and then rewrite the essay in no more than four paragraphs.

```
     I loved East Bay, Nova Scotia. We lived only a
few miles from the shore, and I often spent summer
afternoons sailing on the lake or walking on the
beach.
     I enjoyed my high school because I had a lot of
friends and participated in a lot of activities. I
played softball and football.
     My father was transferred to Toronto when I was
in grade eleven.
     I hated leaving my school and friends but thought
I would be able to adjust.
     I found the move harder to deal with than I
thought.
     Instead of living in a colonial house on a half-
acre lot, we moved into a downtown loft. It was spa-
cious, offered a wonderful view, and had both a
swimming pool and a health club.
     As big as our two-floor loft was, it began to
feel like a submarine. I missed the feel of wind and
fresh air.
     After two years in a city loft, I could not wait
to go to college in Halifax, Nova Scotia.
     The first thing I did when I got my acceptance
letter was to get my sailboat out of storage. I am
never going to live far from grass and water again.
```

_____

_____

_____

_____

_____

_____

_____

_____

_____

_____

_____

_____

_____

_____

_____

_____

Using Paragraph Breaks in Dialogue

Dialogue, direct quotations from a conversation, is hard to follow unless paragraphs show the transitions between speakers. Paragraph breaks show the back and forth nature of a conversation, clearly indicating when one person stops talking and another begins:

I get out of the car. The white man comes over and stands right in front of me. He's almost two feet taller.

"If you're going to drive, why don't you carry your license?" he asks in an accusatory tone.

"I didn't bring it," I say, for lack of any other defense.

I look at the damage to his car. It's minor, only a scratch on the paint and a pimple-sized dent.

"I'm sorry," I say. "Tell me how much it will cost to fix, and I'll pay for it; that's no problem." I'm talking to him in English, and he seems to understand.

"This car isn't mine," he says. "It belongs to the company I work for. I'm sorry, but I've got to report this to the police, so that I don't have to pay for the damage."

"That's no problem," I tell him again. "I can pay for it."

RAMÓN "TIANGUIS" PÉREZ, *Diary of an Undocumented Immigrant*

EXERCISE 6 Using Paragraph Breaks in Dialogue

Rewrite this paragraph to separate the direct quotations of the two speakers.

I love my sister, but often Sharon drives me crazy. Just last week I faced a crisis. I had to drive to school to take a makeup exam before my math teacher had to file her midterm grades. I got dressed, packed up my books, and raced downstairs to my car only to discover I had a flat tire. I raced upstairs and woke Sharon, who was still sleeping. "Sharon, I need to borrow your car," I blurted out. "Why," she asked, upset that I disturbed her. "My car has a flat." "So, this is your day off." "I know, but I have to make up an exam today." "Go tomorrow after work," she said. "No way," I told her. "I have to take the exam today. It's the last possible day for makeups," I argued. "I don't want anyone driving my new car," Sharon mumbled. "New car? It's five years old," I told her. "Well, it is new to me. Take the bus." At that moment the phone rang. Mom was on her way to drop off some clothes. She was only too glad to drop me off at school.

_____

_____

_____

_____

_____

_____

_____

_____

_____

_____

_____

_____

_____

_____

_____

_____

_____

_____

 **GET THINKING**
AND WRITING

CRITICAL THINKING

In two or more paragraphs describe the courses you are taking this semester. Which classes are the most interesting? What is the hardest course? Which course poses the greatest challenge?

WHAT HAVE YOU WRITTEN?

Write out the topic sentence or controlling idea for each paragraph. Is each one clearly stated? Could they be made more precise or more effective with different wording? Do the details in each paragraph support the controlling idea?

Do paragraphs help organize your thoughts and make logical transitions between main points?

Review your sentences for spelling errors (see Chapter 28), fragments (see Chapter 15), run-ons and comma splices (see Chapter 17), and errors in agreement (see Chapter 20 and page 347).

WHAT HAVE YOU LEARNED?

Answer each question about paragraphs True or False.

1. _____ Every paragraph must have a topic sentence.

2. _____ Paragraphs usually consist of three or more sentences.

3. _____ Paragraph breaks are essential when you present dialogue.

4. _____ Topic sentences always open a paragraph.

5. _____ An essay must always have five paragraphs.

Answers appear on the following page.

GET WRITING

Are creativity and personal expression important to you? Would you rather own your own business than work for a large corporation? Does a career mean more to you than money? Contrast the image of a potter in a studio with that of the executive on page 29.

Write a few sentences describing which photograph better expresses your idea of success.

WRITING ON THE WEB

Using a search engine such as AltaVista, Yahoo!, or Google, enter terms such as *paragraph design, modes of development, revising paragraphs,* and *topic sentences* to locate current sites of interest.

1. Review recent online articles and notice how writers select and organize details to support a topic sentence and express a controlling idea.
2. Note how authors use the modes of development to organize paragraphs.

POINTS TO REMEMBER

1. Paragraphs are the building blocks of an essay.
2. Every paragraph must have a controlling idea supported by details.
3. Paragraph breaks signal transitions between main points.
4. Paragraph breaks are used to separate direct quotations in dialogue.
5. Precisely worded topic sentences guide writing, helping you decide what details to include in paragraphs and which details to leave out.

ANSWERS TO WHAT HAVE YOU LEARNED? ON PAGE 43
1. false (see pages 33 and 36), 2. true, 3. true (see pages 31 and 41), 4. false (see page 33), 5. false

4

Supporting Topic Sentences with Details

Write a paragraph describing your reaction to the photograph. Many people perceive Canadians as living in a country where it is winter year round. And Canadians don't always think fondly of snow. Do children like winter? What winter activities are fun? What winter activities to you remember?

What Are Supporting Details?

Paragraphs need a topic sentence and a clear controlling idea. For the controlling idea to be effectively expressed, it must be supported by details—observations, experiences, facts, testimony, statistics, or examples. Without enough support, a topic sentence remains unproven. Irrelevant details can distract readers and weaken the controlling idea.

WHAT DO YOU KNOW?

Read the following paragraph carefully and underline the topic sentence, then cross out the sentences that do not support the controlling idea.

The college must improve its computer system. This semester almost five hundred students did not receive their final grades because of a programming error. The college e-mail system, which is critical to the distance learning department, was down for two weeks, preventing students from turning in assignments. The ten-year-old computer system lacks the speed, capacity, and sophistication our college needs. It's the same with the dorms. They are so old, more students are moving off campus. The school does not have enough parking lots to serve the growing number of adult students who want to come to class directly from work to take night classes. To attract students and expand services, the college must provide cutting-edge information technology the current system cannot support.

Answers appear on the following page.

GET WRITING
AND REVISING

WHAT ARE YOU TRYING TO SAY?

Select one of the topics below or develop one of your own and make a few notes before writing:

gas prices	soap operas	college sports
the evening news	AM radio	planning weddings
party crashers	campaign commercials	campus social life
fast food	car repairs	health insurance

Write a clear topic sentence and develop a paragraph that supports it with relevant details:

_____

_____

_____

_____

_____

_____

_____

_____

_____

_____

_____

_____

_____

◄

ANSWERS TO WHAT DO YOU
KNOW? ON PAGE 46
The college must improve its
computer system. Cross out the
following: *It's the same with the
dorms. They are so old, more
students are moving off campus.
The school does not have enough
parking lots to serve the growing
number of adult students who
want to come to class directly
from work to take night classes.*

WHAT HAVE YOU WRITTEN?

Read your paragraph carefully:

1. Underline the topic sentence. Is it clearly stated? Does it express a focused controlling idea?
2. Do the other sentences support the controlling idea, or do they introduce unrelated information? ◄

Steps to Building Effective Paragraphs

1. Start with a Clear Topic Sentence and Focused Controlling Idea

In Chapter 3 you learned the importance of developing a topic sentence. When you revise something you have written, examine your topic sentences to make sure they state a clear controlling idea.

Weak Topic Sentences	Improved Topic Sentences
My uncle taught me a lot.	My uncle taught me respect and discipline.
The Internet helps poor schools.	The Internet helps poor schools provide online resources their libraries cannot afford.

EXERCISE 1 Improving Topic Sentences

Revise each of the weak topic sentences, adding details to create a more focused controlling idea.

EX: **College is harder than high school.**

College demands more work and provides students with less support than high

school.

1. **Advertising can hurt impressionable teens.**

_____

2. Online dating can be dangerous.

_____

_____

3. Canadians should study foreign languages to help their country.

_____

_____

4. Balancing school and work is hard.

_____

_____

5. Exercise is beneficial.

_____

_____

2. Distinguish between Supporting Detail and Restating the Topic Sentence

Support does not just repeat ideas. A topic sentence makes a statement or expresses a point of view. The sentences that follow should provide additional information, observations, facts, examples, or quotations. In a rough draft you may find yourself repeating ideas rather than introducing support:

> Professional athletes are getting paid too much. Their salaries are out of hand. Teams are spending too much just to pay their players. These outrageous salaries are alienating fans, eroding the ability of teams in smaller markets to attract players, and making the game as a whole less interesting. Players should be compensated, but their salaries should not destroy the game that supports them—especially when they can make millions in lucrative endorsements.

The first sentence states the controlling idea. But the next two sentences simply repeat it and weaken the essay. In addition, there is little factual support for the writer's position. Deleting repetitive sentences and adding facts can strengthen the paragraph:

> Professional athletes are getting paid too much. In the 1970s basketball players' salaries were $100,000, or about twelve times the average teacher's income. Today the Toronto Raptors pay midlevel players millions of dollars, many times more than what a teacher earns. These outrageous salaries are alienating fans, eroding the ability of teams in smaller markets to attract players, and making the game as a whole less interesting. Players should be compensated, but their salaries should not destroy the game that supports them—especially when they can make millions in lucrative endorsements.

3. Support Topic Sentences with Adequate and Relevant Details

Topic sentences state an opinion or observation that requires adequate and relevant support. The other sentences should contain details that directly support the topic sentence—not simply list everything you know or can remember about the topic.

A topic sentence is not a writing prompt to inspire you to write everything you can think of, but a clear statement requiring specific evidence.

Vague

We must stop illegal immigration. We have to keep people from entering Canada by breaking the rules. All over the world people are waiting in refugee camps to enter this country. They take classes and learn English and wait their turn. But every year millions of illegal immigrants swim ashore or hide in shipping containers and ignore the law. People in this country feel they can break whatever law they please. Half the cars going down my street break the speed limit. The high school lawns are scattered with beer bottles. People nowadays have to go through metal detectors to keep them from bringing weapons into airports and courthouses. The convenience store on the corner placed steel bars over its windows to stop the break-ins. We don't need more people to add to this. People who break one law are going to break others. Illegal immigration poses a special threat to our security these days.

This paragraph has a clear topic sentence. But the second sentence simply restates the topic sentence. The sentences about speeders, metal detectors, and public security relate to general lawlessness and have little to do with illegal immigration. The last sentence mentions a "special threat" but provides no detailed support. Eliminating repetition and adding more specific detail can create a more effective paragraph:

Improved

We must stop illegal immigration. All over the world people are waiting in refugee camps to enter this country. They take classes preparing them to find jobs and housing and understand our banking system. They learn English. They follow the rules and pass through security screening before being granted visas. But each year millions of illegal immigrants swim ashore or hide in shipping containers and ignore the law. They enter the country ill equipped to fit into our society. Many become criminals or the victims of criminals. These days illegal immigration poses a special threat to our national security. It is too easy for terrorists to slip into this country across our unprotected borders. The routes illegal aliens and drug smugglers use today can be used tomorrow by terrorists to bring in weapons of mass destruction.

EXERCISE 2 Recognizing Relevant Supporting Details

Read each topic sentence carefully and check those sentences that provide relevant support. Ignore sentences that simply restate the topic sentence or contain irrelevant details.

1. Public schools should not ignore the importance of physical education.

   a. _____ Many school officials ignore the value of physical education.

   b. _____ Physical education provides young people with supervised activities that burn off stress in productive games and sports.

   c. _____ Physical education teaches students the need for proper exercise and nutrition to maintain health and avoid disease.

d. _____ Public schools face dwindling resources and more children needing special assistance.

e. _____ Nearly 40 percent of today's children are overweight because they do not get enough exercise.

2. Vancouver is the fastest-growing city in Canada.

a. _____ Retirees find the moderate climate of the city appealing.

b. _____ Families with young children move to Vancouver to take advantage of the city's highly regarded school system.

c. _____ Vancouver is building housing at a rate higher than that of any other city in Canada.

d. _____ Vancouver has been featured in many motion pictures.

e. _____ Because the city is so popular, residents pay very high property taxes, making home purchases less affordable.

3. Cable television provides filmmakers with the chance to make movies traditional producers and distributors would reject.

a. _____ Cable channels like HBO earn revenue from millions of subscribers, unlike movie studios that have to sell tickets.

b. _____ An art film that might sell only a handful of tickets in one city could attract a significant national audience that makes a cable channel profitable.

c. _____ Cable television fees keep rising.

d. _____ Cable television is noted for showing daring programs.

e. _____ Unlike movie houses, which have limited hours, cable channels screen movies around the clock, so art films can serve as late-night filler if needed.

4. Immigration changed the face of Canadian cities in the early 1900s.

a. _____ Urban neighbourhoods revealed the influence of new arrivals.

b. _____ Immigrants introduced new cuisine, new customs, and new fashions.

c. _____ Streets in Toronto, Calgary, and Vancouver now featured Jewish delis, Irish pubs, German bakeries, and Italian restaurants.

d. _____ The automobiles began to replace the horse, and soon every major city was building an airport.

e. _____ Catholic schools and synagogues sprouted up among the long-established Protestant churches.

5. We must stop the destruction of rain forests.

a. _____ Rain forests produce much of the planet's oxygen.

b. _____ Rain forests must be saved from eradication.

c. _____ Each day thousands of acres of precious rain forest are cut for timber or to provide pastureland for farm animals.

d. _____ Rain forests have rare plants that may contain cures for many deadly human diseases.

e. _____ People take the environment for granted.

Types of Support

Observations and Personal Experiences

Personal observations include details and impressions about a person, place, thing, or situation. If you write an essay about your high school football team, much of the supporting detail would include your memories of the coach, the players, key games, and other teams. A topic sentence stating that high school football builds character could include your observations of friends who developed discipline and became more mature by playing on the team. An essay about urban renewal could contain your observations of new buildings in your neighbourhood.

Like personal observations, accounts from your own life can supply rich details to support a topic sentence. As a college student, you are a participant in postsecondary education. Your experiences as a parent, a car buyer, or a new Canadian can provide insights unavailable in facts and figures.

Personal accounts can humanize an issue and provide gripping evidence. Carol Geddes uses her own childhood experience to demonstrate the extent of culture shock for native children in schools:

> Going to school in Whitehorse was a shock. The clash of native and white values was confusing and frightening. Let me tell you a story. The older boys in our community were already accomplished hunters and fishermen, but since they had to trap beaver in the spring and hunt moose in the fall, and go out trapping in the winter as well, they missed a lot of school. We were all in one classroom and some of my very large teenage cousins had to sit squeezed into little desks. These guys couldn't read very well. We girls had been to school all along, so, of course, we were better readers. One day the teacher was trying to get one of the older boys to read. She was typical of the teachers at the time, insensitive and ignorant of cultural complexities. In an increasingly loud voice, she kept commanding him to "Read it, read it." He couldn't. He sat there completely still, but I could see that he was breaking into a sweat. The teacher then said, "Look, she can read it," and she pointed to me, indicating that I should stand up and read. For a young child to try to show up an older boy is wrong and totally contrary to native cultural values, so I refused. She told me to stand up and I did. My hands were trembling as I held my reader. She yelled at me to read and when I didn't she smashed her pointing stick on the desk to frighten me. In terror, I wet my pants. As I stood there fighting my tears of shame, she said I was disgusting and sent me home. I had to walk a long distance through the bush to get to my home. I remember feeling this tremendous confusion, on top of my humiliation. We were always told the white teachers know best, and so we had to do whatever they said at school. And yet I had a really strong sense of receiving mixed messages about what I was supposed to do in the community and what I was supposed to do at school.

> **"GROWING UP NATIVE"**

TIPS FOR USING PERSONAL OBSERVATIONS AND EXPERIENCES AS SUPPORT

1. **Personal observations and experiences are best suited for personal essays.** They may not be appropriate in objective research papers or business reports.
2. **Make sure your observations and experiences directly support the topic sentence.** Your goal is not to tell a story but provide support. Avoid including unnecessary detail or unrelated events.
3. **Because personal experiences and observations are only one person's opinion or story, balance this support with facts, statistics, or other people's experiences.** Understand the limits of personal experiences as evidence. You may have to prove that your observations or experiences are not isolated events.
4. **Use personal observations and experiences to humanize impersonal data such as numbers and statistics.**

Examples

Examples are specific events, people, objects, or situations that represent a general trend. Although they are individual items, they are not isolated. If you want to support a topic sentence that asserts the need for better campus daycare, you might tell the story of one single parent to demonstrate the problem. To support her view that reading is a complex skill, Eileen Simpson uses specific letters of the alphabet to show how easily they can be confused by children with dyslexia:

> Reading is the most complex skill a child entering school is asked to develop. What makes it complex, in part, is that letters are less constant than objects. A car seen from a distance, close to, from above, or below, or in a mirror still looks like a car even though the optical image changes. The letters of the alphabet are more whimsical. Take the letter *b*. Turned upside down it becomes a *p*. Looked at in a mirror, it becomes a *d*. Capitalized, it becomes something quite different, a *B*. The *M* upside down is a *W*. The *E* flipped over becomes ∃. The reversed *E* is familiar to mothers of normal children who have just begun to go to school. The earliest examples of art work they bring home often have I LOV∃ YOU written on them.
>
> *REVERSALS*

TIPS FOR USING EXAMPLES AS SUPPORT

1. **Make sure your examples are representative — not exceptions.** Listing a half dozen celebrities who are high school dropouts does not adequately support the idea that staying in school is a waste of time.
2. **Use examples people recognize.** Avoid using as examples obscure people or events that require lengthy explanations.
3. **Provide more than one example if you can.**
4. **Blend examples with factual support.** To prove that your example is not an isolated case, provide statistics or expert testimony.

Facts

Facts are observable and objective details that can be checked, examined, and documented by others. A personal observation might state, "Tom has an old car." The term "old" is a personal impression that some people could debate. "Tom has a 1984 Mustang" is a factual statement that anyone can easily verify. Facts are not opinions, but they can be used to support opinions. Opinions are statements that express a personal interpretation or point of view. Opinions can be used as support (see page 54), but they should not be confused with facts:

Opinions	Facts
The building is too tall for the neighbourhood.	The building is twenty-two stories high.
Sarah is too young to live alone.	Sarah is seventeen years old.
This computer is very affordable.	This computer costs $799.95.

Because facts are objective, they can provide powerful support for a topic sentence. In some cases writers choose to let facts speak for themselves and present them without a topic sentence. Although there is no topic sentence, Louise McCready's description of the Montreal Symphony Orchestra has a clear controlling idea:

> In its first season the orchestra gave only seven concerts and was heard by about 5,000 people. Today, each season is made up of forty-five performances and attended by 100,000 people. Dr. Pelletier has a continuing interest in it and often conducts the orchestra. There is never any trouble finding a conductor, however; the Montreal Symphony Orchestra is one of Canada's finest and easily attracts conductors such as Bruno Walter, Charles Munch, Sir Thomas Beecham, Leopold Stokowski and others of similar ability and fame. Artists such as Arthur Rubinstein, Rudolf Serkin and Ezio Pinza also have performed with the orchestra.
>
> *CANADIAN PORTRAITS*

TIPS FOR USING FACTS AS SUPPORT

1. **Facts should directly support the topic sentence or controlling idea, not bring up other issues.**
2. **Use facts from reliable sources readers will recognize and respect.** Facts taken from government publications, encyclopedias, and mainstream magazines will be more convincing than facts from someone's home page or an advertisement.
3. **Use facts to balance personal observations and examples to add credibility to your opinions.**
4. **Make sure you use representative facts.** Don't just pick facts that support your opinion. Try to get the big picture and use facts fairly. Don't take facts out of context.

Statistics

Statistics are facts expressed in numbers. Statistics can make dramatic statements readers can easily understand and remember:

> Over 15 percent of Canadians do not have dental insurance.
> One in nine women will develop breast cancer.
> This year 85 percent of our high school graduates will go on to college or university.

Used properly, statistics are convincing evidence to support a topic sentence. David Foote uses numbers to prove his point that demographics are important:

The tennis boom started in the early 1970s when most of the population were in their teens and 20s. Those are prime tennis-playing years. In the mid-1990s, the boomers are in their 30s and 40s, with the oldest among them pushing 50. Those are prime years for leaving tennis racquets in basements and closets. Of course, many middle-aged and older people still play tennis just as they always have. A former governor general of Canada, Roland Michener, for example, was still playing in his 90s. Nevertheless, the reality is that the average 90-year-old and the average 40-year-old are both less likely to pick up a tennis racquet than the average 20-year-old. The tennis boom was predictable in 1970 to anyone who understood demographics. And the decline in participation was just as predictable in 1970 as it is obvious in the mid-1990s.

BOOM, BUST & ECHO

TIPS FOR USING STATISTICS AS SUPPORT

1. **Make sure the items being counted are clearly defined.** Statistics about juvenile delinquents, for example, are not accurate if people use different definitions of delinquency.
2. **Use statistics from reliable government sources, academic institutions, respected writers, or mainline magazines.**
3. **Make sure you present enough statistics.** Stating that "over 80 percent of Amalgamated Enterprises workers own stock in the company" makes the firm sound employee owned—until you learn the average worker has only a dozen shares. Ninety percent of the stock could be held by outsiders or even a single investor.
4. **Consider alternative interpretations of statistics.** Often numbers can be interpreted differently. If reports of child abuse have risen 50 percent in two years, does this mean more children are being abused or just that more cases are being reported?

Testimony (Quotations)

Testimony includes the words, experiences, opinions, and observations of others. They can be participants in an event, witnesses, or outside experts. Testimony can be stated in direct quotations that repeat word for word what someone wrote or said or in indirect summaries. The words or observations of a single real person can add life to a paragraph.

Matthew McClearn uses the words of a judge to dramatize the problems caused by professionals who snoop in people's garbage:

Certain courts, however, have ruled the opposite. In 1988, the Supreme Court of the United States ruled that the U.S. Constitution's Fourth Amendment (which outlines personal rights against unreasonable searches and seizures) does not prohibit the taking of garbage outside a home. That same reality faced John Krist, a marijuana grower in Pitt Meadows, B.C. Krist was arrested shortly after police found marijuana plants and growing paraphernalia in his garbage. Krist argued that the seizure violated Section 8 of Canada's Charter of Rights and Freedoms, which is similar to the Fourth Amendment. However, successive courts ruled that Krist's trash was fair game. "Putting material in the garbage signifies that the material is no

longer something of value or importance to the person disposing of it,"
wrote Justice Anne Rowles of the Court of Appeal for British Columbia in a
1995 decision. "When trash is abandoned, there is no longer a reasonable
expectation of privacy in respect to it."

"THE LAW OF THE CURB," CANADIAN BUSINESS

TIPS FOR USING TESTIMONY AS SUPPORT

1. **Avoid using quotations from famous people unless they directly support your topic sentence.** Adding quotations by Shakespeare or Martin Luther King, no matter how impressive, will only distract readers unless the words clearly support your controlling idea.
2. **Make sure you quote people accurately.** Don't rely on your memory of what someone said. Try to locate the original source and copy it accurately.
3. **Place direct quotations in quotation marks.** Remember to use quotation marks when you copy word for word what someone else has said or written. (See page 21.)
4. **Do not take quotations out of context.** Make sure that the quotations you use reflect someone's overall attitudes and experiences, not isolated outbursts.
5. **If needed, explain whom you are quoting.** Testimony will be effective only if readers understand the speaker's knowledge or value. Just adding quotations to a paragraph will not impress readers:

The rising crime rate is ruining the South Side. Joe Long said, "I can't take it anymore, so I am moving."

Improved

The rising crime rate is ruining the South Side. Joe Long, who has lived here for thirty-eight years, said, "I can't take it anymore, so I am moving."

6. **Verify the accuracy and validity of opinions.** Opinions can be powerful evidence, as long as the person you are quoting is a respected expert or authority. Avoid biased opinions or those based on little factual support.

Blending Support

Because each type of support has limitations, writers often use more than one to
provide evidence for a topic sentence:

Are welfare recipients more likely than others to commit bank fraud? A recent pilot project conducted by the Van Horne–Victoria branch of the Bank of Nova Scotia in Montreal suggests that they are not. The branch issued automatic teller cards to 100 recipients of social assistance and provided them with a bank account. The card could be used with only the one account, and the study participants could withdraw funds only by waiting for one day for their assistance cheques to clear. After more than three months, "no fraud was detected among the 100 trial accounts," says Branch Manager, Eli Hachem. Subsequently, the size of the test group was increased to 265 accounts and again no fraud was detected. The bank has recently

topic sentence

facts

expert testimony

facts

concluding sentence

increased the number of these accounts by another 100. The results are that the branch's customer base has increased by some 500 new accounts and another stereotype has been successfully challenged.

POINT TO REMEMBER

In selecting support, ask this question: Does this support my controlling idea? In writing the first draft you may remember facts or experiences. New ideas about your subject may come to mind. But unless these details directly support the topic sentence, they do not belong in this paragraph.

EXERCISE 3 Developing Supporting Details

Supply supporting details for each topic sentence. Make sure the details directly support the controlling idea expressed by the topic sentence.

1. Coach Wilson gets the most from his players.

   a. Testimony _____

   b. Example _____

   c. Fact _____

   d. Personal observation _____

2. Single parents face special problems when they attend college.

   a. Statistics _____

   b. Testimony _____

   c. Example _____

   d. Fact _____

3. Hollywood gives young people misleading ideas about adult life.

   a. Testimony _____

   b. Fact _____

   c. Personal observation _____

   d. Example _____

4. Good jobs are almost impossible to find without higher education.

   a. Statistics _____

   b. Fact _____

   c. Example _____

   d. Personal experience _____

5. Young people take their health for granted.

   a. Example _____

   b. Fact _____

c. Statistics _____

d. Personal observations _____

EXERCISE 4 Revising the Paragraph

Revise this paragraph, deleting repetitive and irrelevant details and adding your own ideas that support the topic sentence.

Peer pressure can overwhelm teenagers. The need to feel "in" can consume a teen's life. Without the right clothes, the right makeup, the right shoes, the right palm pilot or cell phone, young people are exiled, ridiculed, and mocked. Children have been known to drop out of school because their families cannot afford the stylish clothes that seem mandatory to win acceptance. This kind of behaviour reinforces the worst kind of values. Societies often have unhealthy values. Not that long ago blacks were barred from certain clubs, schools, and restaurants. The Chinese were once not allowed to own certain businesses. Many universities limited the number of Jewish students who could attend. Today young people learn that style is more important than character and that material possessions are the measure of success. No wonder we are a nation of consumers who can barely pay our credit card bills. We learn too early that things are supposed to make us happy.

EXERCISE 5 Writing Organized Paragraphs

Write a well-organized paragraph that builds on one or more of the following topic sentences.

1. First-year students need discipline to avoid distractions that might jeopardize their academic performance.

2. Men and women have different attitudes about dating.

3. Parents must monitor their children's use of the Internet.

4. Canadians must learn more about the Arab world.

5. The fashion industry gives young girls unrealistic images of women's bodies.

WORKING TOGETHER

Working with a group of students, edit this paragraph from a student paper to eliminate repetition and irrelevant details. Review sentences for fragments (see Chapter 15), comma splices (see pages 263–264), and misspelled words (see Chapter 28).

```
    For the first time in my life. I could not wait
for school to start. I could not wait for summer
vacation to end. Normally I love summer. Throughout
high school, I spent most summers at my parents'
```

beach house, working on the boardwalk with two of my cousins and their friends. But this past summer I worked third shift at a convenience store. The job payed minimun wage. I got the lowest pay the law allows. I had to stand behind a registor, handle drunks demanding beer after hours, and endure hours of endless boredom waiting for seven a.m. By three a.m. my eyes felt like sand paper, my legs ached, and my head ached. When my shift was over I went home but was unable to sleep during the day. I was always tired. I never got enough rest. I was a like a zombie all summer. I may not know what job I want after I finish college, I certainly know what I don't want.

_____

_____

_____

_____

_____

_____

_____

_____

_____

_____

_____

_____

GET THINKING AND WRITING

CRITICAL THINKING

In recent years a number of trials have been broadcast on television. Do you think that cameras in the courtroom distort justice and turn trials into theatre? Or do they teach people about our criminal justice system? Write one or more paragraphs stating an opinion supported by details.

WHAT HAVE YOU WRITTEN?

Read your paragraphs out loud. Is there a clear controlling idea? Have you stated it in a topic sentence? Do you provide enough supporting detail? Are there irrelevant details that should be deleted? Edit your sentences for run-ons and comma splices (see Chapter 17), agreement errors (see Chapter 20), and misplaced modifiers (see Chapter 18).

Compare this image with the one on page 45. Is your reaction to this one different? Do you see a connection between these two photographs? Does our culture glorify guns and violence? How can we prevent juvenile crime? What motivates young people to turn to violence?

Write a paragraph describing what this image symbolizes to you. If you see it as evidence of a social problem, you may wish to outline one or more possible solutions.

WHAT HAVE YOU LEARNED?

Read the following paragraph carefully and underline the topic sentence, then cross out the sentences that do not support the controlling idea.

Obesity is a major problem in the twenty-first century because our bodies were designed to store calories. The human body was designed to store excess food for future times of need. For thousands of years humans lived on what they could hunt, fish, or gather. Even early farmers were forced to go without food until their crops were ready to harvest. The ability to store excess calories helped them survive days or weeks of hunger. But today people have access to food twenty-four hours a day. We eat many more calories than we use and store the rest as fat. We eat a lot more food than we need to. We put on weight because we don't have the sporadic food supply our ancestors faced. The biological feature that helped humans survive centuries ago now causes us to die early of heart disease and diabetes unless we change our lifestyles.

Answers appear on the following page.

WRITING ON THE WEB

Using a search engine such as AltaVista, Yahoo!, or Google, enter terms such as *paragraph design, modes of development, revising paragraphs,* and *topic sentences* to locate current sites of interest.

1. Review recent online articles and notice how writers select and organize details to support a topic sentence and express a controlling idea.
2. Note how authors use the modes of development to organize paragraphs.

POINTS TO REMEMBER

1. Paragraphs must have clearly stated controlling ideas.
2. Topic sentences must be supported with facts, statistics, personal observations and experiences, or testimony.
3. Avoid simply restating the topic sentence.
4. Details should directly support the topic sentence, not introduce new or irrelevant ideas.
5. Each type of support has limitations, so use more than one.

ANSWERS TO WHAT HAVE YOU LEARNED? ON PAGE 59
Obesity is a major problem in the twenty-first century because our bodies were designed to store calories.
Cross out the following: *The human body was designed to store excess food for future times of need. We eat a lot more food than we need to.*

5

Developing Paragraphs Using Description

What is your first reaction when you see this picture? How did it affect you? How do you think the people close to the fire were affected?

Select details and choose words carefully to develop a paragraph that describes the destructive force of a raging forest fire.

What Is Description?

Description presents facts, images, and impressions of people, places, things, and events. It records what we see, hear, feel, taste, touch, and smell. Good description not only presents information but brings subjects to life:

> Saudi Arabia is a striking blend of shopping malls and mosques, camels and BMWs, vast deserts and palatial fountains.

> Exhausted by the six-week trial, Ahmed Rajpour tapped the phone nervously, unsure how to tell his boss about the jury's verdict.

> To maintain its reputation for objective reporting, the student newspaper never endorses student council candidates.

GET WRITING
AND REVISING

WHAT ARE YOU TRYING TO SAY?

Write a paragraph describing one of the following:

- your first car
- your favourite store
- people found at a local store, club, concert, or coffee shop
- your favourite television show
- the best or worst neighbourhood in your town
- the greatest or most disappointing party or restaurant you have experienced

_____

_____

_____

_____

_____

_____

_____

_____

_____

_____

_____

_____

_____

_____

_____

_____

_____

_____

_____

_____

_____

_____

_____

◄

Read your paragraph carefully. Underline those words that provide details about your subject. Does your description give readers a clear impression? Could minor details be deleted? Could your word choices be more precise? ◄

Creating Dominant Impressions

The goal in writing description is not to list every detail you can think of but to highlight a major point by creating dominant impressions readers will remember. If you attempt to provide readers with everything you can remember about your first apartment, your description can become a jumble of obvious and trivial details:

> On August 23, 2001, I moved into my first apartment, the top floor of a duplex on Seaton Street. The living room had a sofa and a coffee table. On the right side of the room was a series of wall units containing books and CDs. On the left side of the room was a small desk and the stereo. The TV was opposite the sofa. Behind the sofa were three large windows and a door, which opened onto a small porch. There were two small bedrooms. They did not have closets but did have built-in wardrobes. The dining room was large with built-in shelves and large windows. The kitchen was a small L-shaped room. It contained a stove, refrigerator, and a large sink. Next to the kitchen was a small bathroom with a bathtub but no shower. Although awkward, the apartment had plenty of space for my friends when they came over. I only lived there a year, but I remember it fondly.

The paragraph provides many details but tells us very little. The writer states he or she recalls the apartment fondly but gives no reasons why. Much of the paragraph is cluttered with unimportant details—the date, the address, and furniture arrangements. It also is filled with obvious details like the living room having a sofa and the kitchen having a stove.

A more effective description deletes minor and obvious details to create a dominant impression:

> My first apartment was a large, poorly designed flat. The spacious living and dining rooms featured large French windows, built-in shelves, palatial mouldings, and ornate doorknobs. In contrast, the L-shaped kitchen was so narrow that only one person could squeeze past the refrigerator at a time. The child-sized bedrooms looked like crew quarters on a battleship. Both were 9x9, made smaller by large built-in wardrobes. However, the large living room was perfect for my friends. I lived only a block from school, and almost every afternoon friends dropped by to crash, eat takeout pizza, watch soaps, play video games, or surf the Internet to conduct research. That oddly shaped flat became a collective hangout, restaurant, and library.

We worked, partied, dated, and tutored each other through our toughest year of college. I've moved to a better apartment, but I will always think of that odd flat as the best place to have spent my first year away from home.

By creating a dominant impression, adding brief narratives to include action, and showing rather than telling why the apartment holds fond memories, the description becomes lively and effective.

POINT TO REMEMBER

The dominant impression is the controlling idea of a description paragraph.

EXAM SKILLS

Many examination questions call for writing one or more description paragraphs. As with any exam, read the question carefully and make sure your paragraph directly responds to it.

*From **Introduction to Abnormal Psychology***

What are the principal characteristics of paranoid schizophrenia?

general description   *Paranoid schizophrenia is one of four main types of schizophrenia, one of the common and most devastating mental illnesses. The main characteristics include delusions of per-*

details   *secution, racing thoughts, delusions of grandeur, illogical and unrealistic thoughts, and hallucinations. Patients may believe they are being spied upon or conspired against. They often are suspicious of doctors, friends, and family members. Social withdrawal and hostile outbursts make it difficult for them to retain relationships or hold down jobs. The disease can be disabling, even life-threatening. Drugs can control symptoms,*

general description   *but many patients do not take their medication because of the side effects.*

The paragraph opens with a general description of the disease, noting that it is one of several types of schizophrenia. The student then provides a list of specific characteristics. The student ends the paragraph by describing current treatment.

EXERCISE 1 Recognizing Dominant Impressions and Supporting Details

Read the following descriptive paragraph and identify the dominant impression and controlling idea and list the supporting details.

You'll be in the right place if you see the smoky lavender of the prairie grass and the burnt yellow of the wild wheat bordering the road. And not much else. No traffic. No life. The road itself will be cracked in the way that only the prairies can sculpt muck. Dried muck like pieces of a jigsaw puzzle . . . one of those jigsaws that's all in tones of one colour. Tones of gray. It won't be easy to see me. I'll be blending right in with the dirt. So, you'll have to be in the right area of the map. Mid-prairies. Mid-desolation. Side-by-side. There's not a lot of relief in either location.

ELLYN PEIRSON, "JOEY"

Dominant impression:

_____

_____

Supporting details:

1. _____

2. _____

3. _____

4. _____

Key words:

1. _____ 2. _____

3. _____ 4. _____

5. _____ 6. _____

7. _____ 8. _____

9. _____ 10. _____

EXERCISE 2 Creating Dominant Impressions

Create a dominant impression for each subject.

1. **Your elementary school**

_____

_____

2. **A talk show host**

_____

_____

3. **People waiting at an airport gate for a late plane**

_____

_____

4. **Favourite childhood game or pastime**

_____

_____

5. **Your boss on a very bad day**

_____

_____

EXERCISE 3 Supporting Dominant Impressions

Select a topic from Exercise 2 and list examples of details that would support the dominant impression.

Dominant impression:

_____

_____

Supporting details:

1. _____

2. _____

3. _____

4. _____

Improving Dominant Impressions and Supporting Detail

To be effective, dominant impressions and supporting details have to be precisely stated. The words you choose and the way readers react to them are critical in developing a description paragraph.

EXERCISE 4 Revising Dominant Impressions and Supporting Details

Revise the following descriptions by inventing details and adding more precise and effective word choices (see pages 202–208 about word choice and connotations).

1 The restaurant was wonderful. We were seated at a good table with an excellent view. The music was perfect. After a nice glass of wine, we enjoyed a great Italian meal. Everything about the food was great. The evening ended with coffee and dessert, which was very good.

2 The movie was terrible. The plot made no sense. The action scenes were confusing and too violent. The lead actress did not act well. Her scenes were so fake. The musical score did not suit the mood of the movie. The ending was very bad.

3 The old college library was great. The furniture and paintings made you feel you were in a historic place. The books were easy to find. The old lamps on the book tables were interesting. You really felt you were in college when you walked in.

4 This year's football team is the best ever. The coach is smart. The quarterback repeatedly shows a lot of skill. The defence has great ability. All the players work so well.

5 I learned a lot delivering papers after school in junior high. The job made me responsible. I had to change my habits. I learned the importance of being organized. Problems forced me to think for myself.

Student Paragraphs

Description of a person:

I'm part of a growing group of people called CBCs or Canadian-born Chinese. My parents came to Canada from Hong Kong thirty years ago. My father, originally from Shanghai, met my mother in Kowloon while he was visiting a relative. I was born in Toronto into a traditional Chinese family. I speak Cantonese with my mother, but she has to correct me all the time. Even though I look Chinese, people in the Chinese community treat me like an outsider because I speak Cantonese so poorly.

Description of a place:

Ground Zero now looks very innocent. From the viewing stand you can see a vast square pit the size of a strip mine. Trucks move back and forth down below like tiny toys. It looks like a construction site on a grand scale. Men in yellow hard hats signal each other with flags. Forklifts carry building materials. The place almost looks hopeful, like the foundation of the world's biggest building. The looks on the faces of tourists who come every day from Japan, Germany, Italy, and Kansas, however, remind you of what happened here.

Description of an event:

Last Saturday Gaye and Alan hosted their second annual "Winter Patio Party"—an outside barbeque in the middle of February. The backyard patio was swept clear of snow and ice and then covered with a red awning that looked like a giant umbrella. Tropical plants and flowers (fake, of course!) were placed around the floor and the giant heater that stood in the centre. Guests, in their parkas and winter coats, sipped fruity drinks while waiting for the main course to come off the grill. Dessert, however, was served inside—it was ice cream!

PUTTING PARAGRAPHS TOGETHER

The First Internet

Over a hundred and fifty years ago, Morse invented the telegraph. <u>Within a few years this invention changed the nineteenth century the way the Internet changed the late twentieth.</u> The telegraph revolutionized how people communicated, how countries received news, and how companies conducted business.

introduction

topic sentence

supporting details

1. How does this paragraph introduce readers to the topic?
2. How does the student describe the impact of the telegraph?

description of communications
before and after telegraph

Before the telegraph, people had to rely on hand-delivered messages or flag signals that could be seen for only a few miles in good weather. The telegraph now made it possible to send a message hundreds or thousands of miles in a few minutes. Now businesses could quickly negotiate with each other in far-off locations. During wartime news was telegraphed nationwide, so that the public could follow events on a daily basis. <u>The telegraph erased distances, sped up the pace of life, and unified the country.</u>

topic sentence

1. How does this paragraph build on the first one?
2. What details does the student include to describe how the telegraph changed people's lives and historical events?
3. The student places the topic sentence last. Is this effective? Why or why not?

topic sentence

<u>The telegraph, like the Internet, empowered average citizens.</u> People could now send telegrams and instantly communicate with friends, family, and clients. A small entrepreneur in Kelowna could now do business in Toronto or Montreal without opening expensive offices. Average citizens could flash telegrams to the prime minister's office. The telegraph captured people's imaginations. One couple living in different cities actually were married by telegraph.

descriptive
details

1. How does this paragraph follow the previous ones?
2. How do the details support the topic sentence?
3. What impact does the last line have?

Readings

As you read these descriptions, notice how writers use details to create dominant impressions.

PROSPECTS GRIM FOR DAVIS INLET

MICHAEL MACDONALD

Michael MacDonald, a Canadian Press reporter, visited Davis Inlet, an isolated Innu community in northern Labrador, describing the ongoing struggle of this forgotten group for survival.

AS YOU READ:

Notice how MacDonald organizes and selects details, mixing objective reporting with strong, powerful imagery of the people and places of Davis inlet.

1　DAVIS INLET, Nfld. (CP)—Sitting in a filthy, two-room house on Labrador's north coast, surrounded by <u>bleary-eyed</u> drunks, Mary Margaret Rich is yelling at the top of her lungs. "I miss my kids," the woman shouts. Trouble is, her brain is so soaked in booze she can't recall how many of them were among the 35 Innu kids recently sent away to be treated for various addictions, including gasoline sniffing. While some of the children from Davis Inlet may be getting the help they need, many of the alcoholic adults appear to be getting worse.

2　And what's even more disturbing is the widely held belief that most of their children will quickly resume gas sniffing once they return to this bleak place. "Nothing will ever change," says Rich, whose ample 39-year-old frame is shrouded in a shapeless, grimy parka. "And I know why. Children sniff because they want to sniff. I don't know what they want."

3　Rich, who was born in Davis Inlet, admits that she used to sniff gas when she was 16 or 17. Then she started drinking. She says she swore off alcohol a year ago, but that's not apparent on this day. Her stringy black hair and bloated face make her look 10 years older than she is. As Rich speaks, two neighbours shuffle closer to add their thoughts. A woman in a red <u>toque</u>, who appears to be in her fifties, wags an index finger and slurs her words so badly not a single syllable makes sense. The other woman, clutching a glass of some kind of hard liquor, spits out a <u>diatribe</u> that starts with: "I lost my wedding dress and I lost my boyfriend."

4　The house itself is a sliver of the Third World. There is paint peeling from the walls, the floor is covered in cold muck and a heap of cigarette butts surrounds a wood stove. There is no plumbing, only a plastic bucket filled with icy water. Hidden somewhere in the back is a 16-ounce bottle of <u>bootleg booze</u> that cost $300. There are many houses like this in Davis Inlet, a graffiti-scarred island community that was settled in 1967 after government officials decided the nomadic Innu should stay in one place. The Innu were lured here with promises of good homes equipped with indoor plumbing. But those promises were never kept. Within a few years, the Innu social order was in ruins as alcoholism crept into many lives.

5　Today, it's easy to spot the hard drinkers as they stumble through the snow. Even on a sunny Saturday morning they seem to outnumber the sober residents. On the back wall of one <u>dilapidated</u> building, someone has spray-painted: Once we were warriors. Know (sic) we are lost. Down the road, Charlie Pokue scrambles out of his house and insists he has something important to say. But first, there's a <u>caveat</u>. "I'm intoxicated right now, so I won't be driving the <u>Ski-Doo</u>— my woman will be driving," he says with a smile as the snowmobile roars to life.

6　Pokue, a stocky man with black, curly hair and a <u>pock-marked</u> face, says gas sniffing is a serious problem in Davis Inlet, but quickly adds:

Words to Know

bleary-eyed having blurred vision

toque a tight-fitting knitted hat or cap
diatribe bitter disapproval of a person or thing

bootleg booze alcohol that has been obtained unlawfully

dilapidated falling to pieces, partially ruined or decayed through neglect
caveat warning
Ski-Doo snowmobile

pock-marked skin scarred as a result of illness or skin conditions

"There's a lot of boozin' going on here, too." Asked if the young gas sniffers would give up their habit if their parents stopped drinking, he says: "I doubt it very much. Nothing will change." ■

CRITICAL THINKING AND DISCUSSION

Understanding Meaning: What Is the Writer Trying to Say?

1. What is the dominant image that MacDonald creates?
2. Does the description of the people and the places they live in clarify the despair of their circumstances?
3. Does this description help you understand why many people in Davis inlet have little hope for the future?

Evaluating Strategy: How Does the Writer Say It?

1. How important are specific details in describing the homes and people of Davis inlet? Underline facts and details you find significant.
2. How does MacDonald use paragraphs to organize his description?

Appreciating Language: What Words Does the Writer Use?

1. MacDonald uses the phrase "Nothing will change" in paragraph one and again in paragraph six. What impact does this repetition have on the overall impression of this article? What is the writer suggesting in terms of the future expectations of the people?
2. Underline words that create the dominant impressions in each paragraph.

Writing Suggestions

1. Write a paragraph describing a poor neighbourhood you have seen. Avoid using general words like "bad" or "crowded." Select specific details and avoid including unimportant facts like dates and addresses.
2. *Collaborative writing:* Work with a group of students and write a paragraph describing the social problems that refugee camps might produce. ◀

CRABBE

WILLIAM BELL

William Bell is a Toronto born, award-winning author. He holds degrees in literature and education and previously taught high school. In this part of his novel, Crabbe, *the protagonist, describes his recently deceased friend Mary.*

AS YOU READ:

Notice that Crabbe *never describes what Mary looks like. The dominant impression is of his friend's values and life perspective, not her appearance.*

1 Mary was a university professor. She went to the University of Toronto, McMaster and Harvard, where she got a Doctor of Philosophy Degree in History. Then she became an assistant prof at Laurentian University. I read the published articles in the pack and I gather she was a <u>left-winger</u> and an environmentalist. She seemed to think society was sick ("out of touch with itself" was the phrase in one article). Society was like a living creature that had picked up an illness, so the organism had to throw lots of resources into fighting the illness, and that threw the whole organism out of whack until either the organism died or the illness died. I didn't understand the whole essay. There was lots of stuff in it about misusing the environment and wasting resources and so on. She didn't say everything was wrong—I don't mean that— but the wrong things had importance and the wrong people had control.

2 There were quite a few articles on historical questions, too. Pretty boring stuff. But she was one smart woman, I'll tell you.

3 But she wasn't *cold* smart. I've met a lot of smart people at different times and most of them seemed <u>stand-offish</u>, unemotional, as if when their brains grew they pushed all feelings out of the way. And most of them seemed to think that *showing* feelings was some kind of weakness. Most of the smart people my father dragged home were boring snobs. He wanted me to be like that.

4 Mary wasn't like that at all. She always seemed to know what I was feeling, and she cared about that. Oh, she didn't treat me like a glass or anything like that. Hell, sometimes she told me off and didn't hold back. But she could do that because I know she cared about *me*, not my clothes or my money or my high marks at school or my father's job or where I lived—*me*. I never met anyone who made me feel *necessary*. Not important: necessary. I mattered to her.

5 What I mean is, Mary was a tremendously wise, smart woman who didn't come across like a <u>dried up</u> old intellectual. ∎

Words to Know

left-winger believer in socialist-style equality in society

stand-offish reserved, aloof

dried up not interesting, dull

CRITICAL THINKING AND DISCUSSION

GET THINKING
AND WRITING

Understanding Meaning: What Is the Writer Trying to Say?

1. What is the dominant image that the narrator creates?
2. What values does Mary represent?
3. What is the point of this description?

Evaluating Strategy: How Does the Writer Say It?

1. What details does the narrator use to support his description of Mary? Which do you find the most significant?
2. Much of the description of Mary is implied (not specifically stated). How successful is this type of description?
3. How does the statement in paragraph five clarify the narrator's feelings about his friend?

Appreciating Language: What Words Does the Writer Use?

1. Underline words that create the dominant impressions in each paragraph.
2. What words does the narrator use to describe his friend? Are they effective?

Writing Suggestions

1. Write a paragraph describing a person you feel represents beliefs or attitudes you value. Describe a coach who taught you the real meaning of sportsmanship or a relative who overcame a difficult challenge. Establish a clear controlling idea to guide what details you include.
2. *Collaborative writing:* Work with a group of students and write a paragraph describing why a country like Canada needs more people like Mary.

STEPS TO WRITING A DESCRIPTION PARAGRPH

1. Study your subject and apply critical thinking by asking key questions:
   Why did I choose this subject?
   What does it mean to me?
   What is important about it?
   What do I want other people to know about?
2. List as many details as you can, keeping your main idea in mind.
3. Review your list of details, highlighting the most important ones, especially those that create a dominant impression.
4. State a controlling idea or topic sentence for your paragraph.
5. Write a first draft of your paragraph.
6. Read your paragraph aloud and consider these questions:
   Is my subject clearly described?
   Do I provide enough details?
   Are there minor or irrelevant ideas that can be deleted?
   Do I use clear, concrete words that create an accurate picture of my subject?
   Do I create a clear dominant impression?
   Does my paragraph tell readers what I want them to know about my topic?

Selecting Topics

Consider these topics for writing description paragraphs:

People
a person who taught you a lesson
a celebrity you admire
a clique in high school or a campus association
the crowd at a local club, spa, coffee house, or student union
a type of employee or customer you encounter at work
the best or worst boss, teacher, or coach you have
your generation's attitude toward a subject like AIDS, sex, terrorism, marriage, or work

Places

your ideal home

college residence

best club, restaurant, gym, or bookstore you know

a place where you worked

your neighbourhood

a place that exposed you to something new

a place you hope you never have to see again

Things

your first car

your computer

a favourite childhood toy and what it represented

a prized possession

something you lost and why you still miss it

a time of day at school, your home, or job

a season of the year

a local newspaper, television show, or website

EXERCISE 5 Planning and Writing Paragraphs

Select a topic from the above lists or choose one of your own and develop details and a topic sentence.

Topic: _____

Possible supporting details:

1. _____

2. _____

3. _____

4. _____

5. _____

Circle the most important details to create a dominant impression.
State your controlling idea and write a topic sentence:

_____

_____

First sentence: topic sentence, first detail, or introductory statement

_____

_____

Supporting details:

1. _____

2. _____

3. _____

4. _____

5. _____

Last sentence: final detail, concluding statement, or topic sentence:

_____

_____

Write out your paragraph and review it by reading it aloud.

WORKING TOGETHER

Working with a group of students, revise this description from a student paper to delete irrelevant or obvious details that do not support the dominant impression and controlling idea. Edit the paragraph for fragments (see Chapter 15), run-ons and comma splices (see Chapter 17), and spelling errors (see Chapter 28).

Growing up in a Toronto high rise, I enjoyed spending weekends at my uncle's cottage on Lake Joseph. Located a little over an hour from the GTA. My uncle built the cottage ten years ago as a gift to his family. He was accountant for Labatt Breweries and he later worked for several law firms that handled tax cases. The A-frame cabin has striking views because of its floor to roof windows overlooking the lake. Sitting on the porch I would watch the sunsets over the lake, hearing only the gentle rustle of leaves and the soft slap of water against the dock. Other people go jogging, or mediate, or play chess to get rid of stress—but none of those things appeal to me. Jogging is to physical and meditation and chess take too much concentration when I am stressed. Away from the city, from traffic, from school, from work I would sit transfixed until the sun went down. Although I loved the swimming, the games, the horsing around with my cousins, those quiet afternoons on the porch were memomorable. Without them I would never have been able to find the peace of mind I needed to juggle work, school, and family. Next year I hope to be better orgainized.

_____

_____

_____

_____

_____

_____

_____

_____

_____

_____

_____

_____

_____

CRITICAL THINKING

Describe the college course you think will be the most important to your future life or career. Explain what you learned and how you hope to apply it in the future.

WHAT HAVE YOU WRITTEN?

Read your paragraphs carefully. Do you clearly describe the course's significance to your future? Do you include specific details? Are the supporting details clearly organized?

Write out the topic sentence or implied controlling idea:

_____

_____

_____

List the main supporting details in your paragraphs:

_____

_____

_____

Do they support your controlling idea and create a dominant impression? Could you improve your description by adding more details? Are there minor facts or trivial details that could be deleted?

GET WRITING

Write a paragraph describing a childhood friend. Select key details to create a dominant impression of your friend's personality. Consider what made this person so special. Why do you still remember him or her? How did he or she change or influence your life? Consider the most important thing you want people to know about your friend.

WRITING ON THE WEB

Using a search engine such as AltaVista, Yahoo!, or Google, enter terms such as *description, writing description,* or *rhetorical mode description* to locate current sites of interest.

1. Review online articles that describe a recent event, person, or situation. Notice how the writers develop controlling ideas, create dominant impressions, use supporting details, and choose particular words.
2. Write an e-mail to a friend describing a recent event on campus, at work, or in your life. Revise your paragraphs to create controlling ideas, build dominant impressions, and organize supporting details.

POINTS TO REMEMBER

1. Description paragraphs present images and impressions of places, people, things, and events.
2. Effective description paragraphs create dominant impressions that state the writer's most important points.
3. Dominant impressions and controlling ideas are supported with specific details.
4. Many description paragraphs do not contain a topic sentence but have a clear controlling idea.

6

Developing Paragraphs Using Narration

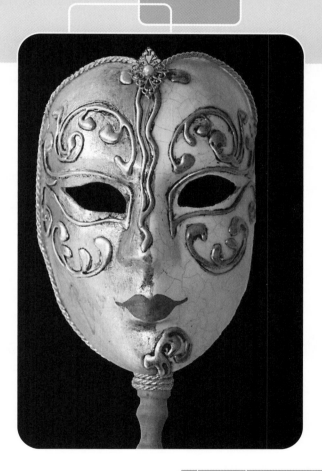

Have you ever been in a situation where you had to hide your feelings? Did you have to mask your fear to appear strong for others, "keep a straight face" to avoid offending people, or act in a professional role different from your personality?

Write a paragraph that tells the story of one of these incidents. Carefully select and organize details that support your main point.

What Is Narration?

The goal of narration is to tell a story or relate a chain of events. History books, newspaper articles, biographies, accident reports, the Bible, Greek myths, and fairy tales are examples of narration. Many of the papers you will write in college will use narration. Narratives explain events:

> After my flight was cancelled, I had to rent a car and drive through the snowstorm at twenty-five kilometres an hour.

> Desperate to stop the flow of skilled workers to the West, East Germany erected the Berlin Wall in 1961.

> After a disappointing start, the team won eight straight games, stunning both fans and sportswriters.

GET WRITING
AND REVISING

WHAT ARE YOU TRYING TO SAY?

Write a paragraph that relates one of the following events:

- a job interview
- an encounter with a stranger you found unforgettable
- a humorous event
- an incident at work you feel most proud or ashamed of
- a childhood event that scared you

Read your paragraph carefully. Does your narrative highlight the most important events, or is it cluttered with minor details? Is your paragraph clearly and logically organized?

Writing Narration: Making a Point

Effective narratives focus on a main point, teaching readers something about the event. In writing a narrative, your job is not to record every single detail but to focus on the most important ones. Narration paragraphs do not always have a topic sentence, but they should have a controlling idea and dramatize a clearly focused point:

Narrative Lacking Focus

   It was June 4, 2003. Eager to start my new job, I woke early and dressed in my brand-new suit and tie. I bought them the week before at The Bay with money I got for my birthday. I polished my shoes. I fiddled with my hair to get it just right. I wanted to make a good impression. I left early so I could run my car through the car wash on Weston Road just in case my new boss saw me pull up. It is an eight-year-old Volvo with over 125,000 kilometres on it. But when it is washed and waxed, it looks quite impressive. I took the highway downtown and got off on Richmond. I pulled up to the building on the corner of Richmond and King and parked right in front where Mrs. Smith had told me to and walked in the main entrance. I showed the receptionist my letter, and she directed me to the second-floor sales office. Anxious to do well, I took a deep breath and went in and introduced myself to Sarah Graham. She smiled and directed me to a tiny cubicle with a computer screen and a telephone headset. That is when I discovered that as an "account rep-resentative" my job consisted of cold calling businesses in the Yellow Pages.

The paragraph recounts someone's first day at work but makes little impact. The writer's main point—the contrast between his expectations and the reality of the job—is lost amid minor details such as the date, addresses, where he pur-chased his suit, and comments about his car. Deleting these details and high-lighting his anticipation emphasizes his final disappointment:

   Eager to start my new job, I woke early and dressed in my brand-new suit and tie. I polished my shoes. I fiddled with my hair to get it just right. I wanted to make a good impression. Advertising is about image, and I wanted to prove to everyone at creative concepts that I was executive material. I had visions of making presentations in polished boardrooms across the country. I even left early, so I could run my car through the car wash just in case my new boss saw me pull up. Entering the spacious lobby of the building, I felt thrilled. I could not wait to start. I introduced myself to Sarah Graham, who directed me to a dim, low-ceilinged room filled with tiny cubicles. Two dozen men and women in sweat shirts, T-shirts, and tat-tered blue jeans sat hunched over telephones, their tiny desks cluttered with candy wrappers, Coke cans, and rumpled newspapers. That is when I discovered that as an "account representative" my job consisted of cold calling businesses in the Yellow Pages.

TIPS FOR MAKING POINTS
1. **In writing a narrative paragraph, keep this question in mind: What is the most important thing I want my reader to know?**
2. **Delete minor details that do not help create your main point.**
3. **Focus on conflict or contrast to create tension or drama.**
4. **Organize details to create strong impressions.**
5. **Use concrete words rather than general or abstract terms to provide dramatic but accurate depictions of events:**

Abstract
The snowstorm affected the campus and made life difficult for the students who had been preparing for midterm examinations.

Concrete
The blizzard paralyzed the campus, knocking out power in classrooms, frustrating students cramming for midterm examinations.

6. **Avoid shifting point of view (from "I" to "you" or "they") unless there is a clear change in focus:**

Awkward Shift
When *I* drive over those train tracks *your* teeth rattle.

Improved
When *I* drive over those train tracks *my* teeth rattle.

or

When *you* drive over those train tracks *your* teeth rattle.

Acceptable Change in Point of View
When *I* was in school ten years ago *I* never had the opportunities *you* have.

7. **Use tense shifts to show logical changes between past and ongoing or current events:**

I *walked* to St. Xavier Blvd., where the city *is constructing* a new bridge.

I *was born* in Winnipeg, which *is* the capital of Manitoba.

We *sing* songs Cole Porter *wrote* sixty years ago.

EXERCISE 1 Making a Point

GET WRITING

Select one of the following subjects, narrow the topic, and establish a controlling idea.

your reaction to an accident you witnessed
an encounter with someone in distress
an argument or confrontation between two people you observed
the plot of your favourite story, book, or movie
an event, situation, or rumour that affected your high school
an event that shaped your attitudes or values
a dispute with a landlord, neighbour, customer, or fellow employee

Narrowed topic: _____

Point or controlling idea: _____

Now develop a narration paragraph that uses details to support the controlling idea. After completing your paragraph, review your subject and your main point. Does your paragraph tell readers what you want them to know? Are there minor details to delete and important details to emphasize?

EXAM SKILLS

Many examination questions call for writing one or more narration paragraphs. As with any exam, read the question carefully and make sure your paragraph directly responds to it. In writing a narrative, remember your goal is not to tell everything that happened or every detail you can remember but to concentrate on an important point. Your narrative should have a clearly stated goal and topic sentence to guide the events you select.

From Canadian History

What was the impact of the Halifax Harbour explosion?

introduction
and summary
of events

On the morning of December 6, 1917, the city of Halifax, Nova Scotia, was a bustling, lively place. However, in less than a second, Halifax became the centre of a tragedy like no other in the history of this country, a tragedy unparalleled in the history of this continent. The French munitions freighter Mont Blanc collided with the Belgian relief ship Imo in Halifax Harbour: the Mont Blanc, full of ammunition, caught fire and exploded, devastating the cities of Halifax and Dartmouth. Sixteen hundred buildings were destroyed, 12,000 were damaged, and 6,000 people were left homeless. The Halifax Harbour explosion was the greatest known man-made explosion until the advent of the atomic bomb. Yet, outside of Nova Scotia, the story of the Halifax explosion is barely known.

details

controlling
idea

Writing Narration: Using Transitions

A narration paragraph explains events that occur in time—whether measured in seconds, minutes, hours, days, weeks, or years. To prevent confusion and help readers follow events, it is important to use transitions to signal shifts in time:

In June 2000 I began working as a cabdriver. The training had been brief, but I thought I was fully prepared. *The first few days* were hectic, but the manager assigned new drivers to shuttle runs. I did not have to answer calls but simply travel back and forth between the airport and downtown hotels. *The next week* I collected my cab and headed out, working on my own. I found it difficult to answer the radio calls. Before I figured out the address, another driver had snatched the call. The dispatcher was rude and cut me off when I tried to ask a question. After paying for the cab rental, gas, and insurance I made only eleven dollars the first week. *By the end of the month* I learned how to handle radio calls and check the paper for downtown events. I got several good fares by hitting theatres as soon as plays let out. *In the next several months* I learned other tricks of the trade, such as having frequent fliers e-mail me to set up airport runs and bypassing the dispatcher. *By the end of the year,* I became a seasoned veteran.

KEY TRANSITION WORDS

before	now	then
after	later	first
after a while	following	finally
next	immediately	suddenly
following	the following day	hours, days, weeks later
while	in the meantime	that morning, afternoon, etc.

EXERCISE 2 Identifying Transitions

Underline transitional statements in the following paragraph.

When I first arrived in Moncton, I rented a car at the airport and followed my sister's directions to the hotel. After checking in, I grabbed a quick lunch and made a few calls. No one was home. I tried my sister's cell phone but could not get through. I took a shower, changed, and unpacked. I plugged in my laptop and checked my e-mail. I tried calling at three o'clock and again at four. I assumed everyone was running errands, getting things ready for the wedding. It was not until after dinner that I finally tracked down my cousin, who offered to drive me to the rehearsal.

Writing Narration: Using Dialogue

Narratives often involve interactions between people. If you are telling a story about an event that involved another person, dialogue—direct quotations—can advance the the story better than a summary of a conversation:

Summary
A good boss has to be a good teacher. My manager, Al Basak, is a nice person, very polite, and often funny. But he never gives people enough information to act on their own when he is out of the office. Last month he left to attend a two-day conference, telling me that if any sales reps called to remind them that their expense reports were due on Monday. I asked what to do if they asked for advances. He told me I could send them something if they needed it. Before I could ask anything else, he was out the door. An hour later, the phone rang. A sales rep in Calgary wanted a thousand-dollar advance. I panicked. Was a thousand too much? I told the sales rep I did not know if I could do that. I promised to call Al and check. I hung up and tried to call Al, but before I could get through to him, another sales rep called asking if he could e-mail his expense report. All I could tell him was that the report was due Monday, but that Al did not tell me whether it could be e-mailed. I promised to call Al and check. I hung up and knew this was going to be a long, long day.

Narrative with Dialogue
A good boss has to be a good teacher. My manager, Al Basak, is a nice person, very polite, and often funny. But he never gives people enough information to act on their own when he is out of the office. Last month he left to attend a

two-day conference, telling me, "If any of the sales reps call, remind them their expense reports are due on Monday."

"What if they need advances?" I asked him.

"Well, you can send them something if they need it."

Before I could ask anything else, he was out the door. An hour later the phone rang. A sales rep in Calgary wanted an advance. "Can you send me a thousand dollars?" she asked.

I panicked. Was a thousand too much? "I don't know if I can send you that much."

"Well, call Al."

"I will."

I hung up and tried to call Al, but before I could get through to him, another sales rep called asking if he could e-mail his expense report. "They are due Monday, but Al never told me if you could e-mail them."

"Are you sure? Call Al and find out."

"OK, I will," I sighed. I hung up and knew this was going to be a long, long day.

- Dialogue brings people to life by letting them speak their own words. Their tone, attitude, and lifestyle can be demonstrated by the words they choose.
- Because dialogue is formatted in short paragraphs, it is faster and easier to read than a long block of text. In addition, direct quotations can reduce the need for statements like "he said" or "she told me."

POINT TO REMEMBER

In writing dialogue, start a new paragraph each time a new person speaks. Because dialogue may include many short paragraphs, including one-word responses such as "No," your essay may appear to be longer than the assigned length. Use a computer word count. A three-page essay with dialogue is often no longer than a page and a half of description.

EXERCISE 3 Writing Narration Using Dialouge

Write a narration paragraph that uses dialogue—direct quotations—to relate an event: a confrontation between two people, an argument, a job interview, or a conversation.

Student Paragraphs

Personal narrative:

    On my first day in Toronto I went to the CN Tower
to have lunch and get a sweeping view of the city.
Using my map, I checked off the sights I wanted to
cover on my two-day layover. I visited the Royal York
Hotel, then explored the vast underground complex of
shops, offices, and tunnels that allow people to travel
throughout downtown without having to face bad weather.
I ended my first day by taking a cab to Casa Loma, the

huge castle like mansion on a hill that features stables, a secret passage, towers, and suits of armour.

Narrative in a history paper:

The 1920s were marked everywhere by a spiralling expansion of business. Technical and industrial advances paced the rising standard of living. In the summer of 1929, industrial production began to slow significantly. In October of that year, the stock market crash heralded unemployment and financial ruin across Canada, as it did elsewhere in the world. Defeated in the 1930 elections, King made way for the Conservatives under Richard Bedford Bennett. Bennett thus had the unenviable responsibility of dealing with the Great Depression. His inability to deal with the crisis, coupled with the severe drought in the prairies, led Canadians to desert the Conservatives. The election of 1935 brought the Liberals back into office, a position they were to continue to hold without interruption for 22 years.

Narrative in psychology midterm:

The reason many mentally ill people are now home-less is that public policy failed to supply enough outpatient clinics and group homes. Throughout much of the twentieth century, mental patients were housed in large state-run institutions. Many were merely warehouses offering little treatment. Patients were often victims of abuse and neglect. By the late 1960s advocates for the mentally ill argued that many patients would be better served by being mainstreamed rather than isolated. The provinces eager to save money closed aging and costly mental hospitals. Men-tally ill people were reintroduced to society, but few had coping skills to find employment or housing. The group homes and outpatient clinics that advocates envisioned never opened. As a result, today we see schizophrenics panhandling and living on the streets.

PUTTING PARAGRAPHS TOGETHER

Dumb and Dumber

introduction

background to event

Sometimes we are so ashamed of something dumb we have done we have to lie. We just can't let anyone know how stupid we have been. Last Canada Day I was getting ready for a picnic with my friends. I was supposed to bring paper plates and plastic cups. I got the supplies ready, then put on a new pair of cream slacks and a white shirt. The boxes were not heavy but bulky, so I carried my car keys so I would not have to try to dig them out of my pocket when I got to the garage. I left my apartment and headed down the hall to the elevator. Just as the elevator reached the lobby and the doors slid open, the boxes shifted and I dropped my car keys. The keys bounced twice and dropped right down the narrow slot between the floor and the elevator. They were gone! I could not believe it! Kneeling, I could see my keys resting two or three feet below.

climax
mistake #1

1. What is the controlling idea of this paragraph? Does it have a topic sentence?
2. How does the student organize the details?
3. How effective is the end of the paragraph? Is it a good place to make a break in the narrative? Why or why not?

Cursing myself, I punched the button and went back up to the third floor. I was running late and had to get my car keys. I dumped the boxes in the hall and ran to my apartment to get a flashlight and a clothes hanger. I was convinced I could hook my key ring with a hanger and be on my way. The elevator floor was dirty, so to be smart I quickly changed into jeans so I would not ruin my new cream slacks. I bent the hanger into the perfect key ring grabber and raced down the hall, letting the apartment door slam behind me.

focus on action

details to emphasize being in a rush

mistake #2

1. How does this paragraph advance the narrative?
2. How does it build on the first paragraph?
3. The student ends the first and second paragraphs by describing mistakes he made. Is this effective? Do the paragraphs highlight the "dumb" things mentioned in the first sentence?

My coat hanger worked perfectly. I snagged the keys on the third try and had them just inches from the floor when the wire slipped and the keys vanished out of sight. Oh well, I thought, I would make a few calls and get them later. When I reached my apartment I dug into my jeans and realized I had left my apartment keys in the new cream slacks I had carefully folded and laid on the bed.

initial good luck

bad luck

topic sentence realizes mistake #2

1. How does this paragraph follow the preceding one?
2. How does the student organize details?
3. Does the last sentence seem like a good place to end a paragraph? Why or why not?

I was now locked out of my car and my apartment. For a moment I thought I would just walk to the

topic sentence

thinks of plan

realizes plan won't work

drugstore and call a cab; then I realized I had no money. My wallet was in the cream slacks along with my cell phone. I was trapped. I raced back to the lobby and spent an hour and a half fishing for my car keys. I managed to finally grab them just as my roommate came through the lobby.

1. How does this paragraph advance the narrative?
2. What are the important details in this paragraph? How do they relate to the idea of doing "something dumb"?

roommate's question

He looked at my smudged clothes and dirty hands and asked, "Hey, I thought you were going to a picnic?"

Playing innocent, I pocketed my car keys and followed him to the elevator. "I had a flat tire," I lied, letting him go ahead so he could open the apartment door.

conclusion

1. How effective is this final paragraph? Does it bring the narrative to a logical close?
2. How does the last line relate to the opening line?
3. How important are final paragraphs in a narrative? How can writers highlight or demonstrate an idea or detail they want readers to remember?

Readings

As you study the readings, notice how each paragraph works and how the paragraphs work together to create a narrative.

TICKETS TO NOWHERE

ANDY ROONEY

Andy Rooney is best known for his humorous commentaries on Sixty Minutes. *A longtime CBS reporter, Rooney began his career writing for* Stars and Stripes *during World War II. In this column Rooney describes the fate of a typical lottery player.*

AS YOU READ:

Notice how Rooney uses different ways to organize his paragraphs in this narration. Some paragraphs use narration to tell a story about Jim Oakland's past. Others use comparison to contrast his dreams of wealth and the reality of his situation.

Things never went very well for Jim Oakland. He dropped out of high school because he was impatient to get rich but after dropping out he lived at home with his parents for two years and didn't earn a dime.

1

2   He finally got a summer job working for the highway department holding up a sign telling oncoming drivers to be careful of the workers ahead. Later that same year, he picked up some extra money putting flyers under the windshield wipers of parked cars.

3   Things just never went very well for Jim and he was 23 before he left home and went to Florida hoping his ship would come in down there. He never lost his desire to get rich but first he needed money for the rent so he took a job near Fort Lauderdale for $4.50 an hour servicing the goldfish aquariums kept by the cashier's counter in a lot of restaurants.

4   Jim was paid in cash once a week by the owner of the goldfish business and the first thing he did was go to the little convenience store near where he lived and buy $20 worth of lottery tickets. He was really determined to get rich.

5   A week ago, the lottery jackpot in Florida reached $54 million. Jim woke up nights thinking what he could do with $54 million. During the days, he daydreamed about it. One morning he was driving along the main street in the boss's old pickup truck with six tanks of goldfish in back. As he drove past a BMW dealer, he looked at the new models in the window.

6   He saw the car he wanted in the showroom window but unfortunately he didn't see the light change. The car in front of him stopped short and Jim slammed on his brakes. The fish tanks slid forward. The tanks broke, the water gushed out and the goldfish slithered and flopped all over the back of the truck. Some fell off into the road.

7   It wasn't a good day for the goldfish or for Jim, of course. He knew he'd have to pay for the tanks and 75 cents each for the fish and if it weren't for the $54 million lottery, he wouldn't have known which way to turn. He had that lucky feeling.

8   For the tanks and the dead goldfish, the boss deducted $114 of Jim's $180 weekly pay. Even though he didn't have enough left for the rent and food, Jim doubled the amount he was going to spend on lottery tickets. He never needed $54 million more.

9   Jim had this system. He took his age and added the last four digits of the telephone number of the last girl he dated. He called it his lucky number . . . even though the last four digits changed quite often and he'd never won with his system. Everyone laughed at Jim and said he'd never win the lottery.

10   Jim put down $40 on the counter that week and the man punched out his tickets. Jim stowed them safely away in his wallet with last week's tickets. He never threw away his lottery tickets until at least a month after the drawing just in case there was some mistake. He'd heard of mistakes.

11   Jim listened to the radio all afternoon the day of the drawing. The people at the radio station he was listening to waited for news of the winning numbers to come over the wires and, even then, the announcers didn't rush to get them on. The station manager thought the people running the lottery ought to pay to have the winning numbers broadcast, just like any other commercial announcement.

Jim fidgeted while they gave the weather and the traffic and the news. Then they played more music. All he wanted to hear were those numbers.

12

"Well," the radio announcer said finally, "we have the lottery numbers some of you have been waiting for. You ready?" Jim was ready. He clutched his ticket with the number 274802.

13

"The winning number," the announcer said, "is 860539. I'll repeat that. 860539." Jim was still a loser.

14

I thought that, with all the human interest stories about lottery winners, we ought to have a story about one of the several million losers. ■

15

GET THINKING
AND WRITING

CRITICAL THINKING AND DISCUSSION

Understanding Meaning: What Is the Writer Trying to Say?

1. How significant is the title? Does it work to shape readers' attitudes even before they read the column?
2. What is the most important thing Rooney wants you to know about Jim Oakland?
3. How does Rooney describe Jim's life? What details stand out? Write one sentence in your own words that describes your view of Jim.
4. What values does Jim have? Are they realistic?
5. What is Rooney's thesis—can you state it in your own words?
6. *Critical thinking:* What seems to have motivated Rooney to write this piece? Are the last lines necessary to get his meaning across, or does his description of Jim Oakland prove his point?

Evaluating Strategy: How Does the Writer Say It?

1. Rooney does not tell readers what Jim looked like. Do you think this is deliberate? Why or why not?
2. What details and examples does Rooney use to demonstrate Jim's values?
3. How does Rooney use paragraph breaks to organize details and show shifts in his train of thought?
4. *Critical thinking:* Rooney notes that the last four digits of the phone number of Jim's last date changed often. What does this detail suggest about Jim's lifestyle?

Appreciating Language: What Words Does the Writer Use?

1. Rooney refers to Jim Oakland by his first name. What impression does this create? Would calling him Oakland throughout the column create a different effect? Why or why not?
2. Rooney notes that "Jim was still a loser" when his number did not come up in the lottery. Does the word "loser" apply to Jim's entire life? What makes a person a "loser"? Would you define Jim as a loser?

Writing Suggestions

1. Write one or more paragraphs that describe your idea of a loser. You may describe the life of a single person or use several examples.

2. *Collaborative writing:* Working with a group of students, write a short paragraph stating whether or not you consider Rooney's column an effective argument against lotteries.

MESSAGE TO PARENTS

TEENAGERS EVERYWHERE

AS YOU READ:

Consider the point of view of teenagers and their struggles with acceptance. In this chilling first-person narrative, the authors speak openly about their feelings of inadequacy in context to the demands of their parents.

1 No, I can't be all that you want me to. No, I can't live the life you want me to eventually see. No, I can't see the positive outcomes of your negative messages. No wonder you can't see life the way I do—you only notice the things I can't, don't, and won't do.

2 Out of all the times you have talked to me, there have only been a fingerful of times when I could truly say I came out with a real true smile. But every single other one (countless) ended up with the feeling of wanting to truly kill myself.

3 It left me empty, feeling like nothing I can do will work. As if everything that I had done meant s**t, which means everything I eventually do will soon have the same damn meaning. Nothing is ever good enough. Nothing! You use examples from other kids that you know about responsible things that they do etc. but don't see that they themselves gawk at the amount of stuff we have to do.

4 I feel bad when all my friends say what great parents I have because they truly could never understand. It seems like this family is just a freaking show and I am just another actor. They all see us as the perfect modern-age family with nothing but happiness and joy on our shoulders but none can truly see what reality has truly bred us to be— a suicidal son, stressed-out mother, an angry and neglected son, a worried son, a rushed father, an overachieved sister, and a spoiled princess. We all just wear our happy faces and move on to hope the next day will be one of the too few good ones.

5 I could put and have put myself in your shoes countless times and all that I can see is stress. This is where all the problems are sourced from. It is this stress that attacks you, which is vented towards us in anger. Like every single thing we do is wrong. Every single step we take to try to help is just another step back.

6 Maybe what we need is less.

7 Maybe we just see too much to have and so buy it with stress and depression. We need less anger, you need less stress. Less stress means

less work, less work means less money, less money means less things to take care of, less things to take care of means less anger. This family has upsized too much, it has truly proven the depressive state that capitalization and consumptionism has toiled down to.

I don't need a huge anything, I don't need money that I can't pay back, I don't need responsibilities and commitments that I can't, don't, and won't see myself carrying out. | 8

Simplify, that's the answer to all questions. Maybe it's the answer to ours. | 9

You will never see this reply because it would be selfish for me to show it to you. The last thing that you need in your life is an answer from someone that never speaks. The last thing I would want to do right now would be to bring you down any more than you already are, 'cause then you just might be as low as me. | 10

I think I was born this way; maybe it was grieving a death that brought it to me. Maybe it is the constant teasing of being stupid and slow at everything. I don't see what the matter is in taking your time with things. The last thing I want to be in would be in a constant rush. | 11

I see where that leads yet I am teased for not doing it. Why? I am called after a turtle because I don't get ready as fast, my name is groaned as a joke because I don't want to rush. Why? | 12

I have already been caught in the act of contemplating death yet still I question it every single day. I wake up in the mornings and wake up to a rush. I fear that the next forty somewhat years (if I make it through this letter) will be spent in some sort of prison where not a single day will go by where I can actually wake up looking forward to what I am going to do for the rest of it. | 13

I can't live life with commitments. I can't live life with commitments. I can't live life with commitments. I can't live life with commitments. I can't live life with commitments. I can't live life with commitments. I can't live life with commitments. I can't live life with commitments. I can't live life with commitments. | 14

I can't look forward to a plan. Yet it seems as if you have my life planned out. You give me plenty of freedoms that lots of my friends don't have, yet you restrict so much of my time that it seems that I can never see them. On every single one of my days off, I know you expect me to be doing chores. | 15

I have come to the point where I now expect myself to be on them. But to say that I can't have friends with me because you don't think that anything will get done, that's unfair. Though that has only happened on one occasion, I know it was worth attempting to fight a high class negotiator like yourself. Never have I come out of a conversation with the feeling that I had one. Someone else always has the last word — no one will ever understand. | 16

The kids haven't changed, the parents have. ■ | 17

CRITICAL THINKING AND DISCUSSION

Understanding Meaning: What Is the Writer Trying to Say?

1. What is the point of the story? What does the writer want his or her readers to understand?
2. Why did the writer include a paragraph about "the perfect modern age family" (paragraph 4)?
3. Why does the narrator seem so angry?
4. How does the narrator perceive his or her life?

Evaluating Strategy: How Does the Writer Say It?

1. Why is the first person narrative used here? How does it change the effect of this piece?
2. How does the level of the language used (colloquial and slang) affect this narrative?

Appreciating Language: What Words Does the Writer Use?

1. Underline the words that dramatize the emotional impact of this narrative.
2. Consider the tone, style, and word choice of this essay. Was it easy to read? Why or why not? What does this suggest about the target audience?

Writing Suggestions

1. Write a paragraph that describes an argument you have had. How did you react? Did you try to reason with the other person? What lesson did you learn? Avoid a description of what was said and focus instead on details that support the point you are trying to make.
2. *Collaborative Writing:* Discuss this essay with a number of students and write a paragraph describing the way they feel teenagers should be treated.

STEPS TO WRITING A NARRATION PARAGRAPH

1. Study your topic and use critical thinking by asking key questions:
     Why did I choose this event to write about?
     What did it mean to me?
     Why do I remember it?
     What is significant about it?
     What do I want other people to know about it?
     What is my most important point?
2. List your point or message as a topic statement to guide your writing (the topic sentence does not have to appear in the finished paragraph).
3. List supporting details that establish your point.
4. Review your list of supporting details, deleting minor ones and highlighting significant ones.
5. If people appear in your narrative, consider using dialogue rather than indirect summaries of conversations. Remember to use paragraph breaks to indicate a shift in speakers. (See pages 33 and 36.)
6. Write a first draft of your paragraph.

(continued)

7. Read your paragraph aloud and consider these questions:
   Does my paragraph make a clear point?
   Does it tell readers what I want them to know?
   Do I provide sufficient details?
   Are there unimportant details that could be deleted?
   Do I use concrete words, especially verbs, to describe action?
   Do I avoid illogical shifts in point of view or tense?
   Do I provide clear transitions to advance the narrative and explain the passage of time?

Selecting Topics

Consider these topics for writing narration paragraphs:

an encounter with a stranger that taught you something
a situation in which you had to give someone bad news
a telephone call that changed your life
taking an exam you were unprepared for
a childhood experience that shaped your values or attitudes
buying a car
voting for the first time
a sporting event you participated in
an argument you witnessed between two people
an event that changed a friend's life
a brief history of your college or employer
an event that occurred in your high school
a sporting event you watched

EXERCISE 4 Planning and Writing Paragraphs

Select a topic from the above list or choose one of your own and develop details and a topic sentence that states the point of your narrative.

Topic: _____

Possible supporting details:

1. _____

2. _____

3. _____

4. _____

5. _____

Circle the most important details that explain the event.
State the point of your narrative and write a topic sentence:

_____

_____

Organize your supporting details chronologically using transitional statements to advance the narrative.

First sentence: topic sentence, first detail, or introductory statement:

_____

_____

Supporting Details:

1. _____
2. _____
3. _____
4. _____
5. _____

Last sentence: final detail, concluding statement, or topic sentence:

_____

_____

Write out your paragraph and review it by reading it aloud.

WORKING TOGETHER

Working with a group of students, revise this paragraph from a student paper to delete irrelevant details, illogical shifts in tense and person, and awkward transitions. Edit the paper for fragments (see Chapter 15), run-ons (see Chapter 17), and misspelled words (see Chapter 28).

Like most days after work, I stop at Tim Hortons for coffee and a chance to read the paper and unwind from the day. It was a wonderfully sunny spring day. I happen to glance over at a nearly table and notice a familiar face. Nancy Sims was older of course and heavier than she was in high school. She wears torn jeans and a sweatshirt with no makeup. In high school she always wearing stylish clothes. You could see her scuffed shoes, broken nails, and matted hair. I returned to reading my paper, not wanting her to see me staring at her. Suddenly, I sense someone standing next to my table. I look up and saw her. I smiled, thinking she is going to ask if I went to Brighton Collegiate. She bent over my table. Her breath is sour and her teeth chipped and stained. "Excuse me, she said, "can you give me your change?" I looked up into her spaced-out eyes and realize she has no idea who I am and push my small pile of coins toward her. She scoops them up greedily and put them in the paper bag she used as a purse and headed to the door. I remembered the last time I saw her at graduation and wondered, what happened to this girl from a nice family who was heading to college with so much hope?

_____

_____

_____

_____

_____

_____

_____

_____

_____

_____

_____

_____

_____

GET THINKING
AND WRITING

CRITICAL THINKING

Have you ever learned a lesson "the hard way"? Did a poor decision ever teach you something? Select an event and summarize what happened and explain the lesson you learned. Develop a strong topic sentence to guide your paragraph.

WHAT HAVE YOU WRITTEN?

Read your paragraph carefully. Do you clearly state your opinion?

Write out the topic sentence or implied controlling idea:

_____

_____

List the main supporting details in your paragraph:

_____

_____

_____

Do they support your controlling idea and provide evidence for your point of view? Could you improve your paragraph by adding more details? Are there minor facts or trivial details that could be deleted?

Have you ever witnessed an event that changed your life? Did you witness an accident, see a celebrity, watch an athletic triumph, or see a performance you cannot forget?

Write a paragraph that tells the story of this event. Focus on creating a strong controlling idea that is supported by relevant details.

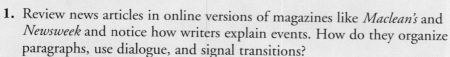

WRITING ON THE WEB

Using a search engine such as AltaVista, Yahoo!, or Google, enter terms such as *narration, writing narration, narrative techniques,* and *first-person narratives* to locate current sites of interest.

1. Review news articles in online versions of magazines like *Maclean's* and *Newsweek* and notice how writers explain events. How do they organize paragraphs, use dialogue, and signal transitions?
2. Write an e-mail to a friend describing something you saw or experienced. Revise your paragraphs to delete minor details and highlight important points.

POINTS TO REMEMBER

1. Narration paragraphs should make a clear point, not simply summarize events.
2. Narratives can be written in first person ("I"), second person ("you"), or third person ("he," "she," or "they"). Avoid illogical shifts:

   I climbed to the top of the hill where *you* can see for miles.

3. Narration can be stated in past or present tense. Avoid illogical shifts:

   I *drove* to the library where I *study* all night.

4. Paragraphs should have clear transition statements to advance the narrative, indicate the passage of time, and prevent confusion.
5. Dialogue—direct quotations—can be more effective than summaries of conversations. Remember to use quotation marks and begin a new paragraph to indicate a shift in speakers.

Developing Paragraphs Using Classification

In a typical classroom, you will find all types of people taking a course. Some are there to learn; others have less dedication to the subject matter.

Write a paragraph identifying the types of students found in a typical classroom.

What Is Classification?

Classification is a type of analysis that helps to make sense of the world by sorting people, experiences, objects, or concepts into groups. We generally classify groups according one unifying principle—a principle that relates to the purpose of the writing:

As far as winter sports go, cross-country, downhill, and freestyle skiing are three of the most popular.

The contents of my closet can be described as "things," "stuff," or "junk."

POINT TO REMEMBER

Classification generally examines three or more related items. The organizing principle, the criteria used to separate the items, should be identifiable, consistent, and apply to all the items being discussed.

WHAT ARE YOU TRYING TO SAY?

GET WRITING
AND REVISING

Identify three categories in the following topics:

- types of stress facing college students
- types of vacations
- types of restaurants
- types of students in college
- types of sports fans

WHAT HAVE YOU WRITTEN?

Read your list carefully. Have you created three groups that can be discussed using the same principle?

EXERCISE 1 Identifying Classifications

Try the following exercise to sharpen your grouping skills. Read each list. First, cross out the one item that has not been classified by the same principle. Then, indicate the principle used to classify the four items.

EX: Classic Films

1. American

2. Japanese

3. Horror

4. French

5. Italian (principle) *Country*

Politicians

1. Liberal

2. Multicultural

3. Conservative

4. Reform

5. NDP   (principle) _____

Music

1. Loud

2. Classical

3. Jazz

4. Blues

5. Rap   (principle) _____

Artists

1. Pissarro

2. Monet

3. Manet

4. Degas

5. Raphael   (principle) _____

Writing Classification Paragraphs

Classification paragraphs help make groups or collections of items easier to understand:

> In a typical college level composition class, there are three major groups of students. In general, you will see the committed, the visitors, and the prisoners.

The group "students" is broken down into three types—"the committed," "the visitors," and "the prisoners." These three groups would then be described in detail in the rest of the paragraph.

> **TIPS FOR USING CLASSIFICATION**
> 1. Identify the shared characteristic (unifying principle).
> 2. Create a strong topic sentence or state a clear controlling idea with three or more identifiable groups.
> 3. Distinguish each type or class from the others by using precise or creative labels.

Using Classification

In using classification, it is important to express a clear principle for the groupings you have created. This principle is simply a rule that explains what your groups will be. Once this information is clear, each category is then further described, using details that distinguish the groups from each other:

> There are several ways to classify memory. One way is to organize types of memory based on the length of time the memory is held. Researchers

have classified three types of memory according to how long the brain takes to process and store the information: sensory memory, short-term memory, and long-term memory. Sensory memory preserves information in its original form, for only a fraction of a second. Short-term memory has a limited capacity (capable of holding about seven chunks of information) and can maintain unrehearsed information for up to about 20 seconds. Short-term memory is working memory and appears to involve more than a simple rehearsal loop. Long-term memory is an unlimited capacity store that may hold information indefinitely. Certain lines of evidence suggest that long-term memory storage may be permanent, but the evidence is not convincing. Some theorists have raised doubts about whether short-term and long-term memory are really separate. Theorists have offered many viewpoints about the structure of memory and how the three types listed above interact.

In this paragraph, the categories were created based on the shared characteristic of time—the duration or length of time that a thought stays in human memory. Each type of memory is organized from shortest to longest and then defined by its "mode of operation" (how it works).

EXERCISE 2 Using Classification to Differentiate

Write a paragraph on one of the following topics. Remember to include a topic sentence or main idea.

types of bosses
types of teachers
types of water sports
types of computer users

_____

_____

_____

_____

_____

_____

_____

_____

_____

_____

_____

_____

_____

_____

_____
_____
_____
_____
_____
_____
_____

WHAT HAVE YOU WRITTEN?

Underline the topic sentence. Does it clearly identify at least three categories? Is the unifying principle clear? Do the categories relate to your main idea or support your point of view? Do some of the categories need to be more specific?

EXAM SKILLS

Some examination questions call for writing classification paragraphs. Read the question carefully to first determine whether or not classification writing is required. Then make sure that your paragraph directly responds to the question. In writing classification, remember that you must first identify the "types" or "categories" related to your topic and then provide sufficient details that clearly show the differences between them.

From English Composition

Describe a portion of society that mirrors society itself.

In many ways, people who take commuter trains form a mini society with its own rules and cliques, much like high school. The first and most prominent are the Seniors, the most established commuters on the train. Similar to in a schoolyard or cafeteria, the senior commuters have seats reserved for their exclusive use and other regular commuters understand and respect this unspoken rule. There are also the Couples, who spend the entire trip immersed in their own private world. They share a newspaper, chat, and gossip in an intimate huddle or even sit in complete silence, but they never interact with the other commuters. Finally, there is the Lone Wolf. The Lone Wolf is not interested in socializing with others, and unlike the Couples, the Lone Wolf travels alone and shuts out the world with a portable audio player or book.

Readings

As you study the following classification model, notice how the writer uses paragraphs to categorize the groups and then uses specific details to describe how each group is different from one another.

'TIS THE SEASON TO BE KISSING

SIDNEY KATZ

Sidney Katz is a freelance Toronto journalist who has written articles for newspapers and magazines.

AS YOU READ:

In this lighthearted article, the writer has classified kissing into three distinct groups that are easily distinguishable from one another. Each paragraph provides specific details and examples that help the reader see how each type of kissing is unique.

1. Kissing, a delightful human activity which peaks on Valentine's Day, is a simple enough act: two people saluting or caressing each other with their lips. But depending on how it's done, the kiss can convey a wide variety of messages—duty, gratitude, curiosity, respect, friendship, sexual passion or undying love. In unsentimental medical jargon, a kiss is described as "the anatomical juxtaposition of the two orbicularis oris muscles in a state of contraction." But to the romantic Greeks, a kiss is "the key to paradise," while Cyrano de Bergerac defined it as "a rosy dot placed on the eye of loving; 'tis a secret told to the mouth instead of to the ear."

2. A widely respected standard for "the perfect kiss" was set more than 50 years ago by Hugh Morris, author of *The Art of Kissing*. The secret, said Morris, lies in concentration. "Kiss as though at that moment nothing else exists in the world. Kiss as though your entire life is wrapped up in the period of the kiss. Kiss as though there is nothing else you would rather be doing."

3. The main types of commonly used kisses can be listed as follows:

4. **The blow kiss.** This comes highly recommended for people who want to avoid physical contact. With a quick gesture of hand and mouth, you can dispatch a kiss to someone at the other end of the room—or to anyone in sight.

5. **The cheek peck.** Widely used, it's a kiss without substance consisting of a quick touch to the cheek. For casual acquaintances.

6. **The cheek nuzzle.** This is more personal than the perfunctory cheek peck and takes longer. You warmly touch the cheek of the recipient with your lips and cheek. Limited to people you genuinely like.

7. **The ear kiss.** Thoughtful people will resort to this kiss if the recipient is a heavily made-up lady who's in fear of seeing her handiwork smeared.

8. **The low-voltage kiss.** For friends you like or for people to whom you wish to express sincere gratitude.

9. **The high-voltage kiss.** To express intense passion and/or love. You should be warned that this kiss triggers a physiological earthquake in the body. The pulse rate shoots up from 72 to 100, the blood pressure and blood sugar level rise and there's a flutter around the heart—the

result of spleen contraction and the addition to the blood of millions of red blood corpuscles.

Although kissing is a pretty safe form of recreation, there are still some hazards to be reckoned with. During a kiss, anywhere between 23 and 280 colonies of bacteria are exchanged, most of them harmless unless you happen to have a cold or some other ailment. In the so-called "Hollywood Kiss" (duration 10 to 12 seconds), twice as many bacteria travel mouth-to-mouth as are transmitted during a perfunctory kiss on the lips. Men with a mustache deliver more bacteria during a kiss than do smooth-shaven ones.

10

Wearers of contact lenses are urged to exercise caution during high-voltage kissing: the vigorous movement of the cheek and jaw muscles during kissing can work the lenses loose and you stand a good chance of losing them. The amount of high-voltage kissing which prevails at any given time must have some bearing on the prosperity (or lack of it) in the optical supplies business.

11

First appeared in *The Globe and Mail* as "'Tis the Season for Kissing." 14 Feb. 1982. Reprinted by permission of the author in *The Harbrace Reader for Canadians*, ed. Joanne Buckley. Harcourt Canada, 2001 [0-7747-3681-X].

GET THINKING
AND WRITING

CRITICAL THINKING AND DISCUSSION

Understanding Meaning: What Is the Writer Trying to Say?

1. What does "perfunctory kiss" mean?
2. What is the general opinion about kissing in this reading?
3. Examine the titles of each category of kiss. What attitude is suggested by these titles?

Evaluating Strategy: How Does the Writer Say It?

1. Would the essay be stronger if the writer used only three categories instead of six?
2. Underline the most significant details of each category. Are they generally positive or negative?
3. What impact does the final paragraph have?

Appreciating Language: What Words Does the Writer Use?

1. The writer has created original labels for each of the six categories. What other labels might be appropriate for this position on kissing?
2. Describe the tone of this reading. Identify the words or phrases that suggest this piece is not totally serious.

Writing Suggestions

1. Write one or more paragraphs classifying your English class colleagues, your neighbours, or people you see every day on your way to school or work.
2. *Collaborative writing:* Working with a group of students, write a short classification paragraph about yourselves.

WHO USES BLOGS?

SHEILA ANN MANUEL COGGINS

Sheila Ann Manuel Coggins, co-owner of the b5media blogging network, has been an Internet enthusiast since 1997. She is a keeper of weblogs, journals, and websites. She regularly hosts podcasts and video blogs.

AS YOU READ:

Pay close attention to the way blog users are categorized and how they are described as four unique groups.

1   Just about anyone can use a blog! In fact, according to reports, there are approximately three million blogs being tracked by mid-2004. And that number is continuously growing as blog software, tools and other applications become more accessible to individuals. Blog users are as varied as the types of blogs available. However, they may be categorized into four main types: personal bloggers, business bloggers, organizational bloggers and professional bloggers.

2   **Personal bloggers** often create blogs that contain diary or journal-type entries. Some focus their blogs on specific themes or topics that they feel passionately about like sports, technology, education, news, politics, pets, writing, art or photography.

3   **Business bloggers** create blogs to promote their products and/or services. Although these business or commercial blogs typically use this online medium as a promotional or marketing tool, the more successful ones do not contain advertisements or *"marketese"* in their blog entries. Their blogs have to offer real, usable information for readers like reviews, comments, links to relevant articles and similar resources.

4   **Organizational bloggers** are people who blog as a way to communicate internally (with fellow employees, students, etc.) and/or externally (with clients, general public, etc.). These types of bloggers may be found in corporations, educational settings, non-profit organizations and community clubs, among others.

5   **Professional bloggers** are considered a rare breed in the blogging community. These are people who are actually hired or paid to blog. They may either propose their own blog topics to a blogging network or they may be hired to write about a specific topic by a network or a company.

6   As the popularity of blogging grows, more and more individuals are finding different ways to use blogs. It will not be surprising, therefore, if more types of people begin to use blogs.

blog short for weblog, an online journal (or newsletter)

marketese a reference to the language of "marketing"

CRITICAL THINKING AND DISCUSSION

Understanding Meaning: What Is the Writer Trying to Say?

1. How successful is the introductory paragraph in identifying the categories of this topic?
2. How relevant are the categories?
3. In the final paragraph, Manuel Coggins suggests that "it will not be surprising . . . if more types of people begin to use blogs." What other types of people could she be referring to?

Evaluating Strategy: How Does the Writer Say It?

1. Examine the descriptions of each category. What kinds of details are provided?
2. Which category is most clearly explained? Why?

Appreciating Language: What Words Does the Writer Use?

1. Consider the term "blog" and the possible reactions to it from different readers. What reaction could you expect from teens? Older people? Computer users?
2. How complete is this essay on blogging? What other details might be necessary to make it more inclusive?

Writing Suggestions

1. Invent your own categories of computer users, using creative labels for each group.
2. *Collaborative writing:* Working with a group of students, identify the types of people who use chat rooms on the Internet. Create specific labels for each group.

STEPS TO WRITING A CLASSIFICATION PARAGRAPH

1. Clearly identify the main topic, the categories that you are going to discuss and the principle by which the categories will be viewed.
2. Consider your readers when you choose the categories. Will they require general explanations or will they require explicit information about the groups you are discussing?
3. Avoid classifying your main topic into more than five groups as it may obscure the purpose of the paper.
4. Keep the assignment criteria in mind.
5. Organize the categories in a clear pattern. You might arrange groups in order of importance, time, or size.
6. Write a draft of your paragraph.
7. Read your paragraph aloud and ask yourself these questions:
    a. Do I have a clear topic sentence that identifies the topic and the categories?
    b. Is each category balanced? That is, is there an equal amount of descriptive information about each group?
    c. Will readers make the connection between the categories and the purpose of the writing?
    d. Can I think of better examples?

Selecting Topics

Consider these topics for developing classification paragraphs.

> types of sports fans
> types of vacations
> methods of negotiation
> types of dieters
> types or styles of parenting
> categories of bad/good employers
> categories of bad/good employees
> types of restaurants

EXERCISE 3 Planning and Writing Classification Paragraphs

Select a topic from the above list or choose one of your own and develop details and a topic sentence that states the goal of your paragraph.

Topics: _____

Possible groups or categories:

1. _____

2. _____

3. _____

Topic Sentence: _____

Category 1 topic sentence _____

   Supporting details about category 1 _____

Category 2 topic sentence _____

   Supporting details about category 2 _____

Category 3 topic sentence _____

   Supporting details about category 3 _____

Concluding statement or final sentence: _____

WORKING TOGETHER

Working with a group of students, turn this list of ideas into a coherent short classification paragraph. Focus on the relationship between the three topics and how, together, the topics help to clarify your point of view.

Topic: Types of dieters

Group 1:   One-month dieters
      start well, good intentioned, but lose focus after thirty days
      go to the gym regularly for one month, but then start to make
        excuses not to go

lose weight quickly, then reward themselves and gain back the
    weight
usually not successful overall

Group 2:   50/50 dieters
have a 50 percent chance of success
make drastic changes in lifestyle and eating habits, but are easily
    discouraged by the number on the scale: if the weight does not
    change significantly, these people return to bad eating habits
require intense motivation from outside sources to keep on track

Group 3:   Successful dieters
dedicated, but set sensible goals (ten pounds or fifty pounds?)
make smart food choices that can be incorporated into daily life
plan regular exercise, but aren't devoted to the gym
accept setbacks calmly, and then continue with their program
    until the goal is reached

Source: http://www.freeessays.tv/d3734.htm

EXERCISE 4 Using Classification to Identify Choices

*The type of holiday you decide to take is determined by many factors including your
level of activity. Would you prefer a week sleeping under a palm tree on a beach?
Sightseeing and enjoying the culture of the destination? Or travelling down the
Amazon in a boat?*

Write a paragraph categorizing different types of vacations based on activity level.

_____

_____

_____

_____

_____

_____

_____

_____

_____

_____

_____

_____

_____

_____

_____

WHAT HAVE YOU WRITTEN?

Read your paragraph carefully. Write out your topic sentence or controlling idea.

_____

What are the three categories you have used?

a. _____

b. _____

c. _____

Are the titles (labels) of your vacation types clear and distinguishable from each other? Are the details describing each group specific? Are they in any particular order (e.g., most extreme to least extreme)?

GET WRITING

"Students use different strategies to study for exams. Some people like to rewrite their class notes, while others prefer to review the text book."

Write a paragraph that identifies the types of study strategies used by college and university students.

WRITING ON THE WEB

Using a search engine such as AltaVista, Yahoo!, or Google, enter terms such as *writing classification, classification essays,* and *classification and division* to locate current sites of interest.

1. Search for news articles that use classification and review how the ideas in the articles have been organized.
2. Write an e-mail to a friend using classification to discuss the types of teachers you have in your current semester.

POINTS TO REMEMBER

1. Classification depends on clearly identifiable groups within a broad topic that are distinguished by precise and accurate details.
2. Classification paragraphs need a strong unifying principle in order to show the relationship of the groups to the main purpose of the writing.
3. The relationship between the groups must be clearly established or else this type of writing will become simply a "shopping list" of details about three separate groups.

8

Developing Paragraphs Using Comparison and Contrast

Do you think men and women bring different qualities to the workplace? Do men and women use different strategies to manage employees, motivate workers, resolve problems, or seek advancement?

Write a paragraph that answers these questions by comparing men and women you have met at work or school.

What Are Comparison and Contrast?

Comparison and contrast measure similarities and differences. Comparison focuses on how two things are alike. Contrast highlights how they are different. Textbooks use comparison and contrast to explain two methods of accounting, two historical figures, two types of poetry, two machines, or two economic philosophies. Your jobs may require you to use comparison to make decisions. As consumers we often use contrast to determine which product to buy, which apartment to rent, or whether we should buy or lease a car. Much of the writing you will do in college or in your job will use comparison and contrast:

Antibiotics are effective in treating most bacterial infections, but they have little or no effect on viral infections.

Coach Wilson always stressed teamwork, but Coach Harris concentrates on two or three key players.

I strongly recommend you consider buying rather than leasing your next car.

GET THINKING AND WRITING

WHAT ARE YOU TRYING TO SAY?

Write a paragraph that compares one of the following pairs:

- high school and college instructors
- amateur and professional sports
- two popular talk shows, soap operas, or sitcoms
- male and female attitudes about dating, marriage, or careers
- two jobs you have had
- two cities or neighbourhoods you have lived in

_____

_____

_____

_____

_____

_____

_____

_____

_____

_____

_____

_____

_____

WHAT HAVE YOU WRITTEN?

Read your paragraph carefully. Underline your topic sentence. Does it clearly state the two topics? What are the important details you listed for the first topic?

a. _____

b. _____

c. _____

What are the important details you listed for the second topic?

a. _____

b. _____

c. _____

Can you think of better details to add? Are there any unrelated details that could be deleted? How could you revise this paragraph to improve its impact?

The Purposes of Comparison and Contrast

Comparison and contrast paragraphs are used for two reasons—to explain and to convince.

Writing to Explain

Comparisons can be used to explain similar topics, showing the differences between air-cooled and water-cooled engines, between state and federal laws, or between African and Indian elephants. You can think of comparisons as two descriptions. The goal of these paragraphs is to teach readers something and to clear up any confusion they may have:

> Many people use the words "jail" and "prison" interchangeably. It is not uncommon, for example, to hear someone say, "He robbed a bank and served ten years in jail." But jails and prisons are very different institutions. City and county jails are short-term facilities. People who are arrested are detained in jail until they are charged or until they go to trial. People convicted of crimes and given short sentences are sent to jail. Jails generally offer minimal services beyond meals and showers. People convicted of serious crimes and sentenced to terms of several months to life are sent to a variety of provincial and federal prisons. Prisons range from minimal facilities to maximum security institutions. Unlike jails, which are designed to detain people for short terms, prisons provide drug counselling, literary programs, and vocational training designed to help convicts start a new life.

TIPS FOR WRITING COMPARISON PARAGRAPHS TO EXPLAIN
1. **Create direct, clearly worded sentences that describe both items.**
2. **Use details and examples to illustrate each type.**
3. **Point out key similarities and key differences.**
4. **Use concrete words rather than general or abstract words.**
5. **Avoid details that require too much explanation or background.**

EXERCISE 1 Using Comparison and Contrast to Explain

Write a paragraph using comparison or contrast to explain the similarities and differences of one of the following topics:

two television shows	two cities or	two bands
AM vs. FM radio	neighbourhoods	PC vs. Macintosh
hybrid vs. gas-	amateur vs. professional	two cell phone plans
powered cars	teams	two airlines

Writing to Convince

In other paragraphs you may use comparison to convince, to prove to readers that one idea is better than another. You might recommend that customers buy one kind of insurance over another or to vote for one candidate rather than an opponent. Comparison paragraphs that are used to convince readers require a clearly stated topic sentence:

> It is rather odd to think that the world's "oldest profession" is considered harmful, and that it must also be illegal. Decriminalizing prostitution, according to many, would have a negative effect on today's society. Anti–red-light activists argue that prostitution and related criminal activity will increase if it is made legal. This forces women (and often men) into illegal prostitution, which is far more destructive to both the individual and the community. Proponents of legalized prostitution, however, argue that decriminalizing this activity will not only reduce crime, but it will also provide better health and safety regulations, which will benefit society as a whole. By looking at the differences between legal and illegal prostitution, and studying the negative effects of illegal prostitution, the potential benefits of legal prostitution should become clear.

TIPS FOR WRITING COMPARISON PARAGRAPHS TO CONVINCE
1. **Create a strong topic sentence clearly stating your choice.**
2. **Provide readers with concrete evidence and examples to support your topic sentence, not just negative comments:**

Ineffective
Illegal prostitution is unfair and should be decriminalized.

Improved
Illegal prostitution fails to protect sex-trade workers, as there are no legal regulations that can provide the health and safety measures to which all members of society are entitled.

3. **Support your topic sentence with examples, facts, quotes, and statistics.**

EXERCISE 2 Using Comparison and Contrast to Convince

GET WRITING ▶ *Choose one of the following topics and write a paragraph that uses comparison or contrast to convince readers that one item in a pair is better than the other.*

talk show hosts	types of parents	new cars
diets	healthcare plans	stores, cafés, or clubs
political candidates	cable news programs	actors, singers, or other performers

Organizing Comparison and Contrast Paragraphs

Because they deal with two topics, comparison and contrast paragraphs can be a challenge to organize clearly:

Confusing

For more than half a century science fiction writers have thrilled and challenged readers with visions of the future and future worlds. These authors offer insight into what they expect man, society, and life to be like at some future time. Ray Bradbury develops this concept in his work *Fahrenheit 451*, a futuristic look at a man and his role in society. Aldous Huxley also uses the concept of society out of control in his science fiction novel *Brave New World*. Bradbury utilizes the luxuries of life in society today, in addition to various occupations and technological advances, to show what life could be like if the future takes a drastic turn for the worse. Written late in his career, *Brave New World* also deals with man in a changed society. He sets man's best friend, the dog, against man, changes the role of public servants, and changes the value of a person. Huxley asks his readers to look at the role of science and literature in the future world, scared that it may be rendered useless and discarded. Unlike Bradbury, Huxley includes in his book a group of people unaffected by the changes in society, a group that still has religious beliefs and marriage, things no longer part of the changed society, to compare and contrast today's culture with his imagined futuristic culture.

The paragraph contains a number of details, but it shifts back and forth between the two topics and so is hard to follow.

There are basically two methods of organizing comparison paragraphs—*subject-by-subject* or *point-by-point.*

Subject-by-Subject

The **subject-by-subject method** divides the paragraph into two parts. The opening line usually introduces the two topics and states the controlling idea. The paragraph describes the first subject, then the second. Most of the actual comparison occurs in the second part of the paragraph:

For more than half a century science fiction writers have thrilled and challenged readers with visions of the future and future worlds. These authors offer insight into what they expect man, society, and life to be like at some future time. Ray Bradbury develops this concept in his work *Fahrenheit 451*, a futuristic look at a man and his role in society. Bradbury utilizes the luxuries of life in society today, in addition to various occupations and technological advances, to show what life could be like if the future takes a drastic turn for the worse. He sets man's best friend, the dog, against man, changes the role of public servants, and changes the value of a person. Aldous Huxley also uses the concept of society out of control in his science fiction novel *Brave New World*. Written late in his career, *Brave New World* also deals with man in a changed society. Huxley asks his readers to look at the role of science and literature in the future world, scared that it may be rendered useless and discarded. Unlike Bradbury, Huxley includes in his book a group of people unaffected by the changes in society, a group that still has religious beliefs and marriage, things no longer part of the changed society, to compare and contrast today's culture with his imagined futuristic culture.

- Subject-by-subject paragraphs may be the simplest to organize because they divide the paragraph into two parts.
- This type of organization works well with longer, more complex comparisons.

Point-by-Point

The **point-by-point method** creates a series of comparisons, showing similarities and differences in specific points:

> For more than half a century science fiction writers have thrilled and challenged readers with visions of the future and future worlds. These authors offer insight into what they expect man, society, and life to be like at some future time. Ray Bradbury develops this concept in his work *Fahrenheit 451*, a futuristic look at a man and his role in society. Aldous Huxley also uses the concept of society out of control in his science fiction novel *Brave New World*. Written late in his career, *Brave New World* also deals with man in a changed society. Bradbury utilizes the luxuries of life in society today, in addition to various occupations and technological advances, to show what life could be like if the future takes a drastic turn for the worse. He sets man's best friend, the dog, against man, changes the role of public

EXAM SKILLS

Many examination questions call for writing one or more narrative paragraphs. As with any exam, read the question carefully and make sure your paragraph directly responds to it. In writing a narrative, remember that your goal is not to tell everything that happened or every detail you can remember but to concentrate on an important point. Your narrative should have a clearly stated goal and topic sentence to guide the events you select.

From Mechanical Engineering

What are the main differences between a gasoline and a diesel engine?

general description — *Gasoline and diesel engines, both developed in Germany in the late nineteenth century, are internal combustion engines used to power motor vehicles. Nickolaus Otto developed*

first subject — *the four-stroke engine in 1876, which was used with Daimler's carburetor to create the first automobile engines. Most cars and light trucks use gasoline engines because of their light weight. Gas engines are only 20–25 percent efficient. Rudolf Diesel developed the diesel engine in 1892, which uses a heavier fuel and achieves efficiencies ranging from 25 to 42 percent.*

second subject — *Diesel engines are heavy, so they are impractical for airplanes and most passenger cars. Diesel engines are used in trains, trucks, and stationary power plants.*

The paragraph states the common details shared by the two engines, then uses the subject-by-subject method to organize a comparison of the engines' development, fuel, weight, efficiency, and current uses.

servants, and changes the value of a person. Huxley also asks his readers to look at the role of science and literature in the future world, scared that it may be rendered useless and discarded. Unlike Bradbury, Huxley includes in his book a group of people unaffected by the changes in society, a group that still has religious beliefs and marriage, things no longer part of the changed society, to compare and contrast today's culture with his imagined futuristic culture.

- Point-by-point comparisons allow you to place specific facts or comments right after each other for easier comparison.
- Point-by-point comparisons can be useful in short comparisons, but they rely on transitional phrases to make the comparison coherent.

Student Paragraphs

Comparison and contrast of two jobs:

My current job allows me to work from home much of the time. For two years I worked nine to five in a claims office. It required a forty-five-minute commute, a six-dollar-a-day parking fee, and a uniform of a suit and tie. I was jammed into a tight cubicle and could take only two five-minute breaks. When the system was down, which happened often, my time was wasted, and all I could do was read the paper and wait. When the accounting department needed our office space, we were given the option of working from home. Now I can sleep an hour later because my commute takes a few seconds. I can wear jeans and a T-shirt and have my whole apartment to work from. I can take breaks when I want. When the system is down, I can run errands, do my wash, work on a school assignment, or take a nap. My neighbours might think I'm unemployed, but I am often working overtime every week.

Comparison and contrast of two television shows:

Sitcoms break down into two types—the family sitcom and the workplace sitcom. In the family sitcom, the action takes place in a living room. It is the oldest kind of show, dating back to the days of *Ozzie and Harriet* and *Father Knows Best. The Cosby Show* and *Everybody Loves Raymond* are updates but really much the same. The focus is on family life and the interactions between husbands and wives and parents and children. Cosby was a doctor who rarely had to leave dinner to see a patient. Raymond was a sportswriter who seemed to spend every night at home. In contrast, the characters in *M.A.S.H.* and *Taxi* seemed to live at work. Workplace sitcoms explore the relationships between bosses and employees, between office rivals and office pals. These shows focus on the two places we spend most of our lives and encounter most of our problems.

Comparison and contrast of two countries:

Iraq and Iran are two Middle Eastern nations that are often in the news, but few Canadians realize how different these neighbours are. Iran, called Persia until 1935, is an ancient nation that goes back thousands of years to biblical times. The people are Persians, not Arabs. They speak Farsi, not Arabic. The population is predominantly Shiite. Under the Shah, Iran was closely linked to Europe and the United States. Today Iran is an Islamic republic seeking to create a new identity. Iraq, on the other hand, is a relatively new country, created by the British after World War I. The people have strong tribal and ethnic ties. The Kurds in the north have a long history of regional independence. Still in turmoil since the fall of Saddam, Iraq's future is unsettled.

PUTTING PARAGRAPHS TOGETHER

introduction
topic sentence

The Civil War lasted longer than many expected and cost more lives than anyone feared because both sides had strong advantages.

1. What is the goal of this paragraph?
2. Is a one-sentence introduction helpful or distracting?

topic sentence
Northern advantges

supporting details

The North had a larger population, better transportation, and a more advanced industrial base than the South. The North had the capital and factories to produce the materials of war: weapons, uniforms, and ammunition. Its extensive merchant fleet and strong navy meant Union forces could import needed supplies. The North had all the resources to build a powerful modern army to crush the weaker Confederate forces.

1. What are the main ideas in this paragraph?
2. How does the student organize this paragraph?

topic sentence
Southern advantges

supporting details

In contrast, the South, though less populated and less industrial, had clear strengths. First, the South basically achieved all its goals by seceding and creating the Confederacy. It only had to protect its borders from attack. Its armies fought on familiar territory and could use this knowledge to wage guerrilla raids against Union forces. Defending armies throughout history have often been able to hold off much larger invading armies. The South hoped recognition and possible support from Great Britain would tip the balance in its favour if it could keep Union forces at bay.

1. How does this paragraph contrast with the previous one?
2. How does the student organize the details?
3. How does this paragraph build on the ideas mentioned in the first one?

Although Southern armies fought hard and inflicted heavy losses on Union forces, they were steadily ground down. They had no resources for a long war, and without outside support the Confederacy slowly crumbled. Despite its inferior position, the South was able to inflict high casualties on the North in America's most costly conflict.

conclusion

details

topic sentence

1. How does this paragraph serve to end the comparison?
2. Does the topic sentence relate to the ideas in the opening paragraph?

Readings

As you study these readings, notice how writers use paragraphs to organize comparisons and make transitions between subjects.

FOR MINORITIES, TIMING IS EVERYTHING

OLIVE JOHNSON

1   Left-handedness and homosexuality both tend to run in families. As my husband's family and mine have some of each, it is not surprising that one of our children is left-handed and another homosexual. Both my left-handed daughter and my homosexual son turned out to be bright, funny, talented people with loving friends and family. But their experience of growing up in different minority groups was a striking contrast and an interesting illustration of how societal attitudes change as sufficient knowledge accumulates to make old beliefs untenable.

2   By the time my daughter was growing up, left-handedness was no longer regarded as a sign of immorality or mental deficiency. Almost everybody knew "openly" left-handed friends, teachers and relatives and viewed them as normal people who wrote differently. Except for a little awkwardness in learning to write at school, my daughter's hand

Words to Know
untenable indefensible; incapable of being justified

preference was simply never an issue. If people noticed it at all, they did so with a shrug. Nobody called her nasty names or banned school library books about left-handed families, as school trustees in Surrey, B.C., recently banned books about gay families. Nobody criticized her left-handed "lifestyle" or suggested that she might be an unfit role model for young children. Nobody claimed that she *chose* to be left-handed and should suffer the consequences.

My gay son did not choose to be different either, but when he was growing up, homosexuality was still too misunderstood to be accepted as just another <u>variant</u> of human sexuality. Because gay people still felt unsafe revealing their sexual orientation, he was deprived of the opportunity of knowing openly gay teachers, friends and relatives. He grew up hearing crude jokes and nasty names for people like him, and he entered adulthood knowing that being openly gay could prevent you from getting a job or renting an apartment. It could also get you assaulted.

variant version; something a little different from others of the same type

Bigotry has never been reserved for homosexuality, of course. I am old enough to remember the time when bigotry directed toward other minorities in Canada was similar to that which is still sometimes aimed at homosexuals. In my Vancouver childhood, Chinese were regularly called "Chinks" (the boys in my high school wore black denim "Chink pants" tailored for them in Chinatown). Black people were "niggers," prohibited from staying in most Vancouver hotels. Kids in the special class were "retards" or "morons." Jews were suspected of all sorts of crazy things, and physically disabled people were often regarded as mental defectives.

Left-handed children were still being punished for writing with their left hand, particularly in the more religious parts of Canada. (When I was a graduate psychology student in Newfoundland doing research on handedness, I discovered that several of my "right-handed" subjects were actually left-handers; at school their left hands had been tied behind their backs by <u>zealous</u> nuns.)

zealous avid; marked by active interest and enthusiasm

The gay children and teachers of my childhood were simply invisible. Two female teachers could live together without raising eyebrows, chiefly because women in those days (especially women *teachers*) were not generally thought of as sexual persons. Two male "bachelors" living together did tend to be suspect, and so gay men brave enough to live together usually kept their living arrangements quiet. "Sissy" boys and "boyish" girls took a lot of teasing, but most people knew too little about homosexuality to draw any conclusions. These boys and girls were expected to grow up and marry people of the opposite sex. Some of them did, divorcing years later to live with one of their own.

Many of the teachers and parents of my childhood who tried to convert left-handed children into right-handers probably believed they were helping children avoid the <u>stigma</u> of being left-handed, just as many misguided therapists tried to "cure" patients of their homosexuality to enable them to avoid the stigma of being gay in a heterosexual world.

stigma mark; a symbol of disgrace; a stain on one's reputation

8　　Thanks to advances in our understanding, left-handedness gradually came to be seen as a natural and <u>innate</u> trait. We know now that people do not *choose* to be more skillful with one hand than the other; they simply are. While researchers are still debating the precise mechanisms that determine hand preference, there is general agreement that left- and right-handedness are just two different (and valid) ways of being. Left-handers are a minority in their own right, not "deviants" from normal right-handedness.

innate natural; inborn characteristic

9　　The same is true for sexual orientation. Although we do not yet clearly understand the mechanisms that determine sexual orientation, all indicators point to the conclusion that it results from interactions between genetic, hormonal and possibly other factors, all beyond the individual's control. Like left-handedness, sexual orientation is an innate trait, not a choice or "lifestyle." Like left-handedness, homosexuality is a valid alternative sexuality, not a deviance from "normal" heterosexuality.

10　　As with other minorities, attitudes toward homosexuality are inevitably becoming more liberal, at least in Canada. A recent poll, commissioned by the B.C. Teachers' Federation, found that almost 70 per cent of B.C. residents think students should be taught in school to accept homosexuals and treat them as they would other people. (Twenty per cent said homosexuality should be discouraged, 9 per cent said they didn't know and 3 per cent refused to answer.) These results indicate that overt bigotry toward homosexuality is increasingly limited to religious extremists. The Surrey school trustees who voted against having gay and lesbian resource materials in schools are probably at about the same stage of cultural evolution as were the Newfoundland nuns who tied children's left hands behind their backs 40 years ago.

11　　Even so, I'm grateful that they're further along the path of enlightenment than their predecessors in medieval Europe, who burned many left-handers and homosexuals at the stake. Being born in the late 20th century was a wise move on the part of my son and daughter. In some things, timing is everything. ■

Source: Johnson, Olive. "For Minorities, Timing Is Everything." *Globe and Mail* 7 July 1997: A14.

CRITICAL THINKING AND DISCUSSION

GET THINKING AND WRITING

Understanding Meaning: What Is the Writer Trying to Say?

1. What are the essential differences between these two "minority" groups?
2. What is the point of a comparison such as this?

Evaluating Strategy: How Does the Writer Say It?

1. This essay is well-balanced, devoting equal amount of information to each topic. How important is "balance" when writing a comparison paper on groups of people?

2. The writer has included some anecdotes (short narrative examples) to made this topic more personal. Is this important? Why or why not?

3. What impact does the final paragraph have?

Appreciating Language: What Words Does the Writer Use?

1. The writer uses some derogatory terms to make this comparison. Does this type of strong language support the purpose of the essay?

2. The writer uses simple and sophisticated language in the same comparison. Is this a successful strategy? Why or why not?

Writing Suggestions

1. If you are familiar with a different culture or a different part of the country, use a single point of reference to show differences. You might compare Toronto and Vancouver taxi drivers, Acadian and Quebecois French, or the East Coast and West Coast.

2. *Collaborative writing:* Discuss the differences between high school and college with a group of students, then select a single point and develop a short comparison paragraph.

NEAT PEOPLE vs. SLOPPY PEOPLE

SUZANNE BRITT

Suzanne Britt has written articles for the New York Times, *the* Boston Globe, Newsweek, *and the* Cleveland Plain Dealer. *Her books include* Show and Tell *and* Images: A Centennial Journey.

AS YOU READ:

Suzanne Britt uses the subject-by-subject method to organize her observations about neat and sloppy people. Think of people you know who fit in these categories.

I've finally figured out the difference between neat people and sloppy people. The distinction is, as always, moral. Neat people are lazier and meaner than sloppy people.

Sloppy people, you see, are not really sloppy. Their sloppiness is merely the unfortunate consequence of their extreme moral <u>rectitude.</u> Sloppy people carry in their mind's eye a heavenly vision, a precise plan, that is so stupendous, so perfect, it can't be achieved in this world or the next.

Sloppy people live in Never-Never Land. Someday is their <u>métier.</u> Someday they are planning to alphabetize all their books and set up home catalogues. Someday they will go through their wardrobes and mark certain items for <u>tentative</u> mending and certain items for passing on to relatives of similar shape and size. Someday sloppy people will make family scrapbooks into which they will put newspaper

Words to Know

rectitude correctness

métier vocation, specialty

tentative hesitant, unsure

clippings, postcards, locks of hair, and the fried corsage from their senior prom. Someday they will file everything on the surface of their desks, including the cash receipts from coffee purchases at the snack shop. Someday they will sit down and read all the back issues of *The New Yorker*.

4   For all these noble reasons and more, sloppy people never get neat. They aim too high and wide. They save everything, planning someday to file, order, and straighten out the world. But while these ambitious plans take clearer and clearer shape in their heads, the books spill from the shelves onto the floor, the clothes pile up in the hamper and closet, the family mementos <u>accumulate</u> in every drawer, the surface of the desk is buried under mounds of paper and the unread magazines threaten to reach the ceiling.

accumulate gather

5   Sloppy people can't bear to part with anything. They give loving attention to every detail. When sloppy people say they're going to tackle the surface of the desk, they really mean it. Not a paper will go unturned; not a rubber band will go unboxed. Four hours or two weeks into the <u>excavation</u>, the desk looks exactly the same, primarily because the sloppy person is <u>meticulously</u> creating new piles of papers with new headings and <u>scrupulously</u> stopping to read all the old book catalogs before he throws them away. A neat person would just bulldoze the desk.

excavation digging
meticulously carefully
scrupulously conscientiously

6   Neat people are bums and clods at heart. They have <u>cavalier</u> attitudes toward possessions, including family heirlooms. Everything is just another dust-catcher to them. If anything collects dust, it's got to go and that's that. Neat people will toy with the idea of throwing the children out of the house just to cut down on the clutter.

cavalier casual, inconsiderate

7   Neat people don't care about process. They like results. What they want to do is get the whole thing over with so they can sit down and watch the rasslin' on TV. Neat people operate on two unvarying principles: Never handle any item twice, and throw everything away.

8   The only thing messy in a neat person's house is the trash can. The minute something comes to a neat person's hand, he will look at it, try to decide if it has immediate use and, finding none, throw it in the trash.

9   Neat people are especially vicious with mail. They never go through their mail unless they are standing directly over a trash can. If the trash can is beside the mailbox, even better. All ads, catalogs, pleas for charitable contributions, church bulletins and money-saving coupons go straight into the trash can without being opened. All letters from home, postcards from Europe, bills and paychecks are opened, immediately responded to, then dropped in the trash can. Neat people keep their receipts only for tax purposes. That's it. No sentimental salvaging of birthday cards or the last letter a dying relative ever wrote. Into the trash it goes.

Neat people place neatness above everything, even economics. They are incredibly wasteful. Neat people throw away several toys every time they walk through the den. I knew a neat person once who threw away a perfectly good dish drainer because it had mold on it. The drainer was too much trouble to wash. And neat people sell their furniture when they move. They will sell a La-Z-Boy recliner while you are reclining in it.

10

Neat people are no good to borrow from. Neat people buy everything in expensive little single portions. They get their flour and sugar in two-pound bags. They wouldn't consider clipping a coupon, saving a left-over, reusing plastic non-dairy whipped cream containers or rinsing off tin foil and draping it over the unmoldy dish drainer. You can never borrow a neat person's newspaper to see what's playing at the movies. Neat people have the paper all wadded up and in the trash by 7:05 a.m.

11

Neat people cut a clean swath through the organic as well as the inorganic world. People, animals, and things are all one to them. They are so insensitive. After they've finished with the pantry, the medicine cabinet, and the attic, they will throw out the red geranium (too many leaves), sell the dog (too many fleas), and send the children off to boarding school (too many scuffmarks on the hardwood floors). ■

12

GET THINKING
AND WRITING

CRITICAL THINKING AND DISCUSSION

Understanding Meaning: What Is the Writer Trying to Say?

1. What are the main differences Britt sees between neat and sloppy people?
2. What does the author mean when she says sloppy people "are not really sloppy"?
3. What motivates sloppy people to keep from organizing things or throwing things out?
4. What does Britt mean when she says sloppy people live in "Never-Never Land"?
5. *Critical thinking:* Britt suggests that neat people are not sentimental. Can you think of exceptions? Do you know people who lovingly organize and catalog their books, pictures, and videos because they want to preserve and protect them?

Evaluating Strategy: How Does the Writer Say It?

1. How does Britt use topic sentences to develop her paragraphs? Why do comparisons require clearly stated controlling ideas?
2. How does Britt use specific examples like cleaning a desk to make her point?

Appreciating Language: What Words Does the Writer Use?

1. Make a list of the words Britt uses to describe neat and sloppy people. Which list contains more positive terms? Which list contains words that suggest aggression or coldness?

2. How could you change the impact of Britt's essay by replacing the words she uses to describe neat and sloppy people?

Writing Suggestions

1. Building upon Britt's observations, write a paragraph stating whether you would rather have a neat or a sloppy person as a roommate.
2. *Collaborative writing:* Discuss Britt's essay with a group of other students, then work together to create one or more paragraphs that contrast spenders vs. savers, dieters vs. eaters, smokers vs. nonsmokers, joggers vs. drivers, those who swear and those who don't, or another pair of opposites.

STEPS TO WRITING A COMPARISON AND CONTRAST PARAGRAPH

1. Narrow your topic and identify key points by creating two lists of details.
2. Determine the goal of your paragraph. Do you plan to explain differences or argue that one subject is better or more desirable than the other?
3. Develop a topic sentence that clearly expresses your main point.
4. Determine whether to use subject-by-subject or point-by-point to organize your details, then make a rough outline.
5. Write a draft of your paragraph, then consider these questions:
   Is my topic sentence clearly stated?
   Are there minor details that should be deleted or replaced?
   Is my paragraph clearly organized?
   Do I provide enough information for readers to understand my comparison or accept my point of view?

Selecting Topics

Consider these topics for developing comparison and contrast paragraphs:

two places you have lived

high school and postsecondary instructors

traditional and Internet courses

attending college or university full-time vs. working and attending part-time

living in residence or at home

best and worst jobs

satellite vs. cable TV

a friend vs. a best friend

your parents' attitudes and your own

two ways of meeting people

two methods of looking for a job

EXERCISE 3 Planning and Writing Comparison and Contrast Paragraphs

GET WRITING

Select a topic from the above list or choose one of your own and develop details and a topic sentence that states the goal of your paragraph.

Topic: _____

Possible supporting details:

Subject 1	**Subject 2**
1. _____	1. _____
2. _____	2. _____
3. _____	3. _____
4. _____	4. _____

Topic sentence:

_____

Organization (subject-by-subject or point-by-point): _____

First sentence: topic sentence, first detail, or introductory statement:

_____

Supporting details in order:

1. _____

2. _____

3. _____

4. _____

Last sentence: final detail, concluding statement, or topic sentence:

_____

Write your paragraph and review it by reading it aloud.

WORKING TOGETHER

Working with a group of students, revise this rough draft of an e-mail to make it easier to read by organizing it in a subject-by-subject or point-by-point pattern. Consider why comparison and contrast writing depends on clear organization to be effective.

Dear Sales Staff:

Until our systems upgrade is complete, we will be using both Federated Express and Air National for shipping. Make sure you use blue labels for Federated Express and yellow labels for Air National packages.

When you have documents to ship, use Federated Express. Bulk packages should go Air National unless going to the Edmonton office. Make sure you register all shipments in the log book. Remember that Air National packages have to have a red stamp before being shipped. The best way to reach Federated Express is at 1-800-555-1500. If you have any questions about Air National, check its website at www.airnational.com. Use Federated for anything going to the Hamilton office.

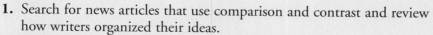
GET WRITING

How have the roles of men and women changed in the last fifty years?

Write one or more paragraphs comparing and contrasting male and female relationships then and now. What has changed? What has remained the same? You may use either subject-by-subject or point-by-point to organize your ideas.

WRITING ON THE WEB

Using a search engine such as AltaVista, Yahoo!, or Google, enter terms such as *writing comparison, comparison and contrast essays, organizing comparison essays, subject-by-subject comparison,* and *comparison point by point* to locate current sites of interest.

1. Search for news articles that use comparison and contrast and review how writers organized their ideas.
2. Write an e-mail to a friend using comparison and contrast to discuss how something has changed or the difference between two classes, two concerts you attended, or two jobs you are considering.

POINTS TO REMEMBER

1. Comparison points out similarities; contrast points out differences.
2. Comparison can be used to explain differences or argue that one subject is superior to another.
3. Comparison paragraphs should have a clear topic sentence expressing your goal.
4. Comparison paragraphs can be organized subject by subject to discuss one topic, then the other; or point by point to discuss both topics in a series of comparisons.
5. Comparison paragraphs depend on clear transitions to prevent confusion.

9

Developing Paragraphs Using Cause and Effect

GET WRITING

Is downloading music without paying for it stealing? What causes some people to see a difference between robbing CDs from a store and using a computer to get them free?

Write a paragraph stating your view about illegal downloading. Do you consider it a crime? Why or why not?

What Is Cause and Effect?

Why did water in Walkerton make people ill? Why did you quit your last job? Why was a popular television show cancelled? How will the legalization of same-sex marriages change the idea of "family" throughout Canada? Will the bankruptcy of airlines such as Jetsgo make people afraid to buy airline tickets directly online? How will rising gas prices affect your driving habits? The answers to all these questions call for cause and effect writing that explains why things happen and examines or predicts results:

Airlines are losing money because of rising fuel costs, decreased business travel, and costly security requirements.

I quit my job at the grocery store because my hours were cut.

People who stay on this diet for more than a month can develop high blood pressure.

Student Paragraph

The Effects of Not Getting Enough Sleep

Without a regular seven to eight hours of sleep a night, I become grumpy, clumsy, and produce poor quality work. My boyfriend can tell through the phone lines when I haven't gotten enough sleep. Fortunately, these days when he calls, I'm usually the happy-go-lucky woman he knows as his "golden girl." However, last semester, I was often sleep deprived. As a result, I got annoyed at him over the most trivial things. For example, he goes to school four hours away, and he called once to tell me that he'd be home later on a Friday evening than he had planned because the guy who normally gives him a ride had to work late. Was it his fault? No, but that didn't matter to me in my grumpy state. I complained about his forthcoming lateness and then grumbled on into a cranky tangent counting all the ways his not owning a car negatively impacted my life. In addition to grumpiness, fatigue also makes me clumsy. After pulling an all-nighter to finish an essay recently, I stumbled and fell down half a flight of stairs on my way to submit the paper. I didn't get hurt; however, a year ago, when I had similarly stayed up all night to finish an assignment, I tripped over my own feet leaving the house, banged my head on my brother's bicycle pedal, and ended up with three stitches in my head. Not only is lack of sleep hazardous to my good humour and my physical health, I never end up producing the kind of quality work that I can turn out with regular sleep. My marks this year attest to that. Last semester, I did everything at the last minute, regularly getting only three to four hours of sleep a night, and struggled to maintain a B average. This semester, aside from that recent essay (which has been my lowest mark this year), I have scheduled time for each assignment, gotten between seven and eight hours of sleep each night, and my average this semester is a solid A. I've decided I like my life a lot better when I'm well rested, so sleep has become a priority rather than something I do when everything else is finally finished.

The topic sentence in the above paragraph is *Without a regular seven to eight hours of sleep a night, I become grumpy, clumsy, and produce poor quality work.* The main effects in the paragraph are

1. I become grumpy.
2. I become clumsy.
3. I produce poor quality work.

Notice that

1. The topic sentence clearly outlines the effects of fatigue upon the writer.
2. Each effect is a direct result of fatigue.
3. The writer maintains the same order throughout the paragraph—grumpiness, clumsiness, poor quality work—as she does in the topic sentence.

WHAT ARE YOU TRYING TO SAY?

Write a paragraph that explains the causes or effects of one of the following topics:

GET WRITING
AND REVISING

Causes for

- students dropping out of high school
- companies outsourcing overseas
- teenagers becoming overweight
- digital cameras being popular

Effects of

- being downsized
- taking too many courses
- having children as a teenager
- working while going to school

_____

_____

_____

_____

_____

_____

_____

_____

_____

_____

_____

_____

_____

_____

_____

_____

WHAT HAVE YOU WRITTEN?

Read your paragraph carefully. Underline the topic sentence. List the main causes or effects in your paragraph:

1. _____

2. _____

3. _____

Do these causes or effects logically relate to your topic sentence? Can you think of better causes or effects? To revise this paragraph, what changes would you make?

Cause and Effect: Critical Thinking

Cause and effect writing calls for careful observation and critical thinking. After studying a problem like drug addiction for years, experts disagree as to what causes people to take narcotics—poverty, genetics, depression, or peer pressure. Even when you write about yourself, you may be unable to clearly determine the reasons for decisions you have made. Why did you decide to attend this school? Which factor was most important—the course offerings, the campus, the location, your parents, the cost?

In determining causes, it is important to look beyond first impressions and assumptions. Make sure you collect enough evidence and avoid rushing to judgment.

As early as the 1920s, doctors began reporting that many lung cancer patients smoked cigarettes. It was not until 1964, however, that scientists collected enough data to establish a cause and effect relationship and declare smoking a health risk. If you spot a stranger leaving your office, then discover your iPod® missing, you might be suspicious. However, you have no proof that the stranger took your iPod® or that it has been stolen and not simply misplaced. Similarly, make sure you avoid jumping to conclusions when you write.

Don't confuse a coincidence or a time relationship for a cause. The fact that you began taking vitamin C in November and did not get a cold all winter does not prove the vitamin is keeping you healthy. It could simply be a coincidence. The fact that your transmission developed problems the day after you had the oil changed does not prove the mechanics did anything wrong with your car. Just because one event happens after another does not prove there is a cause and effect relationship.

EXERCISE 1 Critical Thinking and Cause and Effect

Read each statement and evaluate how effectively the writer uses critical thinking to identify a cause and effect relationship. Write C *for a clear cause,* X *for a time relationship or coincidence, and* P *for a possible cause and effect relationship.*

1. _____ Every time I wash my car it rains. I washed my car this morning; therefore, it will rain today.

2. _____ Teenagers are consuming 35 percent more fast food than their parents' generation did, and less than half report doing any regular exercise. No wonder many young people are overweight.

3. _____ Last year aviation fuel prices soared and ticket sales dropped, causing airline profits to shrink dramatically.

4. _____ A rise in work-related stress coupled with increasingly clogged city streets and major highways explains the rising number of road rage incidents.

5. _____ Bill's kids are always in trouble. It's because he is always away from home on business.

6. _____ Monique speaks French. She would be great working in our bilingual program.

7. _____ Last week a grade eleven student died of a heart attack during training. On Monday a player passed out in the weight room. Coach Ferguson is driving his team too hard.

8. _____ CBC Radio has broadened its target audience to include young people by hiring Sook-Yin Lee, formerly a Much Music VJ, to host "Definitely Not the Opera." Canadian youth love VJs.

9. _____ Britain has double the population of Canada but more than six times as many national newspapers. Canadians don't like to read.

10. _____ I did data entry for fifteen years, and now I need glasses. Looking at a computer screen eight hours a day ruined my eyes.

EXERCISE 2 Identifying Causes

Read the following paragraph, then answer the questions that follow.

Why do celebrities become social activists? At the basest level, it may be simply to garner greater publicity. It may be the newest fashion—to speak out on behalf of causes. Then again, with a growing awareness that we live in a global community, the realization that they are in a position to effect change seems to have spurred some celebrities to take on causes that are important to them. Causes are great forums for publicity. As a spokesperson for PETA (People for the Ethical Treatment of Animals), Pamela Anderson earned almost as much publicity as she did for being a *Baywatch* beauty. Why? It allowed fans to see her in a sympathetic light. Not only is she a physically enhanced lover of bad-boy musicians, but she has an enlightened activist side. Could it be then that being a celebrity activist has become fashionable? Certainly, more and more celebrity biographies include the causes they are affiliated with alongside their acting credits. If activism has become trendy, it's not a new trend—Robert Redford has been promoting solar power since 1975. It does, however, seem to be a growing trend. Angelina Jolie, as a United Nations goodwill ambassador, crusades on behalf of refugees in Africa; Chris Martin of Coldplay speaks out on behalf of beleaguered farmers in Ghana who struggle to survive the tariffs imposed as a result of Western trade practices; and U2 lead singer Bono speaks out about AIDS, trade issues, and world poverty.

1. **What is the topic sentence?** _____

2. **What are the causes? Restate them in your own words:**

   a. _____

   b. _____

   c. _____

   d. _____

   e. _____

EXERCISE 3 Identifying Effects

Read the following paragraph, then answer the questions that follow.

Oil kills birds in many ways. Its first effect is to break down the birds' waterproofing. Water runs off a seabird's back because the bird is protected by a layer of feathers, overlapping like the tiles on a roof. The fine structure of the feathers makes them waterproof. The separate strands, or barbs, in each feather are bound together by rows of tiny hooks, or barbules, into a tight weave that water cannot penetrate. Underneath is a layer of insulating downy feathers that allows the bird's skin to stay warm, and beneath the skin is a layer of body fat that can add some insulation. This waterproof system works like a winter coat whose outer waterproof layer covers a thicker layer of material that traps air, keeping the wearer warm and dry. But it takes very little to disturb the intricate arrangements that make up a seabird's feather "coat." Oil destroys the coat by clogging the barbs and barbules, allowing cold water to soak into the insulating down and reach the skin. Even a small amount of oil—a spot no bigger than a quarter—may be enough to kill a seabird. A healthy seabird maintains a body temperature of 41°C—about two degrees higher than the body temperature of humans—and has no problem swimming and diving in icy waters. But once the bird is touched by oil, its body heat drains away through the "tear" in its protective plumage. The bird tries to maintain its body temperature by burning its energy reserves stored as body fat, but these are soon exhausted. When fat reserves are used up, a bird will burn up its flight muscles to maintain body heat. It may also try to save itself by spending even more energy in search of food. In this pursuit it is handicapped by its extra burden of soaked feathers and weakness, and the exhausted bird will soon die. In the cold waters around the coasts of Canada, hypothermia is usually the cause of death. The bird's other immediate response to oiling is to preen itself to try to restore the feathers' waterproofing. Inevitably, as it preens, the bird inhales and swallows toxic compounds in the oil that can damage its liver, lungs, kidneys, intestines, and other internal organs. This poisoning can kill a seabird, but it is slower to take effect than is loss of body heat. Oil on the feathers of an incubating seabird may also be carried to its eggs, and if the oil soaks through the shell, it can kill the embryo or cause abnormalities in the developing chick.

Source "Oil Pollution and Birds." *Hinterland Who's Who.* 2003. 17 July 2006 <http://www.hww.ca/hww2.asp ?pid=0&cid=4&cid=229>.

1. **What is the topic sentence?** _____

2. **What are the effects? Restate them in your own words:**

    a. _____

    b. _____

EXAM SKILLS

Examination questions often call for cause and effect answers. Given the time limit of most exams, it is important to identify key causes or effects. Because any answer you give will likely be incomplete, you can qualify your answer with a strong introduction or conclusion.

From Earth Science

What are the causes of global warming?

topic sentence cause #1	*Global warming is caused by human activity. Factories, cars, power plants, and cities generate heat and pollution that rise into the atmosphere. Greenhouse gases form a barrier that*
cause #2	*traps the heat and prevents it from leaving the atmosphere. Carbon dioxide is believed to be a primary greenhouse gas. The destruction of the rain forests has reduced the vegetation*
cause #3	*that can absorb carbon dioxide. In some parts of the world farmers use fire to clear forests, destroying plants and producing a great deal of pollution. The rapid industrialization and*
cause #4	*booming consumer economy of China, which has a billion people, will only intensify these causes.*

c. _____

d. _____

e. _____

f. _____

g. _____

Student Paragraphs

Cause paragraph:

When I look back at my high school friends who dropped out, I suppose I could list half a dozen reasons why they decided to leave school. Most of them claimed school bored them. They could not wait to get out. Others hated the teachers. They resented being picked on by the students in higher grades. Some resented the rich kids who could afford designer clothes and drove new cars. A few of my friends even said they hated school because they missed their favourite soap operas. However, the overall reason they dropped out was that they never looked ahead. None of them ever had a plan for what they wanted to do after they dropped out of school.

Effect paragraph:

The annual seal hunt off the East Coast of Canada generates over sixteen million dollars a year for the fishing industry. As gruesome as the hunt seems, it is necessary to control the rapidly growing seal population. In fact, some Atlantic fishermen blame the depletion of cod stocks on the seal boom. In addition to controlling the population explosion, the cull aims to ensure the continued health of seal colonies, and it seems to be working: the harp seal population has tripled since the 1970s. However, the cull has had a negative impact for Canada globally. Anti-hunt activists around the world use graphic images of young seals being clubbed to death to fuel dissent. This year, there were protests in fifty cities around the world. In addition, the Humane Society of the United States is asking the rest of the world to boycott Canadian seafood products in an effort to bully the Canadian government into calling off the hunt. If this boycott is effected, the Canadian fishing industry could forfeit some or all of the three billion dollars earned from exports of seafood to the U.S.

Cause and effect paragraph:

Last year I moved to Montreal to go to school. I moved into an apartment with three younger students. Maybe because I am twenty-three, I found it hard to live with people right out of high school. They were noisy, rude, and disruptive. Working twenty hours a week, I need my sleep. Their TVs and stereos blast well past midnight, even on weekdays. Getting a studio apartment twenty minutes from any school cost more and required a longer commute, but the results have been worth it. I can get to sleep early and take naps when I need to. I have no distractions when I study. I find myself more relaxed, less irritated, and more focused. I now work twenty-five hours a week, get better grades, and experience less stress because I am living alone.

PUTTING PARAGRAPHS TOGETHER

Moving On

Late last year I decided to quit the best job I ever had. I gave up a fun, high-paying job and went back to school because I wanted a future. I was a bartender at one of the busiest pubs in town for over two years. Some weekends I made $500 in tips. I had great friends. We worked hard but had fun. We met celebrities. We hosted sports teams, after-work gatherings, and friends' get-togethers. It was never boring. I became friends with all my coworkers. On our days off we went shopping, swimming, and dating. It was like one endless party, and for the first year I hoped it would never change.

introduction

topic sentence

supporting details

causes

1. How effective is the first sentence? Does it grab your attention?
2. Why are the details about the job important?
3. What is the purpose of this paragraph?

After some time passed, my attitudes changed because I began to see this job as a dead end. I noticed that all my friends had money but no savings. They had plenty of dates but no relationships. They made a lot of money in cash and spent it all on clothes and trips. They were always broke. I had seen them at first as glamorous and fun. However, I saw they were really very shallow, dating one guy after another, going to one party after another. As time

topic sentence
showing transition

supporting details
causes

effects

passed, the gossip and games became empty and tired. The result was I began to hate going to work and putting up with late hours.

> 1. How do the details in this paragraph show a change from the first?
> 2. How does this paragraph use cause and effect?
> 3. How does the student show how something fun became something boring?

topic sentence

effects

I started college in September and feel like I am building a real future. My self-esteem went up because I took courses, read books, and learned computers. The tests and projects gave me something to focus on and plan for. I began to feel like someone living in the adult world. Having to pay for books and tuition forced me to save money and give up partying and shopping. I still work three nights a week and enjoy my friends' company now and then. Right now I have less spending money but am a lot happier because I know I am accomplishing something genuine.

> 1. How does this paragraph build on the one before?
> 2. How does the student use effect to show change?
> 3. How does the student end the paragraph? Does it serve to end the entire writing?

Readings

As you study the readings, notice how writers use paragraphs to highlight main points and signal transitions in writing cause and effect.

WHY WE CRAVE HORROR MOVIES

STEPHEN KING

Stephen King is best known as a writer of horror novels, many of which have been made into motion pictures. His books include The Shining, The Dead Zone, Christine, Misery, *and* The Green Mile.

AS YOU READ:
King uses cause and effect to explain why people love horror films. Notice that King uses examples and narratives to demonstrate reasons for the popularity of scary movies. He uses paragraphs, including one-sentence paragraphs, to organize ideas and highlight transitions.

1   I think that we're all mentally ill; those of us outside the asylums only hide it a little better—and maybe not all that much better, after all. We've all known people who talk to themselves, people who sometimes squinch their faces into horrible grimaces when they believe no one is watching, people who have some hysterical fear—of snakes, the dark, the tight place, the long drop . . . and, of course, those final worms and grubs that are waiting so patiently underground.

2   When we pay our four or five bucks and seat ourselves at tenth-row center in a theater showing a horror movie, we are daring the nightmare.

3   Why? Some of the reasons are simple and obvious. To show that we can, that we are not afraid, that we can ride this roller coaster. Which is not to say that a really good horror movie may not surprise a scream out of us at some point, the way we may scream when the roller coaster twists through a complete 360 or plows through a lake at the bottom of the drop. And horror movies, like roller coasters, have always been the special province of the young; by the time one turns 40 or 50, one's appetite for double twists or 360-degree loops may be considerably depleted.

4   We also go to reestablish our feelings of essential normality; the horror movie is innately conservative, even reactionary. Freda Jackson as the horrible melting woman in *Die, Monster, Die!* confirms for us that no matter how far we may be removed from the beauty of a Robert Redford or a Diana Ross, we are still light-years from true ugliness.

5   And we go to have fun.

6   Ah, but this is where the ground starts to slope away, isn't it? Because this is a very peculiar sort of fun, indeed. The fun comes from seeing others menaced—sometimes killed. One critic has suggested that if pro football has become the voyeur's version of combat, then the horror film has become the modern version of the public lynching.

7   It is true that the mythic, "fairy-tale" horror film intends to take away the shades of gray. . . . It urges us to put away our more civilized and adult penchant for analysis and to become children again, seeing things in pure blacks and whites. It may be that horror movies provide psychic relief on this level because this invitation to lapse into simplicity, irrationality, and even outright madness is extended so rarely. We are told we may allow our emotions a free rein . . . or no rein at all.

8   If we are all insane, then sanity becomes a matter of degree. If your insanity leads you to carve up women, like Jack the Ripper or the Cleveland Torso Murderer, we clap you away in the funny farm (but neither of those two amateur-night surgeons was ever caught, heh-heh-heh); if, on the other hand, your insanity leads you only to talk to yourself when you're under stress or to pick your nose on your morning bus, then you are left alone to go about your business . . . though it is doubtful that you will ever be invited to the best parties.

Words to Know
innately naturally

reactionary backward looking, conservative

voyeur one who enjoys watching others

penchant fondness, liking

exalted glorious

couplets two consecutive
rhyming lines in a poem

coveted popular, highly
desirable

sanctions punishments

remonstrance reprimand,
scolding

morbidity disease,
something unhealthy

The potential lyncher is in almost all of us (excluding saints, past and present; but then, most saints have been crazy in their own ways), and every now and then, he has to be let loose to scream and roll around in the grass. Our emotions and our fears form their own body, and we recognize that it demands its own exercise to maintain proper muscle tone. Certain of these emotional muscles are accepted — even <u>exalted</u>— in civilized society; they are, of course, the emotions that tend to maintain the status quo of civilization itself. Love, friendship, loyalty, kindness — these are all the emotions that we applaud, emotions that have been immortalized in the <u>couplets</u> of Hallmark cards and in the verses (I don't dare call it poetry) of Leonard Nimoy.   9

When we exhibit these emotions, society showers us with positive reinforcement; we learn this even before we get out of diapers. When, as children, we hug our rotten little puke of a sister and give her a kiss, all the aunts and uncles smile and twit and cry, "Isn't he the sweetest little thing?" Such <u>coveted</u> treats as chocolate-covered graham crackers often follow. But if we deliberately slam the rotten little puke of a sister's fingers in the door, <u>sanctions</u> follow — angry <u>remonstrance</u> from parents, aunts and uncles; instead of a chocolate-covered graham cracker, a spanking.   10

But anticivilization emotions don't go away, and they demand periodic exercise. We have such "sick" jokes as, "What's the difference between a truckload of bowling balls and a truckload of dead babies?" (You can't unload a truckload of bowling balls with a pitchfork . . . a joke, by the way, that I heard originally from a ten-year-old.) Such a joke may surprise a laugh or a grin out of us even as we recoil, a possibility that confirms the thesis: If we share a brotherhood of man, then we also share an insanity of man. None of which is intended as a defense of either the sick joke or insanity but merely as an explanation of why the best horror films, like the best fairy tales, manage to be reactionary, anarchistic, and revolutionary all at the same time.   11

The mythic horror movie, like the sick joke, has a dirty job to do. It deliberately appeals to all that is worst in us. It is <u>morbidity</u> unchained, our most base instincts let free, our nastiest fantasies realized . . . , and it all happens, fittingly enough, in the dark. For those reasons, good liberals often shy away from horror films. For myself, I like to see the most aggressive of them—*Dawn of the Dead*, for instance— as lifting a trap door in the civilized forebrain and throwing a basket of raw meat to the hungry alligators swimming around in that subterranean river beneath.   12

Why bother? Because it keeps them from getting out, man. It keeps them down there and me up here. It was Lennon and McCartney who said that all you need is love, and I would agree with that.   13

As long as you keep the gators fed   ■   14

Understanding Meaning: What Is the Writer Trying to Say?

1. King opens his essay with the line "I think that we're all mentally ill." Is this an effective introduction? Why or why not? What does he mean by saying we are a little crazy?

2. What reasons does King give for the popularity of horror movies?

3. How does the fascination of horror films relate to sick jokes in King's view?

4. *Critical thinking:* King suggests that something deeply human draws people to horror films. Do you think this also explains why in the past children loved legends about werewolves, witches, vampires, and haunted houses?

Evaluating Strategy: How Does the Writer Say It?

1. In explaining causes, where does King use narration, description, comparison, and example?

2. How effective is the last line? Does this bring King's essay to a logical conclusion?

3. King uses one-sentence paragraphs in two places. Are they effective? Why or why not? When are short paragraphs like these useful?

Appreciating Language: What Words Does the Writer Use?

1. What do the "hungry alligators" represent? Is this an effective image? Why or why not?

2. What does King mean by his term "psychic relief"?

Writing Suggestions

1. Write several sentences that give reasons why people also enjoy roller coasters and other amusement park rides.

2. *Collaborative writing:* Working with a group of students, provide reasons for the popularity of reality television shows.

I REFUSE TO LIVE IN FEAR

DIANA BLETTER

Diana Bletter was born in New York City but now lives in Israel. She has written articles for Newsday *and the* International Herald Tribune. *Bletter and Samia Zina helped organize Dove of Peace, a friendship organization for Arab and Jewish women.*

AS YOU READ:

In this article Bletter outlines the effects of terrorism in Israel. Her article was written before the terrorist attacks of September 11, 2001. Consider how her comments relate to the way Americans are living in an era of terrorism and security measures.

For most of my life, I thought a shoe box was just a shoe box. Until the afternoon I discovered that it could also be considered a lethal weapon. 1

This is what happened: I had just gone shopping for shoes— one of my favorite pastimes— in the small Mediterranean town of Nahariyya in northern Israel, where I've lived for the last five years. I sat down on a bench to change into my new purchase. I was so busy admiring my feet that I left the shoe box (with my old shoes) on the bench. Fifteen minutes later, I suddenly remembered it and turned back. When I approached the street, I saw crowds of people, barricades and at least five policemen. 2

"What happened?" I asked. 3

"Everyone's been evacuated. Someone reported a suspicious object on a bench down the street." 4

"Oh, no!" I shouted. "My shoes!" 5

Had I arrived even a few seconds later, a special bomb squad— complete with robot— would have imploded my shoe box to deactivate what could have been a bomb hidden inside. The policeman shook his finger at me. "This is the Middle East!" he said angrily. "You can't be careless like that!" 6

Reality Bites, Hard

Moving to Israel from America's tranquil suburbia has taught me about living with the threat of terrorism, something we Americans— after the bomb at Atlanta's Olympic Games and the explosion of TWA Flight 800 — are finally being forced to think about on our own turf. The brutal fact of a terrorist attack is that it shatters the innocent peace of our days, the happy logic of our lives. It inalterably changes the way we live. 7

I can no longer daydream as I walk down a street — now I know that, to stay alive, I have to remain aware of who and what surrounds me. As my fiancé always tells me, "Your eyes are your best friends!" and I use them to keep track of emergency exits, the closest windows, the nearest heavy object that could be used in self-defense. 8

I used to be a reflexive litter-grabber— in my hometown, I never hesitated to pick up a coffee cup from the sidewalk and toss it in a nearby garbage can. In Israel, I've learned not to touch litter and to stay away from garbage cans— on several occasions, bombs have been placed in them. If I see a knapsack, shopping bag or—yes— a shoe box left unattended, I now do three things: One, ask passersby if they forgot the package; two, get away from it as fast as I can; and three, report it to the police. 9

Necessary Inconveniences

Living in a country where terrorism is always a possibility means that at every entrance to a public place, guards search every bag. I forgot this the first time I walked into Nahariyya's lone department store; a guard 10 stopped me to look through my pocketbook. "How could I have shoplifted?" I asked. "I haven't set foot in the store." Then I remembered that in America, people worry about what someone might sneak *out* of a store; in Israel, people worry what weapons or bombs someone might sneak *in* to a store.

11   The first few days after a terrorist attack seem very quiet. Since all of Israel is only the size of New Jersey, everybody usually knows someone who was hurt or killed. The nation slips into mourning: People avoid going out, attending parties, sitting in cafés.

12   Gradually, though, daily life returns to normal. Israelis (and now, Americans) have to prove again and again to potential terrorists that we're not giving in to our fears. If we voluntarily restrict our movements and our lives, terrorists have vanquished us.

13   During the latest hostilities in Lebanon (whose border is about seven miles from Nahariyya), Samia Zina, my dear friend—and a Muslim Arab—dreamed about me, one of those vivid dreams that seems prophetic when you wake. She dreamed that the fighting had forced her to flee her home, and that I'd hidden her and her children in my house (and I certainly would have, had the nightmare been a reality). The next day, Samia popped by to tell me her dream and give me the two stuffed chickens she'd been moved to cook for me.

14   "Thank you," I said, astonished by the food and the dream. "But I know you would have hidden me, too."

15   Terrorists attempt to divide people by fear, but in our community they've brought so-called enemies together: Even Arabs and Jews watch out for each other in public places, knowing that terrorists target everyone. By resisting the temptation to become paranoid and isolated, by sticking up for one another, we remain undefeated.   ∎

CRITICAL THINKING AND DISCUSSION

GET THINKING
AND WRITING

Understanding Meaning: What Is the Writer Trying to Say?

1. What is the point of Bletter's opening story about the shoe box?
2. How has living in Israel changed the way Bletter walks down a street?
3. What three things does she do if she spots an unattended shopping bag or a knapsack on the street? Do you think North Americans will have to learn to live like this?
4. *Critical thinking:* Terrorists in the Middle East plant bombs to create terror and sharpen the divide between Jewish and Arab Israelis. How have these attacks had the opposite effect? What causes Jews and Arabs to depend on each other?

Evaluating Strategy: How Does the Writer Say It?

1. How does Bletter use comparison to develop her point? How is life in the United States different from life in Israel?
2. How effective is the last line? Is this Bletter's thesis?

3. What examples does Bletter use to show the effect terrorism has had on her behaviour?

Appreciating Language: What Words Does the Writer Use?

1. Bletter never defines "terrorism" in her essay. How do you define the word? What is a terrorist in your view?
2. Bletter uses a simple style of language to describe a very complex political situation. Is this effective?

Writing Suggestions

1. Write a paragraph describing the effects terrorism has had on your life since September 11, 2001. Have you encountered more security in airports, known friends who had greater difficulty getting jobs or dealing with immigration authorities?
2. *Collaborative writing:* Discuss Bletter's article with a group of students. In Israel terrorists plant bombs in small packages. In the United States Americans fear terrorists will use biological, chemical, and radioactive weapons. Does the size and mysterious nature make the average citizen feel helpless and vulnerable? Work together and develop a short paragraph about how terrorism affects the way North Americans feel about their personal safety. Do you think people in New York or Washington have more fear than those living in Toronto or Los Angeles?

STEPS TO WRITING A CAUSE AND EFFECT PARAGRAPH

1. Study your topic and use critical thinking by asking key questions:
   Am I going to explain causes or effects or both?
   What is the most important cause or effect I want readers to know?
   Are there any terms I need to define?
   Do readers need any background information?
   What evidence such as facts, examples, or quotations can support my ideas?
2. Develop a topic sentence that clearly states your controlling idea.
3. Review your list of causes or effects and delete minor or confusing details. Organize your ideas by time or by order of importance.
4. Write a draft of your paragraph.
5. Read your paragraph aloud and consider these questions:
   Does the paragraph have a clear topic sentence?
   Are the causes or effects clearly stated and supported by facts, examples, and other evidence?
   Is the paragraph clearly organized?

Selecting Topics

Consider these topics for cause and effect paragraphs:

Explain the causes of one of the following topics:

    teenage pregnancy
    domestic violence

terrorism
a recent scandal
current attitudes about the homeless, an ethnic group, or a political figure
gangs
your choice of major or career
success or failure of a business or sports team

Write a paper measuring the effects of one of the following topics:

the Internet
immigration
welfare reform
gas prices
cell phones
airport security
single-parent families

EXERCISE 4 Planning and Writing Cause and Effect Paragraphs

Select a topic from one of the lists above or choose one of your own. Develop a topic sentence that states your point of view.

GET WRITING

Topic: _____

Causes or effects:

1. _____

2. _____

3. _____

4. _____

First sentence: topic sentence, first cause or effect, or introductory statement:

_____

_____

Causes or effects:

1. _____

2. _____

3. _____

4. _____

Last sentence: final cause or effect, concluding statement, or topic sentence:

_____

_____

Write out your paragraph and review it by reading it aloud.

WORKING TOGETHER

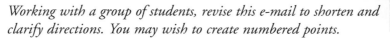

Working with a group of students, revise this e-mail to shorten and clarify directions. You may wish to create numbered points.

Dear Service Staff:

Customers often ask why they can't come behind the counter or enter the garage to look at their cars being serviced. Remember under no circumstances let anyone behind the counter who is not employed by the dealership. People have to understand we have a problem here. Our insurance company will not cover injuries of any customers in the service areas. We work with valuable equipment and it is too easy for people to walk off with electronic components if they are allowed to walk around the shop area. You have to remember, too, that people get in the way when mechanics are trying to work.

Stefan Richard

GET THINKING
AND **WRITING**

CRITICAL THINKING

What effect have twenty-four-hour cable news networks had on the way we see events? Are minor events like car chases exaggerated because they make good television? Are important issues overlooked because they are hard to show on television or because they take place in remote areas? Write a paragraph stating your views.

WHAT HAVE YOU WRITTEN?

Read your paragraph carefully. Write out your topic sentence or controlling idea:

_____

_____

List the effects you identify:

_____

_____

_____

Are they significant effects? Can you think of more significant ones? Could you place them in a different order to make your paragraph stronger and easier to read?

GET WRITING

Many of us are familiar with having suitcases and briefcases searched when we pass through airport customs. However, this is becoming a more common scenario some stores. Employees' purses and knapsacks are searched before they can leave after a shift. Employers who support this policy say it reduces losses due to stolen merchandise, but employees complain that the practice is humiliating and feels like a bad trip through airport customs. The message implied is that employees can't be trusted.

Write a paragraph listing the positive or negative effects of this practice. Do you think searching employees' purses and knapsacks is fair? Do you think this will impact employees' commitment to their jobs?

WRITING ON THE WEB

Using a search engine such as AltaVista, Yahoo!, or Google, enter terms such as *writing cause and effect, cause and effect essays, organizing cause and effect essays,* and *critical thinking and cause and effect.*

1. Search for news articles using cause and effect and review how writers organized their ideas.
2. Write an e-mail to a friend using cause and effect to explain a decision you have made or to give reasons for a problem. times do you revise, edit, and rewrite a simple message?

POINTS TO REMEMBER

1. Cause and effect paragraphs need clear topic sentences.
2. Cause and effect paragraphs depend on critical thinking and evidence. Readers will expect you to prove your points.
3. Qualify your comments and acknowledge alternative interpretations.
4. Peer review can help detect mistakes in critical thinking like hasty generalizations or confusing time relationships for cause and effect.
5. E-mail has become one of the most popular ways to communicate with others. While it's cheap and convenient, it's not a secure form of communication. Therefore, never write information in an e-mail that you wouldn't be comfortable having others read. It takes only a slip of the hand to accidentally forward a confidential message. The rule of thumb is *At work, never write something in an e-mail message that you wouldn't want your boss to read.*

10

Developing Paragraphs Using Persuasion (and Argumentation)

GET WRITING

When we try to convince people of something or change their point of view, we use persuasion. We are effective when the arguments we use are well thought out and organized. Home, school, and work are places we use persuasion.

You want to live in residence instead of living at home while attending college. Write a paragraph about this topic with your parents as the audience. *OR* Wouldn't it be great if your parents were to buy you a car so that you could drive instead of taking public transit to school? Write a paragraph that persuades your parents to do just that.

What Is Persuasion, or Argumentation?

Persuasion is trying to change a person's point of view, or habit, to the one you would like them to have. Salespeople are always trying to persuade us to buy their products. Politicians try to tell us they will bring prosperity to our neighbourhoods in exchange for our votes. These people cite the benefits of their products or services and often appeal to our emotions. Have you ever tried to convince parents, friends, or neighbours to share your point of view? Do you have a part-time job selling? Do you watch advertising on television, listen to it on the radio, or read it on the Internet? What has convinced you to purchase a particular product or service and what has influenced your decision not to make a purchase? Consider all of those factors when you are trying to be persuasive. Persuasion isn't just an emotional plea.

As children we are often told what to do, or bribed with treats to do what our parents want us to do. As adults, we are offended when people tell us what to do. Persuasion is communication for adults. Like kids, adults can be bribed, but we tend to prefer being persuaded by a good argument.

What are the factors that influence a persuasive message? One of the first elements is word choice. If you were a little heavy, wouldn't you rather go to a store that sold clothing for a "mature figure" or advertised "executive sizes" than one that sold "fat" clothing? Would your women friends prefer to be called "skinny" or "slender"? Word choice is important when you are trying to be persuasive. We are similarly influenced by the examples used when someone is trying to persuade us to a point of view. We probably respond more favourably to positive rather than negative examples. Would you prefer hear that successful students get "well-paid and exciting jobs" than to hear that unsuccessful students "won't amount to much in life"? Sometimes the examples are humorous and get us to think about the consequences. Teachers often motivate students by using humour to encourage them to learn new material, try harder, or do better. Sometimes they exaggerate the consequences to encourage students to their point of view. Persuading also uses writing techniques such as analogies, similes, and metaphors. One of the most effective ways to persuade readers and listeners is to use evidence from prestigious sources. Wouldn't you like to know that the head of Bell Canada, who is a successful businessman and communicator, had trouble with his college English course? Whatever you do to persuade people, you must be truthful. It's often evident when someone is not being truthful.

Finally, when you write persuasively, it is important to be organized so that you leave the reader with impact. He or she will remember the last thing read or heard. Infomercials are wonderful at persuading us to buy products and services and often successful. Do you remember trying to persuade your parents to let you stay out later than your curfew? Were you successful?

WRITING PERSUASIVELY

When writing persuasively you need to do the following:

1. Determine the position you want to take and the audience you are trying to convince.

(continued)

2. Have a clear specific topic sentence. What exactly are you trying to persuade the reader to do?
3. Find data and/or sources to support your point of view.
4. Address the gaps in your argument. (It's better for you to find them and talk about them than to give the impression you hadn't fully thought about your topic.)
5. Present some of the benefits and the consequences of your point of view.
6. Be logical.

Transitional expressions make your argument sound more polished and smooth. When one point moves to another, the reader will see your argument as seamless rather than a list of points.

KEY TRANSITION WORDS

first	lastly	nevertheless	hence
second	finally	on the other	consequently
third	because	hand	
another	since	therefore	
next	although	thus	

POINT TO REMEMBER

When writing to persuade, make sure to organize your points. Use credible sources or examples and end with one of your stronger points.

WHAT ARE YOU TRYING TO SAY?

GET WRITING
AND REVISING

Write a persuasive paragraph using one of the following topics:

- joining a union
- becoming a vegetarian
- the benefits of owning a pet
- students having part-time jobs
- starting an exercise program
- learning a second language

_____

_____

_____

_____

_____

_____
_____
_____
_____
_____
_____
_____
_____
_____
_____
_____

WHAT HAVE YOU WRITTEN?

Read your writing carefully. Do you have a specific audience you are trying to convince? Are your ideas in order, with a beginning, middle, and end? Can your audience relate to the facts and sources you have chosen? What details can you include to make your point easier to understand?

WORKING TOGETHER

1. _Working with a small group of your classmates, find an editorial from a local newspaper, or use the one below, then answer the questions that follow._

Danger: System Failure

When a paroled felon in British Columbia kills seven people, and a national review finds nothing major went wrong, the only possible conclusion is that something is rotten in the parole system.

When, in a separate case, the Supreme Court of Canada concludes that the concept of deterrence is not part of sentencing in the youth justice system, some essential flexibility has been lost.

When a superior court judge in Manitoba finds an ex-soldier was so traumatized by war that he was not responsible for his actions in sexually assaulting a 13-year-old girl, a hole has been created in the notion of individual accountability—not to mention the credibility of the courts.

It was that kind of day Thursday. It was a day when those who would clamour for a throw-away-the-key form of justice were given ammunition.

Robert Bruce Moyes of B.C. made the revolving door of justice spin at a dizzying speed. By age 25 he had already been sentenced to 12 separate 15-year terms, including attempted murder after escaping from custody. (He served just five years before winning over the parole board for that one.) Between 1979 and 2000, he was so untrustworthy that he had 47 separate parole hearings. Finally a judge, fed up, sentenced him to life—yet somehow a mere six years later he received parole. He violated it (was anyone surprised?), was put back inside, was promptly released again—and went on his murderous rampage. Where was the hope for reform? Oh yes, he enrolled in a native spirituality program, though he was white. And he wrote lovely letters such as this one: "My plan, although not concrete, does have a solid foundation for success." The great satirist Evelyn Waugh would have given his eyeteeth to write a line like that.

And it worked. Over and over again, he pulled the wool over parole-board eyes. No wonder he was laughing in court last week about how easy it was. And nothing went wrong? Procedures were followed? The rot must surely go deep when Mr. Moyes can laugh after killing seven people while on parole (with a fellow B.C. parolee) and the mandatory joint review by parole and corrections officials finds that nothing major needs fixing. The patient died, the operation was a success. Next!

Everyone who believes in the principle of parole should demand an immediate, independent investigation into that case, and others like it. The principle of monitored early release to enhance community safety is sound, but it will wither and die in a system so rotten. Then the throw-away-the-key faction will be in control.

Everyone who believes in rehabilitation for teenage offenders should insist that Parliament take another look at the youth justice scheme, to ensure the system can distinguish between habitual, hard-core criminals (the 20 percent with five or more crimes on their record) and young people who would benefit from leniency or community-based programs.

And everyone who believes the justice system should punish offenders only when they can be said to have knowingly done wrong should look at the sex-assault case of Roger Borsch, a Canadian soldier who served in Bosnia, and ask whether post-traumatic-stress syndrome would be better considered as a factor in sentencing, rather than in guilt or innocence.

Source: "Danger: System Failure." *Globe and Mail*, 24 June 2006.

What is the main idea of the editorial? Has the writer used data or sources to support the main idea? Were authorities quoted? Did the author use humour or sarcasm? Was it appropriate? Are the consequences explained? Is it proposing a solution? Do you think it is a reasonable or effective argument to show that the parole system is failing?

2. *Compare the editorial your group found, or the one above, with the following editorial that does not contain many examples or quotes. Work with your group to expand this editorial into a piece that is persuasive.*

Away Game

If anyone doubted the fervour of some baseball fans, the news that a U.S. casket-maker will put the logos of their favourite teams on their coffins should set the skeptic straight. According to Reuters, Eternal Image Inc. has "signed a multiyear licensing agreement with Major League Baseball" that lets the company use the teams' names and logos.

Bizarre, yes. But we have another question: In the circumstances, does "multiyear" quite cover it?

Source: "Away Game." *Globe and Mail*, 24 June 2006.

Planning and Writing a Persuasive Paragraph

Completing practice exercises outside of scheduled classes is an important part of the learning process in college. You think that completing practice exercises at home give students

additional practice
time for longer assignments
review

Supporting ideas:

additional practice
  classes too short for adequate practice
  independent practice
time for longer assignments
  compositions
  reports and special projects
  students' different working speeds
review
  new material and old material
  tests and grades

After prewriting and planning, you write the following persuasive paragraph.

Completing practice exercises is an important part of the learning process when you attend college. One reason is that practice exercises give students additional practice of skills covered in class. Sometimes classes are too short to learn a new concept and practise it sufficiently to master it. Students need to be taught a concept, then guided through practice in class, followed by independent practice at home. Another reason is that it provides time to complete longer assignments. For example, the ideal composition process allows time for students to think and to reflect on their ideas, as well as time to revise and to proofread their writing. Also, reports and special projects often require research that cannot always be done at school. And since all students do not work at the same speed, giving students time at home to finish work keeps them from falling behind. Finally, the most important reason for completing practice exercises is that it ensures students will review the material. During the term new material and old material are practised in daily assignments. Students who complete practice exercises every day or every week are prepared for tests and get higher marks. In conclusion, not only is completing practice exercises essential to mastering new skills and maintaining previously learned skills but it also guarantees constant review and provides time for longer assignments, as well as additional time for students who need it. So, do the exercises that are assigned, get better grades, and learn more!

EXERCISE 1 Writing to Influence Opinions

Select one of the following topics and write a persuasive paragraph.

living in a small town
pursuing a hobby

the greatest Canadian athlete
the best winter sport

contributing to a charity

EXERCISE 2 Using Your Experiences to Persuade

Write a paragraph about the benefits of one of the following topics.

attending a private single-sex school	the best sport	your favourite winter sport
the need to learn etiquette	the benefits of reading	
	not using technology	
	walking more often than driving	

_____

_____

_____

_____

_____

_____

_____

_____

_____

_____

_____

_____

_____

_____

_____

_____

_____

PERSUASIVE PARAGRAPH CHECKLIST

1. _____ There is an interesting topic sentence that states clearly what the paragraph is about.
2. _____ The topic sentence is followed by a sentence that states the first reason.
3. _____ There is a clear transition or signal that this is the first reason.
4. _____ The sentence containing the first reason is followed by one or two sentences giving support for the first reason.

(continued)

5. _____ The sentences supporting the first reason are followed by a sentence that states the second reason.

6. _____ There is a clear transition or signal that this is the second reason.

7. _____ The sentence containing the second reason is followed by one or two sentences giving support for the second reason.

8. _____ The sentences supporting the second reason are followed by a sentence that states the third reason.

9. _____ There is a clear transition or signal that this is the third reason.

10. _____ The sentence containing the third reason is followed by one or two sentences giving support for the third reason.

11. _____ There is a closing sentence.

12. _____ The closing has a clear transition or signal.

13. _____ The paragraph is focused; that is, it presents a clear main idea and stays on the topic of that main idea.

EXERCISE 3 Using Your Persuasive Skills

The local newspaper is sponsoring a contest for readers to write about their favourite place to live. They will print the article that gives the best reasons as well as give a cash prize. Choose the one place where you would like to live and explain your reasons in an effort to persuade people that it is the best place to live.

Where Would You Like To Live? _____

Name the place and give reasons why you think it is the best place to live. The reasons could include the things that you can do where you live, the kind of people who live there, or other things that happen to make it a good place to live.

_____

_____

_____

_____

POINTS TO REMEMBER

1. Take time to plan your paragraph.
2. Carefully arrange your ideas.
3. Use vocabulary that convinces readers that your choice is best.
4. Check that your grammar, punctuation, and spelling are correct.

EXAM SKILLS

When writing an exam you may be required to persuade, or put forward an argument on a particular topic. Read the question carefully so that you answer the question that is being asked. Ensure that your answer is thorough, well organized, and covers the key topics. Make sure you mention potential problems with and consequences of your point of view.

From English Literature

In the short story "Miss Brill" why does Miss Brill go to the park every Sunday?

Miss Brill's ritual of visiting the park every Sunday helps her to cope with loneliness. It is clear how much enjoyment the old woman derives from the simple activity as the narrator states, "Oh, how fascinating it was! How she enjoyed it! How she loved sitting here, watching it all!" The weekly outing provides an opportunity for Miss Brill to place herself in the company of others and to leave behind "the little dark room" in which she lives. Miss Brill employs the tactics of listening and watching to passively include herself in the activities of the park crowd. She is expert at "sitting in other people's lives for just a minute" by eavesdropping. This habit of "listening as though she didn't listen" helps her to feel included. Being an avid people watcher, Miss Brill pays rapt attention to those who surround her. By the same care she takes in noticing others, she hopes that "no doubt somebody would have noticed if she hadn't been there" in attendance. This thought allows her to feel a sense of community with the strangers at the park. Miss Brill seizes every opportunity she can to imagine herself as having some connection with the individuals she observes in attempt to garner a sense of belonging. She even likens herself to being a part of the "family" that the band plays to. In effect, the weekly outing provides a means to escape the isolation felt in her solitary existence for a period of time by engaging herself in the happenings at the park. However, as Miss Brill observes and listens, she prefers to view her world through a proverbial set of rose coloured glasses to protect herself from confronting the truth of her lonely existence.

Source: Rambo, Randy. "English Composition 1." Illinois Valley Community College. 20 July 2006 <http://www.ivcc.edu/rambo/eng1001.htm>.

Steps to Writing a Persuasive Paragraph

1. Think about your topic. What are the key points in your argument? What is the best order in which to present them? Have credible sources and examples been used? (*Note:* Wikipedia.org is not considered a credible source.)

2. Develop a topic sentence that clearly states the main idea. Consider using words like must, ought, and should.
3. Review your arguments. Have you included recognized authorities to support your arguments? Have you included responses to potential criticisms of your ideas and/or the consequences of your position?

Readings

As you read, make careful note of the examples, quotes, and credible sources used by the author.

GOVERNOR-GENERAL'S CUP

When the National Hockey League went on strike in 2005, the Stanley Cup Playoffs were cancelled and there was no trophy awarded. Some people suggested that the Stanley Cup, named after Lord Stanley of Preston, a previous Governor General of Canada, be awarded to a women's hockey team, but this did not happen. As a result, Adrienne Clarkson, who was the Governor General in 2005, created the Clarkson Cup for excellence in Canadian women's hockey.

AS YOU READ:

This piece was written in the Globe and Mail. *Written for newspaper readers who need the facts quickly, it uses brief paragraphs. The writer provides facts and statistics to persuade readers of the value and the importance of a national hockey trophy for women.*

1   Like her long-ago predecessor Lord Stanley of Preston, Governor-General Adrienne Clarkson has no way of knowing what passions she will ignite by dedicating a hockey championship trophy, in her case for women. But anyone who has watched the rise of women's hockey over the past few years would not be surprised if, some day, the women's championship absorbs this country's interests, much as the Stanley Cup playoffs do.

2   Women's hockey has a long history in Canada. Isobel Stanley, one of Lord Stanley's two daughters, played the game in the 1890s. By the early 1900s, women's teams existed in much of Canada. Hockey historian Brian McFarlane writes that the women would crouch in front of their goalies, "allowing the hem of their long skirts to spread out and thus foil any attempt by an opposing player to shoot the puck beyond them and into the net." In 1927, McFarlane reports, a female goalie from Queen's University in Kingston, Ont., wore the first mask—a fencing mask.

3   But after the Second World War, women were routinely denied such fun, and so in 1955, eight-year-old Abby Hoffman, a future Olympic runner, disguised herself as a boy so she could join a team. Thankfully,

no girl needs a disguise any more to play. Before the Nagano Olympics in 1998, Hockey Canada had 28,000 girls and women registered in leagues; after the 2002 Salt Lake Olympics, at which the Canadian team, in a memorable final against the United States, won gold, registration soared to 61,000. The quality of play, and in particular of shooting and goaltending, has risen markedly, and one Canadian, Hayley Wickenheiser of Shaunavon, Sask., has even played on a men's professional team in Finland.

Women and girls, it turns out, play the game with the same joy and ferocity as men and boys do. It is sad that, for decades, they did not have the same opportunity as males to express that which can only be expressed with a puck and a stick, on a hockey rink. But now, with Governor-General Clarkson's dedication of a trophy (the precise details of who will play for the championship remain to be worked out), girls and women can be expected to put their stamp on the Canadian game in a way that has never been possible. ∎

4

Source: "Governor-General's Cup." *Globe and Mail,* 12 March 2005: A18.

GET *THINKING*
AND WRITING

CRITICAL THINKING AND DISCUSSION

Understanding Meaning: What Is the Writer Trying to Say?

1. What is the point of the article? What viewpoint is the author trying to persuade the readers to take about a women's hockey trophy?
2. What is the history of women's hockey in Canada?
3. What is the governor-general doing to promote women's hockey in Canada?

Evaluating Strategy: How Does the Writer Say It?

1. What examples from history are used?
2. What current examples are used?

Appreciating Language: What Words Does the Writer Use?

1. Underline words that effectively describe the main idea.
2. List words that have positive connotations.
3. Consider tone and style. Was the vocabulary appropriate? Why or why not? Who is the author trying to convince?

Writing Suggestions

1. Write a paragraph about your favourite sport. Why is it something that classmates should consider watching or playing?
2. *Collaborative Writing:* Discuss this essay with a small group of classmates and write a paragraph about the need for promoting sports specifically for women.

Cellular telephones offer convenience and portability. They also offer security in case of an emergency. Cell phones now come with many features: They can play music, take pictures, or receive text messages. All these features might be fun, but are they necessary?

Write one or more paragraphs persuading a friend to purchase a cell phone for his or her parents or children.

WRITING ON THE WEB

Using a search engine such as AltaVista, Yahoo!, or Google, enter terms such as *writing persuasively, selling through writing, writing for negotiation,* and *influencing with words* to locate current sites of interest.

1. Look at sites that sell products. What do they do that persuades you to use their products or services?
2. Find a chain letter that is convincing. How did the writer make it make a convincing argument?
3. Compose a PowerPoint presentation that would persuade your classmates to buy a particular product or service.

POINTS TO REMEMBER

1. Do not be too strong with your argument or forget other points of view.
2. Be sincere. (Readers can tell when you aren't!)
3. Avoid being whiny, complaining, or aggressive.
4. Omit language that is too emotional.

11

Toward the Essay

What does it take to communicate effectively? Why is it important to consider your reader? If you had to write a charity fund-raising letter, what would you want to know about the readers?

Write a list of questions you would ask about them before writing.

So far in this book you have studied and written different types of paragraphs. Most college assignments, however, demand more than one-paragraph responses. Instructors usually require students to write essays.

What Is an Essay?

An essay is a group of related paragraphs that develops a *thesis,* or main idea. An essay may be written to inform, entertain, or persuade. Essays may consist of facts and statistics or personal thoughts and feelings. Essays can be written about global warming, NAFTA, or your summer vacation. Although written in a variety of styles and lengths, essays generally consist of three main parts:

introduction
body
conclusion

Each part plays an important role in stating the thesis and supporting it with details. Knowing how the parts of an essay work will improve your writing and give you the organizational skills needed to create research papers and business reports in the future.

The Introduction

Introductions should

- grab attention,
- announce the topic,
- address reader concerns, and
- prepare readers for what follows.

Introductions should make strong statements that arouse interest and prepare readers for what follows. Avoid making general statements that simply serve as weak titles that just tell people what you are writing about:

Weak

This paper is about "mad cow" disease. People are afraid to eat beef because they are afraid of contracting this disease. This is bad for the Canadian beef industry.

You can use a number of techniques to create effective introductions:

Open with a Thesis Statement

The threat of continued U.S. border closures to Canadian beef due to bovine spongiform encephalopathy (mad cow disease) is a major threat not only to the Canadian beef industry but to the Canadian economy as a whole.

Begin with a Fact or Statistic

U.S. authorities had planned to reopen the country's borders to Canadian beef in March of 2005;

however, a confirmed case of bovine spongiform encephalopathy (mad cow disease) in January of 2005 jeopardized that plan.

Use a Quotation

Responding to the newest case of mad cow disease in Alberta, analysts speculate that "the new case could ultimately result in significant contraction in the industry and put more pressure on Canadian exports" (Curren).

Open with a Short Example

In 1938, Moishe Lighter invested his life savings— $300.00—to open a steakhouse, Moishe's, on boulevard St-Laurent in Montreal, specializing in prime Canadian beef. Moishe's is now reputed to be the best steakhouse in Montreal, but Canadian beef is no longer served.

The Body

The body of an essay should

- organize supporting details in a logical pattern.

The main part of your paper should be clearly organized so readers can understand the details you present and follow your train of thought.

Weak

Canadian farmers have lost millions of dollars in total because of mad cow disease. The U.S. border has been closed to Canadian beef since 2003. Restaurants, transportation companies, and workers in the beef industry have experienced financial losses. It's important that Canada successfully negotiate with the U.S. to reopen the border; otherwise, more people in more industries will suffer.

To prevent your paper from becoming a confusing jumble of facts and ideas, create a clear pattern people can follow.

- *Organize details by time* and explain them as a chain of events. Tell readers the history of your subject or the way things have changed.
- *Organize details spatially* by dividing them into types. A paper about mad cow disease could discuss how import bans affect farmers, beef industry workers, and transportation companies. A report about drug addiction could be organized by discussing different drugs, different reasons people use drugs, or different treatments. Patients could be discussed by their age, the drug they abuse, or by their income level.
- *Organize ideas by importance* so the paper opens or closes with your most significant points.

The Conclusion

The conclusion of an essay should

- end with a brief summary, a final thought or observation, question, call for action, or prediction.

A short paper or narrative may not require a separate conclusion, but the paper should have a meaningful ending that will make an impression on readers. Avoid summarizing or repeating what you have just written:

Weak

> In conclusion, the U.S. ban on Canadian beef is hurting beef farmers, beef industry workers, and transportation company employees. This is bad for Canada's economy.

A conclusion can make people remember and think about your ideas, if you end on a strong point.

End with a Meaningful Quotation

> Federal Agriculture Minister Andy Mitchell is optimistic that "plans to reopen the border in March will go ahead" (Curren).

End with a Call to Action

> If you care about the future of the Canadian beef industry, buy Canadian steak and make a statement: Canadian beef not only tastes great, it's also safe to eat.

Conclude with a Significant Fact or Statistic Readers Can Remember

> If the border remains closed for another year, more Canadian farmers will be forced out of the beef industry.

End with a Question

> If we want to see the Canadian beef industry thrive again, can we afford not to be proactive?

Developing Topic Sentences in Outlines

One way to develop a well-organized essay is to use a topic sentence outline. After writing your thesis, develop supporting ideas in complete sentences to form a topic sentence for each paragraph:

> Outline: Religion: Bond and Barrier

I   The effects of religion are both positive and negative.

II My grandmother has lived her life with a focus
and hold on her faith.

III The break in relations in our family was a direct
result of religious belief.

IV Not only did my uncle stay away from that wedding, but my atheist uncle, not wanting to be a
part of a celebration that divided our family,
further divided it by refusing to attend.

V For my grandmother, the prayer before a meal is a
time of joined thanksgiving. She didn't argue
with my uncle, but she continued to unite the
table in a few moments of thanksgiving.

Having established clear topic sentences, you can complete the essay by adding details to support each topic sentence:

Religion is often the glue that holds families
together. I've heard that throughout my life. It can
bring people together. I agree. I see it in the way
that my grandmother's deep faith binds our family
together in times of difficulty. However, <u>the effects
of religion are both positive and negative.</u> Religion
also separates. I am a witness to this in my own
family. Religious belief has divided my family at
weddings and it is the reason two of my uncles no
longer speak to each other.

<u>My grandmother has lived her life with a focus
and hold on her faith.</u> It is a faith that to her is
very tangible. She communicates with her god, and
whether we all share her faith or not, we cannot
help but see the results of her faith. Her prayers
really do seem to affect the way things turn out.
Even though I don't share her faith, I frequently
phone her with requests to pray about this or that.
I just want the extra insurance in times of
trouble, and I can't say that it hasn't paid off.
Things work out when she's involved; while they may
not have yet healed rifts in our family, as my aunt
says, "we all come together in Nanna's daily
prayers." It's a nice thought; however, I hope we
will be able to (physically) overcome the barriers
imposed by religious belief and (all) come together
physically again.

<u>The break in relations in our family was a direct
result of religious belief</u>. It began with the division of the church about fifteen years ago. Differing
Biblical interpretations split the church, and the
members of my family who still worship began to
attend two different churches. The division wasn't

felt within the family until three years ago. My uncle, who has always been very close to his nieces and nephews, was barred from attending my cousin's wedding because fifteen years ago he had expressed a different religious opinion than the bride's grandfather (his uncle as it happens). He was told that if he would retract in writing statements made fifteen years ago, he would be invited to the wedding. His ideology won out, and he stayed away.

Not only did my uncle stay away from that wedding, but my atheist uncle, not wanting to be a part of a celebration that divided our family, further divided it by refusing to attend. This resulted in angry words between my uncles. My Christian uncle, in an attempt to "reach out" to his atheist brother, wrote a letter comprising many Bible verses and with Christian literature enclosed. He may have thought he was reaching out, but the result was that his brother moved further away, angry that his own beliefs were not being heard or respected. Unfortunately, this chain of disrespect doesn't stop here. While visiting my grandmother recently, my athiest uncle asked her not to say a prayer of thanksgiving before meals—in her own house!

For my grandmother, the prayer before a meal is a time of joined thanksgiving. She didn't argue with my uncle, but she continued to unite the table in a few moments of thanksgiving. Her message was clear—in my home, you will respect my beliefs and not ask me to silence them (in his home, she respects his beliefs and accepts that meals begin without prayer). This is a strong message, but it's also a fair one. Will my uncles one day be able to follow this example and live their own beliefs while accepting that their brothers, mother, and in-laws have the right to do the same? I don't know. I hope so.

POINT TO REMEMBER

As when they create paragraphs, writers frequently use a method like example, comparison and contrast, or cause and effect to organize an entire essay. Although the overall goal may be to provide an example or make a comparison, the essay may contain paragraphs organized in different ways. Not all paragraphs in a comparison essay will include comparisons. Many will include narrations or descriptions. All the paragraphs, however, work together to support the writer's thesis.

EXERCISE 1 Examining the Essay

Read this student essay and note in the margin where the student uses narration, comparison and contrast, and cause and effect to develop this description of a town.

A Great Place

According to my mother, <u>Woodbridge was a great place to grow up.</u> There were no shopping malls or big box stores nearby. Chapters, Starbucks, and HMV did not exist. My mother and her brothers didn't mind: the open fields and meadows surrounding her childhood home provided all the entertainment that they needed.

<u>Woodbridge was still a small town 40 years ago.</u> When the weather was fine, my mother walked to school with her brothers and the other children on the street, and afterward took a shortcut home through open fields. On warm autumn days, they often stopped to fish in the Humber River. In the winter, they skated on the pond in the meadow across from their house, and built elaborate snow forts. After my grandfather bought the family a snowmobile for Christmas one year, the area surrounding the pond became a crisscross of snowmobile tracks. In the summer, they ventured a few fields over to a neighbour's 200 acre farm, where my mother experienced two memorable firsts: she rode her first horse and kissed her first boy.

<u>It was during her first year of high school that the bulldozers appeared.</u> From that time until now, the meadows and fields of Woodbridge have been steadily filled with houses, shopping plazas, schools, libraries, and, most recently, big box stores. The shortcut from her house to school is now a busy thoroughfare; houses cover the meadow where my mother and her brothers skated, and where there were skidoo tracks, there are now neatly paved driveways dotted with SUVs. Of course the farm disappeared long ago. The fences holding back the horses have been replaced by the walls of an exclusive gated community, and the vast fields that were once overrun with wildflowers are now overrun with subdivisions. Any grass that does remain is enclosed by cement, and the wildflowers that once sprawled across the acres of land don't stand a chance against modern-day pesticides and ride-on lawn mowers.

My grandparents left Woodbridge many years ago. At first they loved driving by their house whenever

they returned to visit friends; however, they stopped
when the changes became too painful to see. When I
drove my grandmother through Woodbridge last year,
she had trouble finding any familiar landmarks.
Finally, she sighed deeply and said, "This can't possibly be Woodbridge. Where is my little town?"

EXERCISE 2 Developing Essay Paragraphs

*Select a topic from the following list or develop one of your own and prewrite for a
few minutes to develop ideas.*

what you want high school students to know about the postsecondary
   experience
the best lesson your parents taught you
the reasons you chose your major or career
your opinion of strikes and lockouts in professional sports
how to explain something difficult like death or divorce to a child
the reason so many people complain of stress
why men and women have problems understanding each other

Introduction and thesis: _____

_____

_____

Topic sentence for supporting paragraph: _____

_____

_____

Topic sentence for supporting paragraph: _____

_____

_____

Topic sentence for supporting paragraph: _____

_____

_____

Final topic sentence or conclusion: _____

_____

EXERCISE 3 Writing Essay Paragraphs

*Using your outline as a guide, write the draft of your essay. When you complete the
essay, review your outline and topic sentences. You may discard ideas and create new
ones in the writing process. Make sure your final version, however, is clearly organized and that all the paragraphs support your thesis.*

GET WRITING
AND REVISING

WORKING TOGETHER

Work with a small group of students and exchange papers. Make copies so each person can make corrections and comments. Discuss what you want to say and ask how what you have written could be improved.

GET THINKING
AND **WRITING**

CRITICAL THINKING

Imagine your brother or sister returns from a late-night party claiming to have hit a mailbox on the way home. The next morning you hear about a hit-and-run accident a block from where the party was held. A witness has given police a description that matches the car your brother or sister was driving. Write three or four paragraphs describing the actions you would take. Would you do nothing, talk to your brother or sister, call the police, or try to find out more about the accident? How would you act if the hit-and-run driver simply sideswiped a car? If the accident involved a death or serious injury, would you behave differently? Why or why not?

WHAT HAVE YOU WRITTEN?

Read your paragraphs carefully. Do you clearly explain the actions you would take?

- How effective is your introduction? Does it engage readers or simply announce what your essay is about?
- How do you organize your main ideas? Do you use paragraphs to signal transitions or highlight main points? Could these paragraphs be better organized or more fully developed? Are there minor or distracting details that should be deleted?
- How do you end your essay? Does it make a final statement readers will remember, or does it just repeat what they have already read?

GET WRITING

How often do people fail to communicate clearly? Do you get letters from your bank or financial aid office that you find hard to read? Have you written papers that received poor grades because you did not explain your ideas clearly?

Write a paragraph describing ways peer review can improve your writing.

WRITING ON THE WEB

Using a search engine such as AltaVista, Yahoo!, or Google, enter terms such as *writing essays, types of essays,* and *composing essays* to locate current sites of interest.

1. Read news articles online and notice how writers develop introductions, create conclusions, and use paragraphs to organize their ideas.
2. Write a multi-paragraph e-mail to a friend. Make sure your message has a clear introduction and conclusion.
3. Pay special attention to the e-mails you send to your professors. Does the topic sentence make it clear why you're writing? Have you included enough information or appropriate reasons (if you're requesting something)? Have you concluded effectively? One way to do this is to politely clarify what you propose to do and what you would like the professor to do. Be sure to use polite commands such as *please let me know* . . . or *could you provide* . . . rather than simply demanding what you need.

POINTS TO REMEMBER

1. An essay states a main idea supported by related paragraphs that provide details.
2. Essays consist of three parts:
   Introduction: grabs attention
                 announces the topic
                 addresses reader concerns
                 prepares readers for what follows
   Body: organizes details in a clear, logical pattern
   Conclusion: ends with a brief summary, a final thought or observation, question, call for action, or prediction
3. Essays often use different types of paragraphs—comparison, example, narration, cause and effect, and description—to support a thesis.
4. In writing essays, consider your readers in presenting ideas, selecting details, and choosing words.

12

Writing at Work

How is writing at work different from writing at school? What do people expect in communications? Have you ever had to write anything for work? Do you expect writing will be important in your career?

Write a brief paragraph describing the writing challenges you expect to face.

Writing on the job is very different from writing in the classroom. Although memos, e-mail, letters, reports, and résumés depend on the writing skills you learn in college or university, they are created in a very different environment, have different readers, and serve different purposes.

- *Business writing occurs in a specific context.* The tone, style, wording, and format of business writing are shaped by the history and standards of the profession, organization, readers, and topic.
- *Business writing is directed to specific readers.* In school you write to a general academic audience. In business you will address specific readers who will have special problems, questions, concerns, and values.
- *Business writing is action oriented.* In school you usually write papers that present ideas. At work you will more often direct people to take action—to buy a product, use a service, accept an explanation, or make an investment.
- *Business writing is sensitive to legal implications.* Letters, reports, and contracts are legal documents. You have to be careful not to make statements that can expose you to legal action.
- *Business writing represents the views of others.* In school your work expresses personal ideas and opinions. At work the e-mail, letters, and reports you write should reflect the values, attitudes, and positions of your employer. Avoid writing personal opinions that may bring you into conflict with your superiors.

WRITING ON THE JOB

This chapter is divided into two subsections: *Writing on the Job* and *Writing to Get a Job*. *Writing on the Job* outlines three of the most common business writing assignments you will face: e-mail messages, memos, and letters. *Writing to Get a Job* focuses on résumés and cover letters.

E-mail

Today most professionals use e-mail to communicate. Some people confuse e-mail with "instant messages" or chat room discussion. They write and answer e-mail without thinking, producing a stream of tangled ideas, missing details, grammatical errors, and inappropriate comments. E-mail, like any kind of writing, takes thought and planning to be effective.

E-mail Format

Type e-mail messages in sentence case. While it's fine to use capital letters to draw attention to important words, writing an entire e-mail in uppercase is akin to shouting at your reader.

Include an informative subject line. Spam—unwanted e-mail messages—uses misleading headings such as "Following up your call" or "This week's meeting" to grab attention. To prevent your e-mail from being overlooked or deleted before it is read, use specific identifying details in the subject such as "RE: Nov. 18th request for additional credit" or "Tredway Furniture Annual Budget Review Meeting."

Include your reader's full name and the date in your inside address.

Keep e-mail direct and concise. People expect e-mail to be direct and easy to read. Avoid complicated sentences and long paragraphs. Use short paragraphs, bulleted points, or numbered points to increase readability.

End the e-mail with a clear summary, request, or direction.

- Summarize important points.
- If you are asking for information or help, clearly state what you need, when you need it, and how you can be reached.
- If you want readers to take action, provide clear directions.

Ask readers for an acknowledgment if you want to make sure they received your message.

E-mail Procedure

Think before you write. E-mail should have a clear goal. Consider whom you are writing to, what the recipients need to know, and how you can persuade them to accept your ideas.

Follow the prewriting, drafting, revising, and editing strategies you would use in writing a paper document. Don't let an e-mail message simply record whatever comes into your head. E-mail should have a clear purpose and an easy-to-follow organization. Plan before you write.

Review, edit, and double-check e-mail before sending. Check your spelling, addresses, names, prices, or figures for accuracy. Read your e-mail out loud to catch missing words, illogical statements, confusing sentences, or awkward phrases.

Print hard copies of important e-mail for future reference.

E-mail Dos and Don'ts

1. **Realize that e-mail is <u>real mail.</u>** For the purposes of business, the language of e-mail should be courteous and professional. E-mail can be stored, distributed, and printed. Unlike a note or memo that can be retrieved or corrected, e-mail, once sent, becomes permanent.

2. **Avoid sending messages you will later regret.** Never send e-mail when you are tired or angry.

3. **Ensure that you use correct grammar and spelling.** Although e-mail is a less formal form of communication, grammar and spelling must be correct. Never use Instant Messenger language in business e-mail.

4. **Make sure to use the correct e-mail address.** E-mail addresses can be complicated and oddly spelled. Often names are shortened or reversed. Laura Bassi might appear as "laurabassi," "lbassi," or "bassil." Double-check addresses.

5. **Do not attempt to send a fifteen-page report by e-mail.** E-mail is considered appropriate for short, informative messages. Longer documents can be sent as attachments.

6. **Do not send personal or sensitive information by e-mail.** E-mail is seen as too informal and too public for confidential correspondence. A good rule: never write anything in an e-mail message from work that you would not be comfortable having your boss or supervisor read.

E-mail Etiquette

1. **Respond to e-mail carefully.** Often e-mail messages will have multiple readers listed. Before sending a reply, determine whether you want everyone or just a few people to see your response. Remember, it can be a struggle for people to wade through the large number of pertinent messages received every day. If you are one of many recipients, consider if it is necessary to respond to everyone or only to the sender.

2. **Understand that humour is subjective.** Many employers frown upon jokes being sent via company e-mail accounts. Know what your employer's stance is on this issue, and use discretion when forwarding humorous or non-business e-mail messages.

Sample E-Mail

TO: Jennifer Kryden, Sylvia Reynolds, Lindsey Tang, Conrad Jergin, Jared Drieves, Kumiko Tosiro, Tim McCullough, Anton Schiebner, Lars Neilson, Akmed Al-Hassan, Paula Sands, Kathrien Wilsche, Maggie Loschuk, Michael McCann, Storm Vessa, Mathieu Richard, Stephanie Evans, Danielle Manset

FROM: Helena Gordon <hgordon@graphictrends.net>

SUBJECT: ART AUCTION AND DINNER   ← Informative subject line
Cc:
Bcc:
Attached:

Hi everyone,

The Print Division is hosting an art auction and dinner at trendy Pavlovich's to raise funds for Tsunami Relief International.   ← States purpose immediately ← The company name doesn't appear in the first line, indicating that this is an internal e-mail.

You and a guest (or guests) are invited to join us for a fabulous evening. It all begins with a "Gallery Walk." After viewing the pieces that will be auctioned later in the evening, enjoy a succulent five course meal to the musical strains of the Leah Sethe band.   ← Adds some details.

It's a great time to get that original piece of art you've always wanted!   ← Setting this apart increases its visibility.

Please invite a friend and join us. Following are the details:

Date:	Thursday, January 21
Time:	Gallery Walk: 6:00 p.m. - 7:00 p.m.
	Dinner: 7:00 p.m. - 8:00 p.m.
	Auction: 8:00 p.m. - 9:30 p.m.
Location:	Pavlovich's, 79 Harbour Square
Cost:	$30.00 per person or $200.00 per table (8/table)
Attire:	Business Casual

← headings in bold and alignment of information make the details easy to see at a glance.

Entrée options for the evening include roast chicken, tomato-basil risotto, and poached salmon.

Clearly states how to → Please RSVP to hgordon@graphictrends.net by January
respond and gives a 17. Indicate the number of people attending and
deadline. →*Note:* Each entrée options in your reply.
recipient needs to reply   Thank you from the Print Division.
only to Helena Gordon. If
everyone hit "Reply to All," Helena Gordon
unnecessary e-mail would
flood each recipient's inbox

EXERCISE 1 Revising E-mail

Revise/edit this e-mail to create a clear, concise, correct message.

Helena

This e-mail is a follow-up to our conversations last
week about the upcoming art auction. I think we need
to call Al Wilsch and discuss some points before next
week. I think we need to get a commitment from
Graphic trends regarding its financial contribution.
We also need to determine if Al Wilsch plans to
invite representatives form Tsunami Relief
International to the auction. And I like I said, I
think we have to do more publicity.

Paul Dykstra

_____

_____

_____

_____

_____

_____

_____

_____

_____

_____

_____

_____

EXERCISE 2 Writing E-mail

*You are interested in pursuing a career in hospitality, and your mother's friend Shirin
Jain, who manages a busy downtown hotel, agreed to meet with you last week so that
you could ask her some questions about the field. She spent over an hour with you
sharing her passion for her field. The meeting has made you more certain than ever
that this is the field for you.*

Your Assignment: Write to Shirin Jain and thank her for meeting with you. Include specific examples of how the meeting was helpful.

_____

_____

_____

_____

_____

_____

_____

_____

_____

_____

_____

_____

_____

_____

_____

_____

Memos

While e-mail has cut down on the number of memos sent, memos are still a very useful form of communication. Memos are used exclusively for communication **within** an organization. As such, use familiar language in memos; however, as with all other forms of business communication, your language should be professional and courteous.

Memo Format

1. **Follow correct memo format.** Memos include the headings DATE, TO, FROM, and SUBJECT as in the following example:

   DATE: March 21, 2006
   TO: Professors, Business and Creative Arts Department
   FROM: Karan Shah, Chair, Business and Creative Arts
              Department KS
   SUBJECT: GRADE AMENDMENTS FOR SPRING 2006

2. **Include first and last names, positions, and departments to ensure that memos are delivered quickly.** In larger organizations where there are many departments, it is essential to include such information for expedient delivery.

3. **Ensure that the subject line is brief yet informative.** Include specific information that clearly indicates if action is required.

4. **Omit the salutation, complimentary close, and signature block.** However, it is appropriate to sign your initials beside your name at the top of the memo. If the memo is being sent electronically, the initials should be typed.

5. **Make use of graphic highlighting within the body of the memo to make the information easy to access.**

   - Use bullets and numbers to highlight things such as questions and options.
   - Use of white space: Use several short paragraphs, and indent bullets and numbers to make them more visible.
   - Use charts to order detailed information.
   - Use boldfaced type to draw attention to important words.

Memo Procedure

1. **Think before you write.** As with e-mail, memos should have a clear goal. Consider your audience, the information you need to convey, and the most effective way to convey it. As memos are internal, use inclusive language: "We need to find a solution"; "The seminar will help us to become a stronger team."

2. **Prewrite, draft, revise, and edit to ensure that your purpose is clear and your directions easy to follow.**

3. **Review memos for correctness.** Ensure that your grammar and spelling are correct; double-check that dates, prices, and figures are accurate. Read the final draft aloud—your tongue will catch mistakes that your eyes have missed.

4. **Cover one topic per memo.** Trying to save time by including details of professional development workshops in a memo that outlines due dates for student grades will only confuse readers.

5. **Clearly outline the action you wish the reader to take** and include contact information (extension number or e-mail address) to make it easy for the recipient(s) to respond.

6. **Use a conversational tone.** Memos are more formal than e-mail messages but less formal than letters.

Sample Memo

DATE:	January 22, 2007
TO:	Emerson employees
FROM:	Raphael Galati, Employee Services Manager RG
SUBJECT:	EMPLOYEE PARKING

Introduces the larger problem, and doesn't presume that employees have intentionally been using reserved spots. →

As we are all aware, there are limited employee parking spaces in the front parking lot. However, some of you may not be aware that the north end of the front parking lot is reserved for customer parking.

In the past month, we have had more than ten complaints from customers about the lack of parking. This is not due to a dramatic increase in customers visiting the showroom, but because employees have been parking in customer-designated spots.

The following areas are available for employee parking:

- the front parking lot where posted signs indicate "employee parking"
- the rear parking lot except in "loading zone" areas
- the east parking lot where posted signs indicate "Emerson employee parking"

We don't want to lose customers because they can't find a place to park; therefore, let's keep customer parking spots available for them.

If you have any questions or concerns, please contact Raphael Galati at extension 427.

← Identifies the specific problem, and explains the cause without placing blame.

← Uses bullets to make the information easily accessible.

← Uses a "we" tone.

← Keeps the lines of communication open.

EXERCISE 3 Revising Memos

Revise this memo to create a clear, concise yet positive *message. Is the format correct?*

DATE: December 15, 2006
TO: All Employees
FROM: Kay Braithwaite
SUBJECT: COMPUTER USE

It has come to management's attention that employees are surfing the Internet and sending/receiving e-mail on company time. Using company computers for personal business is permitted only during breaks and lunch. To combat this trend, we are implementing a new e-mail monitoring system that will allow IT personnel to track what sites you visit and for how long.

_____

_____

_____

_____

_____

_____

_____

_____

_____

_____

_____

_____

_____

_____

_____

EXERCISE 4 Reply Memo

Your boss at Filtrix Inc., Lily Chen, will be at the Filtrix Inc. branch in Halifax from Tuesday, March 1 to Friday, March 4. She has asked you to book her flight and hotel. You have booked a ticket for her on Air Canada flight 672 at 7:00 a.m. on March 1. She will return home on Air Canada flight 673 at 4:00 p.m. on March 4. She is travelling business class both ways. You have arranged for her to stay in a suite at the Halifax Hilton.

You have set up three meetings for Ms. Chen while in Halifax. She is meeting with Hal Smithy in the Filtrix Inc. boardroom at 1:00 p.m. on March 1. She will have a lunch meeting with Samantha Singh in the Orchard Restaurant at the Halifax Hilton on Wednesday at 12:30. Finally, she will meet Richard Fulton for a breakfast meeting on Friday at 8:00 a.m. This will also be in the Orchard Restaurant. In addition, she is scheduled to attend two larger meetings. The first is with the Atlantic Board of Directors for Filtrix Inc. on Thursday at 11:00 a.m. in the Filtrix Inc. boardroom. The second is a business dinner with Doug Holson and Petra Stolski of Filtrix Inc. along with potential investors from the Halifax area. This dinner will be at 7:00 p.m. on Thursday at Hugo's.

Your Assignment: Write a memo to Ms. Chen including the vital information she needs. Use graphic highlighting to make the details of her itinerary easy to read.

_____

_____

_____

_____

_____

_____

_____

_____

_____

_____

_____

_____

_____

_____

_____

Letters

Letters are more formal than e-mail messages or memos. They are used to communicate with people outside of your own organization and to communicate important or sensitive messages to individuals within your own organization.

There are four categories of letters:

1. **Routine letters**—information or action requests and responses; order requests and confirmations/responses; basic claim requests and grants.
2. **Negative news letters**—any letter in which a recipient's request is denied; these might include denying a claim, opting not to hire someone, or saying no to a favour request.
3. **Persuasive letters**—non-routine claim requests; favour requests; sales letters.
4. **Goodwill/special letters**—letters of recommendation, congratulations, appreciation, or sympathy.

Full Block Letter Format

1. **Include a return address in the body of the letter.** It's vital that your contact information is easily accessible.
2. **Ensure that your date is properly formatted.** The correct format for the date is month, day (in numerical form), year (in numerical form). For example, July 2, 2006. The day of the week is not included in the date.
3. **Include the address of the person to whom you are writing.** This is called the **inside address.** When writing persuasive letters (favour requests, non-routine claim letters, and cover letters), try to include the name of the person who will read your letter rather than "Dear Sir or Madame" or "To Whom It May Concern." For example, if you have a problem with a product and the warranty has expired, call the company, and ask who the Customer Service Manager is. If necessary, ask for the spelling of the name.
4. **Address the recipient as Dear + name.** Use first names only if you have a preestablished relationship. If you don't know someone, play it safe and address that person by his or her surname: Dear Ms. Erikson. If you are unsure of the gender of the recipient, address him or her by both first and last names, omitting the title: Dear Pat Bronson. Address women as "Ms." (unless you know for a fact that someone uses the title of Mrs.) and men as "Mr."
5. **End with a complimentary close.** Yours truly, Yours sincerely, Sincerely, and Best regards are appropriate complimentary closes.
6. **Sign your letters—always!** If you are sending a letter electronically (as an attachment to an e-mail, for example), either sign the letter electronically or type your name using a script font.

Yours sincerely,

Mathilde Huettner

Mathilde Huettner

Indicate if you have enclosed documents. If an invoice, account statement, sales receipt, or repair record is enclosed, indicate this by typing "Encl." or "Enclosure" flush with the left margin two spaces below the signature block.

Sample Full Block Letter

Return Address (Sender's Address) →	Healthy Goodness 39 King Street Charlottetown, PE C0M 1T0 (902) 469-7749
Date →	May 19, 2005
Inside Address (Receiver's Address) →	Ms. Lana Fallow Grassroots Inc. 1877 Commercial Avenue Moncton, NB E6L 1L1
Salutation →	Dear Ms. Fallow:
Subject Line →	**INFORMATION ON HERBAL REMEDIES AND INFUSIONS**

Body of Letter →

Would you please send us your most recent catalogue as well as any brochures and other literature pertaining to herbal remedies and infusions. As we have a large number of elderly customers, please include any information that would be tailored to seniors.

In addition, could you please answer the following questions:

1. **Weight Loss Products.** We would like to offer our customers a variety of weight loss herbal remedies; however, we are especially interested in products that do not contain Ephedra sinica. How effective are Ephedra sinica—free products?
2. **Energy Boosters.** Can you recommend an energy booster that pregnant women could safely use?
3. **Blood Cleansers.** We have had many requests for blood cleansers from our elderly customers. Is there any risk involved in these cleansers?

Please send us the above information by the end of the month as we want to have a good selection of herbal remedies in stock for the summer tourist season.

Complimentary Close →	Sincerely,
Signature Block →	Elaine MacCloud Owner

em

Modified Block Letter Format

1. **The subject line should clearly state the purpose of your letter.** Prepare your reader for what is to come. For this reason, subject lines are normally not used in negative news letters.

2. **Break the body up into manageable paragraphs.** It is very difficult for readers to access information from long, dense paragraphs.
3. **Use white space, bullets, numbers, and boldfaced type.** The more visually appealing your letter is, the more likely it will be that the recipient will read it.

Sample Modified Block Letter

Healthy Goodness

39 King Street
Charlottetown, PE C0M 1T0
(902) 469-7749

May 19, 2005
← Date

Ms. Lana Fallow
Grassroots Inc.
1877 Commercial Avenue
Moncton, NB E6L 1L1

Dear Ms. Fallow:

INFORMATION ON HERBAL REMEDIES

← Subject line draws attention to the fact that this is an information request.

Would you please send us your most recent catalogue as well as any brochures and other literature pertaining to herbal remedies. As we have a large number of elderly customers, please include any information that would be tailored to seniors.

← Specifies what information she requires.

← Short paragraphs make the information easier to access

In addition, could you please answer the following questions:

1. **Weight Loss Products.** We would like to offer our customers a variety of weight loss herbal remedies; however, we are especially interested in products that do not contain Ephedra sinica. How effective are Ephedra sinica-free products?

← Numbers effectively organize questions.

2. **Energy Boosters.** Can you recommend an energy booster that pregnant women could safely use?
3. **Blood Cleansers.** We have had many requests for blood cleansers from our elderly customers. Is there any risk involved in these cleansers?

← Uses bold face type to highlight important words.

← White space sets questions apart from the rest of the letter and makes them easy to see at a glance.

Please send us the above information by the end of the month as we want to have a good selection of herbal remedies in stock for the summer tourist season.

← Close with a specific request and a deadline by when information is required.

Sincerely,

Elaine MacCloud
Owner

em

Letter Procedure

Letter procedure is often dictated by the type of letter you are writing.
When writing routine and goodwill letters:

1. **State the problem or purpose immediately.** In a routine claim letter, this may involve asking that your VISA account # 4569 01234 5678 910 be refunded $270.00 to correct a duplicate charge.
2. **Provide specific information and concrete examples.** In an order request, include all the pertinent information such as item numbers and prices. Use bullets or a chart to make your order clear and easy to read. In a letter thanking a recipient for hosting a dinner, refer to the highlights of the evening.
3. **Close with a request for specific action.** Be clear about what you require, and include time deadlines.

When writing persuasive letters:

1. **Grab the reader's attention.** You can do this by complimenting the reader or emphasizing how the reader will benefit. Explain to the recipient of a persuasive favour request why he or she is your preferred choice as a guest speaker or a reference. For example, when inviting someone to speak at your school, you might explain how his or her achievements have inspired you and your classmates. When writing a non-routine letter of complaint, outline how satisfied you have been with past products or service. These letters are referred to as non-routine because your right to a refund or replacement is not cut-and-dried. For example, if you purchased a TV at a store with whom you do a lot of business, and the TV stops functioning two months after the warranty expires, the fact that you have been a longstanding customer may benefit you. *It costs companies 30–40 times more money to attract a new customer than to retain a current customer.*
2. **Build the reader's interest.** It's important to focus on the reader rather than the writer. Point out specific ways in which the reader will benefit.
3. **Reduce any resistance the reader might feel.** Show how the benefits outweigh any negative aspects.
4. **Make it easy for the reader to respond or take action.** Provide contact information. In a sales letter going out to a geographically broad range of customers, include a toll-free number. Include a deadline by which the reader must respond. In a sales letter, this deadline is often attached to free merchandise: "Order before August 1, and receive a complimentary DVD player."

When writing negative news letters:

1. **Begin with a positive statement.** If you open with the bad news, there is a good chance that your reader will not read the whole letter. If you must deny a customer a refund, first thank them for taking the time to write to your company.
2. **Outline the facts logically and objectively when writing a letter of complaint or a claim.** Include concrete details and examples. Explain why your company has a particular policy. For example, if you are writing from a discount store to tell a customer that he or she cannot return merchandise

beyond the 15-day return limit, you can explain that in order to provide your customers with low prices, you must have firm return policies.

3. **Make a goodwill gesture.** Is there anything that you can offer? While you may not be able to replace a television set that is no longer under warranty, you may be able to offer 15 percent off the purchase of a new television. *Warning:* Offer discounts or merchandise only if you are authorized to do so.

4. **Do not encourage further contact regarding the current problem.** You want to resolve the problem and then move on.

EXERCISE 5 Revising Letters

Revise both the body and the format of this letter to create an effective, concise message.

Monday, December 4, 2006

Donald Fischer
The Guardian
165 Prince St. - P.O. Box 760
Charlottetown, PEI

Dear Donald:

Although we have never met, I know from my father that you are a journalist with *The Guardian*. I am very interested in getting into the field of journalism and wondered if you could answer some questions. What college do you think is the best for journalism in Canada? In what way did you most benefit from the program at Holland College? Was there anything lacking in the program that you needed to find elsewhere? How long was the program? Was it more academic learning or hands-on learning, and do you feel that style of learning was appropriate for the course? Did your program at Holland College help you to get a job in journalism? Do you think a journalism degree is essential to working in journalism?

I would appreciate the answers to these questions and any other information you can provide.

Thanks so much,

Tara Rule

_____

_____

_____

_____

_____

_____

_____

_____
_____
_____
_____
_____
_____
_____
_____
_____
_____

EXERCISE 6 Order Request

As the administrative assistant at Web Design Inc. in Edmonton, you are responsible for ordering office supplies. You are currently low on several items and wish to have them delivered by the end of the month. Place an order for ten boxes of staples (item no. T7546)—each box costs $4.49; two No. 3 staplers (item no. A3540)—each costs $8.99; four boxes of photocopy paper (item no. A8890)—each box costs $39.99; and four ink jet print cartridges for an S230 printer (item no. Y2225)—they are $19.29 each.

Your Assignment: Write to Staples Business Depot, 750 Marsh Avenue, Edmonton, AB T5Y 6G3 and order the items needed. Let them know that you have an account with them (account # W777345987433) and wish to be invoiced for this order. Add in any missing information such as Web Design Inc.'s address.

_____
_____
_____
_____
_____
_____
_____
_____
_____
_____
_____
_____

_____

_____

_____

_____

Résumés

Probably the first business documents you will write will be a résumé and cover letter. Before starting work on a résumé, it is important to know what a résumé is and what a résumé is not:

- *A résumé is <u>not</u> a biography or a list of jobs—it is a ten-second ad.* Research shows the average executive spends less than ten seconds looking at each résumé before rejecting it or setting it aside for further reading. A résumé does not have to list every job you have had or every school you attended. It should not be cluttered with employer addresses or names of references. It should briefly but clearly present facts, experiences, skills, and training that relate to a specific job or profession.
- *The goal of a résumé is to get an interview, not a job.* Few people are hired based on a résumé. Résumés only show an employer that you are worth talking to. The goal of a résumé is to generate enough interest to prompt someone to call you for an interview.
- *You may need several résumés.* Companies create different ads for the same product to reach different people. You might need three or four résumés that target specific jobs. A nurse, for example, might create one résumé highlighting her intensive-care experience and another focusing on her work with abused children. Because résumés are quickly screened, they have to communicate at a glance. A résumé that tries to cover too many areas will be vague or confusing.

Strategies for Writing Résumés

1. **Understand that there are no absolute "rules" for writing résumés— only guidelines.** You may have heard people say that a résumé should be only one page or must never include your age. Because the world of work is so varied, there are exceptions.
2. **Develop your résumé by focusing on the job description or company.** Study the wording of want ads or job announcements and highlight skills and experiences that directly match those listed in the ad.
3. **Include your full name, address, telephone number with area code, and e-mail address:**

       Seung Eun Cheung
       990 Broughton Avenue
       Vancouver, BC V9G 2A7
       (604) 555-2957
       secheung@bcnet.com

4. **Provide a clear, objective statement describing the job you seek.**
   Avoid vague objectives like "a position making use of my skills and
   abilities" or "sales, marketing, or public relations." If you have different
   interests, create separate résumés for each field or job:

   ```
   Objective    Retail Sales Management
   ```

5. **Use a brief overview or summary to highlight key skills and
   experience:**

   ```
   Overview     Five years' experience in retail
                sales management. Proven ability to
                hire, train, and motivate sales
                staff. Highly skilled in customer
                relations, point of purchase sales,
                and loss prevention.

   Summary      Retail Sales Management

                • Sales manager, La Senza 2002-2005
                • Loss prevention consultant, Jazzco,
                  2001
                • Developed online sales associate
                  program, lowering training costs 35%
                • Reduced turnover 65% first year
   ```

   You may find it easier to write the overview last, after you have identified
   your key skills and accomplishments.

6. **List your most important credentials first.** If you are a college or university graduate with no professional experience, list education first. If a
   current or recent job relates to the job you seek, list experience first.

7. **Arrange education and job experience by time, beginning with the
   most recent.**

8. **Avoid general job descriptions:**

   ```
                Receptionist responsible for greet-
                ing visitors, maintaining schedules,
                logging incoming calls, scheduling
                appointments, and receiving and dis-
                tributing faxes.
   ```

   Focus on individual accomplishments and demonstrate the significance of
   your experience:

   ```
                Receptionist for 28 sales representa-
                tives generating $54 million in sales
                annually. Individually responsible for
                receiving and distributing faxes used
                to expedite rush orders.
   ```

9. **List training seminars, volunteer work, hobbies, and interests only if they directly relate to the job you want.**
10. **Do not include addresses of employers, names of supervisors, or references.** These details can be supplied after you are called in for an interview.

Recent Graduate with Intern Experience

Seung Eun Cheung
990 Broughton Avenue
Vancouver, BC V6G 2A7
(604) 555-2957
secheung@bcnet.com

GOAL	An entry-level position in nonprofit fund-raising.
OVERVIEW	Associate degree in marketing. Three years' experience in telemarketing, mass mailing, and Internet fund-raising. Demonstrated ability to work within budgets, maximize returns, and resolve problems.
EXPERIENCE Jan.–May 2006	*Intern* BC CENTRE FOR THE PERFORMING ARTS Completed four-month internship, working directly with vice president in charge of fund-raising

• Developed three direct-mail letters used in annual campaign that achieved a 15% return and $257,000 in pledges
• Supervised 15 telemarketers during Pledge Week
• Assisted vice president in press conferences, public appearances, and radio call-in program

EDUCATION	DOUGLAS COLLEGE, Coquitlam, BC Market Management Degree Program, May 2006 Completed courses in business management, accounting, sales and marketing, nonprofit financing, public relations, and communications skills

• 3.5 GPA
• One of six students selected to assist faculty in annual United Way Drive

LANGUAGES	French and Mandarin

References and work samples available on request

Recent Graduate with Unrelated Experience

MARIA SANCHEZ
1732 Andrews Road
Winnipeg, MB R2E 1D2
(204) 555-1171
mariasanchez@earthlink.net

OBJECTIVE	Retail printing management
OVERVIEW	Five years' experience in retail sales management. Fully familiar with state-of-the-art printing equipment and techniques. Proven ability to lower overhead, increase sales, and build customer relations.

- Certified to service and repair all Canon and Xerox copiers

EDUCATION	RED RIVER COLLEGE, Winnipeg, MB Associate Degree, Printing and Publishing, 2006 Completed courses in graphic design, editing, high-speed printing, and equipment repair

- Attended Quadgraphics seminar
- Assisted in design and production of college newspaper

XEROX, Winnipeg, MB
Completed service training program, 2005

EXPERIENCE 2004 –	FAST-PRINT, Winnipeg, MB *Retail sales.* Work twenty hours a week assisting manager in counter sales, customer relations, printing, and inventory in downtown print shop.
1999 – 2004	VINYL CITY MUSIC, Winnipeg, MB *Manager* of retail record outlet with annual gross sales of $2.5 million

- Hired, trained, and supervised 30 employees
- Reduced operating costs 15% first year
- Developed special promotions with radio stations, increasing sales 32%
- Prepared all financial statements

HONOURS	Dean's list, 2005, 2006

References and transcripts available

Cover Letters

Cover letters can be as important as the résumés they introduce. Résumés submitted without letters are often discarded because employers assume that applicants who do not take the time to address them personally are not serious. Résumés tend to be rather cold lists of facts; cover letters allow applicants to present themselves in a more personalized way. The letter allows applicants to explain a job change, a period of unemployment, or a lack of formal education.

Strategies for Writing Cover Letters

In most instances, cover letters are short sales letters using standard business letter formats.

1. Avoid beginning a cover letter with a simple announcement:

   Dear Sir or Madam:

   This letter is to apply for the job of controller advertised in the San Francisco Chronicle last week. . .

2. Open letters on a strong point emphasizing skills or experiences:

   Dear Sir or Madam:

   In the last two years I opened fifty-eight new accounts, increasing sales by nearly $800,000.

3. Use the letter to include information not listed on the résumé. Volunteer work, high school experiences, or travel that might not be suited to a résumé can appear in the letter—if they are career related.

4. Refer to the résumé, indicating how it documents your skills and abilities.

5. End the letter with a brief summary of notable skills and experiences and a request for an interview. To be more assertive, state that you will call the employer in two or three days to schedule an appointment.

Cover Letter Responding to a Want Ad

Seung Eun Cheung
990 Broughton Avenue
Vancouver, BC V6G 2A7
(604) 555-2957
secheung@bcnet.com

May 25, 2006

Vicki Spritzer
Foundation Management Services
45 Robson Street
Vancouver, BC V74 2P9

RE: Fund-raising assistant position advertised in the *Vancouver Sun*, May 24, 2006

Dear Ms. Spritzer:

In 2005, the BC Centre for the Performing Arts raised $209,000 in its April direct-mail campaign. This year the letters I wrote, edited, and tested generated $257,000—a 23% increase.

For the past four months, I have worked directly with Deborah Mandel, vice president of the BC Centre for the Performing Arts, in fund-raising and public relations. I assisted her in all phases of fund-raising, including direct mail, public appearances, telemarketing, and a radio pledge drive.

As my résumé shows, I have just received a degree in market management. In addition to completing courses in business management and communications skills, I took special courses in fund-raising that included extensive research in online fund-raising.

Given my education in marketing and my experience in fund-raising, I believe I would be an effective fund-raising assistant for your firm. I look forward to the opportunity of discussing this position with you at your convenience. I can be reached at (604) 555-2957, or you can e-mail me at secheung@bcnet.com.

I can e-mail you samples of fund-raising letters, flyers, telemarketing scripts, and letters of recommendation if you wish.

Sincerely yours,

Seung Eun Cheung

Cover Letter Responding to Personal Referral

MARIA SANCHEZ
1732 Andrews Road
Winnipeg, MB R2E 1D2
(204) 555-1171
mariasanchez@earthlink.net

May 25, 2006

Linda Burstein
ABC Printing
1212 Front Avenue
Winnipeg, MB R4T 2S3

RE: Manager position for Front Avenue ABC Print Shop

Dear Ms. Burstein:

Sean McLean mentioned that ABC Printing is seeking a manager for its Front Avenue print shop sometime this summer.

As my résumé shows, I have just completed my associate degree in printing and publishing and am fully familiar with all the equipment used by ABC Printing. During the past two years I have been working the counter at one of Fast-Print's busiest downtown locations.

Before deciding to go into printing and publishing, I managed one of Winnipeg's major music stores. I supervised 30 employees, lowered operating costs, generated new accounts, and increased sales by 32%.

Given my knowledge of printing and publishing techniques, practical experience in both print shop operations and retail management, I believe I could be an effective manager for ABC Printing. I would appreciate the opportunity to discuss this position with you at your convenience. I can be reached by phone at (204) 555-1171 or by e-mail at mariasanchez@ earthlink.net.

Sincerely yours,

Maria Sanchez

WORKING TOGETHER

Working with a group of students, discuss the following résumé and cover letter and recommend changes. Delete needless information, reword awkward phrases, eliminate repetitions, and edit for spelling and other mechanical errors.

KARLA MESSER
1434 Douglas Avenue #456
North Bay, ON P1B 3C5
(705) 555-7878

GOAL	To ultimately own my own business. In the meantime seeking a position in restaurant and or hotel management.
EDUCATION	Marshall High School, North Bay, ON Graduated 2003 Was in band, school yearbook, tennis club
	Canadore College, North Bay, ON Graduated 2006 Completed Hotel, Resort, and Restaurant Management Program with courses in business law, hotel law, bookkeeping, food service management, and sales management.
EXPERIENCE 2002	Valentine's 1536 Lower Leeds Avenue, North Bay, ON P1C 3C3 Banquet waitress responsible for serving banquet dishes at banquets, weddings, and business lunches for up to 250 guests.
2003	Valentine's assistant banquet manager responsible for assisting manager in organizing wait staff, menu organization, and working with clients setting up plans for upcoming events at the restaurant.

2004	Bruno's
	756 Main Street, Main Street, North Bay, ON P1C 5V7
	Assistant manager responsible for all lunch wait staff serving up to 200 lunchtime customers in restaurant's pub and grill. Assisted owner in redesining menu offering to increase sales and reduce preparation time.
2005	Holiday Inn-Airport
	2700 Orion Road, North Bay, ON P1A 3G4
	Banquet operations assistant responsible for booking rooms, scheduling wait staff, ordering special supples, confirming reservations, etc.

References	George Avery	Francine Damiani	Margo Silver
	(705) 555-8989	(705) 555-9090	(705) 555-8987

- -

KARLA MESSER
1434 Douglas Avenue #456
North Bay, ON P1B 3C5
(705) 555-7878

May 25, 2006

Dear Ms. Mendoza:

This letter is to reply to the ad in the *North Bay Gazette* that appeared May 22, 2006 last week.

This month I will complete my Hotel, Resort, and Restaurant Management program at Canadore College. I have studied food service administration, bookkeeping, office management, and business law. In addition, I have several years' experience working in restraurants and more recently the Holiday Inn. I have worked in banquet operations, restaurant operations, and convention planning.

I think I have a lot of good ideas that could benefit the Hyatt organization. I would be glad to be able to meet with you and discuss this job and my background. I can be reached at (705) 555-7878.

Thanking you for your attention,

Karla Messer

GET THINKING
AND WRITING

CRITICAL THINKING

Describe the most important aspects of the job you want when you graduate. What is more important to you: a high income or job security? Would you be willing to relocate? How will your first job fit into your life goals?

How do you plan to look for a job when you graduate? Do you plan to use the college placement office, recruiters, employment agencies, want ads, or networking?

Write a paragraph outlining your plans. If you are unsure, consider learning more about the job search process by exploring the Internet and talking to friends and instructors.

WRITING ON THE WEB

Using a search engine like AltaVista, Yahoo!, or Google, enter terms such as *résumés, writing résumés, cover letters,* and *applying for jobs* to locate current sites of interest.

1. Imagine that you need to write an e-mail cover letter. Compose this letter using what you have learned in this chapter. Is your opening effective? Does the body of the letter expand upon the skills and experience outlined in your résumé? Does the ending summarize your notable skills? Have you requested an interview?
2. Edit and revise the letter, asking yourself, "Would I hire this person?" Let others read the letter, and get their input. Save the letter, and update it occasionally as your skills and experience change. When the time comes that you do need a cover letter, you will already have a strong draft to work from.

POINTS TO REMEMBER

1. Business writing occurs in a very different environment from college writing. Be sensitive to the tone, style, and format used in your field.
2. E-mail is real mail. Treat e-mail messages with the professionalism you would in writing a first-class letter.
3. Realize the limits of e-mail. Longer documents should be sent as attachments.
4. All business communiqués should be clear, concise, and direct. Avoid long, rambling messages.
5. Memos are internal communiqués.
6. Memos follow a precise format, beginning with the headings DATE, TO, FROM, and SUBJECT.
7. Letters are more formal than e-mail messages or memos.
8. Letters are used to communicate with people outside of your own organization and to communicate important or sensitive messages to individuals within your own organization.
9. Résumés should be written concisely so they can be scanned in seconds.
10. Résumés should stress important points in your career—avoid including hobbies, high school jobs, and other minor details.
11. Cover letters should emphasize skills and experience and link yourself to the job you want.
12. Cover letters give you the opportunity to explain unrelated experience and add information not suited for the résumé.

Part 3

Writing Sentences

13

Recognizing the Power of Words

GET WRITING

How hard is it to choose the right word?

Write a few sentences describing a situation, such as applying for a job or writing a condolence card to a friend, when you had problems finding words to express what you were trying to say.

The Power of Words

Words are the building blocks of language. They have the power to inform, entertain, and persuade. When we talk, our word choices can be casual and haphazard because we also communicate through eye contact, tone of voice, and gestures. Speech is interactive. We can repeat sentences for emphasis and reword awkward phrases as we talk. If our listeners cannot understand what we are saying, they can ask questions:

"Did you hear him tell us what to do about this thing today?"
"What thing?"
"That deal over there."
"Oh, that thing, sure. We ship it Air."
"Air Express?"
"Right."

However, when we write, our readers cannot ask questions or give us a chance to restate our ideas—we have to get things right the first time. Readers have to rely on the text to understand our meaning. We will not be there to correct false impressions, answer questions, or rephrase statements. Readers also assume our word choices will match the definitions they find in the dictionary.

WHAT DO YOU KNOW?

Choose the appropriate word in each sentence.

1. _____ The prime minister's stance stirred the (conscience/conscious) of the nation.

2. _____ How will this project (effect/affect) my grade?

3. _____ (Its/It's) going to be difficult to repair your car.

4. _____ It is later (then/than) you think.

5. _____ The student (council/counsel) will meet at noon.

6. _____ Her remarks clearly (implied/inferred) that she would support us.

7. _____ Please remove keys and (lose/loose) change from your pockets.

8. _____ The cottage is (further/farther) down the road.

9. _____ Will you (except/accept) out-of-province cheques?

10. _____ I am tired and need to (lay/lie) down.

Answers appear on the following page.

GET WRITING
AND REVISING

WHAT ARE YOU TRYING TO SAY?

Write a paragraph that describes a person you have strong feelings about. Provide details that explain why you like or dislike this person. What are his or her most noticeable characteristics? Choose words that reflect your point of view.

_____

_____

_____

_____

_____

_____

_____

_____

_____

WHAT HAVE YOU WRITTEN?

Underline the key words in your paragraph. Do they give readers a strong impression? Could you improve your statement by choosing different words? Read your description aloud. What changes would you make to increase its impact?

GUIDELINES FOR USING WORDS

- *Use correct words.* Make sure you know a word's precise meaning.
- *Use effective words.* Use clear, concrete language your readers understand.
- *Use appropriate words.* Use words suited to your purpose, subject, audience, and document. Be aware of connotations.

Use Correct Words

English has a number of words that are easily confused or misunderstood:

elicit	to prompt or provoke	His threats failed to *elicit* a response.
illicit	illegal	They found *illicit* drugs.
than	used in comparisons	Leasing is cheaper *than* buying.
then	used in time references	He worked all day, *then* went home.
there	a place or direction	Put it over *there*.
their	possessive of "they"	Put it in *their* mailbox.
they're	contraction of "they are"	*They're* here!
to	preposition *or* infinitive	She went *to* college *to* study marketing.
too	in excess *or* also	It was *too* cold to swim. Are they coming, *too*?
two	a number	We're a *two*-car family now.

ANSWERS TO WHAT DO YOU KNOW? ON PAGE 198
1. conscience, 2. affect, 3. It's, 4. than, 5. council, 6. implied, 7. loose, 8. farther, 9. accept, 10. lie.

(See pages 487–490 for other easily confused words.)

A NOTE ON SPELLING

An important part of using words is making sure you spell them correctly. Spelling errors confuse readers and make your work appear sloppy and unprofessional.

Tips for Improving Your Spelling
- *Pronounce new words.* Reading them aloud can help you recall letters you might overlook, like the *n* in "environment" or the *r* in "government."
- *Write out new words you learn in school and at your job.*
- *Make a list of words you repeatedly misspell and refer to it whenever you write.* Keep copies of this list in your notebook, by your desk, or in your purse, backpack, or briefcase.
- *Use a dictionary to help with spelling.* Get in the habit of writing with your dictionary close at hand. Look up unfamiliar words or words you know you have difficulty spelling.

Tips for Improving Your Word Choice
- *Write out new words you learn in school and at your job.*
- *Make a list of words that you repeatedly mix up; refer to it as you edit your work.*

(See Chapter 28 for further help with spelling.)

EXERCISE 1 Using the Correct Word

Circle the correct word in each sentence.

1. The (principal/principle) asked the teacher to resign.
2. The lifeboat (foundered/floundered) in the heavy surf.
3. (Whether/weather) you go to college or get a job, you will need to learn how to use a computer.
4. We still don't (know/now) if she is going to speak next week.
5. Her speech will depend on (who's/whose) invited.
6. We toured the accident (site/sight).
7. Her parents (emigrated/immigrated) from Poland in the 1970s.
8. The mayor's speech cannot be (preceded/proceeded) by a comedic performance.
9. The prime minister's speech made (allusions/illusions) to World War II.
10. We wondered if (anyone/any one) would call for help.

POINT TO REMEMBER

Words sometimes have special or specific meanings. One college might define a *full-time student* as someone who takes twelve credits, while another school requires students to take sixteen credits. The word *high-rise* means one thing in Toronto, Canada, and another in Lagos, Nigeria. *Make sure your readers understand the exact meanings of the words you use. Define terms with footnotes or a glossary at the end of your document to prevent confusion.*

EXERCISE 2 Understanding Meaning

Define each of the words, then check your answers using a college dictionary.

archaic _____   lucrative _____

collateral _____   optician _____

discriminate _____   patron _____

fundamental _____   surrogate _____

homicide _____   topical _____

How many words have you heard but could not define? How many did you get wrong? Which words have additional meanings you were unaware of?

LEARNING MORE ABOUT WORDS

- Use a college dictionary to look up new or confusing words.
- Study the glossaries in your textbooks to learn special terms and definitions.

DICTIONARIES FOR ESL STUDENTS

If English is your second language, refer to dictionaries like the *Canadian Oxford Dictionary* and the *Collins Canadian Dictionary*. They give not only definitions but rules for combining words. If you look up *future*, for example, you learn that it often appears in phrases such as *predict the future*, *plan the future*, and *face the future*. These dictionaries include sample sentences to show how a word is used in context.

EXERCISE 3 Editing Your Writing

Select one or more writing responses you completed in a previous chapter or the draft of an upcoming assignment and review your use of words. Look for errors in usage. Have you confused there *and* their *or* its *and* it's? *Have you written* affect *for* effect *or* adapt *for* adopt? *List words you have confused in the back of this book or a notebook for future reference.*

Use Effective Words

To communicate effectively, you need to use words that are clear and concrete. Abstract and general terms lack impact:

> I hated my summer job at PizzaXpress. It was awful. I worked in the worst part of the business. It made me depressed. That place always made me feel bad, mentally and physically. I was uncomfortable and felt bad all the time. The whole experience was negative, and it took a toll on every part of me. It ruined my whole summer. Even my free days were like a waste. I was in no mood to do anything I normally liked. For the first time in my life I could not wait for school to start.

Words like *bad, awful* and *negative experience* are vague. The statement simply announces that the writer hated his or her job but does not tell us why. Concrete language, however, creates stronger impressions:

> I hated my summer job at PizzaXpress. The kitchen was hot, noisy, and dangerous. The roar of the oven fans gave me headaches, and the sharp edges of the steel tables cut my arms and thighs. By the second night my hands were sore, swollen, and burned. The stress from demanding customers, rude drivers, and yelling managers ruined my whole summer. Even on free days, I never felt like seeing friends or going to the beach. For the first time in my life I could not wait for school to start.

Instead of *feeling bad mentally and physically*, this version offers specific details such as *sore, swollen, and burned hands*. Readers can understand why *demanding customers, rude drivers, and yelling managers* would ruin the student's summer.

Use Concrete Nouns

Concrete nouns create strong images readers can identify and remember.

Abstract	Concrete
residential rental unit	*apartment*
employment situation	*job*
individual	*boy*
educational facility	*junior high school*

Use Strong Verbs

Verbs should emphasize action. Avoid weak verb phrases that use several words to describe action that could be expressed with a single word.

Weak Verb Phrase	Strong Verb
make an examination	*examine*
effect a change	*change*
offer an apology	*apologize*
develop a plan	*plan*

Avoid Clichés

Clichés are worn-out phrases. They may have been colourful, striking, or entertaining at one time, but like jokes that have been told too often, they are stale and meaningless:

Cliché	Improved
as white as snow	*pure white*
thin as a rail	*thin*
out like a light	*slept soundly*
selling like hotcakes	*popular*

EXERCISE 4 Improving Word Choices

Rewrite each of the following sentences, replacing abstract nouns, weak verb phrases, and clichés.

1. During the summer month of July 1976 an employee of a cotton storage facility in the Sudanese town of Nzara suddenly suffered a condition of shock and died from hemorrhages that proved to be uncontrollable.

_____

_____

_____

2. Days later, two of the man's coworkers exhibited signs of ill health and quickly died of bleeding that was massive in scope.

_____

_____

3. The disease went through the village like a knife through butter, infecting and killing the resident population of Nzara.

_____

_____

4. People who were sick went to the nearby medical facility, which became as crowded as the subway at rush hour.

_____

_____

5. Not having knowledge about the deadly nature of the virus, doctors and nurses of the hospital facility contracted the disease as they made examinations of patients.

_____

_____

6. Soon the medical staff began to die, along with people who were family members of the patients.

_____

_____

7. Then suddenly the epidemic came to an end when the virus ran out of people who were healthy it could infect.

_____

_____

8. Scientific research personnel who made a study of this outbreak called the virus "Ebola," after the nearby Ebola River.

_____

_____

9. Medical experts saw the outbreak as having great significance because it made a suggestion that science had not conquered the problem of infectious disease.

_____

_____

_____

10. Ebola never reached Canada, but within a few years another new virus, AIDS, would create a change in the way scientific research personnel addressed the study of infectious diseases.

_____

_____

_____

Use Appropriate Words

The words you choose should suit your purpose, your audience, and the document. Words, like clothing, can be formal or informal, traditional or trendy. Just as you dress differently for a job interview or a soccer game, you write differently to produce a research paper, a résumé, or an e-mail to your best friend. It is important to use the right level of diction or word choice.

LEVELS OF DICTION

formal/technical	terms used to communicate within a discipline or profession
standard	words commonly used in books, magazines, and newspapers intended for a general audience
informal	regional expressions, jargon used within specialized groups, slang, and text messaging (u for "you" or brb for "be right back")

Use the Appropriate Level of Diction

Doctors, lawyers, engineers, and stockbrokers use **formal** or **technical** terms that may be unfamiliar to most educated people. Many of your college textbooks include glossaries of technical terms. These terms must be understood for people to communicate without confusion. **Standard** words are widely known and used. They are the kind of words found in popular books, magazines, and on most websites. **Informal** English can include slang, jargon used on the job, and expressions spoken by an ethnic group or residents of a particular part of the country. Jazz artists, airline pilots, baseball fans, sailors, computer hackers, bankers, and people in show business all have their own words and phrases.

Formal/technical	Standard	Informal
taken into custody	*arrested*	*busted*
dissociative rage disorder	*violent outburst*	*going postal*
corrective lenses	*glasses*	*specs*

The level of diction writers use depends on their goal, their readers, and the document. Lawyers drafting motions to file in court use formal legal terminology. To communicate to their clients, they use standard terms anyone can understand. In sending e-mails to their office staff, they might use slang and jargon only a few people could understand.

It is important to make sure that you do not use inappropriate diction that may confuse readers or weaken the impact of your writing. Slang words in a research paper or business letter will make a writer seem insincere and unprofessional. Formal language can make a memo difficult to read at a glance.

EXERCISE 5 Selecting Appropriate Words

Revise each sentence to replace words that are inappropriate for a formal research paper.

1. During the war on Iraq, the opposition party pressured Jean Chrétien to get on the ball and send Canadian troops to Iraq.

   _____

   _____

2. Industrial toxicologists discovered the presence of asbestosis in automobile workers was way bad.

   _____

   _____

3. Affirmative action policies that once fired up the administration to employ more minorities have been ignored in order to save a buck.

   _____

   _____

Revise each sentence to remove words that are inappropriate for an informal memo.

4. Tell the shipping department to immediately effectuate a transfer of all financial records to payroll.

   _____

   _____

5. Until our insurance problem is fixed, don't let any of the individuals from the sales department utilize company cars for transportation.

_____

_____

Use Appropriate Idioms

Idioms are expressions or combinations of words that are not always logical. For example, you *ride in a car* but *fly on a plane*. You *run into friends* when you meet them by accident and *run to friends* when you seek their help. Idioms can be a challenge to understand for two reasons. First, some idioms like *pay attention to* can't be easily understood by looking at the meaning of each word. Second, some idioms like *wrap your mind around* or *hit the roof* don't mean what they literally suggest. Idioms are often difficult or impossible to translate word for word into other languages.

In college and business writing you will be expected to use idioms accurately. If you are confused about the meaning of an idiom, refer to multilingual dictionaries like the *Canadian Oxford Dictionary* or the *Collins Canadian Dictionary*.

Commonly Misused Idioms

Incorrect	Correct
act *from* concern	act *out of* concern
bored *of* the idea	bored *with* the idea
different *than* the others	different *from* the others
in / with *regards* to	in / with *regard* to
irritated *with*	irritated *by*
on accident	*by* accident
relate *with*	relate *to*
satisfied *in*	satisfied *with*
superior *than*	superior *to*
type *of a*	type *of*
wait *on* line	wait *in* line

TIPS FOR USING IDIOMS CORRECTLY

As anyone who speaks English as a second language knows, idioms can be one of the greatest challenges. Idioms coupled with prepositions often pose a special problem.

1. Make a note of idioms and how they are used in your readings.
2. Choose three idioms to use regularly for a month. Each month choose another three to add to your vocabulary.

EXERCISE 6 Using the Appropriate Idioms

Write sentences using each of the following idioms correctly.

1. get even with, get out of hand

   _____

2. take off, take on, take over

   _____

3. wait for, wait on

   _____

4. stand a chance, by chance

   _____

5. good at, good for, good with

   _____

Be Aware of Connotations

All words have a **denotation,** or basic meaning. A *car* is a motor vehicle that transports people and goods. A *dwelling* is a place where people live. Some words also have **connotations,** or suggested meanings. A large automobile can be called a *luxury sedan* or a *gas guzzler.* A small vacation house can be called a *summer home,* a *cottage,* or a *shack.* Someone who spends money carefully can be termed *thrifty* or *cheap.* A person who blows up a government building can be denounced as a *terrorist* or praised as a *freedom fighter.* A private upscale school can be called *prestigious* or *elitist.* A discount motel can be *affordable* or *cheap.*

What we call things influences the way people respond to our ideas. Our connotations should match our attitudes. If you like a quiet little restaurant near campus, you are probably going to call it *softly lit, peaceful,* and *intimate* rather than *dark, boring,* and *cramped.* Advertisers use words with appealing connotations like *new, improved, natural,* and *free* to attract consumers. Politicians use connotations to influence voters. They might urge the public to support a project that will "*drain a swamp* to create *new homes* for *families,*" while their opponents argue the same project will "*destroy a wetland* to create *luxury condos* for *the rich.*"

Consider the different impact these words have:

casual	vs.	*sloppy*	*proud*	vs.	*vain*
young	vs.	*immature*	*brave*	vs.	*reckless*
the homeless	vs.	*street people*	*pre-owned*	vs.	*used*
cautious	vs.	*cowardly*	*simplistic*	vs.	*simple*

Connotations shape the way people perceive an event or situation:

In love with the young singer, the *passionate* fan *followed* his *idol* from concert to concert, *begging* to see her.

Obsessed with the young singer, the *deranged* fan *stalked* his *victim* from concert to concert, *demanding* to see her.

Comprised of four *elegant* clock faces, the Peace Tower *soars* over Parliament Hill like a *beacon of hope*.

Comprised of four *enormous* clock faces, the Peace Tower *looms* over Parliament Hill like an *overbearing watchtower*.

Asked to comment on the allegations, the mayor *declined* to answer.

Asked to comment on the allegations, the mayor *refused* to answer.

LEARNING CONNOTATIONS

To make sure you understand a new word's connotation, study how it is used in context. If the word is used in a phrase or sentence that seems negative, the word's connotation is probably negative. If the phrase or sentence seems positive, the word's connotation is probably positive. You can also use a thesaurus to find a word's synonyms and antonyms. If you look up *stubborn*, for example, you will find it means the same as *obstinate* and *pigheaded* and the opposite of *compliant* and *easygoing*.

WORKING TOGETHER

Working with a group of students, review the text of the following e-mail to eliminate negative connotations. Write a more positive version of this message.

```
We regret to inform employees that the bonus cheques
we promised to distribute on March 1 will not be
available until March 30. Because many employees
failed to submit their pay forms on time, we were
unable to process them until last week. If you expect
to be paid on time, make sure you do not fail to
submit reports on time.
```

CRITICAL THINKING

In a paragraph, describe the way you talk—your favourite expressions, words you learned playing sports, working a job, or speaking with friends. What or who has influenced your vocabulary—your parents, friends, television, coworkers? Examine one or more of the greatest influences on your language. If English is not your native language, what English words were easiest for you to learn? Do you ever blend English and another language?

WHAT HAVE YOU LEARNED?

Choose the appropriate word in each sentence:

1. _____ The federal government's policy will (affect/effect) the way colleges charge tuition.

2. _____ We can't (accept/except) late assignments.

3. _____ (They're/There) coming here after the game.

4. _____ The mayor does not seem to be (conscious/conscience) of the budget problems.

5. _____ Hospitals require a (continual/continuous) supply of water.

Choose effective words and phrases in the following sentences:

6. _____ The city (conducted tests of/tested) the water supply for mercury.

7. _____ The heart sensor is (round/round in shape).

8. _____ She predicted that (hurricanes/hurricane activity) could ravage the coast.

9. _____ Scientists will have to (achieve purification of/purify) this substance to make it of medical use.

10. _____ The judge ordered that psychiatrists (render an examination of/examine) the defendant.

Choose the proper level of diction for a college research paper.

11. _____ (The mentally ill/head cases) require expensive treatment.

12. _____ Current juvenile justice policies fail to reform (gangbangers/gang members).

13. _____ The manager insisted he would (eighty-six/dismiss) anyone serving minors.

14. _____ The government wants to (weed out/eliminate) archaic regulations.

15. _____ The accountants will (dope out/assess) the cost of the new equipment.

Choose words with positive connotations:

16. _____ The committee met (secretly/privately) to discuss the lawsuit.

17. _____ The refugees were (expelled/relocated).

18. _____ The lumber mill (devours/processes) five thousand trees a day.

19. _____ The café was (dimly/softly) lit.

20. _____ This facility will store (toxic waste/industrial by-products).

Answers appear on page 211.

GET WRITING

Study this photograph carefully. How would you describe its mood, what the woman is thinking, the importance of her facing away from the camera?

Write a few sentences describing your reactions to this image. Then underline the key words you chose. What are their connotations? Do they express what you are trying to say?

WRITING ON THE WEB

1. Using a database or a search engine like AltaVista, Yahoo!, or Google, look up articles from a variety of magazines. What do you notice about the level of diction, the use of words? How do the styles of the *Harvard Business Review, Criminal Justice Digest, People, Maclean's, Chatelaine,* and your local newspaper differ? What does this say about the writers, the publication, the intended readers?
2. Analyze the language used in Internet chat rooms. Have these electronic communities produced their own slang or jargon? Do chat rooms of car enthusiasts differ from those dedicated to childcare or investments? Do people with special interests bring their particular terminology and culture into cyberspace?
3. Using a search engine like AltaVista, Yahoo!, or Google, enter the following search terms to locate current sites you might find helpful:

diction	*connotation*	*usage*
word choice	*slang*	*vocabulary*

   Write two or three sentences using new words you discover on the web. Determine which are technical, standard, or informal.
4. Ask your instructors for URLs of useful websites. Keep a list and update it when you find other sources.

POINTS TO REMEMBER

1. The words you choose shape the way readers will react to your writing.
2. *Choose correct words.* Check dictionaries to make sure you have selected the right words and spelled them correctly.
3. *Choose effective words.* Use words that are clear and concrete—avoid wordy phrases, clichés, and abstract terms.
4. *Consider connotations.* Be aware of the emotional or psychological impact words may have. Choose words that reflect your message.
5. Review the lists of commonly confused and misspelled words on pages 487–491.
6. Study glossaries in your textbooks to master new terms you encounter in college.
7. Select a good college-level dictionary and get in the habit of referring to it several times a week. Use highlighters or Post-It™ notes to personalize your dictionary.
8. Practice using an online dictionary, especially if you write on a computer.

14

Writing Sentences

Public telephones were once placed in booths so people could make calls behind closed doors. Have cell phones changed our concept of privacy? Have you heard people discuss personal or sensitive issues on cell phones in public places? Should you always let callers know where you are and who might be listening?

Write three or four sentences describing the way you think people should use cell phones in public.

What Is a Sentence?

Everything that happens in life—natural occurrences, historical events, conflicts, thoughts, feelings, opinions, ideas, and experiences—is explained in sentences. A main idea is connected to an action or linked with other words to express a thought. Long before they learn to read, children talk in sentences. Unwritten languages are spoken in sentences. The sentence is basic to all human communication:

This was the noblest Roman of them all.
SHAKESPEARE

Call me Ishmael.
HERMAN MELVILLE

The ballot is stronger than the bullet.
ABRAHAM LINCOLN

I have a dream.
MARTIN LUTHER KING

Things go better with Coke.
ADVERTISING SLOGAN

A **sentence** is a group of words that contains a subject and verb and states a complete thought.

WHAT DO YOU KNOW?

Underline the subjects (main idea) and circle the verbs (action words) in each sentence.

1. Children watch too much television.
2. The House debated the bill until midnight.
3. We can't attend tonight's meeting.
4. Michael and Saleem work third shift.
5. Kim directs student plays and writes movie reviews for the college paper.
6. The faculty and the new administration rejected the budget and demanded a new audit.
7. Although suffering from flu and exhaustion, Ari won a silver medal.
8. Originally developed for use in military aircraft, this system will improve airline safety.
9. The coach, supported by angry players, demanded the referee call for a penalty.
10. France and Germany, once enemies in three wars, cooperate in industrial development.

Answers appear on the following page.

GET WRITING
AND REVISING

WHAT ARE YOU TRYING TO SAY?

Write a one-sentence response to each of the following questions:

1. What is the greatest challenge you face this semester?

_____

2. What was your favourite course in high school?

_____

3. Describe how you commute to school each day—do you walk, drive, or take public transportation?

_____

4. Why did you enroll in college?

_____

5. What would you like to be doing in five years?

_____

WHAT HAVE YOU WRITTEN?

Read each sentence aloud. Have you expressed a complete thought? Does your sentence make sense? Does it state what you were thinking, what you were trying to say?

The Working Parts of a Sentence

This chapter explains the working parts of a basic sentence. By understanding how a sentence works, you not only avoid making mistakes but create writing that is fresh, interesting, and easy to read. To understand how sentences function, it is important to understand the parts of speech—words that have special functions.

PARTS OF SPEECH

Nouns	name persons, places, things, or ideas: *teacher, attic, Italy, book, freedom*
Pronouns	take the place of nouns: *he, she, they, it, this, that, what, which, hers, their*

(continued)

Verbs	express action: *buy, sell, run, walk, create, think, feel, wonder, hope, dream* link ideas: *is, are, was, were*
Adjectives	add information about nouns or pronouns: a *red* car, a *bright* idea, a *lost* cause
Adverbs	add information about verbs: drove *recklessly,* sell *quickly, angrily* denounced add information about adjectives: *very* old teacher, *sadly* dejected leader add information about other adverbs: *rather* hesitantly remarked
Prepositions	link nouns and pronouns, expressing relationships between related words: *in* the house, *around* the corner, *between* the acts, *through* the evening
Conjunctions	link related parts of a sentence: **Coordinating conjunctions** link parts of equal value: *and, or, yet, but, so* He went to college, *and* she got a job. **Subordinating conjunctions** link dependent or less important parts: *When* he went to college, she got a job.
Interjections	express emotion or feeling that is not part of the basic sentence and are set off with commas or used with exclamation points: *Oh,* he's leaving? *Wow!*

Words can function as different parts of speech:

> I bought more *paint* [noun].
> I am going to *paint* [verb] the bedroom.
> Those supplies are stored in the *paint* [adjective] room.

Parts of speech can be single words or phrases, groups of related words that work together:

> Thandi and her entire staff [noun phrase]
> wrote and edited [verb phrase]
> throughout the night [prepositional phrase]

Subjects and Verbs

The two most important parts of any sentence are the subject and verb. The **subject** is the actor or main topic that explains what the sentence is about. Subjects, which generally appear at the beginning of the sentence, may be a single word, several words, or a phrase:

Tom works with toxic chemicals.
Tom and Anna work with toxic chemicals.
Working with toxic chemicals requires skill.

Subjects are usually **nouns** or **pronouns.**

What Are Nouns?

Nouns are names of people, places, ideas, or things:

People	Places	Ideas	Things
teacher	attic	freedom	pencil
children	mountain	tardiness	computer
banker	bank	wealth	penny
driver	car	speed	wheel

Count nouns may be singular or plural:

book	books
child	children

Spelling note: Most nouns become plural by adding an *s,* but some nouns have a plural spelling. See pages 412–414 for further information. Noncount nouns have only one form. Examples: *architecture, furniture.*

Nouns may be **common** or **proper.** Common nouns refer to general or abstract people, places, ideas, or things. Proper nouns refer to specific people, places, ideas, or things.

Common	Proper
high school	Saint John High School
city	Burnaby
teacher	Ms. Mahone
supermarket	Sobeys

Note: Proper nouns are always capitalized. See Chapter 27 for guidelines on capitalization.

ARTICLES

Indefinite articles *a* and *an* are used with singular nouns to indicate a type or kind of something:

Use *a* before a consonant sound—*a* car, *a* girl, *a* loft, *a* wagon.
Use *an* before a vowel sound—*an* apple, *an* error, *an* item, *an* oven.

The definite article *the* is used with singular or plural nouns to indicate something specific: *the* car, *the* apple, *the* girl, *the* girls.

The student borrowed *a* book.   (A specific student borrowed some book.)
A student borrowed *the* book.   (Some student borrowed a specific book.)

What Are Pronouns?

Pronouns take the place of a noun and can be the subject, object, or possessive of a sentence:

Noun	Pronoun
teacher	he *or* she
children	they
pencil	it

The types of pronouns include *personal, relative, demonstrative,* and *indefinite.*

Personal

Personal pronouns refer to people and have three forms, depending on how they are used in a sentence: *subjective, objective,* and *possessive.*

	Subjective		Objective		Possessive	
	Singular	**Plural**	**Singular**	**Plural**	**Singular**	**Plural**
1st person	I	we	me	us	my (mine)	our (ours)
2nd person	you	you	you	you	your (yours)	your (yours)
3rd person	he	they	him	them	his (his)	their (theirs)
	she		her		her (hers)	
	it		it		its (its)	

He drove *their* car to *our* house, so *we* paid *him.*
They rented a cottage because *it* was cheaper than *our* time-share.

Relative

Relative pronouns introduce noun and adjective clauses:

who, whoever, whom, whose   which, whichever   that, what, whatever

I will work with *whoever* volunteers.
Sam was levied a thousand dollar fine, *which* he refused to pay.

Demonstrative

Demonstrative pronouns indicate the noun (antecedent):

this, that, these, those

That car is a lemon.
These books are on sale.

Indefinite

Indefinite pronouns refer to abstract persons or things:

Singular				Plural	Singular or Plural		
everyone	someone	anyone	no one	both	all	more	none
everybody	somebody	anybody	nobody	many	any	most	some
everything	something	anything	nothing	few			
each	another	either	neither				

Everyone promised to come, but *no one* showed up.
Someone should do *something.*

Note: Pronouns must clearly refer to specific nouns called *antecedents* and agree or match their singular or plural form:

Incorrect

The neighbourhood is desolate. Trash litters the street. Abandoned cars jam the alleys. The lawns are choked with weeds. The shabby houses have broken windows. Their front porches are cluttered with old furniture and rubbish. *They* just don't care.

[*Whom* does *they* refer to? Politicians, landlords, tenants, housing officials?]

Revised

The neighbourhood is desolate. Trash litters the street. Abandoned cars jam the alleys. The lawns are choked with weeds. The shabby houses have broken windows. Their front porches are cluttered with old furniture and rubbish. *Slumlords* just don't care.

Incorrect

Every citizen should do *their* best.

Citizen is a singular noun.

Correct

Every citizen should do *his or her* best.
Citizens should do *their* best.

(See Chapter 22 for further information about pronouns.)

CHOOSING SUBJECTS

In some languages, a noun and subjective personal pronoun can be used together as a subject, but in English, you must choose one:

Incorrect: My *teacher she* wrote the book for our class.
Correct: My *teacher* wrote the book for our class.

or

She wrote the book for our class.

EXERCISE 1 Locating Singular and Plural Subjects

Underline the subject—the main idea—in each sentence. If the subject is plural, underline it twice. To identify the subject of the sentence, read the sentence carefully. What is the sentence about? What part is connected to an action or linked to other words?

1. The 2003 forest fires in British Columbia were a major disaster.

2. The summer of 2003 was exceptionally hot and dry.

3. By midsummer, the Kelowna area was parched.

4. British Columbia experienced an unusually high number of forest fires that year.

5. At one point, more than 800 wildfires were burning in the province.

6. Many fires, fanned by strong winds, spread throughout south and southeast Kelowna.

7. Thousands of people had to evacuate their homes.

8. A helicopter pilot was killed when he crashed while fighting the fires.

9. B.C. Premier Gordon Campbell declared a provincewide state of emergency in early August.

10. Damage to many of the province's wineries made news across Canada.

EXERCISE 2 Locating Noun and Pronoun Subjects

Underline the subject in each sentence. Use two lines if the subject is a pronoun.

1. Stephen Leacock was born in Hampshire, England, in 1869 and was the third of eleven children.

2. He immigrated to Canada with his family in 1876.

3. Leacock attended the University of Toronto, where he studied modern and classical languages and literature.

4. He exhibited so much dedication to his studies that he was able to finish two years of courses in a single year.

5. After graduating, Leacock was successful as a humorist, publishing articles in a variety of magazines.

6. Despite this success, Leacock decided to pursue a postgraduate degree in economics and political science.

7. His focus returned to literature once again, and in 1910 he published *Literary Lapses.*

8. This publication transformed Leacock into one of the most popular writers of the time.

9. He continued to write parodies and satires of Canadian life throughout his life.

10. His legacy, the "Stephen Leacock Medal for Humour," is awarded each year to a Canadian writer of humour.

Locating "Hidden Subjects"

Subjects are not always easy to spot. They don't always appear at the beginning of a sentence, and at first glance they may not look like important words. *Subjects are not possessive nouns, and they are not nouns in prepositional phrases.*

Inverted Sentences

In most sentences the subject comes before the verb:

I *bought* a new car.
Last night my father *fixed* the TV.
Every morning we *run* two miles.

In some sentences this pattern is inverted or reversed, so the subject follows the verb:

There *are* people waiting in the lobby.
At the bottom of the steps *lies* a pile of used clothing.
Behind almost every successful comic *is* an unhappy childhood.

Possessives

Many sentences contain a subject that is the object of a possessive:

Harrison's *career* suffered after being sued by her investors.
Karl's *car* needs new tires.
Last year's *models* were poorly received by the public.

The subject in each sentence appears after a possessive. The subject is not "Harrison" but "Harrison's *career*." One way to keep from being confused is to ask yourself who or what is doing the action or being linked to other ideas. What, for instance, "needs new tires"?—"Karl"? or "Karl's *car*"?

EXERCISE 3 Locating Subjects

Underline the subject in each sentence.

1. Behind expert predictions is pure guesswork.
2. The future is difficult to imagine.
3. In the nineteenth century experts feared that by 1900 much of North America would be stripped of trees.
4. The continent's demand for wood to heat homes was growing faster than the ability of forests to regenerate themselves.
5. The experts' calculations may have been correct.
6. But they failed to anticipate that oil would replace wood as an energy source in the twentieth century.
7. Some scientists' studies suggested a coming "gasoline famine."
8. The world, they predicted, would soon run out of oil reserves.
9. However, in the twentieth century, massive oil deposits were discovered in Alberta.
10. Events, scientific research, and new inventions constantly disprove the wisest expert's past predictions.

Prepositional Phrases

Prepositions are words that express relationships between ideas, usually regarding time and place:

above	before	with	across
over	during	without	to
under	after	within	toward
below	since	from	of
around	like	near	off
past	except	like	along
against	inside	outside	

Prepositions can begin phrases: *before the rehearsal, during the night, after the election, up the chimney, under the stairs, around the corner, inside the factory, outside the campus.* Prepositional phrases appear frequently in English:

After the game we walked *around the corner. In the student union,* I met everyone *on the winning team.* They walked *throughout the union* and signed autographs *during the celebration.*

The only thing you have to remember about prepositional phrases is that *the subject of a sentence will not be found in a prepositional phrase.* The subject of the first sentence is *we,* not *game,* which is part of the prepositional phrase *after the game.*

EXERCISE 4 Locating Subjects and Prepositional Phrases

Underline prepositional phrases in the following sentences. Underline the subject of the sentence twice.

1. Many people in the country think of thieves as men in black masks who rob banks or break into houses.

2. In the information age, however, many thieves use computers.

3. About five years ago a group of criminals in California developed a scheme to defraud consumers.

4. Dressed in conservative suits and presenting official-looking credentials, they convinced shopping mall owners to let them install ATMs.

5. The ATMs were dummies that were not connected to any banking network.

6. Customers who swiped their cards in the ATM and punched in their personal identification numbers received an error message.

7. The customers did not know that the rigged ATM had just recorded their account number and PIN.

8. In less than a week, the ATM collected data from fifty people.

9. After a month of complaints, the criminals apologized to the mall owners and removed their defective ATMs.

10. In a few days they stamped out plastic cards with the account numbers and used the PINs in real ATMs to loot bank accounts and max out credit cards held by the unsuspecting shoppers.

EXERCISE 5 Locating Subjects in Your Own Writing

Describe your favourite television program and explain why you like it. After you complete this description, underline the subject of each sentence.

Verbs

Verbs express action, link ideas, or help other verbs.

Action verbs show what the subject is doing:

The teacher *distributed* the test booklets.
Canada *accepted* recommendations by the World Bank.
I *bought* a new computer.

Action verbs also express "invisible" behaviour:

The teacher *hoped* students would pass the test.
Canada *contains* numerous mineral resources.
I *believe* in being optimistic.

Linking verbs connect the subject to related ideas in the sentence. Linking verbs function much like an = sign. Instead of showing action, they express a relationship between ideas:

The teacher *was* late.
Canada *is* a major timber exporter.
I *am* optimistic.

Helping verbs assist the main verb by adding information:

The teacher *will* distribute the test booklets.
Canada *should* win at least four gold medals in the Olympics.
I *could* help next week.

Verbs also tell time, explaining when the action or relationship takes place:

Past	He *drove* home in the storm.	He *was* a driver.
Present	He *drives* home every night.	He *is* a driver.
Future	He *will drive* us home tonight.	He *will be* a driver.

(See pages 323–324 for further information on verb tense.)

Verbs are either singular or plural:

Singular	He *drives* to school.	He *is* a driver.
Plural	They *drive* to school.	They *are* drivers.

Verbs must "agree with," or match, their subjects. Many subjects that look like plurals are singular:

Six days <u>is</u> not enough time.   The *jury* <u>is</u> deliberating until noon.
The *United Nations* <u>is</u> sending aid.   The *price of books* <u>is</u> increasing.

(See Chapter 20 for further information on subject–verb agreement.)

EXERCISE 6 Locating Action Verbs

Underline the action verbs in each of the following sentences.

1. In the early morning hours of August 31, 1888, a London policeman discovered the stabbed and mutilated body of Polly Nichols.
2. A week later police found the slashed body of Annie Chapman.
3. These murders in London's impoverished East End gripped the public.
4. Radicals and reformers used the murders to demand social change.
5. When two more women were murdered in a single night, political pressure mounted against the government.

6. Someone claiming to be the killer sent the press a letter, signing it Jack the Ripper.

7. On November 9, authorities discovered the slashed remains of Mary Kelly, whose heart had been cut out.

8. Then the Ripper murders mysteriously stopped.

9. Four years later the police closed the case, leaving the murders unsolved.

10. Over a century later, "Ripperologists" debate the identity of the first-known serial killer.

EXERCISE 7 Locating Linking and Helping Verbs

Underline linking verbs once and helping verbs twice.

1. Airships are aircraft lifted by lighter-than-air gases rather than engines.

2. After World War I, airships were the largest aircraft to carry passengers and freight.

3. Unlike existing airplanes, airships could carry passengers across continents and oceans.

4. Commercial airships were majestic aircraft with ornate staterooms and gourmet meal service.

5. Their reign, however, was brief.

6. By the 1930s, commercial airplanes could carry passengers faster and cheaper than massive airships.

7. Airplanes could operate from smaller fields.

8. Photographs of the dramatic crash of the *Hindenburg* in 1937 would shock the public.

9. This single accident would change aviation history.

10. Airships, however, are sparking new interest as surveillance platforms to fight terrorism and direct traffic.

EXERCISE 8 Locating Action, Linking, and Helping Verbs

If you completed Exercise 5, read through your response and circle the action verbs. Underline linking verbs once and place two lines under helping verbs.

PHRASAL VERBS

Sometimes a verb consists of more than one word. This type of verb is called a *phrasal verb*. It consists of a verb and an *adverbial particle* such as *down, on,* or *up.* The adverbial particle may explain that something is completed, as in *finish up* or *close down.* Some phrasal verbs use idioms such as "She *ran up* a huge bill" or "That old building *cries out* for repairs." The literal meaning of *ran up* or *cries out* does not explain the verb's action.

(continued)

> **PHRASAL VERBS** *(continued)*
>
> Most phrasal verbs can be separated by pronouns or short noun phrases:
>
> I *picked* Joe's uncle *up* at noon.
> I *picked* him *up* at noon.
>
> Some phrasal verbs cannot be separated:
>
> We *went over* the paper together.
>
> Standard dictionaries may not include phrasal verbs. If you cannot understand a phrasal verb in context, refer to a dictionary like the *Gage Canadian Dictionary* or the *Canadian Oxford Dictionary.*

EXERCISE 9 Locating Subjects and Verbs

Circle the subject of each sentence and underline action and linking verbs. Underline helping verbs twice.

1. The word *laser* stands for **l**ight **a**mplification by **s**timulated **e**mission of **r**adiation.

2. Lasers emit an intense narrow beam of light.

3. The beam from a flashlight diffuses in a conelike pattern.

4. In contrast, a laser beam will appear like a glowing tube.

5. Geographers and mapmakers use lasers to accurately measure distances.

6. Industrial lasers are powerful enough to cut steel.

7. Powerful laser weapons in outer space could disable satellites and disrupt television broadcasts and telephone communications.

8. No one on earth would be killed by a laser on a battlefield.

9. However, the loss of key satellites could ruin a nation's economy.

10. Whether used in peace or war, lasers are key instruments in the twenty-first century.

Building Sentences: Independent and Dependent Clauses

Sentences are made up of **clauses,** groups of related words that contain both a subject and a verb. There are two types of clauses: **dependent** and **independent.**

Dependent clauses contain a subject and verb but do *not* express a complete thought and are not sentences:

While I waited for the bus
Before we lost the game
After I moved to Orillia

Dependent clauses have to be joined to an independent clause to create a sentence that expresses a complete thought:

While I waited for the bus, it began to rain.
He thought highly of us before we lost the game.
After I moved to Orillia, I bought a new car.

Independent clauses are groups of related words with a subject and verb that express a complete thought. They are sentences:

I waited for the bus.
We lost the game.
The college cancelled night school this semester.

Every sentence contains at least one independent clause.

Sentence Length

A sentence can consist of a single word—if it expresses a complete thought:

Run!
Stop!
Go!

In giving commands, the subject "you" is implied or understood, so it does not have to actually appear in print for a sentence to state a complete thought. A long train of words, however, is not necessarily a sentence:

Because the basketball team, which includes two all-province champions, practised an additional six days this summer.

Although there is a subject ("team") and a verb ("practised"), the words do not express a complete thought. If you read the sentence aloud, it sounds incomplete, like the introduction to an idea that does not appear. It leaves us wondering what happened because the team practised six extra days. Incomplete sentences—phrases and dependent clauses—are called **fragments.**

A NOTE ON FRAGMENTS

Incomplete sentences that fail to express a complete thought are called *fragments*—a common writing error. Although sometimes written for emphasis, fragments should be avoided in college writing.
See Chapter 15 for help on avoiding fragments.

WORKING TOGETHER

Working with a group of students, revise the following paragraph to change linking verbs to action verbs.

The Student Union is the organizer of all campus events. People who are interested in using the facilities for parties, lectures, performances, or seminars must contact Mariah Bond. As Student Union coordinator, she is the person who approves all requests. She is also the editor of the Student Union newsletter.

CRITICAL THINKING

People complain about crime, pollution, taxes, racial profiling, and poverty. But in many elections half the eligible voters do not vote. Why don't more Canadians vote? What reasons do people give? Write a paragraph that explains why so many people fail to vote.

WHAT HAVE YOU WRITTEN?

Read your paragraph carefully. Circle the subjects and underline the verbs in each sentence. If you are unsure whether some of your sentences are complete, see Chapter 15.
Choose one of your sentences and write it below:

_____

Does the sentence clearly express what you were trying to say? Is the subject clearly defined? Is the verb effective? Could more concrete words or stronger verbs (see pages 202–203) improve this sentence?
Summarize your observations with one sentence. What is the main reason many Canadians don't vote?

_____

Read this sentence carefully. Circle the subject and underline the verb. How effective is your word choice (see Chapter 13)?
Does this sentence fully express your ideas? Try writing a different version:

_____

Ask a fellow student to read and comment on both sentences. Can your reader understand what you are trying to say?

WHAT HAVE YOU LEARNED?

Circle the subjects (main idea) and underline the verbs (action and linking words) in each sentence. Underline helping verbs twice.

1. Parents should monitor their children's use of the Internet.

2. Woody Allen's movies are usually set in New York.

3. The price of gasoline varies across the country.

4. Many Hollywood stars were born in Canada.

5. Parliament Hill's security systems are continually updated.

6. My parents' house is being painted.

7. *Midnight's Children* was written by Salman Rushdie.

8. The printer's toner cartridge was replaced yesterday.

9. It was published last year.

10. Bobby Orr was born in 1948.

Answers appear on page 228.

Get Writing

How much privacy should high school students have? Should school authorities be able to search backpacks for weapons or let the police search lockers for drugs?

Write three or four sentences stating your views on student privacy.

WRITING ON THE WEB

The Internet offers resources on sentence structure and style.

1. Using a search engine like AltaVista, Yahoo!, or Google, enter terms such as *sentence structure, parts of speech,* and *independent clauses* to locate current sites of interest.
2. Review e-mails you have sent. What changes would you make in your writing? What would make your sentences more effective?

POINTS TO REMEMBER

1. The sentence is the basic unit of written English.
2. Sentences contain a subject and verb and express a complete thought.
3. Subjects explain what the sentence is about.
4. Verbs express action or link the subject to other words.
5. Phrases are groups of related words that form parts of sentences.
6. Dependent clauses are groups of related words with a subject and verb but do not state a complete thought.
7. Independent clauses are groups of related words that contain a subject and verb and express a complete thought.
8. All sentences contain at least one independent clause.

ANSWERS TO WHAT HAVE YOU LEARNED? ON PAGE 226

1. subject: *parents*, verb: *should monitor*; 2. subject: *movies*, verb: *are set*; 3. subject: *price*, verb: *varies*; 4. subject: *stars*, verb: *were born*; 5. subject: *security systems*, verb: *are updated*; 6. subject: *house*, verb: *is being painted*; 7. subject: *Midnight's Children*, verb: *was written*, 8. subject: *cartridge*, verb: *was replaced*; 9. subject: *it*, verb: *was published*; 10. subject: *Bobby Orr*, verb: *was born*

Avoiding Fragments

Write three or four sentences describing your first impression of this picture. Does it represent traditional or outdated values? What does it suggest about the role of women in society? Do you see this as something desirable or irrelevant? Does it bring back happy memories?

In order to express yourself clearly, you have to write in sentences—groups of words that have a subject and a verb and express a complete thought:

I bought a new car.
Susha has to work tonight.
Should Tom and I drive you to the airport?

Each of these sentences states a complete thought and can stand on its own. They are **independent clauses.** They make sense all by themselves. Each sentence forms a pattern in which the subject—*I, Susha, Tom and I*—is connected to a verb expressing action—*bought, has to work, drive.* (See pages 214–224.)

In speaking we don't always express ourselves with complete sentences, especially when we are talking to people we know. In person, we communicate not only with words but with gestures, tone, and facial expressions. We may stop midsentence and move to the next idea when we see that people are following our train of thought. Because our communication is interactive, listeners can interrupt us with questions if they become confused:

"Going to the computer lab?"
"After lunch."
"Sure?"
"Got to."
"Really?"
"Forgot the econ project is due."
"See you later. Got to get my disks from the car."
"You drove?"
"Overslept. Missed the bus."
"Get a ride home?"
"Not leaving until four or five."
"No problem."

When we write, our readers can rely only on the text we give them. If we don't write in complete sentences, we fail to express complete thoughts:

Bought a new car.	[Who bought the new car?]
Because Susha has to work tonight.	[Then what happens?]
Should Tom and I?	[Should Tom and I do what?]

Because we often think faster than we can write, it is easy to make mistakes in expressing ideas. We skip words, shift our train of thought midsentence, and break off phrases. Instead of creating a complete statement, we leave our readers with partial sentences called **fragments:**

Last night we saw a movie. Then we went to the new coffee house. *Located by the airport.* It was crowded. *Because all new places are popular. At least for a while.*

Revised

Last night we saw a movie. Then we went to the new coffee house located by the airport. It was crowded. All new places are popular, at least for a while.

WHAT DO YOU KNOW?

Label each sentence OK for a complete sentence and F for a sentence fragment.

1. _____ Reporting they are unable to secure funds for additional construction projects.

2. _____ Take two aspirin and call me in the morning.

3. _____ Lowering automobile emissions has proven to be a challenge to scientists and engineers.

4. _____ The city council, which will fund the new playground.

5. _____ Available at any time for further consultation.

Answers appear on the following page.

What Are Fragments?

Fragments are incomplete sentences. A fragment is a sentence that is missing a key element. It sometimes lacks a subject or a complete verb.

Subject Missing
Worked all night. [Who worked *all night*?]

Revised
He worked all night. [*He* (the one performing the action) is the subject of the sentence.]

Verb Missing
Juan the new building. [What was Juan doing?]

Revised
Juan designed the new building. [*Designed* (the action word) is the verb.]

Incomplete Verb
Juan designing the new building. [-*ing* verbs cannot stand alone.]

Revised
Juan is designing the new building. [Adding *is* to the verb *designing* transforms it into a complete verb.]

or

Juan designed the new building.

A fragment may contain both a subject and a verb and yet not be a complete sentence. In order to be complete, a sentence has to make sense on its own, and it has to express a complete thought.

If one of the following words begins a sentence, that part of the sentence will be a dependent clause—it does not make sense on its own—and must be joined to an independent clause (one that makes sense on its own).

SUBORDINATORS

after	even though	until	which
although	if	what	whichever
as	in order that	whatever	while
as if	provided that	when	who
as long as	since	whenever	whom
as soon as	so that	where	whose
because	that	wherever	
before	though	whereas	
even if	unless	whether	

Incomplete Thought
Although Juan designed the building. [It has a subject and verb but fails to express a whole idea.]

Revised
Juan designed the building.

or

Although Juan designed the building, he did not receive any recognition.

The term *fragment* is misleading because it suggests something small; length actually has nothing to do with writing complete sentences. A sentence can consist of a single word:

Run!

The subject "you" is understood. Commands express complete thoughts. A long trail of words, even those with subjects and verbs, can be a fragment if it fails to state a whole idea:

Because physical activity, even moderate exercise such as walking, has been shown to lower blood pressure, reduce stress, and enhance a sense of well-being.

Although it looks like a long sentence, these words do not express a complete thought. Readers are left wondering: Because exercise is good . . . then what?

INCLUDING ALL VERBS

All parts of the verb phrase must be included to create a complete sentence. Be sure to include helping and linking verbs where needed:

Sentence needing a helping verb: The popularity of basketball $\overset{is}{\wedge}$ growing.
Sentence needing a linking verb: It $\overset{is}{\wedge}$ widespread in Latin America.

POINT TO REMEMBER

Reading aloud can help identify fragments. Ask yourself, "Does this statement express a complete thought?"

WHAT ARE YOU TRYING TO SAY?

GET WRITING
AND REVISING

Write a brief response to each question.

1. What sport do you enjoy watching the most and why?

   _____

   _____

2. What can parents do to make their children appreciate the importance of nutrition and exercise?

   _____

   _____

3. What is your opinion of reality television shows?

   _____

   _____

   _____

4. What do you admire most about your best friend?

   _____

   _____

   _____

5. How should government officials be prosecuted when funds are misappropriated?

   _____

   _____

   _____

WHAT HAVE YOU WRITTEN?

Read each of your responses aloud. Have you written complete sentences? Does each have a subject and verb? Can each sentence stand alone? Do any statements sound incomplete, like introductions to another idea? Rewrite any sentence fragments you discover.

EXERCISE 1 Identifying Fragments

Label each sentence OK *for a complete sentence and* F *for a sentence fragment.*

1. _____ When he was just twenty-one, Terry Fox lost a leg to cancer.

2. _____ Thwarted his plans of becoming a gym teacher.

3. _____ Just two years after losing his leg, Terry began his "Marathon of Hope."

4. _____ On April 12, 1980, he started his run across Canada in St. John's, Newfoundland.

5. _____ Only small crowds watching him as he ran through Atlantic Canada.

6. _____ As he got closer to Ontario, word of his achievement had begun to spread.

7. _____ Popular, and even celebrities began coming out to meet him on the road so that they could run a short distance with him.

8. _____ His health took a turn for the worse as he neared Thunder Bay.

9. _____ Discovered the cancer had spread to his lungs.

10. _____ Although Terry Fox died in 1981, the Terry Fox Foundation continues to raise millions of dollars every year.

Correcting Fragments

There are two ways of correcting fragments:

1. Turn the fragment into a complete sentence by making sure it expresses a complete thought:

   Fragments
   Memorial University being the centre for this research
   Public opinion surveys
   The mayor designated

   Revised
   Memorial University is the centre for this research. [complete verb added]
   The new study is based on public opinion surveys. [subject and verb added]
   The mayor designated Sandy Gomez to head the commission. [words added to express a complete thought]

2. Attach the fragment to a sentence to state a complete thought. (Often fragments occur when you write quickly and break off part of a sentence.)

   Fragments
   He bought a car. *While living in Regina.*
   Constructed in 1873. The old church needs major repairs.

   Revised
   He bought a car while living in Regina.
   Constructed in 1973, the old church needs major repairs.

EXERCISE 2 Identifying and Correcting Fragments

Identify and correct the fragments by adding missing words or connecting them to another sentence. Some items may be correct.

1. Throngs of people visiting Ottawa every year to celebrate the tulip festival.

   _____

   _____

2. To enjoy the millions of tulips.

   _____

   _____

3. Many don't know how the tulip festival began.

   _____

   _____

4. Tulips a gift of appreciation from Queen Juliana of the Netherlands.

   _____

   _____

5. During World War Two, the Dutch Royal Family was in exile.

   _____

   _____

6. And found refuge in Ottawa.

   _____

   _____

7. Queen Juliana was pregnant with her third child.

   _____

   _____

8. A special parliamentary law making her rooms at the Ottawa Civic Hospital "extraterritorial."

   _____

   _____

9. Allowed her daughter to be born on temporarily declared Dutch soil.

   _____

   _____

10. In appreciation of Canada's aid to her family and her country, began sending a gift of tulips every year.

    _____

    _____

EXERCISE 3 Identifying and Correcting Fragments

Identify and correct the fragments by adding missing words or connecting them to another sentence. Some items may be correct.

1. Although computers have revolutionized writing and publishing. Some historians are concerned about the effect technology will have on written records.

   _____

   _____

2. For hundreds of years, historians, biographers, and journalists have relied on written records.

   _____

   _____

3. In addition, literary scholars have been able to view various drafts of a play or poem. Allowing them to see how a writer like Ibsen or Poe worked.

   _____

   _____

4. In the future many scholars fear they will have only final copies to work with. Writers having made revisions electronically so that earlier versions were erased.

   _____

   _____

5. Journalists also wondering if computers will make it easier for political and business leaders to alter records.

   _____

   _____

6. Because technology changes quickly. Future researchers being unable to access records stored on obsolete software.

   _____

   _____

7. For instance, many records from 1960s census are stored on reel-to-reel magnetic tapes that cannot be read by today's computers.

   _____

   _____

8. Terrorists or hackers may be able to enter data banks and alter historical records.

   _____

   _____

9. On the other hand, computers and the Internet allowing today's researchers to examine documents held by libraries around the world.

   _____

   _____

10. No longer do students have to visit a library or museum to conduct research.

    _____

    _____

EXERCISE 4 Correcting Fragments

Revise the following paragraph to correct fragments.

Jim Carrey, born in Newmarket, Ontario, in 1962, the son of a frequently out-of-work performer. At fifteen, Carrey began doing standup comedy routines at Yuk-Yuk's in Toronto. Discovered his talent for celebrity impressions. In 1979, Carrey moved to Los Angeles. At the age of nineteen. He started out doing standup comedy but soon landed a role in the trendy TV show *In Living Color*. This was followed by his first starring role in a movie, *Ace Ventura: Pet Detective*. Carrey was a hit. He went on to make *Mask, Dumb and Dumber,* and *The Cable Guy*. Became famous for his ability to mould his face into cartoonish expressions. Carrey wanted to prove that he was more than a comedic actor. In 1998 starred in his first dramatic film. He portrayed the deluded main character in *The Truman Show*. However, it was for a comedic role in *Liar Liar* that he received a Golden Globe Best Actor nomination. Luckily for his fans, Carrey's career hasn't slowed down at all. Nor has he limited himself to a single genre. His comedic roles have been expansive. Including starring roles in *Me, Myself, and Irene, How the Grinch Stole Christmas, Bruce Almighty,* and *Lemony Snicket's A Series of Unfortunate Events*. Interspersed among these comedies, his more serious roles in *Man on the Moon* and *Eternal Sunshine of the Spotless Mind*. The latter wowed audiences and showed Carrey's enormous talent as a dramatic actor.

EXERCISE 5 Correcting Fragments

Revise the following paragraph to correct fragments.

Long before people could communicate using the Internet, telephones, or the telegraph. They saw the need to relay information quickly. Without electricity all messages having to be delivered by coach or runner. During the French Revolution, a young engineer proposing a signalling system to connect Paris and Lille using semaphores. Claude Chappe, who received backing from the government. Working with his brother, Claude Chappe constructed a series of towers eight to sixteen kilometres apart. The towers were equipped with two telescopes and two long wooden arms that could be set in forty-nine different positions, each signalling a letter or symbol. Letter by letter, the operator in one tower would set the wooden arms to send a message to the operator in the next tower who watched through a telescope. He would then copy the message, setting the arms on his tower to signal the next tower. Although expensive and cumbersome, the system could send a message across the countryside in hours instead of days. These windmill-like towers soon dotted the hills of Europe, connecting major cities. In Nova Scotia, the Pony Express serving much the same purpose before the advent of the telegraph.

_____

_____

_____

_____

_____

_____

_____

_____

_____

_____

_____

_____

_____

_____

_____

WORKING TOGETHER

Working with a group of students, revise this e-mail to eliminate any fragments.

National Convention, March 24—27, Edmonton, AB

This year's national convention held in Edmonton at the Argyll Plaza Hotel from March 24 to March 27. The deadline for registration is March 1. Make sure to include both your business and home addresses on the attached form. Reservations for flights and hotel rooms. Must be arranged through the convention committee to receive discounts. If you have any questions. Contact the convention office at natconv @vica.org.

CRITICAL THINKING

Living in the shadow of the United States, it is difficult for us as Canadians not to compare ourselves to the U.S. Do you think that Canada is a smaller version of the United States, or do you think that there are distinct cultural differences that set us apart from our southern neighbours? In what ways are we similar? How are we different? Do you think that people from around the world view Canadians as being "American" or not? Write a short paragraph stating your opinion.

WHAT HAVE YOU WRITTEN?

When you finish writing, identify and correct any fragments by adding missing elements or attaching the fragment to a related sentence.

1. Select one of your sentences and write it below:

   _____

   _____

2. Circle the subject and underline the verb.
3. Why does this sentence state a complete thought? What relationship is there between the subject and the verb?
4. Read the sentence aloud. Could you make the sentence more effective by replacing abstract words with concrete nouns and stronger verbs (see pages 202–203)? Try writing a different version of your sentence:

   _____

   _____

WHAT HAVE YOU LEARNED?

Label each sentence OK *for a complete sentence and* F *for a sentence fragment.*

1. _____ The computer has revolutionized the workplace.

2. _____ Move to the rear of the aircraft.

3. _____ While he was running for a seat in Parliament and condemning other candidates for being hypocrites.

4. _____ After the game, the defeated team was surprisingly upbeat.

5. _____ Caught in the glare of the headlights.

Answers appear on the following page.

WHAT HAVE YOU WRITTEN?

Review writing exercises in this book, papers written for other courses, work you did in high school, and e-mail sent to friends for fragments. Do you have a tendency to forget words or break off phrases, creating incomplete sentences? If you discover fragments or continue to make them in upcoming assignments, review this chapter. When you write, refer to page 463 in the handbook.

GET WRITING

Write a brief response to this photograph. How do your feelings about this image contrast with those about the picture on page 229? Do you find it humorous, acceptable, or offensive? Why?

Review what you have written. Could your sentences be improved by combining ideas into single sentences? Should some combined sentences be separated?

WRITING ON THE WEB

Using a search engine such as AltaVista, Yahoo!, or Google, enter the terms *sentence fragment*, *grammar*, and *sentence structure* to locate current sites of interest.

POINTS TO REMEMBER

1. Sentences contain a subject and verb and express a complete thought.
2. Sentence fragments are incomplete sentences—they lack a subject or verb or fail to express a complete thought.
3. Fragments can be used for special effect to dramatize words, re-create dialogue, or isolate a key phrase. They should be avoided in formal writing.
4. Reading a sentence aloud is the best way to detect a fragment. If a sentence sounds incomplete or like an introduction to something unstated, it is probably a fragment.
5. Fragments can be corrected in two ways:
   a. Create a complete sentence by adding missing elements.
   b. Attach the fragment to a sentence to state a complete thought.

ANSWERS TO WHAT HAVE YOU LEARNED? ON PAGES 239–240
1. OK, 2. OK, 3. F, 4. OK, 5. F

Building Sentences Using Coordination and Subordination

Immigration experiences vary widely. In 1947, so many Irish families arrived with typhoid fever that the Canadian government, fearing the "Irish Plague," quarantined immigrants on Partridge Island. Over six hundred died between May and October 1947. In the spring of 1992, Mira left her hometown of Sarajevo to vacation with her children in Croatia; her husband was to join them. Before he could, armed conflict began in Sarajevo. Mira and her children fled to Canada as refugees, leaving all of their possessions behind. Her husband followed six months later. Kirsten came to Canada from Germany as a nanny. Her plan was to improve her English and then return to school in Germany. That changed when she met Alec, a Canadian. They began dating and ultimately were married. She calls herself "the accidental immigrant."

Write a paragraph comparing your own or someone else's immigrant experience to the Partridge Island immigrants', Mira's, or Kirsten's.

We communicate in sentences—independent clauses that have a subject and verb and express a complete thought. Chapter 14 explains the working parts of a basic or *simple sentence,* a sentence with a single independent clause. However, we do not always write in simple sentences. In telling a story, describing a person, making a comparison, or stating an argument, we often *coordinate* ideas, creating sentences with more than one complete thought. We place two or three independent clauses in a single sentence to demonstrate how one idea affects another:

I took History 101 in the summer, so I will take 102 this fall.
Pasqual wanted to fly, but we insisted on taking the train.

In other cases we may *subordinate* a minor idea, reducing it to a dependent clause connected to an independent clause to create a sentence:

Because it started to rain, we cancelled the hike.
Marina's grades improved after she began using a computer.

Without coordination and subordination, writing can become a list of choppy and repetitive simple sentences:

I attended George Brown College. I worked at Mega-Tours Travel. It was only two years old. Mega-Tours was one of the most successful travel agencies in Toronto. Mega-Tours offered a wide range of travel services. It specialized in organizing adventure travel packages. I worked with Cecile Skilling. She was the daughter of the owner. She had a great personality. She was very helpful.

Joining ideas with coordination and subordination creates writing that is more interesting and easier to follow:

While I attended George Brown College, I worked at Mega-Tours Travel. Although it was only two years old, Mega-Tours was one of the most successful travel agencies in Toronto. Mega-Tours offered a wide range of travel services, but it specialized in organizing adventure travel packages. I worked with Cecile Skilling, who was the daughter of the owner. She had a great personality, and she was very helpful.

WHAT DO YOU KNOW?

Place a C *next to sentences that use coordination to join independent clauses and an* S *next to sentences that use subordination to join dependent clauses to independent clauses. Mark simple sentences—those with one independent clause—with an* X.

1. _____ Although the dealer slashed prices, the cars did not sell.

2. _____ Stock prices can be volatile, but bonds have fixed values.

3. _____ Victoria is the capital of British Columbia; St. John's is the capital of Newfoundland and Labrador.

4. _____ The Cabot Trail is one of the most picturesque and awe-inspiring routes on the East Coast.

5. _____ José rented a loft apartment in Halifax, but the rest of us stayed in Bedford.

6. _____ Don't delay; call 911 now!

7. _____ The Great Wall of China is believed to be the only structure that can be seen from the moon.

8. _____ Children don't get enough exercise; they spend too much time watching television.

9. _____ Developing new methods of detecting computer viruses will be vital to protecting our ability to communicate and process data.

10. _____ Because they cannot attract new accounts, these companies have to provide new products and services to existing customers.

Answers appear on page 246.

What Are Coordination and Subordination?

Coordination creates *compound sentences* that join independent clauses using semi-colons or commas and coordinating conjunctions (*and, or, nor, for, yet, but, so*):

The U.S. is Canada's greatest trading partner; Japan is the second.
The U.S. is Canada's greatest trading partner, and Japan is the second.

Subordination creates *complex sentences* that join independent clauses stating a complete thought with dependent clauses that add additional information or state a less important idea:

I took a cab because my car wouldn't start.
Because my car wouldn't start, I took a cab.

Note: When the dependent clause begins a sentence, it is set off with a comma.

Note: Subordination is a way of avoiding *fragments* (Chapter 15), by connecting dependent clauses to independent ones.

CHOOSING THE RIGHT CONJUNCTION

You can connect clauses with either a subordinating or a coordinating conjunction—but not both. Use one or the other:

Incorrect
Although we returned to campus early, *but* there were long lines at the bookstore.

Correct
Although we returned to campus early, there were long lines at the bookstore.

We returned to campus early, *but* there were long lines at the bookstore.

WHAT ARE YOU TRYING TO SAY?

*GET **WRITING***
AND REVISING

Write a paragraph that tells a story or relates the details of a recent decision you made. Why did you decide to enroll in college? What led you to buy a car, sell your home, select a daycare centre, start or quit a job, or join a health club?

_____

_____

_____

_____

_____

_____

_____

_____

_____

_____

_____

_____

_____

WHAT HAVE YOU WRITTEN?

Underline the independent clauses in your paragraph—groups of words that have a subject and verb and express a complete thought. Do some sentences contain more than one complete thought? Did you create any sentences that contained a dependent clause (a group of words with a subject and verb that does not state a complete thought)?

If all the sentences are single independent clauses or simple sentences, read your paragraph aloud. Would your ideas be clearer if some of these sentences were combined into a single statement?

ANSWERS TO WHAT DO YOU
KNOW? ON PAGE 244
1. S, 2. C, 3. C, 4. X, 5. C, 6. C,
7. X, 8. C, 9. X, 10. S

Types of Sentences

Just as writers make choices about using different words to express an idea, they also use different types of sentences. Sentence types are determined by the number and kind of clauses they contain.

A **simple sentence** consists of a single independent clause. A simple sentence is not necessarily short or "simple" to read. Although it may contain multiple subjects and verbs and numerous phrases set off with commas, it expresses a single thought:

> Thomas sings.
> Thomas and Elsa sing and dance at the newly opened El Morocco.
> Seeking to reenter show business, Thomas and Elsa sing and dance at the newly opened El Morocco, located near Bathurst Street and Lakeshore Blvd.

A **compound sentence** contains two or more independent clauses but no dependent clauses. You can think of compound sentences as "double" or "triple" sentences because they express two or more complete thoughts:

> Thomas studied dance at York; Elsa studied music at Humber.
> [*two independent clauses joined by a semicolon*]
> Thomas wants to stay in Toronto, but Elsa longs to move to Berlin.
> [two independent clauses joined with a comma and coordinating conjunction]

A **complex sentence** contains one independent clause and one or more dependent clauses:

> *Thomas and Elsa are studying dance and music* because they want to perform on Broadway.
> Because they want to perform on Broadway, *Thomas and Elsa are studying dance and music.*
> [*When a dependent clause begins a complex sentence, it is set off with a comma.*]

A **compound-complex sentence** contains at least two independent clauses and one or more dependent clauses:

> Thomas and Elsa perform Sinatra classics, and they often dress in forties clothing *because the El Morocco draws an older crowd.*
>
> *Because the El Morocco draws an older crowd,* Thomas and Elsa perform Sinatra classics, and they often dress in forties clothing.

The type of sentence you write should reflect your thoughts. Important ideas should be stated in simple sentences to highlight their significance. Equally important ideas can be connected in compound sentences to show cause and effect, choice, or contrast. Minor ideas can be linked to complete thoughts in complex sentences as dependent clauses.

Coordination

Coordination creates *compound sentences* by linking two or more simple sentences (independent clauses). There are two methods of joining simple sentences:

1. Use a comma [**,**] and a coordinating conjunction (*and, or, nor, for, yet, but, so*).
2. Use a semicolon [**;**].

Coordinating Conjunctions

Coordinating conjunctions join simple sentences and show the relationship between the two complete thoughts:

and	adds an idea	We flew to Amsterdam, *and* we rented a hotel room.
or	shows choice	I will get a job, *or* I will sell the car.
nor	adds an idea when the first is negative	He was not a scholar, *nor* was he a gentleman.
but	shows contrast	He studied hard, *but* he failed the test.
yet		She never studied, *yet* she got an A.
for	shows a reason	He left town, *for* he had lost his job.
so	shows cause and effect	I had a headache, *so* I left work early.

A simple diagram can demonstrate the way to use coordinating conjunctions:

Independent clause**,** *and* independent clause.
or
nor
but
yet
for
so

Note: A comma always comes before the coordinating conjunction.

In some cases no coordinating conjunction is used. Parallel independent clauses can be linked with a semicolon (see Chapter 19).

Winnipeg handles our Canadian accounts**;** Chicago handles our American ones.

The Senate supports the budget**;** the House is undecided.

Semicolons are also used to join independent clauses with adverbial conjunctions (*however, meanwhile*, etc.), which are set off with commas:

Winnipeg handles our Canadian accounts; however, Chicago handles our American ones.

The Senate supports the budget; nevertheless, the House is undecided.

Adverbial Conjunctions

Adverbial conjunctions link independent clauses, but unlike coordinating conjunctions—*and, or, nor, for, yet, but, so*—they are set off with a comma and require a semicolon:

Independent clause; *adverbial conjunction*, independent clause.

Common Adverbial Conjunctions

To Add Ideas

in addition	likewise	besides
moreover	furthermore	

She speaks French; *in addition,* she knows some Italian.
They refused to pay their bill; *furthermore,* they threatened to sue.

To Show Choice

instead	otherwise

He did not go to the library; *instead,* he used the Internet.
We sold the car; *otherwise,* we could not pay the rent.

To Show Contrast

however	nonetheless	nevertheless

We left early; *however,* we arrived two hours late.
He lost every game; *nevertheless,* he loved the tournament.

To Show Time

meanwhile	while	whenever

The company lowered prices; *meanwhile,* customers sought bargains.
He worked hard; *while* he was working, everyone else went shopping.

To Show Cause and Effect

thus	therefore	consequently
accordingly	hence	

We lost our tickets; *hence,* we had to cancel our trip.
Our sales dropped; *therefore,* our profits are down.

To Show Emphasis

indeed	in fact

The housing market is tight; *indeed,* only four houses are for sale.
He was a gifted actor; *in fact,* he was nominated for a Genie Award.

Note: You don't have to memorize all the adverbial conjunctions. Just remember you need to use a semicolon unless independent clauses are joined with *and, or, for, nor, yet, but, so.*

Note: If you fail to join two independent clauses with a comma and a coordinating conjunction or a semicolon, you create errors called *run-ons* and *comma splices.*
See Chapter 17 for strategies to spot and repair run-ons and comma splices.

EXERCISE 1 Combining Simple Sentences (Independent Clauses) Using Coordinating Conjunctions and Commas

1. Write two simple sentences joined by *and*:

   _____

   _____

2. Write two simple sentences joined by *or*:

   _____

   _____

3. Write two simple sentences joined by *but*:

   _____

   _____

4. Write two simple sentences joined by *yet*:

   _____

   _____

5. Write two simple sentences joined by *so*:

   _____

   _____

EXERCISE 2 Combining Simple Sentences (Independent Clauses) Using Coordinating Conjunctions and Commas

Combine each pair of sentences using a comma and a coordinating conjunction.

1. **Lee De Forest developed the sound-on-film technique. It revolutionized the film industry.**

   _____

   _____

2. **Now actors could talk and sing. Sound created problems.**

   _____

   _____

3. **Immigrant stars with heavy accents seemed laughable playing cowboys and cops. Their careers were ruined.**

   _____

   _____

4. A single studio orchestra now supplied the background score.
   Thousands of musicians who had played in silent theatres were unemployed.

   _____

   _____

5. Hollywood's English-language films lost foreign markets.
   Dubbing techniques had to be created.

   _____

   _____

EXERCISE 3 Combining Simple Sentences (Independent Clauses) Using Coordinating Conjunctions

Add a second independent clause using the coordinating conjunction indicated. Read the sentence aloud to make sure it makes sense.

1. The university purchased new computers, *but* _____

   _____

2. The blizzard swept up the East Coast, *and* _____

   _____

3. The company received a large government contract, *so* _____

   _____

4. You can take a bus, *or* _____

   _____

5. My uncle's store lost money for years, *yet* _____

   _____

EXERCISE 4 Combining Simple Sentences (Independent Clauses) Using Semicolons

Write a sentence joining two independent clauses with a semicolon. Make sure the statement you add is a complete sentence.

1. _____ ;

   _____

2. _____ ;

   _____

3. _____ ; therefore,

   _____

4. _____ ; however,

   _____

5. _____ ; in fact,

   _____

EXERCISE 5 Combining Simple Sentences (Independent Clauses) with Semicolons

Add a second independent clause to each sentence. Read each sentence aloud to make sure it makes sense.

1. I love watching football at Mel's; _____

   _____

2. The Mercedes was polished this morning; _____

   _____

3. The CN Tower is the tallest free-standing structure in the world; _____

   _____

4. Brazil is the largest country in South America; _____

   _____

WORKING TOGETHER

Working with a group of students, revise this paragraph to eliminate choppy sentences by creating compound sentences using coordination.

        Few Americans have heard about the Fenian invasion. Many Canadians remember the group's ill-fated attack. The potato famine of the 1840s ravaged Ireland. Millions emigrated to escape hunger and disease. Hundreds of thousands of Irish immigrated to the U.S. They struggled to build new lives in the New World. Many harboured resentment against Great Britain. They blamed Great Britain for their suffering. Tens of thousands of Irishmen fought in the American Civil War. After the war some Irish veterans wanted to use their army training to attack Britain. They did not have any method of crossing the Atlantic. They decided to attack Canada. In 1866 about eight hundred Fenian soldiers crossed the border and captured Fort Erie. They were supported by a secondary force of five thousand men. Canadian forces and American troops frustrated their plans. They were forced to withdraw. The movement staged additional raids until the 1870s. All of them proved unsuccessful.

Subordination

Subordination creates *complex* sentences by joining an independent clause with one or more dependent clauses. Dependent clauses contain a subject and verb but cannot stand alone. They are incomplete thoughts and need to be joined to an independent clause to make sense:

Dependent Clause Stating an Incomplete Thought
Because I drive to school
After we went to the game

Dependent clauses are *fragments* and should not stand alone (see Chapter 15).

Dependent Clause Linked to an Independent Clause Stating a Complete Thought
Because I drive to school, the bus strike did not affect me.
After we went to the game, we drove to Jane's for coffee.

POINTS TO REMEMBER

Place a comma after a dependent clause when it comes before an independent clause.

Because I missed the bus, I was late for school.
I was late for school because I missed the bus. [no comma needed]

USING SUBORDINATING CONJUNCTIONS IN DEPENDENT CLAUSES

Begin clauses with a subordinating conjunction rather than a preposition.

Incorrect
My mother's family moved to Canada *because of* they wanted a better life.

Correct
My mother's family moved to Canada *because* they wanted a better life.

Because is a subordinating conjunction. *Because of* is a two-word preposition that must be followed by a noun or pronoun.

The flight was delayed *because of* fog.
We were delayed *because of* him.

Subordination helps distinguish between important ideas and minor details. Without subordination, writing can be awkward and hard to follow:

I was born in Ottawa. I grew up in St. John's. My father was a professor. He took a job in Newfoundland. I was five. He retired last year. He started writing a novel.

Revised
Although I was born in Ottawa, I grew up in St. John's. My father was a professor. He took a job in Newfoundland when I was five. After he retired last year, he started writing a novel.

Dependent clauses can be placed at the beginning, within, and at the end of an independent clause. When they come first or within an independent clause, they are set off with commas:

Primary Idea	Secondary Idea
I could not attend summer school.	I could not get a loan.
I met the mayor.	I was working at city hall that summer.
The house was sold.	I rented it every summer.

Complex Sentences

I could not attend summer school *because I could not get a loan.*
While I was working at city hall that summer, I met the mayor.
The house, *which I rented every summer,* was sold.

EXERCISE 6 Combining Ideas Using Subordination

Create complex sentences by joining the dependent and independent clauses. If the dependent clause comes first, set it off with a comma.

1. **I loved skating on the canal.**
   When I lived in Ottawa.

   _____

   _____

2. **Even though it was constructed in 2001.**
   The bridge shows signs of wear and tear.

   _____

   _____

3. **Many children still delight in old-fashioned puppet shows.**
   Although people are accustomed to watching television.

   _____

   _____

   _____

   _____

4. **Ming Sun avoided her favourite restaurants.**
   When she was on a diet.

   _____

   _____

5. **Although he completed only four major plays.**
   Chekhov is considered one of the world's greatest dramatists.

   _____

   _____

   _____

   _____

EXERCISE 7 Combining Ideas Using Subordination

Create complex sentences by turning one of the simple sentences into a dependent clause and connecting it with the more important idea. You may change the wording of the clauses, but do not alter their basic meaning. Remember that dependent clauses that open or come in the middle of a sentence are set off with commas.

EX: **Many people watched Donovan Bailey win Olympic gold in 1996. Few know that he is also a successful businessman.**

Although many people watched Donovan Bailey win Olympic gold in 1996, few know

that he is also a successful businessman.

1. **Donovan Bailey was born in Manchester, Jamaica. He became one of the most inspiring sprinters in Canadian history.**

   _____

   _____

2. **Bailey immigrated to Canada with his parents and four brothers. He was thirteen years old.**

   _____

   _____

3. **After graduating from high school, Bailey went to Sheridan College. He earned a degree in economics.**

   _____

   _____

4. **Bailey was a star basketball player at Sheridan. It was for his success at track and field that he gained the most attention from his coaches and peers.**

   _____

   _____

5. **Bailey won his first major event in Sweden. He won the men's 100-metre race. He became a Canadian world champion. This was in 1995.**

   _____

   _____

6. **In 1996, he went to the Olympic Games in Atlanta. He won two gold medals. His winning time was 9.84 seconds. He was named the Canadian athlete of the year.**

   _____

   _____

7. **The following year, he challenged U.S. sprint champion Michael Johnson to a 150-metre sprint race. This was to determine who the faster runner was. The race took place at the Skydome in Toronto.**

   _____

   _____

8. **The winner earned one million dollars plus the title of World's Fastest Man. Bailey won. Johnson couldn't run the race because of a leg injury. Bailey accused him of being afraid to lose.**

   _____

   _____

9. Bailey experienced a series of injuries. He also had a serious car accident. He retired from running in 2001.

_____

_____

10. Donovan Bailey returned to his business roots. He now invests his time building his stock-brokerage company. He owns it with one of his four brothers.

_____

_____

WHAT ARE YOU TRYING TO SAY?

GET WRITING
AND REVISING

Write a simple sentence (an independent clause) that expresses a complete thought about a person, place, thing, event, or situation. Then write a dependent clause that adds additional information to the main idea. Join the two clauses to create a complex sentence. Remember to set off dependent clauses with commas when they are placed at the opening or within a sentence.

Example:

Simple sentence: *I missed the midterm exam.* _____

Dependent clause: *Because I had jury duty.* _____

Complex sentence: *I missed the midterm exam because I had jury duty.* _____

1. Simple sentence: _____

   Dependent clause: _____

   Complex sentence: _____

   _____

   _____

2. Simple sentence: _____

   Dependent clause: _____

   Complex sentence: _____

   _____

   _____

3. Simple sentence: _____

   Dependent clause: _____

   Complex sentence: _____

   _____

   _____

Read the complex sentences. Do they make sense? Should the dependent clause be placed in another part of the sentence? Should the dependent clause be made into an independent clause that stands alone as its own sentence?

EXERCISE 8 Using Coordination and Subordination

The following passage is stated in simple sentences. Revise it and create compound and complex sentences to make it more interesting and easier to read.

In 1933 the U.S. Federal Bureau of Prisons opened a new complex on Alcatraz. It is an island in San Francisco Bay. The prison was not like others. Alcatraz was designed to punish. It made no attempt to rehabilitate inmates. Prisoners were isolated in one-man cells. Mail was limited. Family visits were restricted. Newspapers were forbidden. Inmates received no news of the outside world. At first prisoners were not even allowed to speak during meals. The strict discipline proved stressful. Some inmates suffered nervous breakdowns. The prison soon got a reputation for severity. It was nicknamed "the Rock." The prison was very expensive to operate. There was no water supply on the island. Tons of water had to be shipped to Alcatraz each day. Visitors and employees had to be ferried back and forth. This was costly. By the 1960s the prison seemed outdated. In 1963 the U.S. government decided to close the facility.

After completing your draft, read it aloud. Have you reduced choppy and awkward sentences? Does your version make the essay easier to follow?

GET **THINKING**
AND **WRITING**

CRITICAL THINKING

How well do high schools prepare students for college? Do courses and teachers provide the skills and knowledge needed to succeed in higher education? Do you have any suggestions to improve schools? Use simple, compound, and complex sentences to develop a paragraph stating your views.

When you complete your paragraph, read over your work. Underline each independent clause once and each dependent clause twice. Did you create effective compound and complex sentences and punctuate them correctly? Read your sentences aloud. Are there missing words, awkward phrases, or confusing shifts that need revising?

1. Select one of the compound sentences and write it below:

_____

_____

_____

Are the independent clauses closely related? Do they belong in the same sentence? Could you subordinate one of the ideas to create a complex sentence? Try writing a complex sentence that logically reflects the relationship between the ideas:

_____

_____

_____

Does this complex sentence make sense—or does a compound sentence better express what you are trying to say?

Have you used the best method to join the two ideas? If you used a comma and coordinating conjunction, rewrite the sentence using a semicolon:

_____

_____

_____

How does this version affect meaning? Does it make sense? Why are coordinating conjunctions important?

2. Select one of your complex sentences and write it below:

_____

_____

_____

Underline the independent clause. Is it the more important idea? Does the dependent clause express only additional or less important information?

Turn the dependent clause into an independent one and create a compound sentence. Remember to use a semicolon or a comma with _and, or, nor, for, yet, but,_ or _so_ to join the two clauses:

_____

_____

_____

Does the compound sentence better express what you are trying to say, or does it appear illogical or awkward?

Write the two independent clauses as separate simple sentences:

_____

_____

_____

How does stating these ideas in two sentences alter the impact of your ideas? Does it better express what you are trying to say or only create two choppy sentences?

When you are trying to express an important or complex idea, consider writing two or more versions using simple, compound, and complex sentences. Read them aloud and select the sentences that best reflect your ideas.

GET WRITING

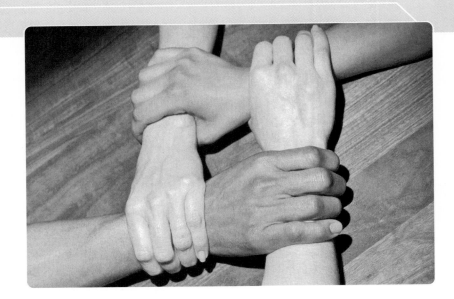

How will today's immigrants change Canadian society? What new values, cultures, insights will they represent? Do immigrants help Canadian compete in a global economy? Without immigrants, could Canada become an isolated nation?

Write a paragraph on the influence of today's immigrants. Are they different from those immigrants described on page 242?

WHAT HAVE YOU LEARNED?

Place a C next to sentences that use coordination to join independent clauses and an S next to sentences that use subordination to join dependent clauses to independent clauses. Mark simple sentences—those with one independent clause—with an X.

1. ____ Contrary to popular belief, the Reversing Falls in Saint John does not flow backward continuously; the backward flow happens only around high tide.

2. ____ Most baseballs are manufactured in Haiti.

3. ____ Gasoline was rationed during World War II to conserve the nation's limited supply of rubber tires.

4. ____ Confederation Bridge connects P.E.I. to New Brunswick, and the Wood Island Ferry runs between P.E.I. and Nova Scotia.

5. _____ The Saskatchewan Roughriders play in Regina tonight, but the Calgary Stampeders play in Montreal.

6. _____ Because new drugs can have dangerous side effects, they must be thoroughly tested.

7. _____ We moved our sales office to Trois-Rivières after we won a major provincial construction contract.

8. _____ Kazuo Ishiguro was born in Nagasaki, Japan, but he immigrated to England when he was six.

9. _____ Donald Sutherland was expelled from his Victoria College residence when he threw a sink out of the window.

10. _____ Toronto suffered a devastating SARS outbreak in 2003.

Answers appear below.

WRITING ON THE WEB

Using a search engine such as AltaVista, Yahoo!, or Google, enter terms such as *simple sentence, compound sentence, complex sentence, independent clause,* and *dependent clause* to locate current sites of interest.

POINTS TO REMEMBER

1. Simple sentences contain one independent clause and express a single complete thought.
2. Compound sentences link two or more independent clauses with a semicolon (;) or a comma (,) and a coordinating conjunction (*and, or, yet, but, so, for, nor*).
3. Complex sentences link one or more dependent clauses with a single independent clause.
4. Compound-complex sentences link one or more dependent clauses to two or more independent clauses.
5. Use compound sentences to *coordinate* ideas of equal importance.
6. Use complex sentences to link an important idea with a dependent clause adding secondary information.
7. Use sentence structure to demonstrate the relationship between your ideas.

ANSWERS TO WHAT HAVE YOU LEARNED? ON PAGES 258–259
1. C, 2. X, 3. X, 4. C, 5. C, 6. S, 7. S, 8. C, 9. S, 10. X

17

Repairing Run-ons and Comma Splices

GET WRITING

How do you communicate when you have a problem? Think of a time when you had a disagreement with your landlord, supervisor, professor, neighbour, or a government official about a problem. How did your tone, facial expressions, and gestures add meaning to your words? Did you depend on reading the other person's face to tell if he or she understood what you were trying to say?

Think of the last time you had such a conversation. Try to recapture it in a few sentences or a short paragraph. Do you find it hard to re-create the mood or feeling on paper? Why?

260

NEL

What Are Run-ons?

Run-ons are not wordy sentences that "run on" too long. **Run-ons** are incorrectly punctuated compound sentences. Chapter 16 explains how independent clauses are coordinated to create compound sentences that join two or more complete thoughts. You can think of them as "double" or "triple" sentences. Compound sentences demonstrate the relationship between closely related ideas that might be awkward or confusing if stated separately:

Keith speaks fluent Korean.   The army sent him to Germany.

Revised
Keith speaks fluent Korean, but the army sent him to Germany.
  [The coordinating conjunction *but* dramatizes the irony of a Korean
  speaker being sent to Germany.]

The city is responsible for road repairs.   The county is responsible for
                                              bridge repairs.

Revised
*The city is responsible for road repairs; the county is responsible for
bridge repairs.*
  [The semicolon links the two matching sentences as an equal pair.]

To be effective, compound sentences have to be accurately punctuated to avoid causing confusion. There are two methods of joining independent clauses:

Use a semicolon:
Independent clause**;** independent clause.

or

Use a comma with a coordinating conjunction:
Independent clause**,** *and* independent clause.

or

but

yet

so

nor

for

If you fail to use the right punctuation, you create a run-on. Run-on sentences—also called *fused sentences*—and a related error called *comma splices,* or *comma faults,* are some of the most common errors found in college writing. Because thoughts occur to us in a stream rather than a series of separate ideas, we can easily run them together in writing:

*The college is facing a financial crisis but most students don't seem to be
aware of it.* Unless the provincial legislature supports the new funding bill,
the school will have to make drastic cuts. *Faculty will be laid off student services will be cut.* Construction of the new dorms will be halted. *I can't understand why no one seems concerned about two hundred classes may be
cancelled next semester.*

Revised

The college is facing a financial crisis, but most students don't seem to be aware of it. Unless the provincial legislature supports the new funding bill, the school will have to make drastic cuts. Faculty will be laid off, and student services will be cut. Construction of the new dorms will be halted. I can't understand why no one seems concerned. About two hundred classes may be cancelled next semester.

Run-ons can be of any length. Just as fragments can be long, run-ons can be very short:

I asked no one answered.   Let's drive Jacinda knows the way.

Revised   *Revised*

I asked, but no one answered.   Let's drive; Jacinda knows the way.

POINT TO REMEMBER

Unlike fragments, there are no acceptable run-ons. Run-ons are never written for special effect. We don't speak in run-ons. We usually pause between complete thoughts or connect them with words like *and* or *but*. In writing it is important to keep complete thoughts from being confused with others. Some teachers and editors, however, will use only a comma to connect independent clauses in sentences with no other punctuation:

She can help, that's her job.   Let's go, we'll be late.

WHAT DO YOU KNOW?

Label each sentence OK *for correct or* RO *for run-on.*

1. _____ Jazz originated in New Orleans but Chicago played an important part in its history.

2. _____ Hypertension is called a silent killer many people have no symptoms until they suffer a heart attack.

3. _____ Although he was born of French parents in a small village in Nigeria and spoke no English until he was eight years old, Jakob felt right at home in Regina.

4. _____ The car won't start the battery cables are corroded.

5. _____ The students were eager to help the flood victims, who needed food, shelter, and dry clothes.

   Answers appear on the following page.

GET WRITING AND REVISING

WHAT ARE YOU TRYING TO SAY?

Write a brief narrative about a recent important event. Explain who was involved. Describe what happened and why it happened. Try to create compound sentences to show cause and effect, contrast, or choice.

Example:

Last week, in the middle of the day, two men tried to steal a car out of a driveway. They managed to break into the car and to get it started without anyone noticing them; however, in their hurry to get away undetected, they didn't notice another car pull into the driveway behind them. They were so surprised by the resulting crash that they jumped out of the car while it was still in reverse and ran away. Luckily for the police, one of the would-be thieves dropped his wallet in his haste and was arrested a few hours later.

_____

_____

_____

_____

_____

_____

_____

_____

WHAT HAVE YOU WRITTEN?

Read your draft carefully. Have you created any compound sentences—sentences that contain two independent clauses, two complete thoughts? Are the compound sentences properly punctuated? Do you join the independent clauses with semicolons or with commas and coordinating conjunctions (and, or, yet, but, so, for, nor)?

Run-ons: Fused Sentences and Comma Splices

Some writing teachers use the term *run-on* to refer to all errors in compound sentences, while others break these errors into two types: fused sentences and comma splices.

Fused Sentences

Fused sentences lack the punctuation needed to join two independent clauses. The two independent clauses are *fused,* or joined, without a comma or semicolon:

Travis entered the contest he won first prize.

ANSWERS TO WHAT DO YOU KNOW? ON PAGE 262
1. RO (comma needed after *New Orleans*), 2. RO (semicolon needed after *killer*), 3. OK, 4. RO (comma + *and* needed after *start*), 5. OK

Revised

Travis entered the contest, and he won first prize.

or

Travis entered the contest; he won first prize.

Jolene speaks Spanish but she has trouble reading it.

Revised

Jolene speaks Spanish, but she has trouble reading it.

or

Although Jolene speaks Spanish, she has trouble reading it.

Comma Splices

Comma splices are compound sentences where a comma is used instead of a semicolon:

My sister lives in Iqaluit, my brother lives in Lethbridge.

Revised

My sister lives in Iqaluit; my brother lives in Lethbridge.

The lake is frozen solid, it is safe to drive on.

Revised

The lake is frozen solid; it is safe to drive on.

Identifying Run-ons

To identify run-ons, do two things:

1. Read the sentence carefully. Determine if it is a compound sentence. Ask yourself if you can divide the sentence into two or more independent clauses (simple sentences).

   Sam entered college but dropped out after six months.

   Sam entered college . . . [independent clause (simple sentence)] dropped out after six months . . . [not a sentence]

   [not a compound sentence]

   Nathalia graduated in May but she signed up for summer courses.

   Nathalia graduated in May . . . [independent clause (simple sentence)] she signed up for summer courses . . . [independent clause (simple sentence)]

   [compound sentence]

2. If you have two or more independent clauses, determine if they should be joined. Is there a logical relationship between them? What is the best way of connecting them? Independent clauses can be joined with a comma and *and, or, nor, for, yet, but, so,* or with a semicolon.

   Nathalia graduated in May, but she signed up for summer courses.

   But indicates a logical contrast between two ideas. Inserting the missing comma quickly repairs this run-on.

EXERCISE 1 Identifying Run-ons: Comma Splices and Fused Sentences

Label each item OK *for correct,* CS *for comma splice, or* F *for fused sentence. If your instructor prefers, you can label any error* RO *for run-on.*

1. _____ Tuberculosis, or TB, is a serious infectious disease that primarily affects the lungs, though other organs may be involved.

2. _____ Unlike AIDS, TB can be spread by indirect contact, a patient's sneeze can disperse infectious droplets to others.

3. _____ The TB bacillus is very hardy and can survive outside the body for months, a person's clothing and bedding can be sources of transmission.

4. _____ The first symptoms resemble those of a bad cold people suffer coughing, fever, and fatigue.

5. _____ TB patients may linger for years as the disease slowly robs them of breath eventually they die of exhaustion, lung hemorrhages, or secondary infections.

6. _____ Although the disease was known in the ancient world, it did not become a major killer until the nineteenth century.

7. _____ TB spread rapidly in the crowded industrial cities of Europe and North America, millions became infected.

8. _____ For centuries doctors had no effective treatment; they could only prescribe bed rest and fresh air.

9. _____ In the 1940s new drugs were discovered they effectively treated TB and prevented it from spreading.

10. _____ By the 1980s TB seemed like a disease of the past but a new drug-resistant form has recently been discovered and it nearly always proves fatal.

EXERCISE 2 Identifying Run-ons: Comma Splices and Fused Sentences

Underline the comma splices and fused sentences in the following paragraph. If your instructor prefers, you can indicate fused sentences by underlining them twice.

Today's college students are accustomed to using notebook computers they are smaller and lighter than the portable typewriters of earlier generations. These slim models bear no relation to their ancestors. The first generation of computers were massive contraptions they filled entire rooms. They used thousands of vacuum tubes, which tended to burn out quickly. To keep the computers running, people had to run up and down aisles, they pushed shopping carts full of replacement tubes. Because of their size, computers had limited military value. None could fit into an airplane, but during World War II some ships featured computers that weighed several tons. Early computers were expensive to operate only the government could afford to use them to make calculations. One expert thought that the United States would need only three computers. No one in the early 1950s could imagine that one day millions of North Americans would own personal computers.

Repairing Run-ons: Minor Repairs

A fused sentence or comma splice may need only a minor repair. Sometimes in writing quickly we mistakenly use a comma when a semicolon is needed:

> The Senate likes the finance minister's budget, the House still has questions.

> *Revised*
> The Senate likes the finance minister's budget; the House still has questions.

In other cases we may forget a comma or drop one of the coordinating conjunctions:

> The Senate likes the finance minister's budget but the House still has questions.

> Senators approve of the budget, they want to meet with the finance minister's staff.

> *Revised*
> The Senate likes the finance minister's budget, but the House still has questions.

> Senators approve of the budget, and they want to meet with the finance minister's staff.

Critical Thinking: Run-ons Needing Major Repairs

In other cases run-ons require more extensive repairs. Sometimes we create run-ons when our ideas are not clearly stated or fully thought out:

> Chrétien was prime minister during the 1995 referendum and a majority of Quebecois voted to remain part of Canada.

Adding the needed comma eliminates a mechanical error but leaves the sentence cumbersome and unclear:

> Chrétien was prime minister during the 1995 referendum, and a majority of Quebecois voted to remain part of Canada.

Repairing this kind of run-on requires critical thinking. A compound sentence joins two complete thoughts, and there should be a clear relationship between them. It may be better to revise the entire sentence, changing it from a compound to a complex sentence:

> *Revised*
> Chrétien was prime minister during the 1995 referendum when a majority of Quebecois voted to remain part of Canada.

In some instances you may find it easier to break the run-on into two simple sentences, especially if there is no strong relationship between the main ideas:

> Swansea is a port city in Wales that was severely bombed in World War II and Dylan Thomas was born there in 1914.

> *Revised*
> Swansea is a port city in Wales that was severely bombed in World War II. Dylan Thomas was born there in 1914.

POINT TO REMEMBER

A compound sentence should be used to join independent clauses that state ideas of equal importance. Avoid using an independent clause to state a minor detail that could be contained in a dependent clause or a phrase:

Awkward
My brother lives in Yellowknife, and he is an architect.

Revised
My brother, who lives in Yellowknife, is an architect.
My brother in Yellowknife is an architect.

Methods of Repairing Run-ons

There are a number of methods for repairing run-ons.

1. Put a period between the sentences.

Sometimes in first drafts we connect ideas that have no logical relationship:
John graduated in 2005, and the football team had a winning season.

Revised
John graduated in 2005. The football team had a winning season.

Even if the two sentences are closely related, your thoughts might be clearer if they were stated in two simple sentences. Blending two sentences into one can weaken the impact of an idea you may want to stress:

The alderman asked for emergency aid, and the mayor refused.

Revised
The alderman asked for emergency aid. The mayor refused.

2. Insert a semicolon between the sentences to show a balanced relationship between closely related statements:

Fredericton is the capital of New Brunswick; Charlottetown is the capital of Prince Edward Island.
Employees want more benefits; shareholders want more dividends.

3. Connect the sentences with a comma and *and, or, nor, for, yet, but,* or *so* to show a logical relationship between them:

I am tired, *so* I am going home.	[indicates one idea causes another]
I am tired, for I have worked a lot of overtime.	[indicates one idea causes another]
I am tired, *but* I will work overtime.	[shows unexpected contrast between ideas]
I am tired, *yet* I will work harder.	
I am tired, *and* I feel very weak.	[adds two similar ideas]

| I will take a nap, *or* I will go home early. | [indicates one of two alternatives] |
| I am not tired, *nor* am I bored. | [indicates relationship between two negatives] |

4. Rewrite the run-on, making it a simple or complex sentence to reduce wordiness or show a clearer relationship between ideas:

Hector developed a computer program and he later sold it to Microsoft.

Jennifer moved to Vancouver to live with her brother while she went to law school she wanted to save money.

Revised

Hector developed a computer program he later sold to Microsoft.

[simple sentence]

Jennifer moved to Vancouver to live with her brother while she attended law school because she wanted to save money.

[complex sentence]

POINTS TO REMEMBER

Often in revising a paper, you may wonder, "Should this comma be a semicolon?" To determine which mark of punctuation is correct, apply this simple test:

1. Read the sentence aloud. Ask yourself if you can divide the sentence into independent clauses (simple sentences that can stand alone).
2. Where the independent clauses are joined, you should see a semicolon or a comma with *and, or, nor, for, yet, but,* or *so.*
3. If *and, or, nor, for, yet, but,* or *so* are missing, the comma should be a semicolon.

Remember, a semicolon is a period over a comma—it signals that you are connecting two complete sentences.

WORKING TOGETHER

Working with a group of students, correct the fused sentences by using each method identified below. Have each member provide four solutions, then share your responses. Determine who came up with the most logical, easy-to-read sentence.

1. The community centre is unable to maintain its current services the cost of a new roof demanded by provincial inspectors will bankrupt the organization.

Two simple sentences:

_____

_____

Two types of compound sentences:

_____

_____

One complex sentence:

_____

_____

2. The FDA will license this new headache remedy doctors believe it will be a major breakthrough in treating migraines.

Two simple sentences:

_____

_____

Two types of compound sentences:

_____

_____

One complex sentence:

_____

_____

3. Computers and fax machines have increased demand for phone lines new area codes have been introduced in many cities.

Two simple sentences:

_____

_____

Two types of compound sentences:

_____

_____

One complex sentence:

_____

_____

EXERCISE 3 Correcting Run-ons: Fused Sentences

Correct each fused sentence using each method. Notice the impact each correction has. When you finish each item, circle the revision you think is most effective.

1. Cyberspace has created virtual communities criminals lurk in these electronic neighbourhoods.

    a. Place a period between the two main ideas, making two sentences.

    _____

    _____

    b. Connect the main ideas using a comma with *and, or, nor, for, yet, but,* or *so.*

    _____

    _____

    c. Connect the main ideas with a semicolon.

    _____

    _____

    d. Revise the sentence, making it either simple or complex.

    _____

    _____

2. Her novel was a great success the movie was a major disappointment and financial disaster.

    a. Place a period between the two main ideas, making two sentences.

    _____

    _____

    b. Connect the main ideas using a comma with *and, or, nor, for, yet, but,* or *so.*

    _____

    _____

    c. Connect the main ideas with a semicolon.

    _____

    _____

    d. Revise the sentence, making it either simple or complex.

    _____

    _____

3. Arctic scientists have to be inventive their environment's cold temperatures require special scientific techniques.

    a. Place a period between the two main ideas, making two sentences.

    _____

    _____

    b. Connect the main ideas using a comma with *and, or, nor, for, yet, but,* or, *so.*

    _____

    _____

    c. Connect the main ideas with a semicolon.

    _____

    _____

d. Revise the sentence, making it either simple or complex.

_____

_____

EXERCISE 4 Correcting Run-ons: Fused Sentences

Rewrite the fused sentences, creating correctly punctuated compound, complex, or simple sentences.

1. Television sets went on sale in the late 1930s they cost almost as much as new cars.

   _____

   _____

2. The picture tubes were long and they had to be placed vertically.

   _____

   _____

3. No one could see the screen facing the ceiling viewers used a tilted mirror.

   _____

   _____

4. Television stations broadcast only a few hours a week their programming was dull and unimaginative.

   _____

   _____

5. World War II began in 1939 and civilian broadcasting was terminated until 1945.

   _____

   _____

EXERCISE 5 Repairing Comma Splices and Fused Sentences with Commas and Semicolons

Revise each of the following sentences to correct run-ons by inserting commas and semicolons.

1. Recovering alcoholics sometimes call themselves Friends of Bill W. he was a founder of Alcoholics Anonymous.

2. Bill Wilson was not a doctor or a therapist he was a stockbroker and alcoholic.

3. He tried to remain sober and focus on rebuilding his career but the temptation to drink often overwhelmed him.

4. On a business trip in Ohio, Wilson had a sudden inspiration in later years it would change the lives of millions.

5. To keep himself from drinking he knew he needed to talk to someone and he began calling churches listed in a hotel directory.

6. He talked to several ministers he did not ask them for guidance but for the name of a local alcoholic.

7. Wilson was put in touch with Dr. Robert Smith he was a prominent physician whose life and career had been nearly destroyed by drinking.

8. As Wilson and Dr. Smith talked, they made an important discovery although they were strangers, they had much in common.

9. They shared the guilt about broken promises to their wives they knew how alcohol affected their judgment, their character, and their health.

10. Both men sensed they had learned something important only an alcoholic could help another alcoholic and this meeting led to the founding of Alcoholics Anonymous.

EXERCISE 6 Repairing Comma Splices and Fused Sentences

Rewrite the following passage, correcting comma splices and fused sentences.

"Kanadian Korner," also known as "The Great White North" was one of the strangest series of skits ever made but it served a purpose. On September 19, 1980, the first skit aired in the final minutes of the CBC series *SCTV,* featuring Rick Moranis and Dave Thomas as beer guzzling Canadian brothers Bob and Doug McKenzie, it was an instant success.

Many people don't know the reason behind the development of this offbeat yet cultishly successful part of the *SCTV* series. CBC demanded that *SCTV* include more Canadian content on the show Moranis and Thomas balked at being told what to include in the show. In an attempt to illuminate what they considered the ridiculousness of the request, they asked if they should wear toques and parkas and lounge in front of a map of Canada while guzzling beer. To their surprise, CBC loved the idea and Bob and Doug McKenzie were born.

The McKenzie brothers and their oddly endearing behaviour, expressions (*Good day, eh*), and theme "song" ("Ka-roo-koo-koo-a-koo-koo-koo") were such a hit that "Kanadian Korner" became a mainstay on *SCTV,* wrapping up the show every week. As the credits rolled, Bob and Doug discussed such illuminating topics as back bacon, snow chains, and disco music Canadian viewers couldn't get enough of this mockery of Canadians by Canadians.

Capitalizing on the popularity of the skits, Moranis and Thomas decided to take the McKenzie brothers beyond television in 1981, they recorded the album *Great White North,* which comprised seventeen of their best skits, including their own take on the "Twelve Days of Christmas." Their debut on the big screen followed in 1983 with the release of the feature film *Strange Brew.*

Rick Moranis and Dave Thomas left *SCTV* at the end of the third season to pursue film careers. Numerous successful movies later, both actors remain famous for thumbing their noses at Canadian content rules while creating two of TV's most offbeat characters.

WORKING TOGETHER

Working with a group of students, revise this e-mail to eliminate fused sentences and comma splices.

Attention all students and faculty:

Recent environmental tests have revealed unacceptable air quality in several buildings Fischer Hall will be closed March 1. Renovations are expected to take one month classes will be relocated. English classes meeting in Fischer Hall will be held in the Lévesque Theatre building on 9th Street, all other liberal arts classes will meet in the Women's Centre. The college website lists all room changes maps include new parking instructions.

CRITICAL THINKING

Many corporations use hidden surveillance cameras to monitor employees. How would you feel if you learned that your workstation was being videotaped? Have you ever heard of this happening to anyone? How did that person respond? Do you think companies should be allowed to review their employees' behaviour? If you owned a business, would you feel you had the right to see if your employees were doing their jobs, treating customers with respect, and following government regulations? Select one of these questions and write a response that clearly states your views.

GET THINKING AND WRITING

WHAT HAVE YOU WRITTEN?

Read your response carefully and underline the compound sentences—those containing two or more independent clauses. Did you avoid run-ons? Did you join the independent clauses with a semicolon or a comma with and, or, nor, for, yet, but, so?

Select one of your compound sentences and write it out below:

_____

_____

1. Why did you place more than one complete idea in this sentence? Are the independent clauses logically related? Does your compound sentence link ideas of equal importance, show cause and effect, demonstrate a choice, or highlight a contrast? Could you improve the impact of your sentence by using a different coordinating conjunction?

2. If the ideas are not of equal importance, would it be better to subordinate one of them?

   Unequal
   My cousin lives in Waterloo, and he won a Governor General's Literary Award.

Revised
My cousin, who lives in Waterloo, won a Governor General's Literary Award.

Select a simple sentence—a single independent clause—and write it out below:

_____

Think about the main idea you were trying to express, and write another sentence about the same topic:

_____

3. Read the two sentences. Should these ideas remain in separate sentences, or would it be more effective to join them in a compound sentence to demonstrate their relationship?

When you are trying to express an important or complex idea, consider writing two or more versions using simple, compound, and complex sentences. Read them aloud and select the sentences that best reflect your ideas.

GET WRITING

Do you find writing different from talking? Have you found it harder to write an e-mail to a friend than talking on the phone? Why is choosing the right word more important in writing than speaking?

Write a paragraph describing the main differences between speaking and writing a message.

WHAT HAVE YOU LEARNED?

Label each sentence OK *for correct or* RO *for run-on.*

1. _____ After working for years in the coal mines, many miners reported unexplained health problems.

2. _____ Saudi Arabia is rich in oil but it lacks water.

3. _____ Dimitry completed law school and is prepared to take the bar exam this month.

4. _____ Alistair Court bought a boat in North Rustico and began a deep sea fishing business.

5. _____ Parents rushed to see the coach they wanted to congratulate her for winning the championship.

   Answers appear below.

WRITING ON THE WEB

Using a search engine such as AltaVista, Yahoo!, or Google, enter terms such as *run-on, comma splice, comma fault, compound sentence, complex sentence,* and *sentence types* to locate current sites of interest.

POINTS TO REMEMBER

1. Run-ons are common writing errors.
2. A run-on is an incorrectly punctuated compound sentence.
3. Compound sentences join two or more related independent clauses using semicolons or commas with *and, or, nor, for, yet, but,* or *so.*
4. Run-ons can be corrected in two ways:
   a. If the sentence makes sense when you read it aloud, and the independent clauses are related, add the missing words or punctuation:

   Independent clause; *independent clause.*
   or
   Independent clause, and *independent clause.*
   or
   nor
   for
   yet
   but
   so

   b. If the sentence does not make sense, reword it or break it into separate simple or complex sentences.

ANSWERS TO WHAT HAVE YOU LEARNED? ON PAGE 275
1. OK, 2. RO (see page 267), 3. OK, 4. OK, 5. RO (see page 267).

18

Correcting Misplaced and Dangling Modifiers

How hard is it for people to work together, to keep a common goal and stay motivated? Have you ever been part of or witnessed a group at work or a team that failed to keep its goal in mind? Have you noticed that some people can compromise and work with others and other people can't?

Write a paragraph about an experience you or someone you know had working with others. Why did the group succeed or fail?

What Are Modifiers?

Modifiers describe words and phrases. Whether they are adjectives (*hot, green, new, stolen, creative*), adverbs (*hotly, creatively, slightly, deeply*), or participial phrases (*driving to school, leading the team to victory, playing his mother's violin*), they must be clearly linked to what they modify. Changing the position of a modifier in a sentence alters the meaning:

Sentence	Meaning
Only Tom ordered tea for lunch.	Tom was the one person to order tea.
Tom ordered *only* tea for lunch.	Tom ordered tea and nothing else.
Tom ordered tea *only* for lunch.	Tom ordered tea for lunch but not for other meals.

Misplaced Modifiers

Misplaced Modifiers can occur anywhere in a sentence. Because they are often not set off by commas, they can be harder to detect:

Misplaced Modifier
I saw the quarterback who threw two touchdown passes in the post office yesterday.

Correct
Yesterday at the post office, I saw the quarterback who threw two touchdown passes.

Misplaced Modifier
The film won an Academy Award, which cost less than a million dollars to produce.

Correct
The film, which cost less than a million dollars to produce, won an Academy Award.

Reading sentences aloud can help you detect misplaced modifiers, but even this may not help you avoid some of them. Because the ideas are clear in your mind, you may have a hard time recognizing the confusion your sentence creates. You know that you saw the quarterback in the post office, not that he threw two touchdown passes in the post office. You know that it was the film, not the award, that cost less than a million dollars. Readers, however, rely on the way your words appear on the page.

Dangling Modifiers

A **dangling modifier** is a modifier attached to the beginning or end of a sentence and not clearly linked to what it is supposed to describe:

Dangling Modifier
Running a red light, two children   [Who ran the red light—two children?]
were hit by a cab.

Correct
Running a red light, a cab hit two children.

Dangling Modifier

I cancelled my trip, having caught   [Who caught a bad cold—my trip?]
a bad cold.

Correct

Having caught a bad cold, I cancelled my trip.

WHAT DO YOU KNOW?

Put an X *next to each sentence with a misplaced or dangling modifier and* OK *next to each correct sentence.*

1. _____ Rowing across the lake, a pale moon rose over the mountains.

2. _____ First sold in the late 1930s, televisions did not become popular until the 1950s.

3. _____ Sir Wilfred Laurier became the first French Canadian prime minister elected in 1896.

4. _____ Basing his film on the life of William Randolph Hearst, Orson Welles's *Citizen Kane* became a classic.

5. _____ Faced with declining sales, many car companies in the 1970s laid off workers, closed plants, and borrowed heavily.

6. _____ Last night I sat up looking at my old yearbooks and drinking tea, which filled me with nostalgia.

7. _____ I saw the man who won the Boston Marathon in the airport last week.

8. _____ We missed the bus, so we had to take the car to the game with bad tires.

9. _____ She stayed at the King Edward, one of the most famous hotels in Toronto.

10. _____ Painted by Picasso in the 1920s, the auctioneer was disappointed so few people bid on the portrait.

Answers appear on the following page.

GET WRITING
AND REVISING

WHAT ARE YOU TRYING TO SAY?

Write a paragraph describing someone who influenced your values or shaped your direction in life—a family member, a friend, a boss, a teacher, a coach. Provide adjectives that describe this person's characteristics and adverbs to describe this person's actions.

_____

_____

_____

_____

_____

_____

_____

_____

_____

_____

_____

_____

_____

_____

_____

_____

_____

_____

WHAT HAVE YOU WRITTEN?

Circle each modifying word or phrase and underline the word or words it describes. Are they clearly linked? Are any sentences confusing? Could any sentences be interpreted in different ways? Could your modifiers be located closer to what they describe?

EXERCISE 1 Detecting Misplaced Modifiers

Write OK *for each correct sentence and* MM *for sentences containing a misplaced modifier.*

1. _____ One of the ideals of the Olympic Games is fostering peace through international athletic competition free of politics and ideology.

2. _____ The games, however, could not be fully shielded from world events, which often led to protests and cancellations.

3. _____ The first modern Olympics were held in Greece, where the ancient games were held in 1896.

ANSWERS TO WHAT DO YOU KNOW? ON PAGE 278
1. X (the moon did not row), 2. OK, 3. X (*elected in 1896* modifies *Laurier,* not *French Canadian prime minister*), 4. X (*Basing his film* has to modify Welles, not *Citizen Kane*), 5. OK, 6. X (yearbooks, not tea, caused nostalgia), 7. X (the runner did not win a marathon *in the airport*), 8. X (the car, not the game, had *bad tires*), 9. OK, 10. X (the auctioneer was not *painted by Picasso*)

4. _____ World War I cancelled the 1916 games, which claimed the lives of an entire generation of young athletes.

5. _____ The Olympic Games resumed after the war made more popular by the advent of radio and motion pictures.

6. _____ The 1932 games were held in Los Angeles, which desperately needed economic stimulation during the Depression.

7. _____ Hitler used the 1936 Berlin games to showcase his nation's achievements, eager to impress foreign visitors.

8. _____ In Berlin the Germans constructed a massive new stadium Hitler hoped to make the most impressive capital city in the world.

9. _____ The Nazis removed anti-Jewish signs that might temporarily offend foreign visitors.

10. _____ Hitler could not avoid controversy although attempting to be a gracious host.

11. _____ He was accused of shunning black athletes who refused to shake hands with the winners.

12. _____ The Nazi Olympics troubled many observers, who felt the games were exploited for propaganda purposes.

13. _____ Hitler's invasion of Poland started World War II and caused the cancellation of the Olympic Games three years later.

14. _____ The games flourished after the war still shadowed by politics and controversy.

15. _____ During the 1968 games in Mexico City two African American athletes raised their fists during an awards ceremony seen as a celebration of black power.

16. _____ Many Mexican students were beaten and shot by police seeking to use the games to bring attention to their antigovernment protests.

17. _____ Eleven Israeli athletes were murdered by Arab terrorists at the 1972 Munich games watched by millions around the world.

18. _____ U.S. President Jimmy Carter pulled the United States out of the Moscow Olympics to protest the Soviet invasion of Afghanistan in 1980.

19. _____ Four years later when the games were held in Los Angeles, the Soviets, citing security reasons, refused to send athletes.

20. _____ In recent years, members of the International Olympic Committee have been accused of taking bribes from representatives of cities hoping to host future games.

EXERCISE 2 Correcting Misplaced Modifiers

Rewrite each of the following sentences to eliminate misplaced modifiers. Add needed words or phrases, but do not alter the basic meaning of the sentence.

1. The mayor tried to calm the anxious crowd speaking on television.

   _____

   _____

2. The paramedics who were badly injured rushed accident victims to the hospital.

   _____

   _____

3. The tourists requested Paris attorneys, unfamiliar with French law.

   _____

   _____

4. The judge ordered psychiatric counselling for the defendant who feared the young woman might attempt suicide.

   _____

   _____

5. We served lamb chops to our guests covered in mint sauce.

   _____

   _____

Avoiding Dangling Modifiers

We frequently start or end sentences with modifying words, phrases, or clauses:

Constructed entirely of plastic . . .
First described by Italian explorers . . .
Available in three colours . . .

These modifiers make sense only if they are correctly linked with what they are supposed to modify:

Constructed entirely of plastic, the valve we use weighs less than 180 grams.
Tourists are amazed by the volcano, *first described by Italian explorers.*
Available in three colours, these raincoats are popular with children.

In writing, however, it is easy to create sentences that are confusing or illogical:

Constructed entirely of plastic, we use a valve that weighs less than 180 grams.
The volcano amazes tourists, *first described by Italian explorers.*
Available in three colours, children love these raincoats.

Because the ideas are clear in your mind, even reading your sentences aloud may not help you spot a dangling modifier. Keep this simple diagram in mind:

Modifier, main sentence

Think of the comma as a hook or hinge that links the modifier with what it describes:

> One of the most popular sports cars is <u>the Corvette</u>, *introduced in 1953*.
> *Located near the airport*, <u>the hotel</u> is convenient for conventioneers.

The comma links *introduced in 1953* with *Corvette* and *located near the airport* with *the hotel*.

TESTING FOR DANGLING MODIFIERS

Dangling modifiers can be easily missed in routine editing. When you find a sentence that opens or ends with a modifier, apply this simple test:

1. Read the sentence, then turn the modifier into a question, asking who or what is being described?

   <u>Question</u>, <u>Answer</u>

2. The answer to the question follows the comma. If the answer makes sense, the sentence is probably correct. If the answer does not make sense, the sentence likely contains a dangling modifier and requires revision.

Examples:

Running across the street, I was almost hit by a car.
Question: *Who ran across the street?*   Answer: *I*
                          correct

Having run marathons, the five-kilometre race was no challenge.
Question: *Who has run marathons?*   Answer: *the five-kilometre race*
                 incorrect and needs revision
Having run marathons, I found the five-kilometre race no challenge.

EXERCISE 3 Detecting Dangling Modifiers

Write OK *for each correct sentence and* DM *to indicate those with dangling modifiers.*

1. _____ Many Canadian students assume that slavery never existed in Canada, having read *Uncle Tom's Cabin*.

2. _____ Heavily dependent on cheap, skilled labourers to help build cities such as Halifax, slaves were frequently resold in the American Colonies when they were no longer needed.

3. _____ In return for their allegiance during the War of Independence, slaves were promised free land in Canada.

4. _____ Arriving in Canada to claim their land, plots were found to be rocky and difficult to farm.

5. _____ In contrast to Canada, slavery was a feature of Brazilian society for three centuries.

6. _____ Having received more slaves from Africa than any other nation, slave labour was an important element of the Brazilian economy.

7. _____ As in Canada, slavery was eliminated by the Brazilians without a war.

8. _____ Forced to work in very dangerous conditions, slaves in Brazil had a very high death rate.

9. _____ Relying on fresh shipments of slaves from Africa, Brazil faced a crisis when the international slave trade was abolished in 1850.

10. _____ Confronted with increasing labour shortages, slaves were shipped from one region of Brazil to another.

11. _____ Inspired in part by Canada's abolition of slavery in 1834, slavery was opposed by many Brazilians.

12. _____ Brazilian abolitionists wanted to free the slaves, demanding reform.

13. _____ Needing slave labour, emancipation was blocked by the nation's wealthy coffee growers.

14. _____ Although resisted by many slave owners, the Brazilian government took steps to eradicate slavery.

15. _____ As in Canada, the abolishment of slavery was forwarded by a strong anti-slavery movement.

16. _____ Seeking to dismantle slavery in stages, children born to slaves after 1871 were declared free.

17. _____ Many coffee growers rebelled against the federal government, hoping to preserve slavery.

18. _____ Although it claimed several thousand lives, the conflict to end slavery in Brazil was finally successful.

19. _____ Having depended on slave labour to harvest coffee beans, the Brazilian economy feared a labour shortage would damage its economy.

20. _____ Benefiting from the world's increasing demand for rubber, the Brazilian economy was able to flourish despite the loss of slave labour.

EXERCISE 4 Detecting Dangling Modifiers

Write OK _for each correct sentence and_ DM _to indicate those with dangling modifiers._

1. _____ David Suzuki has become one of the most popular scientists in Canada, born in Vancouver in 1936.

2. _____ Interned in a B.C. camp during World War Two, Suzuki and his parents found their rights as Canadian citizens snatched away.

3. _____ Migrating east after the war, Suzuki relocated to London, Ontario, where he went to high school.

4. _____ After finishing high school, Amherst College in Massachusetts, from which he graduated with Honours, was the next step.

5. _____ In 1961, he earned a Ph.D. in zoology from the University of Chicago.

6. _____ Hired as a full professor, Suzuki taught at the University of British Columbia from 1969 to 2001.

7. _____ Deeply committed to research, the EWR Steacie Memorial Fellowship award from 1969 to 1972 for "Outstanding Canadian Research Scientist under the Age of 35" was received.

8. _____ With more than fifteen honorary degrees from Canada, the U. S., and Australia, educating people about environmental issues seems to be an endless passion.

9. _____ Unlike some scientists, Suzuki speaks simply and with deep passion about how we can save our planet.

10. _____ As host of *The Nature of Things* on CBC, environmental issues are brought into our homes.

11. _____ Including a UNESCO prize for science, a United Nations Environment Program medal, and the Order of Canada, his many awards from around the globe testify to his passion for the environment.

12. _____ Encouraging everyday Canadians to do their part, David regularly speaks throughout the world on behalf of the environment.

13. _____ Having authored more than 30 books, sustainable ecology is an outstanding passion.

14. _____ Incorporated in 1990, about 40,000 members comprise the David Suzuki Foundation.

15. _____ Along with several other board members, the *Declaration of Interdependence* for the United Nations' Earth Summit in 1992, was written by David Suzuki.

16. _____ Based on the *Declaration of Interdependence*, Symphony no. 6, also called *Interdependence*, was written by Finnish composer Pehr Henrik Nordgren in 2001.

17. _____ Serving as lyrics, the words from the *Declaration of Interdependence* were coupled with Nordgren's music to create a performance piece.

18. _____ Advocating on behalf of future generations, the eradication of coal burning plants has been encouraged.

19. _____ Concerned about the fate of wild salmon, a brochure about the dangers of farmed salmon was published by the David Suzuki Foundation.

20. _____ Even while focused on governmental solutions, Suzuki repeatedly asks the question "What can *you* do?," calling on individuals to step up to the plate.

EXERCISE 5 Opening Sentences with Modifiers

Create a complete sentence by adding an independent clause to logically follow the opening modifying phrase. Test each sentence to make sure you avoid a dangling modifier. Make sure you create a complete sentence and not a fragment (see Chapter 15).

1. Popular with teenagers, _____

_____

2. Imported from France, _____

_____

3. Having worked all night, _____

_____

4. Damaged by last night's storm, _____

_____

5. Widely advertised on television, _____

_____

EXERCISE 6 Ending Sentences with Modifiers

Create a complete sentence by adding an independent clause to logically precede the modifying phrase. Test each sentence to make sure you avoid a dangling modifier. Make sure you create a complete sentence and not a fragment (see Chapter 15).

1. _____

_____, facing a massive lawsuit.

2. _____

_____, driving late at night with little sleep.

3. _____

_____, suffering from a serious knee injury.

4. _____

_____, unwilling to talk to reporters.

5. _____

_____, written by Michael Ondaatje.

EXERCISE 7 Eliminating Dangling Modifiers

Rewrite each of the following sentences to eliminate dangling modifiers. Add needed words or phrases, but do not alter the basic meaning of the sentence.

1. Facing eviction, the landlord demanded police protection from angry tenants.

_____

_____

2. Opened just four years ago, city officials were dismayed that the stadium needed major repairs.

_____

_____

3. Having won eight games in a row, fans cheered when the coach appeared.

_____

_____

4. Heading north to avoid the storm, the passengers were informed by the captain that their arrival would be delayed.

_____

_____

5. *Harry Potter* has enthralled readers all over the world, having been translated into dozens of languages.

_____

_____

EXERCISE 8 Detecting Misplaced and Dangling Modifiers in Context

Underline misplaced and dangling modifiers in the following passage.

No other radio program had more impact on the American public than Orson Welles's famous "War of the Worlds" broadcast. Only twenty-three at the time, Welles's newly formed Mercury Theatre aired weekly radio productions of original and classic dramas. On October 30, 1938, an Americanized version of H. G. Wells's science fiction novel *The War of the Worlds* was aired by the Mercury Theatre, which described a Martian invasion.

Regular listeners understood the broadcast was fiction and sat back to enjoy the popular program. The play opened with the sounds of a dance band. Suddenly, the music was interrupted by a news report that astronomers on the surface of Mars had detected strange explosions. The broadcast returned to dance music. But soon the music was interrupted again with reports of a meteor crash in Grovers Mills, New Jersey. The broadcast then dispensed with music, and a dramatic stream of reports covered the rapidly unfolding events.

Equipped with eerie special effects, the strange scene in the New Jersey countryside was described by anxious reporters. The crater, listeners were told, was not caused by a meteor but by some strange spacecraft. A large, octopuslike creature emerged from the crater, presumably coming from Mars, and blasted onlookers with powerful death rays.

Regular listeners were gripped by this realistic-sounding drama. However, people who tuned in after the play started assumed the fictional news reports were genuine. New Jersey police stations were bombarded with phone calls from citizens asking about the invasion. Listeners in New Orleans and San Francisco called the police who had friends and relatives in New Jersey asking for news. Assuming the Martians would head toward New York, businesses closed. Bars and restaurants emptied as customers fled to rescue loved ones. Fearing attack, farmers on Long Island grabbed shotguns and stood guard.

The following day, stories about the broadcast made headlines across the country. Reports of accidental shootings and suicides were probably exaggerations, but many newspapers called for congressional hearings, angered that the new medium of radio had been misused. Criticized for creating a panic, Orson Welles reminded people that his show had been broadcast on the eve of Halloween, a day devoted to monsters and mischief.

Oddly enough, this was not the last time the mythic invasion was to cause controversy. In 1944 a Spanish version of the radio drama led listeners in Santiago to panic, believing that Chile was being invaded by Martians. Five years later, a broadcast of the play in Ecuador had a similar result. Angered by the false news of an alien invasion, the Quito radio station was attacked and burned to the ground by a mob.

EXERCISE 9 Using Modifiers

Insert the modifier into each sentence by placing it next to the word or words it describes.

1. **Caroline took Monika to Prince Edward Island this summer.**
   Insert: *who was born in Charlottetown,* to refer to Caroline

   _____

   _____

2. **The RCMP closed the offices on Monday.**
   Insert: *which had been conducting an investigation for weeks,* to refer to the RCMP

   _____

   _____

3. **The television show cost the network millions in lost advertising revenue.**
   Insert: *which suffered low ratings*

   _____

   _____

4. **Donna Augustine was instrumental in bringing the traditional spiritual ways back to the Mi'kmaq people.**
   Insert: *who is a Native traditionalist from Elsipogtog, New Brunswick*

   _____

   _____

5. **The missing girl was last seen by her mother.**
   Insert: *who is only three years old*

   _____

   _____

WORKING TOGETHER

Working with a group of students, revise this notice to eliminate misplaced and dangling modifiers.

Summer Parking Restrictions

This summer campus parking will be greatly limited because of major construction projects. Beginning

June 1, students registered for summer classes will have to use orange parking passes. A map of campus parking lots can be found on the college website, www.ualberta.edu, for summer use. Faculty and administrators are only allowed to use the 114 Street parking lot. Cars will be towed by campus security guards not displaying orange parking passes on their visors.

EXERCISE 10 Cumulative Exercise

Revise each sentence for misplaced or dangling modifiers, fragments, and run-ons.

1. Assisted by his grandson, the crowd surrounding the injured man as he emerged from the train.

   _____

   _____

2. The police focused their entire investigation on Selena Anderson the RCMP uncovered evidence implicating other suspects.

   _____

   _____

3. Shot entirely on location, critics praising the film for its realism.

   _____

   _____

4. Our company purchases paper products from National Office Supply but we order all other office products from Business Depot.

   _____

   _____

5. We will have to take the bus cars are not allowed beyond this point.

   _____

   _____

CRITICAL THINKING

Do you want to own your own home? Why or why not? Do people who own a home feel different from those who rent? Do most people view owning a home as a major goal in life? Write a paragraph stating your views about owning a home.

WHAT HAVE YOU WRITTEN?

Underline the modifiers in each sentence. Are they properly placed? Are there any sentences that are confusing or could be interpreted in two ways?

WHAT HAVE YOU LEARNED?

Put an X next to each sentence with a misplaced or dangling modifier and OK next to each correct sentence.

1. _____ Reporting engine trouble, the control tower directed the pilot to make a forced landing.

2. _____ Operating throughout Canada, Tim Hortons has become a national enterprise.

3. _____ Facing his accusers, the defendant insisted he would be acquitted.

4. _____ The cake was appreciated by everyone made of chocolate.

5. _____ Having failed two courses, the dean suggested Diana see a tutor.

6. _____ Although she never owned a pet, Kristin's mother left her entire estate to an animal shelter.

7. _____ The movie tells the story of a young woman coping with depression after the death of her lover in nineteenth-century Russia.

8. _____ Opened only recently, the public was disgusted by the art exhibit.

9. _____ Having grown up in Mexico, Raul speaks excellent Spanish.

10. _____ Afraid of getting another speeding ticket, Sarah drove no faster than 100 kilometres per hour on the highway.

Answers appear on the following page.

GET WRITING

What makes a good leader? Describe a boss, teacher, coach, or politician you think demonstrates effective leadership skills.

Write a paragraph that uses examples and short narratives to support your point of view.

WRITING ON THE WEB

Using a search engine such as AltaVista, Yahoo!, or Google, enter terms such as *dangling modifier* and *misplaced modifier* to locate current sites of interest.

1. Review some current online journals or newspapers to see how writers place modifying words and phrases in sentences.
2. Write a brief e-mail to a friend, then review it for dangling and misplaced modifiers and other errors.

POINTS TO REMEMBER

1. Modifiers are words or phrases that describe other words. To prevent confusion, they must be placed next to what they modify.
2. If sentences begin or end with a modifier, apply this simple test:

Read the sentence, then turn the modifier into a question, asking who or what is being described:
   Question, Answer

If the answer makes sense, the sentence is probably correct:

   Born on Christmas, I never have a birthday party.
   Q: Who was born on Christmas?   A: I

                    Correct

If the sentence does not make sense, it probably contains a dangling modifier and needs revision:

   Filmed in Iraq, critics praise the movie for its realism.
   Q: What was filmed in Iraq?   A: critics

                    Incorrect

Revisions:
   Filmed in Iraq, the movie was praised by critics for its realism.
   Critics praised the movie filmed in Iraq for its realism.

3. In revising papers, underline modifying words and phrases and circle the words or ideas they are supposed to modify to test for clear connections.

ANSWERS TO WHAT HAVE YOU LEARNED? ON PAGE 289
1. X (see page 282), 2. OK, 3. OK, 4. X (see page 277), 5. X (see page 282), 6. OK, 7. X (see page 277), 8. X (see page 282), 9. OK, 10. OK

Understanding Parallelism

What can the Canadian government do to reduce the increasing number of gun-related crimes? Should it focus on social programs, prevention, stiffer penalties, or a national gun registry?

Write a paragraph that describes one or two things the Canadian government can do to make the country safer.

What Is Parallelism?

At first glance, the word *parallelism* may remind you of geometry. Perhaps it reminds you of parallel parking. All the cars are facing the same way? Some students find parallel structure abstract and confusing but it doesn't have to be. If you made a shopping list you would put how many of each item you wanted to purchase and then the item description. Using this pattern makes the list not only easy to read but also *parallel.* The concept is very simple: To make sentences easy to understand, pairs and lists of words have to *match;* they have to be all nouns, all adjectives, all adverbs, or all verbs in the same form. To be balanced, pairs and lists should be all phrases or clauses with matching word patterns. In most instances, we use parallelism without any problems. When we write a shopping list, we automatically write in parallel form:

We need *pens, pencils, paper, stamps,* and *envelopes.* [all nouns]

It is easy, however, to make errors when, instead of listing single nouns, you list phrases:

The department chair must approve faculty workload changes, schedule classes, order textbooks, and when the dean is unavailable take her place.

The last item, *when the dean is unavailable take her place,* does not match the other items in the list:

The department chair <u>must</u> . . . *approve* faculty workload changes
. . . *schedule* classes
. . . *order* textbooks
. . . *when the dean* is unavailable take her place

Revised
The department chair <u>must</u> *approve* faculty workload changes, *schedule* classes, *order* textbooks, and *take* the dean's place when she is unavailable.

Not Parallel
Both *running* and *to swim* are good exercise.

We walked *slowly, quietly, and felt fear.*

Anger, doubting, and *depression* nagged him.

Students should *read* carefully, *review* lecture notes, and *assignments* should be completed on time.

Parallel
Both *running* and *swimming* are good exercise.

We walked *slowly, quietly,* and *fearfully.*

Anger, doubt, and *depression* nagged him.

Students should *read* carefully, *review* lecture notes, and *complete* assignments on time.

WHAT DO YOU KNOW?

Label each sentence OK *for correct and* FP *for faulty parallelism.*

1. _____ The concert was loud, colourful, and many people attended.

2. _____ The film lacked a clear narrative, logical transitions, and the dialogue was unbelievable.

3. _____ The prime minister's policy divided his caucus, angered critics, and alienated voters.

4. _____ Taking care of the elderly and the education of children are important elements of our plan.

5. _____ She was unable to speak or sing and had to be replaced by her understudy at the last minute.

Answers appear on the following page.

WHAT ARE YOU TRYING TO SAY?

GET WRITING
AND REVISING

Most jobs require special skills, abilities, or aptitudes. Describe the job skills needed in the career you hope to pursue, or explain the abilities people needed—or lacked— in a job you had in the past.

_____

_____

_____

_____

_____

_____

_____

_____

_____

_____

_____

_____

_____

_____

WHAT HAVE YOU WRITTEN?

Read your sentences aloud. Did you create sentences that contain pairs of words or phrases or lists? If so, are the items parallel—do they match each other?

Overcoming Parallelism Errors

Mistakes in parallelism are easy to make. If you are describing a close friend, for example, a number of ideas, words, or phrases may come to mind. They may be nouns, adjectives, or verbs:

> *bright   caring   works well with students   teacher*

When putting these ideas together, make sure they are parallel:

Not Parallel
She is a teacher who is bright, caring, and works well with students.

Parallel
She is a bright, caring teacher who works well with students.
She is a teacher who is bright, caring, and good with students.

TESTING FOR PARALLELISM

The simplest way of determining if a sentence is parallel is to test each element to see if it matches the base sentence:

> Example: The car is new, well maintained, and costs very little.

The car is *new*.
The car is *well maintained*.
The car is *costs very little*.

The last item does not match and should be revised:

The car is new, well maintained, and inexpensive.
The car is *new*.
The car is *well maintained*.
The car is *inexpensive*.

A TIP ON REVISING FAULTY PARALLELISM

Sometimes you may find it difficult to make all the items in a sentence match. You might not be able to think of a suitable noun form for an adjective. In making the sentence parallel, you may find yourself having to change a phrase you like or create something that sounds awkward. In some cases you may have simply been trying to get too many ideas in a single sentence.

It may be easier in some instances to break up an unparallel sentence. It is easier to make two short sentences parallel than one long one.

(continued)

Not Parallel

Example: The new dean will be responsible for scheduling new courses, expanding student services, upgrading the old computer labs, and most important, become a strong advocate for students.

Parallel

The new dean will be responsible for *scheduling* new courses, *expanding* student services, and *upgrading* the old computer labs. Most important, she must become a strong advocate for students.

EXERCISE 1 Detecting Faulty Parallelism

Write OK *by each correct sentence and* NP *by each sentence that is not parallel.*

1. _____ CFL football is exciting, fast paced, and can captivate fans.

2. _____ The origins of the game remain open to debate and controversial.

3. _____ Sports historians agree that Canadian football includes the speed of soccer and the contact of rugby.

4. _____ In the early 1800s American college students played a running game that was often marked by violent confrontations, and serious injuries often occurred.

5. _____ The games were more like gang fights, having few officials, limited rules, and excessive violence not being penalized.

6. _____ Harvard and Yale briefly banned these games, disturbed by the players' violence and fans behaving poorly.

7. _____ The first Grey Cup was played in 1909 between the University of Toronto and Parkdale at Varsity Stadium in Toronto, in front of 3,807 fans, and the winner of the game was Toronto.

8. _____ Following soccer rules, players advanced the ball down the field by kicking the ball or striking it with their heads.

9. _____ Then, in 1882, two brothers from Ottawa, Fred and Jackson Booth, introduced Queen's athletes to the game of "rugby football," an older version of modern rugby and the game from which football at Queen's evolved.

10. _____ In 1874 McGill University was invited to play Harvard, and this historic game created the rules and set the tone for modern football.

11. _____ During practice Harvard students watched the Canadian players catch, hold, and to run with the ball.

12. _____ McGill students were playing rugby, a game Harvard players had never seen or played.

13. _____ To create a fair game, the teams decided on a compromise, using soccer rules in the first half and to follow rugby rules in the second half.

14. _____ Allowing soccer players to catch the ball and running down the field introduced elements that would be incorporated into a whole new game.

15. _____ In 1962 the infamous "Fog Bowl" was played between the Hamilton Tiger-Cats and the Winnipeg Blue Bombers, took place over two days, and was played in Winnipeg and Toronto.

16. _____ Early football games, however, remained violent and boredom.

17. _____ On offence, players formed a wedge and trying to plough through the defensive line.

18. _____ Resembling tug-of-war, these games saw little movement and touchdowns were few.

19. _____ In later years, coaches introduced new rules to the game to make it faster, less violent, and more exciting to watch.

20. _____ Knute Rockne energized the sport by emphasizing the forward pass, creating the sharply competitive and high-scoring game of modern football.

EXERCISE 2 Revising Sentences to Eliminate Faulty Parallelism

Rewrite each sentence to eliminate faulty parallelism. You may have to add words or invent phrases, but do not alter the meaning of the sentence. In some cases, you may create two sentences.

1. In the 1990s the Internet revolutionized business, education, the media, even a grandmother keeping in touch with her children.

2. Today, for instance, someone interested in restoring Model T's can easily and without a lot of expense connect with Model T enthusiasts all over the world.

3. A small entrepreneur can participate in the global economy without the cost of maintaining branch offices, mailing catalogues, or television commercials.

4. People who never thought they would use a computer now e-mail friends, search the web for recipes and childcare tips, buy airline tickets online, and tracking their stock portfolios.

5. No single person invented the Internet, but Robert E. Taylor played a role in designing the first networks and to overcome numerous obstacles.

6. While working for the U.S. Department of Defense in the late 1960s, Taylor explored ways to connect computer networks and making them work together.

_____

_____

_____

7. At that time computers were like paper notebooks, so that whatever was entered into one could not be transferred to another without reentering the data, which was costly and took a lot of time.

_____

_____

_____

8. The military wanted to streamline and simplifying its procurement process.

_____

_____

_____

9. The government provided grants to corporations and universities to stimulate research into connecting computers, overcome incompatibility, and developing standards.

_____

_____

_____

10. When personal computers became affordable, it was only a matter of time before the Internet would link individuals to a worldwide network, revolutionize education and business, and entire subcultures would be created.

_____

_____

_____

EXERCISE 3 Revising Sentences to Eliminate Faulty Parallelism

Rewrite each sentence to eliminate faulty parallelism. You may have to add words or invent phrases, but do not alter the meaning of the sentence. In some cases, you may create two sentences.

1. The system is large and convenient, and it does not cost very much.

_____

_____

2. The processor sends either a ready function code or standby function code.

_____

_____

3. The log is a record of problems that have occurred and of the services performed.

_____

_____

_____

4. The committee feels that the present system has three disadvantages: it causes delay in the distribution of incoming mail, duplicates work, and unnecessary delays are created in the work of several other departments.

_____

_____

_____

5. In our first list we inadvertently omitted the seven lathes in room B-101, milling machines in room B-117, and from the next room, B-118, we also forgot sixteen shapers.

_____

_____

_____

6. This product offers ease of operation, economy, and it is easily available.

_____

_____

_____

7. The manual gives instructions for operating the machine and to adjust it.

_____

_____

_____

8. Three of the applicants were given promotions, and transfers were arranged for the other four applicants.

_____

_____

9. To analyze the data, carry out the following steps: Examine all the details carefully, eliminate all the unnecessary details, and a chart showing the flow of work should then be prepared.

_____

_____

_____

10. We have found that the new system has four disadvantages: too costly to operate, it causes delays, fails to use any of the existing equipment, and it permits only one in-process examination.

_____

_____

_____

11. The design is simple, inexpensive, and can be used effectively.

_____

_____

_____

12. Management was slow to recognize the problem and even slower understanding it.

_____

_____

_____

EXERCISE 4 Writing Parallel Sentences

Complete each sentence by adding missing elements, making sure they create a matched pair or a list of matching words or phrases in order to be parallel.

1. To stay healthy, many people exercise regularly, avoid junk food, and _____ _____ .

2. Jogging, swimming, and _____ are good forms of exercise.

3. To be healthy, your meals should be balanced and _____ .

4. You should also avoid environmental hazards such as secondhand smoke, asbestos, and _____ .

5. Taking short naps, talking to friends, listening to soft music, and _____ _____ can help decrease stress.

6. Getting enough sleep and _____ are important to maintaining mental health and emotional _____ .

7. Some people spend a great deal of time and money on expensive running shoes, costly health club memberships, and _____ .

8. However, all you really need are a good pair of running shoes and _____ to get started.

9. Too many people attempt to do too much and become so sore and _____ they quit.

10. People who want to lose weight should set realistic goals, consult a physician before starting any radical diets, and _____ _____ .

WORKING TOGETHER

Working with a group of students, revise the following announcement to eliminate errors in parallelism. Notice how collaborative editing can help detect errors you may have missed.

Job Announcement

The Student Federation Council is seeking a bright, hardworking undergraduate to serve as a special assistant to the president. The ideal candidate will have a 3.5 GPA or better, good communication skills, and be able to organize clearly. Students with desktop publishing skills, sales ability, and having experience in working in a fast-paced environment are encouraged to apply. Applications can be picked up in B3027 or downloading from the Student Federation Council website, www.sfcouncil.ca.

GET THINKING AND WRITING

CRITICAL THINKING

Write a list of tips to help high school students prepare for college. Try to create at least five recommendations.

WHAT HAVE YOU WRITTEN?

Review each item in your list for faulty parallelism.

GET WRITING

Natural disasters are now recorded by tourists with video cameras and cellular telephones that can take pictures. They allow the world to see natural destruction instantaneously. Should television newscasts show these videos and pictures? Should people be paid for the pictures they take?

Write a short paragraph stating your opinion and give examples.

WHAT HAVE YOU LEARNED?

Label each sentence OK *for correct or* FP *for faulty parallelism.*

1. _____ The new mayor was colourful, energetic, and known for having a hot temper.

2. _____ The dessert had three layers: one filled with chocolate, one lined with pineapple slices, and one using strawberries for decoration.

3. _____ The Canada Day celebration was subdued, having no fireworks, few picnics, and not a single parade.

4. _____ The circus performers were agile, highly trained, and they surprised us by being so articulate.

5. _____ The drought was responsible for destroying crops, creating fire hazards, and decimating cattle herds.

Answers appear on the following page.

WRITING ON THE WEB

Using a search engine such as AltaVista, Yahoo!, or Google, enter terms such as *faulty parallelism* and *writing parallel sentences* to locate current sites of interest.

1. Review some current online journals or newspapers to see how writers state ideas in parallel form.
2. Write a brief e-mail to a friend describing some recent activities or a person you have met. Review your sentences to see if pairs and lists of words and phrases are parallel.

POINTS TO REMEMBER

1. Words and phrases that appear as pairs or lists must be parallel—they must match and be nouns, adverbs, adjectives, or verbs in the same form:

Not Parallel	*Parallel*
Swimming and *to fish* are fun.	*Swimming* and *fishing* are fun.
She is *bright, witty,* and *has charm*.	She is *bright, witty,* and *charming*.
He must *design* the building, *establish* the budget, and *workers* must be hired.	He must *design* the building, *establish* the budget, and *hire* workers.

2. You can discover errors in parallelism by testing each element in the pair or series with the rest of the sentence to see if it matches:

Whomever we hire will have to collect the mail, file reports, answer the phone, update the website, and accurate records must be maintained.

(continued)

POINTS TO REMEMBER *(continued)*

Whomever we hire will have to . . . *collect the mail*
file reports
answer the phone
update the website
accurate records must be
maintained

The last item does not match *will have to* and needs to be revised to be parallel with the other phrases in the list:

Whomever we hire will have to collect the mail, file reports, answer the phone, update the website, and *maintain accurate records*.

3. If you find it difficult to make a long or complicated sentence parallel, consider creating two sentences. In some instances, it is easier to write two short parallel lists than a single long one.

ANSWERS TO WHAT HAVE YOU LEARNED? ON PAGE 301
1. FP (see page 260), 2. FP (see page 260), 3. OK, 4. FP (see page 260), 5. OK

Part 4

Understanding Grammar

20

Subject–Verb Agreement

GET WRITING

What does this image mean to you? Is it just a picture of a woman in a uniform, or does it show how attitudes about men and women have changed?

Write a paragraph describing what this picture represents to you.

What Is Subject-Verb Agreement?

The most important parts of any sentence are the *subject*—the actor or main idea—and the *verb*—a word or words that express action (*run, walk, argue*) or link the subject with other ideas (*is, are, was, were*). The subject and verb work together to state a *complete thought* and create a sentence:

Ahmed *sells* insurance. Ahmed *is* smart.

To make sentences clear, it is important that subjects and verbs agree—that they match in number. *Singular subjects require singular verbs; plural subjects require plural verbs:*

Singular	*Plural*
The <u>boy</u> *walks* to school.	The <u>boys</u> *walk* to school.
The <u>bus</u> *was* late.	The <u>buses</u> *were* late.
The <u>memo</u> *is* on your desk.	The <u>memos</u> *are* on your desk.

In most cases you add an *s* or *es* to a noun to make it plural and add an *s* or *es* to a verb to make it singular.

Singular and plural verbs occur only in first and third person:

	Singular	*Plural*
First person:	I *am*	We *are*
Third person:	He *was*	They *were*

In second person, only the plural verb is used:

You *are* a person I can trust. You *are* people I can trust.

WHAT DO YOU KNOW?

Select the correct verb in each sentence.

1. _____ The principal, backed by students and parents, (refuses/refuse) to cancel the prom.

2. _____ Fifteen days (don't/doesn't) give us enough time to finish the project.

3. _____ Where (is/are) the plan the students promised to send to the faculty committee?

4. _____ One of our students (works/work) at the mall.

5. _____ She (don't/doesn't) seem to understand the problem.

Answers appear on the following page.

WHAT ARE YOU TRYING TO SAY?

Write a brief paragraph describing activities you and your family enjoy.

_____

_____

_____

_____

_____

_____

_____

_____

_____

_____

_____

_____

_____

_____

ANSWERS TO WHAT DO YOU KNOW? ON PAGE 306
1. refuses (*principal* is singular; *students and parents,* set off by commas, is not part of the subject), 2. doesn't (units of time and amounts of money are singular), 3. is (*Where* refers to *plan,* which is singular), 4. works (*One* is singular), 5. doesn't (*she* is singular)

WHAT HAVE YOU WRITTEN?

Circle the subjects and underline the verbs in each sentence. Do the subjects and verbs match so that your sentences clearly identify which activities are singular and which are plural? Do your verbs show which things your family enjoys as a group and which are enjoyed by a single person?

Grammar Choices and Meaning

Matching subjects and verbs is not just a matter of avoiding a grammar mistake but of making your meaning clear. Changing a verb from singular to plural changes the meaning of a sentence:

Sentence	Meaning
Singular	
My accountant and adviser *is* coming.	*One person is both an accountant and an adviser.*
Plural	
My accountant and adviser *are* coming.	*The accountant and adviser are two individuals.*
Singular	
The desk and chair *is* on sale.	*The desk and chair are sold as one item.*

Plural	
The desk and chair *are* on sale.	*The desk and chair are sold separately.*
Singular	
His drinking and driving *is* unacceptable.	*One activity, indicating drunk driving.*
Plural	
His drinking and driving *are* unacceptable.	*Two activities, indicating excessive drinking and bad driving but not necessarily drunk driving.*
Singular	
Bacon and eggs *is* on the menu.	*Bacon and eggs served as a single dish.*
Plural	
Bacon and eggs *are* on the menu.	*The menu lists both bacon and egg dishes.*

Before the Civil War, for example, the noun *United States* often appeared as a plural to emphasize the independence of each state. After the Civil War, in a desire to unite the country, writers began using *United States* as a singular noun.

EXERCISE 1 Choosing the Correct Verb

Write out the subject and correct verb in each sentence.

	Subject	Verb
1. The stock market (attracts/attract) speculators and investors.	_____	_____
2. A speculator (expects/expect) to make a fortune with a fast deal or a hot tip.	_____	_____
3. Investors (plans/plan) to increase their wealth over time by researching the market.	_____	_____
4. Both speculators and investors (has/have) been known to achieve great wealth.	_____	_____
5. Investors (buy/buys) a variety of stocks.	_____	_____
6. A speculator, however, (is/are) likely to gamble everything on a single tip.	_____	_____
7. Speculators (rely/relies) on getting the odd bit of information about a buyout or a lawsuit.	_____	_____
8. Most people (has/have) no access to this kind of information.	_____	_____
9. A person saving for retirement (need/needs) to be careful about following a stock tip.	_____	_____
10. Too often tips (is/are) inaccurate or misleading.	_____	_____

Special Nouns and Pronouns

In most cases it is easy to tell whether a noun is singular or plural: most nouns add an *s* to become plural. But some nouns are misleading.

- Not all nouns add an *s* to become plural:

  deer   children   women   people

- Some nouns that end in *s* and look like plurals are singular:

  economics   mathematics   athletics   physics
  Mathematics *is* my toughest course.   Economics *demands* accurate data.

- Some nouns that may refer to one item are plural:

  pants   gloves   scissors   fireworks
  My scissors *are* dull.   *Are* these your gloves?

- Proper nouns that look plural are singular if they are names of companies, organizations, or titles of books, movies, television shows, or works of art:

  General Motors   *The Three Musketeers*   The Urban League
  General Motors *is* building a   *The Three Musketeers is*
  new engine.   funny.

- Units of time and amounts of money are generally singular:

  Twenty-five dollars *is* a lot for a T-shirt.   Two weeks *is* not enough
                                                  time.

  They appear as plurals to indicate separate items:

  Three loonies *were* lying on the table.   My last weeks at camp *were*
                                             unbearable.

Group Nouns

Group nouns—nouns that describe something with more than one unit or member—can be singular or plural, depending on the meaning of the sentence.

COMMON GROUP NOUNS

audience	committee	faculty	number
board	company	family	public
class	crowd	jury	team

In most instances, group nouns are singular because they describe a group working together as a unit:

"Faculty Accepts Council of   [headline describing teachers
Presidents' Offer"   acting as a group]

Group nouns are plural when they describe a group working independently:

"Faculty Protest Council of Presidents' Offer"	[headline describing teachers acting individually]

Some group nouns are conventionally used as plurals because we think of them as individuals rather than a single unit:

The Rolling Stones *are* releasing a new CD.	The Toronto Raptors *play* the New York Knicks on Sunday.

EXERCISE 2 **Choosing the Correct Verb with Special and Group Nouns**

Circle the correct verb in each sentence.

1. The United Nations (is/are) headquartered in New York City.
2. *The Chronicles of Narnia* (is/are) available on DVD.
3. The Imperial Order of the Daughters of the Empire (sponsor/sponsors) upcoming debates.
4. My trousers (is/are) ripped.
5. After six days of tense deliberations, the jury now (declares/declare) a verdict.
6. Our football team (plays/play) only five games on the road next season.
7. The Blue Jays (is/are) heading to the dugout.
8. Physics (is/are) challenging.
9. Naturally, you (plans/plan) to take a long vacation this summer, don't you?
10. The male chorus (travels/travel) by bus.

Hidden Subjects

In some sentences the subject is not easily spotted, and it is easy to make mistakes in choosing the right verb.

- *Subjects followed by prepositional phrases:*

Incorrect
One of my oldest friends are visiting from Calgary.

Correct
One of my oldest friends *is* visiting from Calgary.

[*Friends* is plural, but it is not the subject of the sentence; the subject is *One,* which is singular.]

Incorrect
Development of housing projects and public highways demand public support.

Correct
Development of housing projects and public highways demand**s** public support.

[*Projects* and *highways* are plural, but the subject is *Development,* which is singular.]

Remember, the subject of a sentence does not appear in a prepositional phrase.

Make sure that you identify the key word of a subject and determine whether it is singular or plural:

The *price* of textbooks and school supplies *is* rising.   [singular]

The *prices* of gold *are* rising.   [plural]

Prepositions are words that express relationships between ideas, usually regarding time and place:

above	before	with	across
over	during	without	to
under	after	within	toward
below	since	from	of
around	like	near	off
past	except	like	along
against	inside	outside	among

- *Subjects followed by subordinate words and phrases.* In many sentences the subject is followed by words or phrases set off by commas. These additional words are subordinate—extra information that is not part of the main sentence. They should not be mistaken for compound subjects:

The teacher <u>and</u> the students *are* filing a complaint with the Board of Governors.
[Plural *and* links *teacher* + *students* to form a compound subject.]
The teacher, supported by students, *is* filing a complaint with the Board of Governors.
[Singular *is* and commas indicate students are subordinate and not part of the subject.]

- *Subjects following possessives.* It can be easy to choose the wrong verb if the subject follows a possessive noun:

Incorrect
The town's business leaders is debating the new legislation.

Correct
The town's business leaders *are* debating the new legislation.
[The subject is not *town* but *leaders,* which is plural.]

Incorrect
The students' proposal fail to address the problem.

Correct
The students' proposal *fails* to address the problem.
[The subject is not *students* but *proposal,* which is singular.]

POINT TO REMEMBER

The subject is never the word with the apostrophe but what follows it.

- *Inverted subjects and verbs.* In some sentences the usual subject-verb order is inverted or reversed, so the subject follows the verb:

Singular	*Plural*
Here *is* a <u>book</u> you will like.	Here *are* the <u>books</u> you ordered.
There *is* a <u>letter</u> for you.	There *are* several <u>letters</u> for you.
There *was* no <u>call</u> for you today.	There *were* two <u>calls</u> for you today.
Outside the city *lives* a <u>poor family</u>.	Outside the city *live* <u>the poor</u>.

EXERCISE 3 Choosing the Correct Verb with Hidden or Complex Subjects

Circle the correct verb in each sentence.

1. The creativity and originality of Canadian independent filmmakers (has/have) excited both critics and fans around the world.
2. When (is/are) the coach and several players meeting with the dean to seek more funds?
3. The prime minister, pressured by key members of caucus, (is/are) going to address Parliament.
4. There (is/are) no children attending the party.
5. Who (buys/buy) a car with cash these days?
6. After the blizzard, the unavailability of snowplows and trucks (was/were) frustrating.
7. Key supporters of the mayor (was/were) unwilling to believe the growing reports of corruption in city hall.
8. There (is/are) no plans for urban renewal or community development in the new budget.
9. Why (is/are) no reports available on your accident?
10. The new drug's effects (is/are) more powerful than expected.

"Either . . . Or" Subjects

More than one subject may appear in a sentence, but that does not automatically mean that the verb should be plural:

| My aunt *and* my sister *are* taking me to the airport. | [aunt + sister = two people (plural)] |
| My aunt *or* my sister *is* taking me to the airport. | [aunt OR sister = one person (singular)] |

Remember, the conjunctions *or* and *nor* mean "one or the other but not both."

- If both subjects are singular, the verb is singular:

Neither the teacher *nor* the principal *is* responsible.
Mathematics *or* physics *was* required.
My father *or* my brother *drives* us to school.

- If both subjects are plural, the verb is plural:

  Neither the teachers *nor* the parents *are* responsible.
  Mathematics books *or* physics lectures *were* helpful.
  Our fathers *or* our brothers *drive* us to school.

- If one subject is singular and one subject is plural, the subject closer to the verb determines whether it is singular or plural:

  Neither the teacher *nor* the parents *are* responsible.   [plural]
  A mathematics book *or* the physics lectures *are* helpful.   [plural]
  Our fathers *or* my brother *drives* us to school.   [singular]

With "either . . . or" sentences, it is important to focus on special and group nouns:

Neither the judge nor the jury *is* going to decide her ultimate fate.   ["*Jury*" is singular.]

The parents or the class *complains* about the new teacher.   ["*Class*" is singular.]

English or social studies *is* going to be taught online this fall.   ["*Social studies*" is singular.]

Indefinite Pronouns

Indefinite pronouns can be singular or plural, but most are singular.

INDEFINITE PRONOUNS

Singular Indefinite Pronouns

another	each	everything	nothing
anybody	either	neither	somebody
anyone	everybody	nobody	someone
anything	everyone	no one	something

<u>Anything</u> *is* possible.   <u>No one</u> *attends* those meetings.   <u>Someone</u> *is* coming.

Plural Indefinite Pronouns

both	few	many	several

<u>Both</u> *are* missing.   <u>Few</u> *are* available.   <u>Many</u> *are* called.

Indefinite Pronouns That Can Be Singular or Plural Depending on Meaning

all	any	more	most
none	some		

The children were in a bus crash. <u>Some</u> [*Some* refers to *children*. (plural)] *were* injured.

Snow fell all night. <u>Some</u> *has* melted.   [*Some* refers to *snow*. (singular)]

Security is tight. But <u>more</u> *is* needed.   [*More* refers to *security*. (singular)]

Security guards are present. But <u>more</u> *are* needed.   [*More* refers to *guards*. (plural)]

EXERCISE 4 Choosing the Right Verb with "Either . . . Or" and Indefinite Pronouns

Circle the correct verb in each sentence.

1. Either the G8 or a coalition of developing nations (is/are) going to organize a policy to reduce third-world debt.

2. Anyone concerned with eliminating poverty (has/have) to be concerned about the effect debt has on emerging nations.

3. Either business leaders or a skilled diplomat (is/are) needed to resolve the problem.

4. In the 1970s many (was/were) convinced that massive loans to poor countries would provide resources needed to reduce poverty and stimulate economic growth.

5. Few (was/were) able to predict that these loans would have a crippling effect on many poor countries.

6. Unfortunately, corruption or mismanagement (was/were) responsible for making poor use of the borrowed funds.

7. Some ventures failed, and many (was/were) barely profitable.

8. In Africa rapid population growth or AIDS (was/were) responsible for placing unexpected stress on already fragile economies.

9. Most (believes/believe) poor countries cannot repay the debts.

10. Leading economists or celebrities (has/have) brought public attention to the problem of third-world debt.

Relative Pronouns: *Who, Which,* and *That*

The words *who, which,* and *that* can be singular or plural, depending on the noun they replace:

Who
Sandy is a person who really *cares*. [*Who* refers to "a person." (singular)]
They are people who really *care*. [*Who* refers to "people." (plural)]

Which
He bought a bond, which *was* worthless. [*Which* refers to "a bond." (singular)]
He bought bonds, which *were* worthless. [*Which* refers to "bonds." (plural)]

That
She bought a car that *has* no engine. [*That* refers to "a car." (singular)]
She bought cars that *have* no engines. [*That* refers to "cars." (plural)]

It is important to locate the exact noun these words refer to in order to avoid making errors:

Incorrect
Vicki is among the athletes who trains off-season. [*Who* refers to "athletes," not "Vicki."]

Correct

Min is among the athletes who
train off-season.   [plural]

Incorrect

David or Bruce is joining the   [*Who* refers to "students," not "David or
students who is demonstrating.   Bruce."]

Correct

David or Bruce is joining the
students who *are* demonstrating.   [plural]

Incorrect

Listed in the newspapers is a   [*That* refers to "story," not
story that reveal a scandal.   "newspapers."]

Correct

Listed in the newspapers is a   [singular]
story that *reveals* a scandal.

EXERCISE 5 Choosing the Right Verb with *Who, Which,* and *That*

Underline the correct verb in each sentence.

1. The cost of the books that (was/were) ordered last year has doubled.

2. Each of the students who (was/were) chosen by the dean for recognition attended the dinner.

3. Either Valerie or Amin will join the teachers who (is/are) reviewing the budget.

4. We spent all our time shopping in stores that (was/were) crowded and overpriced.

5. Dale's parents joined a committee that (meet/meets) every Friday evening.

6. The United Nations' hunger program that (was/were) so successful in Asia will be expanded next year.

7. Fixing the car cost $890, which (was/were) more than I made all week.

8. Did you see the three loonies that (was/were) left on the table?

9. Juan is one of those students who (is/are) heading to Banff during spring break.

10. I test drove each of the cars that (has/have) been recalled.

EXERCISE 6 Choosing the Right Verb

Underline the correct verb in each sentence.

1. Few people today (is/are) old enough to remember a quiz show called *Twenty-One* that changed television history and triggered a national scandal.

2. The lure of fame and money (was/were) to ruin the career of a rising academic.

3. Allegations by a previously unknown college student (was/were) to expose a scandal that led to congressional hearings and a national moral debate.

4. Herb Stempel was a twenty-nine-year-old college student when he wrote the producers who (was/were) selecting new contestants for *Twenty-One*.

5. Producers selected Stempel, whose photographic memory and knowledge of obscure topics (was/were) to astound viewers.

6. Week after week, millions of Americans (was/were) amazed at Stempel's ability to correctly answer tough questions.

7. Few viewers understood that many of the moments of high drama on the show (was/were) staged.

8. Before the shows, Stempel (was/were) coached by producers, who went over answers and told him when to pause and mop his brow to build tension.

9. Stempel appeared week after week and won a great sum of money, but producers and sponsors (was/were) disappointed by the show's ratings.

10. According to the producers, a more appealing contestant (was/were) needed.

11. Stempel, following instructions from producers, (was/were) told to take a dive, deliberately missing a simple question about his favourite movie.

12. The new winner, Charles Van Doren, (was/were) a handsome young Columbia University professor and son of the noted scholar Mark Van Doren.

13. Also coached on answers, Van Doren appeared week after week, becoming so popular that he (was/were) soon becoming a household name, his face appearing on the cover of *Time* magazine.

14. Seen as a genius, Van Doren was given a lucrative contract to appear on *The Today Show,* but Stempel (was/were) beginning to feel cheated and revealed that the game show was rigged.

15. Admitting before Congress his part in the scheme, Van Doren (was/were) disgraced, losing his television contract, resigning from Columbia, and dropping out of public life.

EXERCISE 7 Making Subjects and Verbs Agree

Complete each of the following sentences, making sure that the verb matches the subject. Write in the present tense—walk/walks, sing/sings, and so on.

1. **One of my neighbours** _____

_____

2. **Both my parents** _____

_____

3. **Either the lawyers or the judge** _____

_____

4. The price of these houses _____

_____

5. The premier, troubled by protests and demonstrations, _____

_____

CRITICAL THINKING

Do you think public schools should require students to take both English and French? Would Canada benefit from having more citizens who can speak both official languages, French and English? Why or why not? Write a paragraph stating your opinion.

WHAT HAVE YOU WRITTEN?

1. _Select two sentences with singular verbs from your paragraph and write them below:_

_____

_____

Read the sentences aloud. Have you identified the right word or words as the subject? Is the subject singular?

2. _Select two sentences with plural verbs and write them below:_

_____

_____

Read the sentences aloud. Have you identified the right word or words as the subject? Is the subject plural?

3. _Edit your paragraph for fragments (see Chapter 15), comma splices (see Chapter 17), and run-ons (see Chapter 17)._

EXERCISE 8 Cumulative Exercise

Rewrite this passage to eliminate errors in subject-verb agreement, fragments, and run-ons.

Today many colleges offer courses through the Internet. The idea of broadcasting classes are not new, for decades, universities, colleges, and technical institutions has used television to teach classes. Unlike educational television programs, Internet courses are interactive. Professors can use chat rooms to hold virtual office hours and class discussions so that a student feel less isolated. Everyone in the class are able to post a paper on a computer bulletin board. Then the professor or other students adds comments. Course websites with links containing text, audio, and video material. Because of the flexibility of the Internet. A last-minute change or instructions about an upcoming exam can be easily posted for students.

_____

_____

_____
_____
_____
_____
_____
_____
_____
_____

WORKING TOGETHER

Working with a group of students, read this letter and circle any errors in subject-verb agreement. Note how collaborative editing can help detect errors you may have missed on your own.

Dear Student:

The Student Federation Council are hosting a summer job seminar April 15-20. Any student who are interested in finding a job this summer will find this seminar valuable. United Dynamics are sponsoring this program and will be providing information to anyone who are looking for work. All meetings will be held at the Student Life Centre, Upper Lounge. Members of the Council is available for additional information beginning April 1. A representative or a recruiter from Dewy, Soakim, and Howe, a temporary employment agency, will meet with interested students Wednesday, April 17 from 1:00 to 4:00 p.m. See the Student Federation Council website for a complete schedule and last-minute updates.

GET WRITING

How were boys and girls raised in the past? Did giving boys and girls clear-cut roles limit their opportunities? Are today's children growing up with more options or less direction?

Write a paragraph about this picture. Does it imply that boys are socially programmed to be violent?

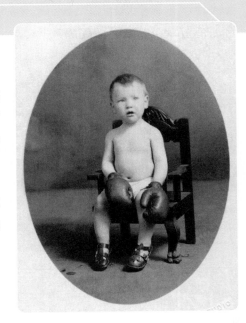

WHAT HAVE YOU LEARNED?

Select the correct verb in each sentence.

1. _____ Each of the children's mothers (expect/expects) a phone call.

2. _____ The farmworkers or the farmer (needs/need) to get a lawyer to help with the negotiations.

3. _____ WestJet (fly/flies) to Vancouver more than six times a day.

4. _____ Here (is/are) the winning lottery numbers.

5. _____ Where (is/are) the memos I sent last week?

Answers appear on the following page.

WRITING ON THE WEB

Using a search engine such as AltaVista, Yahoo!, or Google, enter terms such as *subject-verb agreement, verbs,* and *verb agreement* to locate current sites of interest.

1. Read online articles from magazines or newspapers and notice the number of group words such as *committee, jury,* or *parliament.*
2. Send an e-mail to a friend and make sure you choose the right verbs in sentences containing "either . . . or" and "which."

POINTS TO REMEMBER

1. Subjects and verbs agree, or match, in number:

   Singular subjects take singular verbs:

   The boy *walks* to school.
   The bus *is* late.

   Plural subjects take plural verbs:

   The boys *walk* to school.
   The buses *are* late.

2. Verb choice affects meaning:

   The desk and chair *is* on sale.   [The items are sold as a set. (singular)]
   The desk and chair *are* on sale. [The items are sold separately. (plural)]

3. Group nouns, units of time and money, and some words that appear plural are singular:

   The jury *is* deliberating.
   Fifty dollars *is* not enough.

4. Some nouns that refer to a single item are plural:

   My scissors *are* dull.
   The fireworks *are* starting.

(continued)

POINTS TO REMEMBER *(continued)*

5. *Here* and *there* can precede singular or plural verbs depending on the subject:

   There *is* one girl who wants to join the team.
   Here *are* three girls who want to join the team.

6. The subject of a sentence never appears in a prepositional phrase:

One of my friends *lives* in Peterborough.	[*One* is the subject, not *friends*.]
The prices of oil *are* rising.	[*Prices* is the subject, not *oil*.]

7. Nouns set off by commas following the subject are not part of the subject:

   The professor, supported by students, *is* protesting. [singular]

8. The subject may follow a possessive:

Tom's cars *are* brand-new.	[*Cars* is the subject.]
The children's playground *is* open.	[*Playground* is the subject.]

9. *Either . . . or* constructions can be singular or plural:

   If both subjects are singular, the verb is singular:

   Either my aunt or my sister *is* taking me to the airport.

   If both subjects are plural, the verb is plural:

   Either the boys or the girls *are* hosting the party.

   If one subject is singular and the other is plural, the subject closest to the verb determines whether it is singular or plural:

   Either the boy or the girls *are* hosting the party.
   Either the girls or the boy *is* hosting the party.

10. Some indefinite pronouns are singular:

another	each	everything	nothing
anybody	either	neither	somebody
anyone	everybody	nobody	someone
anything	everyone	no one	something

    Anything *is* possible.   Nothing *is* missing.

11. Some indefinite pronouns are plural:

both	few	many	several

    Both *are* missing.   Few *are* available.

12. Some indefinite pronouns can be singular or plural:

all	any	more	most
none	some		

    All the money *is* gone.   All the children *are* gone.

ANSWERS TO WHAT HAVE YOU LEARNED? ON PAGE 319
1. expects (see page 313), 2. needs (see page 313), 3. flies (see page 309), 4. are (see page 309), 5. are (see page 309)

21

Verb Tense, Mood, and Voice

GET WRITING

Did you attend daycare? Have you sent a child to daycare?

Consider your observations and experiences and those of others, and then write a paragraph that compares good and bad daycare. Include details and use examples to support your views.

NEL

321

WHAT DO YOU KNOW?

Select the correct verb in each sentence.

1. _____ I (didn't/don't) work on Tuesdays.

2. _____ I (didn't/don't) work last Monday.

3. _____ She was born in Regina, which (is/was) the capital of Saskatchewan.

4. _____ If I (was/were) unemployed, I would be upset, too.

5. _____ Yesterday, I (drive/drove) home with a flat tire.

6. _____ She (sneak/sneaked) into the dorm after curfew last night.

7. _____ Let's (rise/raise) our glasses to congratulate Ted and Nancy!

8. _____ Don't (sit/set) there; the paint is still wet.

9. _____ She jogs and (swims/swam) to keep in shape.

10. _____ The children have (laid/lain) down for a nap.

Answers appear on the following page.

GET **WRITING**
AND REVISING

WHAT ARE YOU TRYING TO SAY?

Write a brief paragraph explaining an experience that taught you a lesson. How did a high school coach's lessons on discipline affect how you approach problems today? How did a car accident in high school influence the way you drive now? How did getting into credit card debt a few years ago change your buying habits?

_____

_____

_____

WHAT HAVE YOU WRITTEN?

Read your paragraph aloud and underline the verbs. How did you use verbs to tell time? Is it clear what events or actions took place in the past, which ones began in the past and continue into the present, and which ones take place only in the present?

What Is Tense?

Tense refers to time. In addition to expressing action or linking the subject to other words, verbs tell the time. All actions, events, and conditions take place in time. To communicate effectively, we have to state time relationships accurately. A jury listening to witnesses of an auto accident would pay attention to the timing of events. Did the witness hear the horn before or after the car hit the pedestrian? Did the driver call 911 or her lawyer first? Were the police present at the time a witness claims she saw the driver throw away a liquor bottle? Timing is critical in many sentences. Explaining *when* something happened can be just as important as telling readers *what* happened.

Helping Verbs

Verb *tenses* tell when events or actions occur. ***Helping verbs,*** also called *auxiliary verbs,* often appear with verbs to create tense. Common helping verbs are *be, do, have, can, could, may, might, must, shall, should, will,* and *would.*

Tenses

Tense	Use	Example
present	shows current and ongoing actions	I *drive* to school.
simple past	shows actions that occurred in the past and do not continue into the present	I *drove* to school last week.
future	shows future actions	I *will drive* to school next week.
present perfect	shows actions that began in the past and concluded in the present	I *have* just *driven* to school.
past perfect	shows actions concluded in the past before another action occurred	I *had driven* to school before the storm started on Monday.

ANSWERS TO WHAT DO YOU KNOW? ON PAGE 322
1. don't (present tense needed), 2. didn't (past tense needed), 3. is (present, Austin remains the capital), 4. were (subjunctive mood), 5. drove (past tense needed), 6. sneaked, 7. raise, 8. sit, 9. swims (present tense needed to match *jogs*), 10. lain

Tense	Use	Example
future perfect	shows future actions preceding an action or event further in the future	I *will have driven* 5,000 miles by the time I graduate next May.
present progressive	shows ongoing action	I *am driving* to school.
past progressive	shows actions that were in progress in the past	I *was driving* my old Chevy to school in those days.
future progressive	shows ongoing future actions	Next year I *will be driving* to college.
present perfect progressive	shows actions that began in the past and continue in the present	I *have been driving* to school this winter.
past perfect progressive	shows actions in progress in the past before another past action	I *had been driving* to school until bus service resumed last fall.
future perfect progressive	shows future ongoing actions taking place before a future event	I *will have been driving* for years by the time bus service resumes in March.

This chart may seem complicated, but we use tense every day to express ourselves. Consider the difference in these responses to a question about a friend's health:

She *was* sick.	[past tense (indicates she has recovered from a past illness)]
She *is* sick.	[present tense (indicates she is currently ill)]
She *has been* sick.	[past perfect (indicates past illnesses that continue or an unsure recovery)]
She *will be* sick.	[future (indicates she will be ill in the future)]

We use perfect tenses to explain the differences between events in the recent past and distant past or between the near and far future:

She had won two Grammys when MTV asked her to host a show in 2002.
He will have twenty credits in history by the time he graduates next year.

PROGRESSIVE TENSE

Some verbs express actions: *run, buy, sell, paint, create, drive*. Other verbs express conditions, emotions, relationships, or thoughts: *cost, believe, belong, contain, know, prefer, want*. These verbs don't generally use the progressive form:

Incorrect   Citizens of developing countries *are wanting* a higher standard of living.

Correct   Citizens of developing countries *want* a higher standard of living.

Regular and Irregular Verbs

Most verbs are called "regular" because they follow a regular, or standard, form to show tense changes. We add -*ed* to words ending with consonants and -*d* to words ending with an *e*:

Present	Past	Past Participle
walk	walked	walked
create	created	created
cap	capped	capped
develop	developed	developed
paint	painted	painted
rush	rushed	rushed
wash	washed	washed
Xerox	Xeroxed	Xeroxed

VERB ENDING

The verb endings -*s* and -*ed* may be hard to hear when added to words that end in similar sounds. Some people don't pronounce these verb endings in speaking. Make sure to add them when you are writing.

Incorrect	They were *suppose* to give their presentation yesterday. She *learn* quickly.
Correct	They were *supposed* to give their presentation yesterday. She *learns* quickly.

Irregular verbs do not follow the -*ed* pattern.

- Some irregular verbs require no spelling change to indicate shifts in tense:

Present	Past	Past Participle
bet	bet	bet
cost	cost	cost
cut	cut	cut
fit	fit	fit
hit	hit	hit
hurt	hurt	hurt
put	put	put
quit	quit	quit
read	read	read
set	set	set
spread	spread	spread

- Most irregular verbs require a spelling change rather than adding -*ed*:

Present	Past	Past Participle
awake	awoke	awoken
be	was, were	been

Present	Past	Past Participle
bear	bore	borne (not *born*)
become	became	become
begin	began	begun
blow	blew	blown
break	broke	broken
bring	brought	brought
build	built	built
buy	bought	bought
catch	caught	caught
choose	chose	chosen
come	came	come
dive	dived (dove)	dived
do	did	done
draw	drew	drawn
drink	drank	drunk
drive	drove	driven
eat	ate	eaten
feed	fed	fed
feel	felt	felt
fight	fought	fought
fly	flew	flown
forget	forgot	forgotten
forgive	forgave	forgiven
freeze	froze	frozen
get	got	gotten (got)
go	went	gone
grow	grew	grown
hang (objects)	hung	hung
hang (people)	hanged	hanged
have	had	had
hold	held	held
know	knew	known
lay (place)	laid	laid
lead	led	led
leave	left	left
lie (recline)	lay	lain
lose	lost	lost
make	made	made
mean	meant	meant
meet	met	met
pay	paid	paid
ride	rode	ridden
ring	rang	rung
rise	rose	risen
run	ran	run
say	said	said
see	saw	seen
seek	sought	sought

Present	Past	Past Participle
sell	sold	sold
shine	shone	shone
shoot	shot	shot
sing	sang	sung
sink	sank	sunk
sleep	slept	slept
sneak	sneaked	sneaked
speak	spoke	spoken
spend	spent	spent
steal	stole	stolen
sting	stung	stung
strike	struck	struck
strive	strove	striven
swear	swore	sworn
sweep	swept	swept
swim	swam	swum
swing	swung	swung
take	took	taken
teach	taught	taught
tear	tore	torn
tell	told	told
think	thought	thought
throw	threw	thrown
understand	understood	understood
wake	woke	woken
weave	wove	woven
win	won	won
write	wrote	written

EXERCISE 1 Supplying the Right Verb

Complete the following sentences by supplying the correct verb form.

1. **Present**   I speak to youth groups.

   Past   I _____ to youth groups.

   Past participle   I have _____ to youth groups.

2. **Present**   I supply computers to schools.

   Past   I _____ computers to schools.

   Past participle   I have _____ computers to schools.

3. **Present**   They buy silk from China.

   Past   They _____ silk from China.

   Past participle   They have _____ silk from China.

4. **Present**   The clothes fit in my suitcase.

   Past   The clothes _____ in my suitcase.

   Past participle   The clothes have _____ in my suitcase.

5. **Present**   Hope springs eternal.

   Past   Hope _____ eternal.

   Past participle Hope has _____ eternal.

EXERCISE 2 Choosing the Correct Verb

Underline the correct verb form in each sentence.

1. During World War II the world oil supply (is/was) interrupted.

2. German U-boats (sinked/sank) oil tankers crossing the Atlantic.

3. Military and industrial needs (eat/ate) into Britain's limited oil supply.

4. Most English drivers (put/putted) their cars in storage for the duration of the war.

5. Even when convoys (begin/began) to successfully transport oil to Britain, the Allies (face/faced) problems.

6. Once they (invade/invaded) Europe, they would need fuel for tanks, planes, and trucks to succeed.

7. Engineers (design/designed) PLUTO—or Pipe Line Under The Ocean—to pump oil under the English Channel to France.

8. Cut off from imports, the Germans (bore/beared) even greater problems in securing fuel.

9. Scientists had (created/create) a process for converting coal to synthetic gasoline.

10. These efforts, however, (produce/produced) less fuel than needed, so that at war's end many German army vehicles had to be (tow/towed) by farm animals.

EXERCISE 3 Revising Tense Errors

Revise the tense errors in the following passage.

The summer of 1961 seen a great season for the New York Yankees. Two players, Roger Maris and Mickey Mantle, challenge Babe Ruth's record of hitting sixty home runs in a season. The 1927 record seem unbreakable. Despite a slow start that season, Maris soon begin hitting one home run after another, keeping pace with Mickey Mantle. Call the "M&M boys" by sportswriters, Maris and Mantle become national heroes.

As the summer wear on, and both players had hitted over forty home runs, attention grew. Even President Kennedy stop the nation's business to follow their progress. Not everyone is enthusiastic about their hitting. Many Ruth fans, including the baseball commissioner, do not want to saw the classic record breaked. Maris had only play with the Yankees one year, and many New York fans do not consider him worthy to replace Babe Ruth as the home run king. Because the 1961 season is eight games longer than the 1927 season, the baseball commissioner argued it would been unfair to Ruth if a player beated the record because he has extra games.

When Maris break the record during the extended season, he was honoured for hitting sixty-one home runs. But the record books placed an * after his name to indicate his season is longer than Ruth's. The * tarnish Maris's reputation. In 1991, six years after Maris die, the asterisk was remove from official records.

_____

_____

_____

_____

_____

_____

_____

_____

_____

_____

_____

_____

_____

_____

_____

_____

_____

Problem Verbs: *Lie/Lay, Rise/Raise, Set/Sit*

Some verbs are easily confused. Because they are spelled alike and express similar actions, they are commonly misused. In each pair, only one verb can take direct objects. The verbs *lay, raise,* and *set* take direct objects; *lie, rise,* and *sit* do not.

Lie/Lay

To lie means to rest or recline. You "lie down for nap" or "lie on a sofa." *To lay* means to put something down or set something into position. You "lay a book on a table" or "lay flooring."

Present	Past	Past Participle
lie	lay	lain
lay	laid	laid

To Lie
I love to lie on the beach.
She is lying under the umbrella.

To Lay
We lay ceramic tile using special glues.
They are laying the subfloor today.

Yesterday, I lay on the sofa all day.   Yesterday, we laid the kitchen tile.
I have lain in the sun all summer.   I have laid tile like that before.

Remember: Lie expresses an action done *by* someone or something:

Farah called 911, then *lay* on the sofa waiting for the paramedics.

Lay expresses action done *to* someone or something:

The paramedics *laid* Farah on the floor to administer CPR.

Rise/Raise

To rise means to get up or move up on your own. You "rise and shine" or "rise to the occasion." *To raise* means to lift something or grow something. You "raise a window" or "raise children."

Present	Past	Past Participle
rise	rose	risen
raise	raised	raised

To Rise
They rise every day at six.
He is rising to attention.
The children have risen from their naps.

He rose from the hot tub.

To Raise
Every morning they raise the flag.
He is raising wheat.
The merchants have raised prices again.
He raised his hand for help.

Remember: Rise can refer to objects as well as people:

The bread rises in the oven.   Oil prices are rising.

Set/Sit

To set means to put something in position or arrange in place. You "set down a glass" or "set down some notes." *Set* always takes a direct object. *To sit* means to assume a sitting position. You "sit in a chair" or "sit on a committee."

Present	Past	Past Participle
set	set	set
sit	sat	sat

To Set
The referee sets the ball on the goal line.
She is setting the table.
He set a new Olympic record.
They have set prices even lower.

To Sit
The player sits on the bench.
He is sitting at the table.
She sat in the airport all night.
Eric has sat on the Supreme Court for ten years.

EXERCISE 4 Choosing the Correct Verb

Underline the correct verb in each sentence.

1. The contractors (lay/laid) the plywood on my driveway.

2. Our prices are (rising/raising), but no one seems to be complaining.

3. Don't let the dogs (sit/set) in the sun without water.

4. The children's behaviour (raised/rose) alarm in parents across the country.

5. We (rise/raise) the temperature slowly to prevent damaging the ovens.

6. They (set/sat) down guidelines for all future competitions.

7. We (had laid/had lain) in the snow for hours before help arrived.

8. They (had laid/had lain) the tiles in a random pattern.

9. (Sit/Set) the packages on the table.

10. We (have risen/have raised) the water level in the tanks.

Shifts in Tense

Events occur in time. In writing, it is important to avoid awkward or illogical shifts in time and write in a consistent tense:

Awkward
I *drove* to the beach and *see* Karen working out with Eli.
  past   present

Consistent
I *drove* to the beach and *saw* Karen working out with Eli.
  past   past

or

I *drive* to the beach and *see* Karen working out with Eli.
  present   present

You can change tenses to show a logical shift or change in time:

I *was born* in Regina but *live* in Saskatoon. Next year I *will move* to Yellowknife.
  past   present   future

You can shift tense to distinguish between past events and subjects that are permanent or still operating:

I *worked* in Ottawa, which *is* the capital of Canada.
  past   present

[Using the past tense *was* to refer to Ottawa might lead readers to believe the city is no longer the state capital.]

Changing shifts in tense alters meaning:

Sandy *wrote* for the *Toronto Star*, which *is* the largest newspaper in the city.
    past   present

[Meaning: Sandy once wrote for the largest newspaper in the city.]

Sandy *writes* for the *Toronto Star*, which *was* the largest paper in the city.
    present   past

[Meaning: Sandy currently writes for a newspaper that used to be the city's largest.]

Sandy *wrote* for the Toronto Star, which
  past
was the largest paper in the city.
  past

[Meaning: Sandy once wrote for a newspaper that is no longer the city's largest or has gone out of business.]

In writing about literature and film, you can relate the plot's events in either past or present tense, as long as you are consistent:

Present
In *Death of a Salesman* the hero *is* frustrated by his lack of success. He *is* especially tormented by his son's rejection of his values. At sixty-three he *struggles* to make sense of a world he *cannot* control.

Past
In *Death of a Salesman* the hero *was* frustrated by his lack of success. He *was* especially tormented by his son's rejection of his values. At sixty-three he *struggled* to make sense of a world he *could* not control.

One of the most common errors student writers make is beginning a passage in one tense, then shifting when there is no change in time:

present

I wake up and face another tough day on the job. The building site is getting busier, and the work is getting tougher. I walk to the corner and take the bus to Ben's house, who drives us to work. We stop for coffee, where Ben *broke* the news. He *told* me he *was* thinking of quitting. "I just can't take the stress anymore," he *said* softly. I look at him and realize how exhausted he is.

past
present

Revised—Present Tense
I wake up and face another tough day on the job. The building site is getting busier, and the work is getting tougher. I walk to the corner and take the bus to Ben's house, who drives us to work. We stop for coffee, where Ben *breaks* the news. He *tells* me he *is* thinking of quitting. "I just can't take the stress anymore," he *says* softly. I look at him and realize how exhausted he is.

Revised—Past Tense
I *woke* up and *faced* another tough day on the job. The building site *was* getting busier, and the work *was* getting tougher. I *walked* to the corner and *took* the bus to Ben's house, who *drove* us to work. We *stopped* for coffee, where Ben broke the news. He told me he was thinking of quitting. "I just can't take the stress anymore," he said softly. I *looked* at him and *realized* how exhausted he *was*.

Note: The best way to check your work for awkward shifts in tense is to read your essay aloud. It is often easier to hear than to see awkward shifts. Remember to shift tense only where there is a clear change in time.

WORKING TOGETHER

Revise this passage from a student essay to eliminate awkward and illogical shifts in tense. Note: *Some shifts in this passage logically distinguish between past events and current or ongoing conditions or situations.*

I was born in Toronto and grew up in Peterborough, where my parents live. I planned to become a contractor like my father and my two brothers, both of whom work for a company that installed and repairs swimming pools.

The summer after I graduated high school, I work for a tree-trimming service in Lawrence. The job is tough. I had to climb trees, saw branches, even cut down whole trees. It was backbreaking work, and even with gloves and protective gear my hands and arms get cut and scraped. I get paid $18.50 an hour but was too exhausted on the weekends to spend much.

One day in August I fell from a tree and break my leg. Unable to work the rest of the summer, I watch TV and surf the Internet. To kill time I even start my own web page. Then it hit me, and I called my boss. I got the idea to have a website for the tree service, showing residents different types of trees, tree diseases, planting problems, and landscaping tips.

My boss ended up hiring me to create a bigger website that let people e-mail pictures of their landscaping problems for preliminary estimate. People like the idea of being able to use the Internet to send in a picture of a tree or some bushes rather than try to explain their problem on the phone. And it saved the company a lot of time and money.

Active and Passive Voice

English has two voices, active and passive. **Active voice** emphasizes the subject—who did the act. **Passive voice** emphasizes to whom or to what an act was done.

Active
The mayor vetoed the bill.
The children greeted their parents.

Sidney selected the restaurant.

Passive
The bill was vetoed by the mayor.
The parents were greeted by their children.
The restaurant was selected by Sidney.

Grammar Choices and Meaning

Active voice is generally preferred because it is direct, strong, and clear:

Active
Century 21 sold the house on the corner.
Karen painted the kitchen last night.
Judge Wilson authorized a wiretap.

Passive voice tends to reverse the order, emphasizing the recipient of the action over the performer of the action sometimes creating a sentence that reports an action without clearly naming who is doing it:

> *Passive*
> The house on the corner was sold by Century 21.
> The kitchen was painted last night by Karen.
> The wiretap was authorized.

Passive voice is used when the act is more significant than its cause:

> *Passive*
> The plane was refuelled by Aviation Services.
> My sister's wedding was delayed by rain.
> The first baseman was hit by a line drive.

Police officers and other investigators are trained to use passive voice in writing reports to avoid jumping to conclusions. Since using the active voice makes a strong connection between the performer of the action and the action itself (the verb), it can lead writers to make assumptions. By writing in the passive voice, reporting can be made more objective. Facts are presented and events related without stressing cause and effect or assigning responsibility:

> *Passive*
> The office manager was found shot to death in his office. His partner was detained for questioning. Traces of gunpowder were found on his hands and clothing. Bloodstains matching the victim's blood type were found on his shirtsleeve.

However, passive voice is also used to *avoid* assigning responsibility:

> *Passive*
> Efforts to resuscitate him were made.
> Complaints against the teachers were filed.
> After the accident, photographs were taken.
> Tests were performed on the engine.

In all these questions the "who" is missing. Who tried to resuscitate him? Who filed complaints? Who took the photographs? Who performed tests?

EXERCISE 5 **Identifying Active and Passive Voice**

Write an A *next to sentences in active voice and* P *next to sentences in passive voice.*

1. _____ Erin showed us the new house.
2. _____ The car was examined thoroughly by the police.
3. _____ DNA results were made available to the press.
4. _____ We washed the dishes before we went to bed.
5. _____ My car was stolen last night.
6. _____ Thieves robbed the art museum during the night.
7. _____ The policy was widely rejected by voters.

8. _____ Several arrests were made.

9. _____ The plane landed safely.

10. _____ Students supported the new budget.

EXERCISE 6 Changing Passive to Active Voice

Rewrite these sentences to change them from passive to active voice. (Note: In some cases you will have to invent a missing subject.)

1. The contract was signed by Jason Andrews.

   _____

2. New dorms were constructed by the university.

   _____

3. The children were rushed to the hospital.

   _____

4. The drinks were served by the waiter.

   _____

5. The bridge was repaired.

   _____

Other Verb Problems

Could Have, Must Have, Should Have, Would Have

Because *have* and *of* sound alike in speaking, it is easy to mistakenly write "could *of*" instead of "could *have*." *Have* is used in verb phrases. *Of* is a preposition showing a relationship:

Have
He could *have* bought a house.
She should *have* called by now.
You must *have* gotten your bill by now.

Of
The price *of* gas is rising.
He is the new chief *of* staff.
Your bill *of* sale is ready.

EXERCISE 7 Revising Common Verb Problems

Rewrite incorrect sentences. Mark correct sentences OK.

1. We should of taken a cab to the airport.

   _____

2. She must have been the centre of attention.

   _____

3. You should of never paid them in cash.

   _____

4. We would have come if only you could of called.

   _____

5. They should of been sued for breach of contract.

   _____

Double Negatives

Use only one negative to express a negative idea. Don't create **double negatives** using words like *hardly, scarcely, no, not,* or *never:*

Double Negative	*Correct*
I never have no money.	I never have any money.
We can't hardly wait for spring break.	We can hardly wait for spring break.
I didn't buy no concert tickets.	I didn't buy any concert tickets.

AVOIDING DOUBLE NEGATIVES

Double negatives are common in some languages and in some English dialects. If you are a native speaker of one of these languages or dialects, be careful to use only one negative word in each clause.

EXERCISE 8 Eliminating Double Negatives

Rewrite the following sentences to eliminate double negatives.

1. She didn't have no car insurance.

   _____

2. The law school never offered no paralegal courses.

   _____

3. The patients were so weak they could hardly take no steps.

   _____

4. The police never found no evidence of fraud.

   _____

5. Mary didn't scarcely have no time to play sports.

   _____

GET THINKING
AND WRITING

CRITICAL THINKING

Write a paragraph describing how your life plans have or have not changed over the years. What did you want to do as a child? What plans did you make in high school? What are your plans now? What would you like to do in the future?

WHAT HAVE YOU WRITTEN?

When you finish writing, review your use of tense, mood, and voice.

1. Write out one of your sentences stated in past tense:

   _____

   Have you used the proper verb to show past tense?

2. Write out one of your sentences stated in present tense:

   _____

   Does the verb state the present tense? Does it match the subject?

3. **Have you avoided errors with verbs such as** *lie* **and** *lay, raise* **and** *rise, set* **and** *sit*?

4. **Have you written** *of* **instead of** *have* **in** *should have* **or** *would have*?

Do you think it is better for a child to be brought up by a full-time parent rather than in daycare? Is this the ideal family situation, or is it just old-fashioned?

Write a paragraph stating your views. Support your points with examples.

WHAT HAVE YOU LEARNED?

Select the right verb in each sentence:

1. _____ If I (was/were) the boss, I'd fire him immediately.

2. _____ The sun (rose/raised) over the clouds.

3. _____ We should (of/have) complained to the dean.

4. _____ I (rung/rang) the bell twice.

5. _____ Jose (struck/striked) out three times in last night's game.

6. _____ Karen worked in Halifax, which (is/was) the largest city in Nova Scotia.

7. _____ Don't (lie/lay) anything on top of the printer.

8. _____ If we (set/sit) any longer we will miss the bus.

9. _____ They left us with hardly (any/no) money.

10. _____ She had (laid/lain) down for a nap when her son arrived.

Answers appear on the following page.

WRITING ON THE WEB

Using a search engine such as Google, Yahoo!, or AltaVista, enter terms such as *verb tense, past tense, past perfect tense, present progressive tense, irregular verbs, subjunctive,* and *passive voice* to locate current sites of interest.

1. Read online newspaper and magazine articles about an issue that interests you and notice how writers use tense to show shifts from past to present.
2. Write an e-mail to a friend about what you did last week. Choose verbs carefully to distinguish past events from ongoing ones.

POINTS TO REMEMBER

1. Explaining *when* something happens is as important as explaining *what* happens.
2. Regular verbs add *-d* or *-ed* to show past tense:

call	called
talk	talked
show	showed
want	wanted

3. Irregular verbs do not add *-d* or *-ed* to show past tense:

set	set
get	got
thrust	thrust
make	made

4. *Lie/lay, rise/raise,* and *set/sit* are often confused:

	To lie means "to rest or recline."		*To lay* means "to place."	
present	lie	*lie down*	lay	*lay tile*
past	lay		laid	
past participle	lain		laid	

	To raise means "to lift."		*To rise* means "to get up."	
present	raise	*raise prices*	rise	*Rise up!*
past	raised		rose	
past participle	raised		risen	

(continued)

POINTS TO REMEMBER *(continued)*

To set means "to place." *To sit* means "to recline."

present	set	*set prices*	sit	*Sit down!*
past	set		sat	
past participle	set		sat	

5. Avoid awkward shifts in tense or time:

Awkward   We *drove* to the pier and *see* the whales.
Correct   We *drove* to the pier and *saw* the whales.

6. Avoid mistaking *of* for *have* in *should have* and *could have:*

I could *have* passed. *not* I could *of* passed.

7. Avoid double negatives:

I don't have any cash. *not* I don't have no cash.

ANSWERS TO WHAT HAVE YOU LEARNED? ON PAGE 337–338
1. were, 2. rose (see page 326), 3. have (see page 335), 4. rang (see page 326), 5. struck (see page 327), 6. is (see page 322), 7. lay (see page 329), 8. sit (see page 330), 9. any (page 336), 10. lain (see page 330)

Pronoun Reference, Agreement, and Case

Do high school sports build character or distract students from their studies?

Write a paragraph describing the positive or negative impact of high school athletics. Support your views with examples.

What Are Pronouns?

Pronouns take the place of nouns. Without pronouns, your writing would be cumbersome:

> Kaitlin drove Kaitlin's new car home for the weekend. Kaitlin visited Kaitlin's parents. Kaitlin's parents were impressed with Kaitlin's new car, but Kaitlin's parents wondered if Kaitlin was spending too much of Kaitlin's salary on new purchases. Kaitlin's parents worried that Kaitlin's parents' daughter was not saving enough money.

Pronouns eliminate needless repetition:

> Kaitlin drove *her* new car home for the weekend. Kaitlin visited *her* parents. *They* were impressed with *her* new car, but *they* wondered if Kaitlin was spending too much of *her* salary on new purchases. *They* worried that *their* daughter was not saving enough money.

WHAT DO YOU KNOW?

Select the correct pronoun in each sentence.

1. _____ (He/him) and Arras are driving to Newfoundland this summer.

2. _____ Between you and (I/me), I think we need a new dean.

3. _____ Either Tina or Ann will lend me (their/her) car.

4. _____ Each of the girls has (their/her) dorm assignment.

5. _____ When I finally got to the top of the CN Tower, all (I/you) could see was fog.

6. _____ The jury is making (its/their) decision as we speak.

7. _____ We are concerned about (him/his) driving.

8. _____ Please give (this/these) documents to someone (who/whom) you can trust.

9. _____ It is (I/me).

10. _____ Was it (he/him) who ran for help?

   Answers appear on the following page.

WHAT ARE YOU TRYING TO SAY?

GET WRITING
AND REVISING

Summarize the plot of one of your favourite movies or television shows in a paragraph. Explain the main characters and events in the story.

_____

_____

_____

_____
_____
_____
_____
_____
_____
_____
_____
_____
_____
_____
_____

WHAT HAVE YOU WRITTEN?

Underline all the pronouns in your paragraphs.

1. Can you circle the noun (antecedent) each pronoun represents?
2. Are plural nouns represented by plural pronouns? Are singular nouns represented by singular pronouns?
3. Are the pronouns in the right case? Do you use *I, we, he, she, they, it* as subjects? Do you use *me, us, him, her, them* as objects? Do you use *my, our, his, hers, their, its* to show possession?

TYPES OF PRONOUNS

The types of pronouns include *personal, indefinite, relative,* and *demonstrative.*

Personal pronouns refer to people and have three forms, depending on how they are used in a sentence: *subjective, objective,* and *possessive.*

	Subjective		Objective		Possessive	
	Singular	Plural	Singular	Plural	Singular	Plural
1st person	I	we	me	us	my (mine)	our (ours)
2nd person	you	you	you	you	your (yours)	your (yours)
3rd person	he	they	him	them	his (his)	their (theirs)
	she		her		her (hers)	
	it		it		its (its)	

He drove *their* car to *our* house, so *we* paid *him.*
They rented a cottage because *it* was cheaper than *our* time-share.

(continued)

Relative pronouns introduce noun and adjective clauses:

who, whoever, whom, whose   which, whichever   that, what, whatever

I will work with *whoever* volunteers.
Tom was levied a thousand-dollar fine, *which* he refused to pay.

Demonstrative pronouns indicate the noun (antecedent):

this, that, these, those

That car is a lemon.
These books are on sale.

Indefinite pronouns refer to abstract persons or things:

Singular				Plural		Singular or Plural		
everyone	someone	anyone	no one	both	few	all	more	none
everybody	somebody	anybody	nobody	many		any	most	some
everything	something	anything	nothing					
each	another	either	neither					

Everyone should do his or her best.   *More* security is needed.
Both girls are attending summer school.   *More* security guards are needed.

Using Pronouns

To prevent confusion, pronouns have to be used with precision.

- Pronouns have to be clearly linked to **antecedents**—the nouns or other pronouns they represent.

Unclear Reference
The walls are covered with graffiti, and the hallways are cluttered with trash.
They just don't care.
 [Whom does *they* refer to—residents, landlords, city inspectors?]

Clear Reference
Tenants cover the walls with graffiti and clutter the hallways with trash.
They just don't care.
 [*They* refers to *tenants*.]

Unclear Reference
Darshini asked Erica to revise *her* report.
 [Whose report is it—Darshini's or Erica's?]

Clear Reference
Darshini sent *her* report to Erica for revision.
Darshini reviewed Erica's report, then asked Erica to revise it.

- Pronouns have to agree with, or match, the antecedent in number:

Incorrect
Every student should bring *their* books to class.
 [*Student* is singular; *their* is plural.]

Singular
Every student should bring *his or her* books to class.
    [Singular *his or her* refers to singular *student.*]

Plural
The students should bring *their* books to class.
    [Plural *their* refers to plural *students.*]

- Pronouns have to agree or match in person:

Incorrect
We went up to the roof where *you* could see the CN Tower.
    [Awkward shift between *we* (first person) and *you* (second person)]

Revised
We went up to the roof where *we* could see the CN Tower.

- Pronouns have to be used in the right case:

Subjective
He took the money to the bank.

Objective
Maria gave *him* the bill.

Possessive
Juanita drove *his* car to the garage.

Reflexive
He did the work *himself.*

- Unnecessary pronouns should be eliminated:

Unnecessary Pronouns
George *he* should buy a new car.
The budget *it* makes no sense.
The teachers *they* are on strike.

Revised
George should buy a new car.
The budget makes no sense.
The teachers are on strike.

Pronoun Reference

To express yourself clearly, pronouns have to be used precisely. Because you know what you want to say, it is very easy to write sentences that make perfect sense to you but will leave your readers confused. The pronoun *he,* for example, can refer to any single male. It is easy to create sentences in which the word could refer to more than one person:

> Paul opened a limo service right after high school. *His* best friend, John, owned a cab service. *They* combined their forces and started Cream City Car Service. Business increased rapidly, but *he* soon found it hard to work with a partner.

Whom does the *he* in the last sentence refer to—Paul or John? Inserting the **antecedent,** the person's name in this case, eliminates confusion:

Paul opened a limo service right after high school. *His* best friend, John, owned a cab service. *They* combined their forces and started Cream City Car Service. Business increased rapidly, but *John* soon found it hard to work with a partner.

Without a clear link between the pronoun (*I, we, you, he, she, they,* and *it*) and the antecedent or noun it represents, sentences can be misleading:

Confusing
The teachers met with the students to discuss their proposal.

Revised
The teachers met with the students to discuss the faculty proposal.
The students discussed their proposal at a meeting with teachers.

In order to correct reference errors, you may have to make only minor repairs to a sentence:

Unclear Reference
Jana gave Sylvia her keys.

Clear Reference
Jana gave her keys to Sylvia.

In other circumstances, you may have to reword the sentence to prevent confusion:

Unclear Reference
Jana gave Sylvia her keys.

Reworded
Jana returned Sylvia's keys.

EXERCISE 1 Eliminating Unclear Pronoun References

Revise the following sentences to eliminate unclear pronoun references. You may add words or change sentence structure.

1. Sara took Carla to her favourite restaurant in Winnipeg.

_____

_____

2. Jamil encouraged Sid to review his tax return for errors.

_____

_____

3. My cousin worked with Fred until he moved to Regina.

_____

_____

4. The children asked their parents to change their clothes before they met with the principal.

_____

_____

5. Armando's nephew told Mr. Mendoza his car needed new tires.

_____

_____

USING *THEY* WITHOUT AN ANTECEDENT

The pronoun *they* is often used without a clear antecedent. In conversation, we frequently use *they* as an abstract reference to people with authority or power:

> "*They* put too much sex and violence on TV."
> "Can you believe what *they* are paying pro athletes these days?"
> "Why don't *they* fix this road?"

In writing, you should be more precise. Make sure every time *they* appears in your paper it is clearly linked to a specific plural noun. Replace unlinked *they*'s with concrete nouns:

> Networks put too much sex and violence on TV.
> Too much sex and violence appears on TV.

> Can you believe what owners are paying pro athletes these days?
> Can you believe what pro athletes are paid these days?

> Why doesn't the county fix this road?
> Why isn't this road fixed?

In editing papers, read them aloud. Pause when you see *they* and determine if it clearly refers to a noun. Revise sentences with unlinked *they*'s to eliminate confusion.

EXERCISE 2 Eliminating Unclear Uses of *They*

Rewrite the following sentences to eliminate unlinked uses of they. *You can revise the sentence to create a clear antecedent (noun) for* they *or eliminate the pronoun by supplying a noun.*

1. The classrooms are dusty. The halls are marked by graffiti. The lockers are smashed. They just don't care about their school.

_____

_____

2. I don't like the way they advertise candy to children.

_____

_____

3. You would think they would take better care of fragile artwork.

_____

_____

4. **Did you see *Sixty Minutes* last night? They showed how they use the Internet to steal people's credit card information.**

_____

_____

5. **When are they going to build cars with better engines?**

_____

_____

Pronoun Agreement

Just as singular subjects take singular verbs, singular nouns take singular pronouns:

teacher	he *or* she
school	it
Miss Khan	she
Eric	he
the goalie	he *or* she
the nun	she
citizen	he *or* she

Miss Landers retired early because *she* wanted to move to Victoria.
The school closed early on Monday, but *it* will open early on Tuesday.
The citizen plays an important role in shaping society. *He or she* votes.

Plural nouns take plural pronouns:

teachers	they
schools	they
the Khans	they
the quarterbacks	they
the nuns	they
citizens	they

The teachers retired early because *they* wanted to take advantage of the new pension.
The schools closed early on Monday, but *they* will open early on Tuesday.
Citizens play an important role in shaping society. *They* vote.

Singular and Plural Nouns and Pronouns

- Indefinite pronouns refer to no specific person, idea, or object and are always singular:

another	either	nobody	somebody
anybody	everybody	no one	someone
anyone	everyone	none	something
anything	everything	nothing	
each	neither	one	

Another boy is missing, and *he* is only six years old.
Somebody left *his* shoulder guards in the locker room.
Neither girl is going to get *her* paycheck on time.
Each citizen must cast *his or her* vote.

- Some nouns that end in *s* and look like plurals are singular:

    economics   mathematics   athletics   physics

    Mathematics is a tough course. *It* demands a lot of time.

- Some nouns that may refer to one item are plural:

    pants   gloves   scissors   fireworks

    My scissors are dull. *They* need sharpening.

- Proper nouns that look plural are singular if they are names of companies, organizations, or titles of books, movies, television shows, or works of art:

    General Motors   *The Three Musketeers*   The League of Women Voters

    I love *The Three Musketeers* because *it* is funny.

- Units of time and amounts of money are generally singular:

    Two hundred dollars is not enough; *it* won't even pay for my plane ticket.

- They appear as plurals to indicate separate items:

    Three loonies *were* lying on the table. *They* were brand new.

Avoiding Sexism

Because singular pronouns refer to only one sex or the other—*he* or *she*—it can be easy to create sentences that fail to include both males and females. It is acceptable, however, to use only *he* or *she* when writing about a single person or a group of people of the same sex:

Michel has a cold, but *he* came to work this morning.
Each of the boys rode *his* bicycle to school.
Kelly is going to night school because *she* wants an associate degree.
Neither woman wanted to lose *her* place in line.

When writing about people in general, it is important to avoid sexist pronoun use:

Sexist
Every citizen must cast *his* vote.   [Aren't women citizens?]
A nurse must use *her* judgment.   [What about male nurses?]

Methods of Avoiding Sexism

- Provide both male and female singular pronouns:

    Every citizen must cast *his or her* vote.
- Use plural antecedents:

    Citizens must cast *their* votes.

- Reword the sentence to eliminate the need for pronouns:

Every citizen must vote.

USING *THEY* TO AVOID SEXISM

In speaking, people often use *they* rather than *he or she* to reduce awkwardness:

Every student should do *their* best.
Each employee is required to meet *their* supervisor before *they* can apply for a raise.
A good teacher knows *their* students.

This agreement error is often accepted in speech, but writing requires more formal methods of eliminating sexism. If you find yourself using *they* to refer to a singular noun or pronoun, use these methods to avoid both sexism and an error in agreement.

1. Use plural nouns and pronouns to match *they:*

All *students* should do *their* best.
All *employees* are required to meet *their* supervisors before *they* can apply for raises.
Good *teachers* know *their* students.

2. Eliminate the need for pronouns:

A student should study hard.
Every employee must have approval from a supervisor to apply for a raise.
A good teacher knows students.

3. State as commands:

Employees—meet with your supervisor before applying for a raise.

EXERCISE 3 **Selecting the Right Pronoun**

Underline the right pronoun in each sentence.

1. Canadians can go to the Library and Archives Canada website to get information about (its/their) prime ministers.

2. The site examines the prime ministers' political careers as well as (his/her/their) private lives.

3. All Canadians should know that Sir John A. Macdonald was its/their first prime minister.

4. The Bank of Canada honoured Sir John A. Macdonald by putting his picture on (its/their) ten-dollar bills.

5. Lester B. Pearson was Canada's fourteenth prime minister. In 1984, Torontonians honoured him by naming (its/their) airport the Lester B. Pearson International Airport.

6. Canada's first female prime minister was Kim Campbell; she was also (its/their) first native British Columbian prime minister.

7. Canadians will be surprised to learn that (its/their) first woman prime minister was also the first former prime minister to be given a diplomatic post after leaving office.

8. Canada will never forget Jean Chrétien, (its/their) twentieth prime minister.

9. Canadians will remember that Chrétien was Canada's last twentieth-century prime minister and (its/their) first prime minister of the twenty-first century.

10. In recognition of (his/her/their) contributions, our deceased prime ministers have been designated as persons of national historic significance.

Avoiding Shifts in Point of View

Pronouns express three persons:

	First	**Second**	**Third**
singular	I, me, my, mine	you, you, your, yours	he, him, his, his/she, her, her, hers/it
plural	we, us, our, ours	you, you, your, yours	they, them, their, theirs, its

Avoid making illogical shifts when writing. Maintain a consistent point of view.

Shift
We went bird watching, but *you* couldn't even find a robin.
When *I* went to college, *you* couldn't go to law school part-time.

Revised

We went bird watching, but *we* couldn't even find a robin.	[consistent use of plural first person]
When *I* went to college, students couldn't go to law school part-time.	[use of *students* eliminates need for second pronoun]

EXERCISE 4 Eliminating Pronoun Shifts in Point of View

Revise the following sentences to eliminate illogical pronoun shifts in point of view.

1. When he moved to Vancouver, you could find a nice apartment for three hundred dollars a month.

_____

_____

2. If one wants to succeed these days, you really should know computers.

_____

_____

3. We always thought he would be a star—you could tell by watching him rehearse.

   _____

   _____

4. I moved to Toronto, but the heat in the summer is more than you can tolerate.

   _____

   _____

5. We went to the beach to swim, but it was so cold you had to stay inside.

   _____

   _____

Using the Right Case

Nouns serve different functions in sentences. They can be subjects or objects, and they can be possessive. Pronouns appear in different forms to show how they function:

They gave _her_ car to _him_.
Subject   possessive   object

These different forms are called "cases."

PRONOUN CASES

	Subjective	Objective	Possessive	Reflexive/Intensive
singular	I	me	my, mine	myself
	you	you	you, yours	yourself
	he	him	his	himself
	she	her	her, hers	herself
	it	it	its	itself
plural	we	us	our, ours	ourselves
	you	you	your, yours	yourselves
	they	them	their, theirs	themselves
singular or plural	who	whom	whose	

In most sentences we automatically use pronouns in the right case, telling our readers the role the pronoun plays:

Subjective pronouns serve the subject of a verb:

_We_ are driving to Florida on Monday.
This week _she_ is moving to New York.

Objective pronouns serve as objects:

The rental agency reserved a car for *us*.
Give *him* the money.

Possessive pronouns demonstrate the pronoun owns something:

Our car is being repaired.
The garage lost *her* car keys.

Note: Because these pronouns already indicate possession, no apostrophes are needed.

USING POSSESSIVE PRONOUNS

In English, possessive pronouns—*my, your, his, her, our, their*—must agree with the nouns they represent, not the words they modify.

Incorrect   The club members advertised *its* bake sale on TV.

Correct   The club members advertised *their* bake sale on TV.

The possessive pronoun *their* agrees with *club members*, not *bake sale*.

Reflexive pronouns refer to other pronouns:

We moved the furniture *ourselves*.

Intensive pronouns add emphasis:

I myself repaired the roof.

There are, however, some pronoun uses that can be confusing, including plurals, comparisons, and sentences using certain words.

Plural Constructions

Using a single pronoun as a subject or object is generally easy:

He gave the money to Paul.
Paul gave the money to *him*.

However, when pronouns are part of plural subjects and objects, many writers make mistakes:

Incorrect
Jane, Jordan, William, and *him* gave the money to Paul.
Paul gave the money to Jane, Jordan, William, and *he*.

Correct
Jane, Jordan, William, and *he* gave the money to Paul. [subjective case]
Paul gave the money to Jane, Jordan, William, and *him*. [objective case]

When editing, the quickest method of checking case is to simplify the sentence by eliminating the other nouns:

. . . *he* gave the money to Paul.
Paul gave the money to . . . *him*.

Between

Pronouns that serve as objects of prepositions use the objective case—*him, her, me, them.* Most constructions give writers few problems—to *him,* for *them,* with *her.* However, the preposition *between* is often misused:

Incorrect (Subjective Case)	Correct (Objective Case)
between you and *I*	between you and *me*
between you and *he*	between you and *him*
between you and *she*	between you and *her*
between *he* and *she*	between *him* and *her*
between *they* and the teachers	between *them* and the teachers

Although people often use the subjective case with *between* in speaking, the objective case is correct and should be used in writing.

Comparisons

Comparisons using *than* or *as* use the subjective case:

He is taller than *I.*	*not*	He is taller than *me.*
Nancy is smarter than *he.*	*not*	Nancy is smarter than *him.*

These constructions are confusing because the second verb is usually omitted. To test which pronoun to use, add the missing verb to see which pronoun sounds correct:

He is taller than *I am.*	*not*	He is taller than *me am.*
Nancy is smarter than *he is.*	*not*	Nancy is smarter than *him is.*

The Verb *To Be*

Subjective pronouns follow *to be* verbs:

It is *she* on the phone.	*not*	It is *her* on the phone.
It is *I.*	*not*	It is *me.*
Was it *they* in the car?	*not*	Was it *them* in the car?

Because we often use phrases like "It's me" or "Is that her talking?" when we speak, the correct forms can sound awkward. The subjective case is correct and should be used in writing.

If your sentences still sound awkward, rewrite them to alter the *to be–pronoun* form:

She is on the phone.
I am at the door.
Did *they* take the car?

Who and Whom

Who and *whom* are easily confused because they are generally used in questions and change the usual word pattern. *Who* is subjective and serves as the subject of a verb:

Who is at the door?   *Who* bought the car?   *Who* is going to summer school?

Whom is objective and serves as the object of a verb or a preposition:

Give the money to *whom*?   To *whom* it may concern.   For *whom* is this intended?

To help choose the right word, substitute *he* and *him.* If *he* sounds better, use *who.* If *him* sounds better, use *whom.*

(Who/whom) called?
(*He*/him) called.   [Use *who.* "Who called?"]

Take it from (whoever/whomever) can help.
(*He*/him) can help.   [Use *whoever.* "whoever can help"]

For (who/whom) are you looking?
For (he/him).   [Use *whom.* "for whom"]

This and *That*, *These* and *Those*

This and *that* are singular:

This book is overdue.   *That* boy is in trouble.   *This* is a fine day.

These and *those* are plural:

These books are overdue.   *Those* boys are in trouble.   *These* are fine days.

They and *Them*

They is subjective and used when subject to a verb:

They are leaving town on Monday.   You know *they* don't work on Sunday.

Them is objective and used as an object of prepositions or verbs:

Give the money to *them.*   We can't get *them* to work on Sunday.

UNNECESSARY PRONOUNS

Although in speaking people sometimes insert a pronoun directly after a noun, they are unnecessary and should be eliminated:

Unnecessary
Nathalie *she* is going to retire early.
The children *they* won't listen.
The book *it* doesn't make sense.

Revised
Nathalie is going to retire early.
The children won't listen.
The book doesn't make sense.

EXERCISE 5 Selecting the Right Pronoun Case

Select the right pronoun in each sentence.

1. Lino and (I/me) are going to the festival tomorrow.
2. The manager promised free tickets to Lino and (I/me) for helping them last year.
3. That gives (we/us) enough time to finish the job.
4. The faculty, the parents, and (he/him) will have to settle this issue.
5. The school board offered greater funding to the faculty and (him/he).
6. That is more work than (we/us) can handle.
7. She is offering more money to (we/us).
8. Ted, Frank, and (she/her) are leaving early to avoid the rush.
9. The airport limo was sent for Ted, Frank, and (she/her).
10. You know (he/him) and (I/me) went to the same grade school?

EXERCISE 6 Selecting the Right Pronoun

Select the right pronoun in each sentence.

1. Between (they/them) and (we/us) there is little desire for compromise.
2. Vince, Sissy, Eric, Rumy, and (I/me) are going to the library.
3. We could never afford (those/this) house.
4. The administration won't let (they/them) work on weekends.
5. (These/This) players are faster than (they/them).
6. Does Ted or (I/me) owe any money?
7. Give all the money either to Sue or to (he/him).
8. Don't let (she/her) work too hard.
9. It is (he/him) again.
10. We want to have a party for Élise and (he/him) next week.

WORKING TOGETHER

Working with a group of students, revise the pronoun errors in the following e-mail:

New employees must submit pay forms to their supervisors no later than May 1. If your supervisor does not receive this form, they cannot request payment and you will not receive you cheque on time. If you have questions, please feel free to call Faraz Rehman, Janet Sherman, or I. We are usually in our offices in the afternoon. If you are unsure which

supervisor you should report to, call Frank Fallon's
office or e-mail he at frank.fallon@abc.com.

Ted Matthews

EXERCISE 7 Cumulative Exercise

Rewrite each of the sentences, correcting errors in pronoun use, subject–verb agreement, run-ons, and fragments.

1. Jim or me are working on July 1.

   _____

   _____

2. Having worked all summer, her was upset when bonuses were cancelled.

   _____

   _____

3. The teachers and them discussed the new textbook it comes with free CDs.

   _____

   _____

4. Terry and him working all weekend.

   _____

   _____

5. They gave the job to we students but they never provided the supplies we needed.

   _____

   _____

*GET THINKING
AND WRITING*

CRITICAL THINKING

What is the toughest challenge you face at this point in the semester? Is it an upcoming exam or paper? Is it finding time to study or juggling work and school? Write a paragraph describing the challenge you face and how you plan to meet it.

WHAT HAVE YOU WRITTEN?

1. Underline all the pronouns and circle their antecedents. Is there a clear link between the pronouns and the nouns or pronouns they represent?
   - Pay attention to uses of *they.*
2. Do nouns and pronouns agree in number? Do plural nouns have plural pronouns? Do singular nouns have singular pronouns?
   - Pay attention to nouns that look plural but are singular—*economics, committee, jury.*
   - Remember that indefinite pronouns like *each, everyone, anyone, someone,* and *somebody* are singular.
3. Review your use of case.
   - Use the subjective case in comparisons and with pronouns following *to be* verbs: "taller than I" or "It is I."
   - Use objective case with between: "between him and me."

WHAT HAVE YOU LEARNED?

Select the right pronoun in each sentence.

1. _____ You have to choose between Sally and (I/me).

2. _____ Chris Lafleur, Kelly Samson, and (I/me) were late.

3. _____ (This/These) plans of yours are very impressive.

4. _____ Is that Max and (she/her) in the lobby?

5. _____ Each student must bring (their/his or her) lab report to class.

6. _____ How will the new policy affect (we/us)?

7. _____ Give the door prize to (whomever/whoever) arrives first.

8. _____ (We/Us) boys will get a new gym next year.

9. _____ The school is telling the teachers, parents, and (we/us) to expect a change.

10. _____ You and (she/her) work too hard.

Answers appear on the following page.

GET WRITING

Compare this picture with the one on page 340. Do you think playing sports affects high school girls differently than it does boys? Do they learn different lessons? Do they face more or less pressure than male athletes?

Write a short paragraph comparing male and female high school athletes.

WRITING ON THE WEB

Using a search engine such as AltaVista, Yahoo!, or Google, enter *pronoun, pronoun agreement, using pronouns,* and *pronoun cases* to locate current sites of interest.

Review e-mails you may have sent and look at your past use of pronouns. Can you locate errors in your writing? Which pronoun constructions have given you the most trouble in the past? Mark pages in this chapter for future reference.

POINTS TO REMEMBER

Pronouns have to be used with precision to prevent confusion.

1. Pronouns must clearly refer to a noun:

    Unclear Reference
    Jana gave Vicki *her* keys.

    Clear Reference
    Jana gave *her* keys to Vicki.

2. Pronouns and nouns match in number:

    Each girl took *her* car.   [singular]
    The *girls* took *their* cars.   [plural]

3. Pronouns use consistent point of view:

    Inconsistent
    When *one* visits Peterborough, *you* have to dine at St. Veronus.
    When *I* work overtime, *it* gets boring.

    Consistent
    When *you* visit Peterborough, *you* have to dine at St. Veronus.
    When *I* work overtime, *I* get bored.

4. Pronouns must appear in the right case:

    Subjective Case
    Who is at the door?
    She is smarter than I.
    It is I.
    Was that she on the phone?

    Objective Case
    To whom it may concern.
    Between you and me, the film is too long.

5. Pronouns directly following nouns they represent are unnecessary:

    Unnecessary
    The school *it* closed last week.
    Frank *he* works weekends.

    Revised
    The school closed last week.
    Frank works weekends.

ANSWERS TO WHAT HAVE YOU LEARNED? ON PAGE 357
1. me (see page 353), 2. I (see page 352), 3. These (see page 343), 4. she (see page 353), 5. his or her (see page 343), 6. us (see page 351), 7. whoever (see page 354), 8. We (see page 352), 9. us (see page 351), 10. she (see page 351)

23

Adjectives and Adverbs

GET WRITING

How has the Internet changed society? Does it make life easier, create jobs, and link people to information that can improve their lives? Or does it divide society into those with access and those without? Jobs are now posted on the Internet. Does this make it harder for some people to find employment?

Write a paragraph describing one or more positive or negative effects of the Internet. If you use the Internet, describe your online experiences.

What Are Adjectives and Adverbs?

The most important words in a sentence are the subject—the actor or main idea—and the verb, which connects the subject to actions or other words. Adjectives and adverbs add meaning to a basic sentence by telling us more about nouns and verbs.

Adjectives are words and phrases that describe nouns and pronouns:

a *red* hat   he was *smart*   a *restored antique* car

Adverbs are words and phrases that describe verbs, adjectives, and other adverbs. They generally end in *-ly:*

She walked *slowly.*   *hotly* debated   a *newly* restored antique car

Both add meaning to basic sentences:

Basic Sentence
Mary bought a car.

Basic Sentence Enhanced with Adjectives
Mary bought a *repainted used* car that was *affordable* and *easy to repair.*

Basic Sentence Enhanced with Adjectives and Adverbs
Mary *impulsively* bought a *recently* repainted used car that was affordable and *very* easy to repair.

WHAT DO YOU KNOW?

Identify the modifiers in each sentence by underlining adjectives and circling adverbs.

1. Recently discovered documents reveal a former city councillor accepted questionable campaign contributions from convicted criminals.

2. My favourite movie is *Curse of the Jade Scorpion* starring Woody Allen, who plays a humble insurance investigator who becomes a jewel thief after being hypnotized.

3. The Canadian Association of Women Executives & Entrepreneurs is holding its annual convention in Ottawa in late December.

4. She drove carefully during the blizzard, slowly following the map Carrie gave her.

5. Laura Kensington was a noted forties singer whose carefully phrased versions of jazz classics made her a popular radio star.

6. Erik cautiously opened the dented lid of the just discovered trunk.

7. The pension board methodically investigates new stock certificates before investing in new companies.

8. Jenna is seriously looking for a two-bedroom apartment near campus that is affordable and easy to clean.

9. The freshly waxed furniture looked brand-new.

10. The office is so unbelievably old it has dial phones, typewriters, adding machines, and a 1930s mimeograph.

Answers appear on the following page.

WHAT ARE YOU TRYING TO SAY?

GET WRITING AND REVISING

Describe a recent movie or television program you found interesting. Explain what made it fascinating—the plot, the characters, the style, the theme?

_____

_____

_____

_____

_____

_____

_____

_____

_____

_____

_____

_____

_____

WHAT HAVE YOU WRITTEN?

Read through your description and underline each adjective and circle each adverb. Notice how important modifiers are in expressing your ideas. If you eliminated the adjectives and adverbs, would your writing have the same effect? Would readers be able to appreciate your opinions or understand what you are trying to say?

Understanding Adjectives

Some words are clearly adjectives because they describe other words. They add information about nouns and pronouns, telling us about their age, shape, colour, quality, quantity, or character:

new	round	red	rich	numerous
old	square	yellow	poor	many
recent	oval	tan	mediocre	few
classic	pear-shaped	purple	stable	single

Some adjectives are formed from nouns and verbs and have distinct endings.

Noun Form	Adjective	Verb Form	Adjective
South	Southern	slice	sliced
automobile	automotive	paint	painted
law	legal	choreograph	choreographed
medicine	medical	audit	audited

Past participles—past-tense verbs—are adjectives: *broken* window, *torn* shirt, *forgotten* keys, *frozen* pizza.

Other nouns and verbs appear as adjectives with no spelling change. You can tell they are adjectives only by context, their position in a sentence:

We bought *automobile* insurance.	Put that in the *paint* display.
I read a *law* book.	She liked the *choreography* director.
The aspirin is in the *medicine* cabinet.	There is going to be an *audit* review.

These words serve as adjectives because they add meaning to nouns:

What kind of insurance?	*automobile* insurance	Which display?	*paint* display
What kind of book?	*law* book	Which director?	*choreography* director
Which cabinet?	*medicine* cabinet	What kind of review?	*audit* review

ADJECTIVES AND PLURAL NOUNS

In many languages, such as Spanish, adjectives must agree with the nouns they modify. In English there is only one adjective form for both singular and plural nouns.

Singular   He wore an *old* suit.
Plural   He wore *old* suits.

EXERCISE 1 Identifying Adjectives

Underline the adjectives in each sentence.

1. On December 6, 1917, an extremely powerful explosion shattered the wartime port of Halifax.

2. The collision of a Belgian relief vessel, the *Imo,* and a French munitions carrier, the *Mont Blanc,* in Halifax Harbour during World War I caused the world's largest man-made explosion before Hiroshima.

3. The morning of December 6, 1917, was clear and sunny but by the end of that historic day, more than a thousand people would die.

4. Nine thousand more would be injured and maimed by the explosive reverberations resulting from the collision.

5. The Mont Blanc rammed Pier 6, setting its wood pilings on fire.

6. Water around the ship vaporized, a huge wave flooded the streets of Halifax and Dartmouth and swept many people back into the harbour, where they drowned.

7. The Halifax hit by the explosion was unattractive, poorly serviced, and outmoded, said sociologists.

8. The massive reconstruction that followed transformed the north end of Halifax.

9. The sadness and hard work that followed the explosion has inspired writers ever since.

10. The best-known work is Hugh MacLennan's 1941 novel, *Barometer Rising*.

EXERCISE 2 Using Adjectives

Add adjectives in each sentence.

1. I drove Jorge's car, which was _____ and _____.

2. The _____ school was closed for _____ repairs.

3. We had lunch at a _____ restaurant, which was _____ and _____.

4. Her _____ speeches created _____ reactions from her _____ listeners.

5. The _____ apartment building was _____ and _____.

6. The _____ show was _____ and _____.

7. He was a _____ and _____ musician.

8. The job requires applicants who are _____, _____, and _____.

9. The _____ store is selling _____ clothing at _____ prices.

10. The school's _____ policy angered _____ students who were _____.

EXERCISE 3 Using Participles

Past participles are adjectives. Often in speaking, however, people drop the -ed endings and forget to add them in writing. In each sentence, underline the misused past participle and write out the correct adjective form.

1. It was so hot we drank ice tea all afternoon.   _____

2. We drove a rent car to Toronto.   _____

3. They served us mash potatoes and steam carrots.   _____

4. The salad has cheese and dice ham.   _____

5. Sara had to wear a borrow dress to the wedding.   _____

6. Those confuse policies wasted our funds.   _____

7. The date material is totally obsolete.   _____

8. It's the greatest thing since slice bread.   _____

9. She had coffee and a soft-boil egg.   _____

10. Her reason arguments won over her critics.   _____

COMMAS AND ADJECTIVES

Place a comma between two unrelated adjectives describing one noun or pronoun:

We saw a new, fascinating film.   They offered us a nutritious, inexpensive meal.

Do not place a comma between two related adjectives describing one noun or pronoun:

We saw a new Woody Allen film.   They offered us hot apple pie.

Apply this simple test to see if you need commas: Read the sentence aloud and place the word *and* between the two adjectives. If the sentence sounds OK, add a comma:

We saw a new *and* fascinating film. [sounds OK, add comma]

If the sentence sounds awkward, do not add a comma:

We saw a new *and* Woody Allen film. [sounds awkward, no comma needed]

ORDER OF MULTIPLE ADJECTIVES

When using two or more adjectives to modify the same noun, you must arrange them according to their meanings. Follow the order indicated below:

- Evaluation   charming, painful, valid
- Size   enormous, large, tiny
- Shape   rectangular, round, square
- Age   youthful, middle-aged, ancient
- Colour   orange, blue, brown
- Nationality   Libyan, Chinese, Canadian
- Religion   Hindu, Catholic, Muslim
- Material   concrete, stone, adobe

Examples:
We rented rooms in a *charming old Spanish* castle.
A *tall young African* gentleman stood behind the pulpit.

Understanding Adverbs

Adverbs describe verbs, adjectives, and other adverbs. Adverbs are usually formed by adding *-ly* to the adjective form:

adjective	+ -*ly*	=	adverb	adjective	+ -*ly*	=	adverb
careful	-*ly*		carefully	delicate	-*ly*		delicately
cautious	-*ly*		cautiously	soft	-*ly*		softly

adjective +	-ly	=	adverb	adjective +	-ly	=	adverb
hot	-ly		hotly	methodical	-ly		methodically
legal	-ly		legally	beautiful	-ly		beautifully

Other adverbs do not end in -ly:

fast   hard   just   right   straight

EXERCISE 4 Identifying Adverbs

Underline the adverbs in each sentence.

1. Unlike football, basketball was developed by an undeniably creative individual.

2. This all-American game was actually invented by a Canadian-born minister, who was greatly concerned about young people and athletics.

3. Dr. James Naismith, who is largely unknown to today's fans, developed this quick-moving, fast-paced game.

4. While working as the athletics director of a YMCA, Naismith sought to overcome a routinely vexing problem.

5. During the winter young people became increasingly bored with indoor gymnastics.

6. Naismith wanted to invent a game people could play easily with little equipment.

7. Considering the limitations of most gyms, he carefully developed an indoor game using just one ball and a basket.

8. Today's NBA fans would find Naismith's game unbelievably crude.

9. The first basket was actually a peach basket carefully suspended above the court.

10. Someone had to stand patiently on a ladder to retrieve the ball every time a player made a basket.

EXERCISE 5 Using Adverbs

Add adverbs in each sentence.

1. Avril moved very _____ and spoke very _____.

2. Ann speaks Chinese _____ and Bill understands Spanish _____; however, neither is _____ bilingual.

3. The soup tastes _____, but the salad tastes _____.

4. My work is quite _____ and when I come home, I need to sit _____ and relax.

5. I _____ watch television, and _____ I read a book.

6. He studied _____, but he failed the math test.

7. I woke _____, dressed _____ but I arrived _____.

8. My supervisor _____ reprimanded me and told me to start working _____.

9. I promised myself that I would go to bed _____ and get out of bed _____ when the alarm rings.

10. When I am at work, I serve customers _____ and clean the tables _____.

Grammar Choices and Meaning

Because both adjectives and adverbs modify other words, they can be easily confused. Changing an adjective to an adverb changes meaning:

Form	Meaning
adjective + adjective fresh sliced bread	bread that is both fresh and sliced
adverb + adjective freshly sliced bread	bread (fresh or stale) that has just been sliced
adjective + adjective new waxed floor	a floor that is both new and waxed
adverb + adjective newly waxed floor	a floor (new or old) that has just been waxed
adjective + adjective great, expanded program	a program that is both great and expanded
adverb + adjective greatly expanded program	a program (of any quality) that has vastly expanded

Use adjectives and adverbs precisely in modifying verbs of sense—*see, hear, feel, smell, touch,* and *taste.*

Adjective: I feel poor after the accident. [*Poor* modifies the noun *I,* suggesting the writer feels broke or financially distressed by the accident.]

Adverb: I feel poorly after the accident. [*Poorly* modifies the verb *feel,* suggesting the writer is injured or in ill health following the accident.]

POINT TO REMEMBER

In speaking, people commonly use the shorter adjective form when an adverb is needed:

"Drive careful, now."   instead of   "Drive careful<u>ly</u>, now."
"Do the tax work accurate."   "Do the tax work accurate<u>ly</u>."
"That's real good coffee."   "That is real<u>ly</u> good coffee."

(continued)

"He drove real slow."   "He drove really slowly."
"She acted crazy."   "She acted crazily."

In writing, make sure you use adverbs (which often end in -ly) to modify verbs, adjectives, and other adverbs.

Good/Well, Bad/Badly

Two adjective/adverb pairs commonly confused are *good/well* and *bad/badly*.

Good *and* bad *are adjectives:*

You look good. [You appear attractive.]

I feel bad. [I am depressed or sad.]

Well *and* badly *are adverbs:*

You look well. [You appear healthy.]

I feel badly. [I have difficulty sensing touch.]

Good *and* bad *modify nouns and pronouns:*

She looked *good* despite her recent accident.

She had a *bad* fracture in her right arm.

Well *and* badly *modify verbs, adjectives, and other adverbs:*

She walked *well* despite injuring her leg.

Her right arm was *badly* fractured.

Good and *bad* and *well* and *badly* have special comparative and superlative forms:

Basic	Comparative	Superlative
good	better	best
bad	worse	worst
well	better	best
badly	worse	worst

That pasta was *good,* but the *best* pasta in town is served at Rocco's.
Your spare tire is *bad,* but mine is *worse.*
I sing *well,* but I have to admit he is *better.*
That is a *badly* designed house, but the *worst* designed structure in town is the bank.

EXERCISE 6 Using Adjectives and Adverbs

Select the correct adjective or adverb in each sentence.

1. The Toronto Blue Jays have a (good/well) pitching staff this year.

2. The Montreal Canadiens are playing (good/well) this season.

3. The new stadium will offer (better/best) seating than the old stadium.

4. I visit ten or fifteen airports a year, and this is by far the (worse/worst) one.

5. The grade ten class is (better/best) in math and science than the grade eleven class.

6. You will do (good/well) on the exam if you don't get too anxious.

7. She sings (good/well) songs for a young audience.

8. I felt (bad/badly) about Isaac losing his job.

9. The streets were so (bad/badly) paved, the city is suing the contractor.

10. They played so (bad/badly) even the most loyal fans walked out in the first quarter.

EXERCISE 7 Choosing Adjectives and Adverbs

Underline the correct modifier in each sentence. Remember that adjectives modify nouns and pronouns, and adverbs modify verbs, adjectives, and other adverbs.

1. The press has (frequent/frequently) used the term "crime of the century" to describe a (particular/particularly) infamous criminal act.

2. The nation was (deep/deeply) shocked in March 1932 when newspaper headlines and radio broadcasts announced that Charles Lindbergh Jr. had been taken from his crib.

3. Following instructions by the kidnapper, Lindbergh (ready/readily) paid the $50,000 ransom, but his son was not returned.

4. The (intense/intensely) search for the missing child took bizarre turns.

5. Al Capone offered to help find the Lindbergh baby, provided he was released from prison so he could use his (vast/vastly) underground network.

6. Two months later the (bad/badly) decomposed body of Charles Lindbergh Jr. was discovered less than two miles from the Lindbergh home.

7. In 1934 a man paid a New York gas station attendant with a ten-dollar bill authorities (quick/quickly) identified as ransom money.

8. Hauptmann maintained his innocence, but New Jersey's attorney general, who prosecuted the case, presented jurors with an (overwhelming/overwhelmingly) barrage of evidence.

9. Hauptmann was convicted and sentenced to death, and despite a new investigation ordered by the (new/newly) elected governor, he was executed in 1936.

10. The Lindbergh case remains controversial. In 1976 Anthony Hopkins played Hauptmann in a movie that depicted him as guilty; twenty years later, Stephen Rea portrayed Hauptmann as an innocent victim of circumstances in a movie (ironic/ironically) called *The Crime of the Century.*

Comparisons

Adjectives and adverbs are often used in comparing two things. There are three basic rules for showing comparisons:

1. Add -*er* for adjectives and adverbs with one syllable:

Adjectives

Jiang is *tall.*	Jiang is *taller* than Jim.
The house is *old.*	The house is *older* than you think.
The street is *wet.*	The street is *wetter* than the sidewalk.

Adverbs

He sang *loud*.   He sang *louder* than Blair.
She worked *hard*.   She worked *harder* than last week.
They drive *fast*.   They drive *faster* than they should.

2. Use *more* for adjectives with more than one syllable that do not end in *-y:*

The car is *expensive*.   The car is *more expensive* than I can afford.
He is *intelligent*.   He is *more intelligent*.

Use *more* for adverbs; others require adding *-er* to the base form (never use *more* and *-er*):

He spoke *boldly*.   She spoke *more boldly* than before.
He ran *fast*.   She ran *faster*.

3. Add *-ier* after dropping the *-y* for adjectives and adverbs ending in *-y:*

Adjective
The game is *easy*. The game is *easier* than you think.

Adverb
She felt *lucky*.   She felt luckier than her sister.

EXERCISE 8 Using Adjectives and Adverbs in Comparisons

Write out the proper comparative form of each adjective and adverb, then use it in a sentence.

1. **effective** _____

   _____

2. **lazy** _____

   _____

3. **rusty** _____

   _____

4. **loud** _____

   _____

5. **happy** _____

   _____

6. **icy** _____

   _____

7. **cold** _____

   _____

8. **costly** _____

   _____

9. fragile _____

_____

10. fascinating _____

_____

AVOIDING DOUBLE COMPARISONS

When speaking, some people use double comparisons:

Sara is *more smarter* than Beth.
This car is *more older* than mine.
The final is *more harder* than the midterm.

Because both *more* and *-er* indicate something greater; only one is needed:

Sara is *smarter* than Beth.
This car is *older* than mine.
The final is *harder* than the midterm.

Using Superlatives

Comparisons show a difference between two items:

Luc is *older* than Sean.

To show differences between three or more items, use superlative forms:

Luc is the *oldest* boy in class.

There are three basic rules for creating superlative adjectives and adverbs:

1. Add *-est* to adjectives and adverbs with one syllable:

Basic	Comparative	Superlative
hot	hotter	hottest
bold	bolder	boldest
fast	faster	fastest

2. Add *-iest* after dropping the *-y* in adjectives and adverbs that end in *-y:*

Basic	Comparative	Superlative
pretty	prettier	prettiest
easy	easier	easiest
silly	sillier	silliest

3. Use *most* for adjectives and adverbs with two or more syllables that do not end in *-y:*

Basic	Comparative	Superlative
exciting	more exciting	most exciting
relaxing	more relaxing	most relaxing
suitable	more suitable	most suitable

POINTS TO REMEMBER

Remember that superlatives—which usually end in *-est*—are used only when writing about three or more items. Many people mistakenly use superlatives instead of comparisons when writing about only two items:

Incorrect Use of Superlatives
Ambreen is the *eldest* of our two daughters.
In comparing Toronto and Halifax, Toronto is the *biggest*.

Correct Use of Comparison
Ambreen is the *elder* of our two daughters.
In comparing Toronto and Halifax, Toronto is *bigger*.

Do not use superlatives with absolute words such as *impossible, perfect, round, destroyed,* or *demolished.* These terms have no degree. If something is *impossible,* it means that it is not possible, not just difficult. If a building is *destroyed,* it is damaged beyond all repair. To say it is "completely destroyed" is repetitive, like saying someone is "completely dead."

Incorrect
The house was completely demolished.
The room was perfectly round.

Correct
The house was demolished.
The room was round.

EXERCISE 9 Eliminating Errors in Adjective and Adverb Use

Revise each of the following sentences to eliminate errors in using adjectives and adverbs.

1. Born to former slaves, Sarah Walker was orphaned at seven, married at fourteen, and widowed at twenty, enduring one of the worse upbringings possible.

   _____

   _____

2. She laboured steady for twenty years as a laundress to support her daughter.

   _____

   _____

3. Her life radical changed when she invented a remarkably line of hair-care products for black women.

   _____

   _____

4. She sold her new developed products door-to-door, and eventual opened her own company.

   _____

   _____

5. Soon Sarah Walker's company was employing hundreds of newly workers.

_____

_____

6. Walker opened a beauty college to train black beauticians, when most black women were usual limited to working as cooks or maids.

_____

_____

7. Walker's rapid expanding enterprise also trained women to become sales agents and salon operators, allowing many black women to form independently businesses.

_____

_____

8. Soon dubbed Madam Walker, she became one of the most successfully women in North America.

_____

_____

9. She became a respect figure in black society and was active involved in the civil rights movement.

_____

_____

10. High regarded by many politicians, Sarah Walker met with President Woodrow Wilson, urging him to make lynching a federal crime.

_____

_____

WORKING TOGETHER

Working with a group of students, review this e-mail for errors in adjective and adverb use. Underline mistakes and discuss corrections. Note how changing modifiers changes meaning.

Dear Sid:

I got your report last night. Please go over your figures careful. Are we really losing that much in the East Coast malls? I think your suggestions to increase sales are more better than those presented last month at the annually convention. Your report does make a clearly impression, especially about the Moncton and Halifax stores. Halifax is the best place of the two to expand. It seems cheap priced merchandise sells more better in Moncton.

Your point about telemarketing and online sales catalogues makes a lot of sense. We have lagged behind the other department stores. It is totally impossible for us to compete unless we go after the high prof- itable Internet market.

See you next week in Charlottetown,

Perry Rand

_____

_____

_____

_____

_____

_____

_____

_____

_____

_____

_____

_____

_____

CRITICAL THINKING

GET THINKING AND WRITING

Write a paragraph describing how attending college has changed your life. Have you learned new skills, gained confidence, made new friends? Has attending college changed your personal life—forced you to work less or spend less time with family and friends? What are the positive and negative effects of college?

WHAT HAVE YOU WRITTEN?

Read your paragraphs, underlining each adjective and circling each adverb. Review the rules explained in this chapter. Have you used modifiers correctly?

WHAT HAVE YOU LEARNED?

Select the right adjective or adverb in each sentence.

1. _____ We drove over the (bad/badly) roads all night.

2. _____ We could not believe how (poor/poorly) maintained these roads were.

3. _____ The potholes only got (worse/worst) as we got closer to the campgrounds.

4. _____ It was (impossible/totally impossible) to make the trip in less than two hours.

5. _____ Because we arrived late, we could not get assigned the (best/better) of the two campgrounds.

6. _____ The north site is (better/more better) than the old south site.

7. _____ We did manage to put up our (borrow/borrowed) tents before it got dark.

8. _____ A (sudden, powerful/sudden powerful) thunderstorm woke us up at midnight.

9. _____ Our (soak/soaked) tent began to leak.

10. _____ It got (much worse/much worser), so we slept in the SUV.

Answers appear on the following page.

GET WRITING

Can technology be overwhelming? Do you know anyone who is afraid of computers?

Write a paragraph describing people who seem locked out of the information age. Can they live without computers or the Internet, or are they losing opportunities and options?

WRITING ON THE WEB

Using a search engine such as AltaVista, Yahoo!, or Google, enter terms such as *adjective, adverb,* and *modifier* to locate current sites of interest.

ANSWERS TO WHAT HAVE YOU LEARNED? ON PAGES 373–374
1. bad (see page 361), 2. poorly (see page 364), 3. worse (see page 367), 4. impossible (see page 371), 5. better (see page 364), 6. better (see page 370), 7. borrowed (see page 360), 8. sudden, powerful (see page 364), 9. soaked (see page 360), 10. much worse (see page 370)

POINTS TO REMEMBER

1. Adjectives modify nouns and pronouns; adverbs modify verbs, adjectives, and other adverbs. *Note:* Use adjectives and adverbs carefully when modifying verbs like *see, hear, feel, smell, touch,* and *taste:*

   adjective: I see *good* coming from this.   [I predict good results.]
   adverb: I see *well.*   [I have good eyesight.]

2. Past participles are adjectives:

   a *rented* car   a *broken* window   *mashed* potatoes

   Note: When speaking, many people drop the *-ed* ending, but it should always be used in writing. Write "mashed potatoes," *not* "mash potatoes."

3. Most adverbs end in *-ly,* with some exceptions:

   hard   fast   right   just   straight

   Note: When speaking, many people commonly drop adverb endings, but they should always be used in writing. Write "drive carefully," not "drive careful."

4. Adjective and adverb use affects meaning:

   fresh sliced bread   = sliced bread that is fresh
   freshly sliced bread = bread (fresh or stale) that has just been sliced

5. *Good* and *bad* are adjectives that describe nouns and pronouns:

   I feel good. = I am healthy or happy.   I feel bad. = I am sad.

   Well and *badly* are adverbs that describe verbs, adjectives, or other adverbs:

   I feel well. = I have a good   I feel badly. = I have a poor
              sense of touch.   sense of touch.

6. Use proper comparative form to discuss two items:

   Jiang is *taller* than Barry.   My car is *more* expensive than hers.

   Note: Avoid using double comparisons—"more better."

7. Use proper superlative form to discuss three or more items:

   Jiang is the *tallest* boy.   My car is the *most expensive.*

   Note: Avoid using superlatives to compare only two items—

   "eldest of my two girls."

8. Do not use superlatives with words like *impossible, destroyed, perfect, demolished, round:*

Incorrect	*Correct*
The house was completely destroyed.	The house was destroyed.
That is totally impossible.	That is impossible.
The room was perfectly round.	The room was round.

24

Using Prepositions

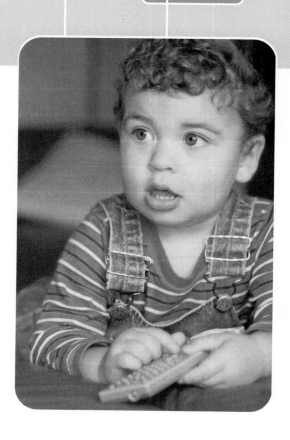

Do you think enough parents monitor what young children watch on TV?

Write a paragraph or develop a list of sentences stating guidelines parents should follow. How can you control what children watch when you are not at home?

What Are Prepositions?

Prepositions show relationships. They can express a geographical relationship—*above, below, inside;* a time relationship—*after, before, during;* or a connection between ideas or words—*with, without, for.* There are so many prepositions that you won't be able to remember all of them. But if you study a list, you will be able to recognize them when they appear in sentences:

about	at	beyond	in	out	toward
above	before	by	into	outside	under
across	behind	despite	inside	over	until
after	below	down	like	past	up
against	beneath	during	near	since	upon
along	beside	except	of	through	with
among	besides	for	off	throughout	within
around	between	from	on	to	without

Phrasal prepositions contain more than one word:

according to	because of	in case of
along with	by means of	in front of
apart from	by way of	in place of
as for	except for	in spite of
as to	in addition to	on account of

Prepositions often appear with nouns as their objects to create **prepositional phrases:**

above the counter	before the mail arrives	toward the park
after the game	behind the times	under the desk
against the grain	beside the freeway	without a clue
the cost of gas	the burden of debts	one of my classmates

UNNECESSARY PREPOSITIONS

Prepositions are not used before the following words:

- *today, tonight, tomorrow, yesterday*
- *here, there, home, downtown, uptown* when they follow verbs showing motion
- *last* and *next* when they modify the object of a preposition

Incorrect
We leave *on* tomorrow.
They went *to* downtown.
He went *to* home last Friday.

Correct
We leave tomorrow.
They went downtown.
He went home last Friday.

We often create sentences that contain so many prepositional phrases they are hard to count:

> *During the game* fans *in the bleachers* tossed debris *on the field for the first time in the memory of parents in the area.* [seven prepositional phrases]

POINT TO REMEMBER

The subject of a clause never appears in a prepositional phrase:

One *of my friends* is sick.   [The subject is *one,* Not *"friends."*]
The prices *of oil* are rising.   [The subject is *prices,* Not *oil.*]

To avoid errors in subject-verb agreement, make sure you do not mistake the object of a preposition for the subject. (*See Chapter 20*)

WHAT DO YOU KNOW?

Circle the prepositions in each sentence.

1. Jean Chrétien was born on January 11, 1934, in Shawinigan, Québec.

2. He was educated at Laval University, where he studied law.

3. He was called to the bar in 1958 and then established a law practice with four partners.

4. In 1963, Chrétien was elected to the House of Commons and, during his political career, has held many positions within the Canadian government.

5. He was elected leader of the Liberal Party in 1990, becoming the Leader of the Opposition in the House of Commons.

6. He was elected prime minister of Canada in 1993.

7. During his three terms as prime minister, Chrétien represented Canada on the national as well as the international stage.

8. For example, Chrétien announced that Canada would not participate in a military invasion of Iraq unless there was a new resolution of the Security Council.

9. But after many years in politics, Chrétien announced that he would step down December 12, 2003—two months earlier than anticipated.

10. One of his last acts as prime minister was a trip to Nigeria for a meeting of Commonwealth nations.

   Answers appear on the following page.

GET WRITING AND REVISING

WHAT ARE YOU TRYING TO SAY?

Write a paragraph describing a rule or policy you would like to see changed. Explain your reasons why a college rule, a traffic law, a criminal statute, or a regulation in sports should be abolished or altered. Should the drinking age be changed? Should students have to take fewer classes to be considered full-time? Should your company's medical benefits be changed? Describe the problem the rule creates and explain how a change would provide a solution.

_____

_____

_____

_____

_____

_____

_____

_____

_____

_____

_____

_____

_____

WHAT HAVE YOU WRITTEN?

Underline the prepositions and prepositional phrases. Circle the subject of each sentence. Make sure subjects do not appear in prepositional phrases.

Incorrect
The problems <u>with</u> the rule *is* . . . [The subject is *problems*, not *rule*.]

Correct
The problems <u>with</u> the rule *are* . . .

EXERCISE 1 Identifying Prepositions

Underline the preposition in each sentence.

1. Everyone was invited except Tim.
2. We must finish this by Monday.
3. We live in Fort McMurray.
4. I took her to school.
5. SARS swept through Toronto.
6. That should be a secret among friends.

ANSWERS TO WHAT DO YOU KNOW? ON PAGE 378
1. on, in; 2. at; 3. to, in, with; 4. In, to, of, during, within; 5. of, in, of, in, of; 6. of, in; 7. During, as, on; 8. For, in, of, of; 9. after, in; 10: of, as, to, for, of.

7. We have tea at four.

8. He is running for city manager.

9. She was promoted to vice president.

10. They seem without hope.

EXERCISE 2 Identifying Prepositional Phrases

Underline the prepositional phrases in each sentence.

1. During the night road crews cleared debris left by the storm.

2. Despite rising costs, these cars remain popular with drivers under thirty.

3. Against his doctor's advice, Sam flew to Europe and biked through the mountains.

4. The passengers waited outside the terminal until the security guards searched through their baggage.

5. In the morning delivery trucks will arrive from Calgary with textbooks for the public schools.

6. I was so tired from running the marathon on Sunday that I slept until noon on Monday.

7. The dispute between the mayor and the city council stems from a long argument over property taxes.

8. Despite her best efforts, our office costs soared over budget and we failed to get the shipment out on time.

9. We walked along the beach in the rain.

10. She drives past our house on her way to work in the morning.

EXERCISE 3 Identifying Subjects and Prepositional Phrases

Underline the subject of each clause twice and underline prepositional phrases once. Remember, subjects never appear in prepositional phrases.

1. Benito Juarez is one of the most important figures in Mexican history.

2. Born in a small village in the state of Oaxaca, Juarez was an orphan and runaway.

3. Despite many obstacles, Juarez graduated from a seminary.

4. Following his election as governor, Juarez developed programs to help the poor in Oaxaca.

5. During his term as governor Juarez initiated policies that brought him into conflict with powerful forces that began to align against him.

6. One of the most powerful leaders in Mexico at the time was Santa Anna, who exiled Juarez to New Orleans.

7. After liberals assumed power, they recalled Juarez from exile to become the Minister of Justice.

8. In this position Juarez wrote a law that limited the power of military tribunals.

9. In 1857 he was elected chief justice of the Mexican Supreme Court.

10. After a year on the Supreme Court, Juarez assumed the presidency.

Commonly Confused Prepositions

We use most prepositions without a problem, automatically placing them in sentences to connect words and ideas. Some prepositions, however, are easily confused because their spellings or meanings are similar:

beside/besides

Beside means "next to":

> Walk *beside* me.

Besides means "in addition (to)":

> *Besides* a skull fracture, he suffered a broken arm.

between/among

Between refers to two items:

> That should be settled *between* father and son.

Among refers to three or more items:

> That should be settled *among* players in the NHL.

due to/because

Due to should not be used in place of *because of:*

Incorrect
The flight was delayed *due to* thunderstorms.

Correct
The flight was delayed *because of* thunderstorms.

like/as

Like is a preposition and should be followed by a noun:

> It hit me *like* a *sledgehammer.*
> She ran *like* a *race horse.*

As is usually a conjunction, which should be followed by a clause (a group of words with a subject and verb). However, it acts as a preposition and can be followed by a noun when it means "functioning in the capacity of." Be sure your meaning is clear.

> It hit me *as I walked* under the bridge.
> She ran *as if she was chasing* a racehorse.
> Ambreen was working *as a clerk* when I met her.

of

Of is not needed when other prepositions like *inside, outside,* and *off* appear:

I went inside the house.	*not*	I went inside *of* the house.
It fell off the table.	*not*	It fell off *of* the table.
She worked outside the law.	*not*	She worked outside *of* the law.

through/throughout

Through means "from one end to the other":

> We drove *through* Hamilton without hitting a red light.
> He went *through* high school with straight A's.

Throughout means "in every part":

> We drove *throughout* Cornerbrook looking for her lost dog.
> He went *throughout* the high school distributing flyers.

toward/towards

Both are correct:

> She walked *toward* the stage.
> She ran *towards* the audience.

IDIOMS WITH PREPOSITIONS

In English, certain nouns, verbs, and adjectives combine with prepositions to form idiomatic expressions:

Noun + Preposition	Verb + Preposition	Adjective + Preposition
criticism of	apologize for	different from
curiosity about	believe in	familiar with
dependence on	rely on	similar to

If you are unsure which preposition to use, refer to dictionaries like the *Gage Canadian Dictionary*.

Locating Prepositions

Prepositions and prepositional phrases often serve as modifiers. They add extra information to a sentence. Like other adjectives and adverbs, they must be clearly linked to the words they describe to prevent confusion:

Confusing
We met the forward who scored the winning goal *in the supermarket*.
There is too much sex and violence viewed by children *on television*.
The crime wave angered voters, forcing the mayor to resign *in the Toronto*.

Revised
When we were *in the supermarket,* we met the forward who scored the winning goal.
Children view too much sex and violence *on television*.
The crime wave angered voters *in Toronto,* forcing the mayor to resign.

EXERCISE 4 Eliminating Misplaced Prepositional Phrases

Rewrite the following sentences to eliminate confusion caused by misplaced prepositional phrases.

1. Tim was exhausted and passed out in the locker room by the marathon.

_____

_____

2. Mistrust can ruin a workplace among employees.

_____

_____

3. I want a sandwich for lunch without mustard.

_____

_____

4. She was the first student to get an athletic scholarship with disabilities.

_____

_____

5. We watched the children skating from the window on the lake.

_____

_____

6. I read the new book about terrorism on the bus.

_____

_____

7. The hikers took shelter from the sudden blizzard in a cave.

_____

_____

8. Because of the leaking roof tenants refused to pay rent on the top floor.

_____

_____

9. Tickets will be available for the midnight game at noon.

_____

_____

10. The children made so much noise that we had to close the window on the playground.

_____

_____

WORKING TOGETHER

Working with a group of students, revise this section of a student psychology paper to eliminate errors in preposition use.

Although it affects the lives of millions, schizophrenia is widely misunderstood. Many people outside of the medical profession think schizophrenics have a "split personality" as Jekyll and Hyde. The root *schiz* refers to a "split" but not a dual personality. It really means a patient is "split," or separated, of reality. Patients have difficulty functioning on society and often show poor social skills. Some hear voices and suffer from hallucinations. Beside these

```
symptoms, patients may become extremely paranoid or
agitated.
     In recent years various medications have proved
useful in helping schizophrenics lead more normal
lives. There is no dispute among patients and doctors
that the drugs are frequently effective. One of the
main problems is that patients complain of side
effects, such as lethargy and weight gain. Patients
forget or refuse to take their drugs, and inside of
a few days severe symptoms return.
     Due to the fact that schizophrenia affects so
many people, more research is needed to develop
better drugs with fewer side effects.
```

_____

_____

_____

_____

_____

_____

_____

_____

_____

_____

_____

_____

_____

_____

EXERCISE 5 Cumulative Exercise

Revise this passage to eliminate faulty parallelism, fragments, run-ons, and dangling or misplaced modifiers.

Expecting veterans to be tall, battle-scarred warriors, Audie Murphy struck the American public as an unlikely hero. Standing only five feet five inches and with a weight of only 112 pounds, the boyish twenty-year-old Texan had been thought unfit for combat. But having killed 241 enemy soldiers in seven bitter campaigns. Murphy emerged in 1945 as the most decorated soldier in American history. He appeared on the cover of *Life* magazine his smiling good looks fascinated the public. Impressed by the young man's charm, Audie Murphy was invited to Hollywood by Jimmy Cagney. Still recovering from war wounds, Murphy studied acting and working to soften his Texas accent. Murphy began appearing in movies and he wrote an autobiography of his war experiences. Having grown up in Texas and loving horses, producers saw Murphy as a natural for Westerns. But fame and having money troubled Murphy, who feared fellow veterans might feel he was "cashing in" on his war record.

During the 1960s the unpopular war in Vietnam tarnished the image of war heroes and Murphy's film career faltered. Needing money, the public was dismayed when newspapers began linking Murphy with organized crime figures and gamblers. When he died in a plane crash in 1971, the media dismissed him as a relic of a bygone age and symbolizing old-fashioned values. Commenting on his friend's troubled last years and early death, cartoonist Bill Mauldin observed, "Long before his plane flew into a mountain, he was nibbled to death by ducks."

_____

_____

_____

_____

_____

_____

_____

_____

_____

_____

_____

_____

_____

_____

_____

_____

_____

_____

_____

_____

_____

_____

CRITICAL THINKING

Write a paragraph describing your composing style at this point in the course. Do you write longhand or use a computer? Do you make outlines or plunge into writing? What prewriting methods, if any, do you use? What aspect of writing do you find the hardest? How could you improve the way you write?

WHAT HAVE YOU WRITTEN?

Read your paragraph aloud and examine it for logic and clarity. Do you avoid errors in sentence structure and preposition use?

1. Underline each preposition.
2. Do you avoid mistaking an object of a preposition for the subject in any sentences?
3. Do you make errors with easily confused prepositions such as *like* and *as* and *beside* and *besides*?

Do you think families spend too much time watching television? Would families benefit more by playing games, working on hobbies, or engaging in sports? Is watching television together a group activity?

Write a paragraph describing how families should spend their time together.

WRITING ON THE WEB

Using a search engine such as AltaVista, Yahoo!, or Google, enter terms such as *preposition, prepositional phrase, like and as,* and *beside and besides* to locate current sites of interest.

WHAT HAVE YOU LEARNED?

Circle the correct word in each sentence.

1. One of the most important automotive figures in Europe (was/were) André Citroën.

2. His influence on France was (as/like) Henry Ford's in North America.

3. (Beside/Besides) building low-priced cars, Citroën helped introduce mass production techniques to French automaking.

4. (As/Like) Ford, Citroën believed cars should not just serve as luxury vehicles for the rich.

5. Low-priced cars and trucks, he thought, would revolutionize transport, freeing the public from bus and rail lines to travel (through/throughout) France when they wished.

6. (Inside/Inside of) a few years after their introduction, small two- and four-cylinder Citroëns became a common sight in Paris.

7. (Beside/Besides) using advertising, Citroën sponsored car expeditions to Africa and Asia to popularize his cars with drivers.

8. (Because of/due to) financial problems during the depression, Citroën was forced to declare bankruptcy and lost control over his car company.

9. On the streets of Paris, the vintage Citroën remains a common sight (as/like) a man with a beret.

10. (Among/Between) North American tourists the cheap little cars became something of a joke (due to the fact that/because) the name Citroën sounds like *citron,* which is French for *lemon.*

Answers appear on the following page.

POINTS TO REMEMBER

1. Prepositions are words that show relationships between ideas:

Time	Location	Connection
before	above	with
after	under	without
during	inside	except

(continued)

POINTS TO REMEMBER *(continued)*

2. Prepositional phrases include a noun as a prepositional object:

The cost of *books*.   It's time for *fun*.   She was without *hope*.

3. The subject of a sentence is never the object of a preposition:

One of the players is injured.   [The subject is *One*, not *players*.]
Her choice of clothes is strange. [The subject is *choice*, not *clothes*.]

4. Use the correct preposition:

besides = in addition (to)   Besides gas, we need oil.
beside = next to   Sit beside me.

between = two items   between mother and father
among   = three or more   among the schoolchildren

Due to should not be used in place of *because of*:

The game was cancelled *because of rain*.   not   The game was cancelled
                                                       due to rain.

Like is a preposition and should be followed by a noun:

She moved *like a dancer*.

As is usually a conjunction and should be followed by a clause:

She moved *as the dancers took the stage*.

Of is not needed with other prepositions like *inside, outside, off*:

inside the house   *not*   inside *of* the house

through = from one end to the other

We drove *through* the Niagara region.

throughout = in every part

Repairs were made *throughout* the Greater Toronto Area.

toward/towards   Both are correct.

5. When using a preposition to modify other words, place it next to the
word or words it modifies to prevent confusion.

Confusing
I met the quarterback who sued the CFL *in the airport*.

Correct
In the airport I met the quarterback who sued the CFL.

Part 5

Using Punctuation and Mechanics

25

Using Commas and Semicolons

Many people now work at home. For some it means being more productive and having more free time because they don't spend hours commuting. They save money on parking and daycare. Others find working at home means a loss of privacy because they feel tied to their work twenty-four hours a day.

Write a paragraph explaining why you would or would not like to work at home.

What Are Commas and Semicolons?

Commas [,] and semicolons [;] are two of the most common, and often misused, marks of punctuation. Because they function like road signs, directing the way we read sentences, they are very important.

WHAT DO YOU KNOW?

Insert commas and semicolons where needed in the following sentences.

1. Anyone who wants to lose weight must have concentration willpower and energy.

2. My brother who wants to quit smoking has tried the patch hypnosis and psychotherapy.

3. The August 14 2003 blackout that affected Ontario and the Eastern United States demonstrated defects in the power grid and it may have shown terrorists a way to cripple our economy.

4. Children no matter how young should be taught about the dangers of drugs.

5. First let me explain why I am here.

6. Toronto the capital of Ontario is nicknamed "Hogtown" by the media.

7. Edmonton is the largest city in Alberta Montreal is the largest city in Quebec.

8. Her brother works in Fredericton her sister works in Moncton.

9. The film symposium included Norman Jewison a director Robert Lantos a producer Paul Gross an actor and Garth Drabinsky a former industry spokesperson.

10. Because parking is limited we are asking students to carpool.

Answers appear on the following page.

GET WRITING
AND REVISING

WHAT ARE YOU TRYING TO SAY?

Write a paragraph describing a place you go to when you want to be alone.

_____

_____

_____

_____

_____

_____

_____

_____

_____

_____

_____

_____

_____

_____

_____

_____

WHAT HAVE YOU WRITTEN?

Circle the commas and semicolons that appear in your paragraph.

1. Can you provide a reason for inserting each comma?
2. Do you insert commas almost on reflex, without thought?
3. Do you sometimes think you miss needed commas or put them where they don't belong?
4. Do you know if any of your commas should be semicolons?

ANSWERS TO WHAT DO YOU KNOW? ON PAGE 392

1. Anyone who wants to lose weight must have concentration, willpower, and energy.
2. My brother, who wants to quit smoking, has tried the patch, hypnosis, and psychotherapy.
3. The August 14, 2003, blackout that affected Ontario and the Eastern United States demonstrated defects in the power grid, and it may have shown terrorists a way to cripple our economy.
4. Children, no matter how young, should be taught about the dangers of drugs.
5. First, let me explain why I am here.
6. Toronto, the capital of Ontario, is nicknamed "Hogtown" by the media.
7. Edmonton is the largest city in Alberta; Montreal is the largest city in Quebec.
8. Her brother works in Fredericton; her sister works in Moncton.
9. The film symposium included Norman Jewison, a director; Robert Lantos, a producer; Paul Gross, an actor; and Garth Drabinsky, a former industry spokesperson.
10. Because parking is limited, we are asking students to carpool.

Comma ,

In speaking, we pause to separate ideas or create emphasis. In writing, we use commas to signal pauses and shifts in our flow of words. Commas are the most common mark of punctuation used within sentences. By habit you may automatically insert the proper commas just as you remember to capitalize a person's name or place a period at the end of a sentence. No doubt, however, there are some places where you forget to use commas or wonder if the comma you added is needed at all.

Commas work like hooks to attach additional ideas to a basic sentence:

Imalah won a scholarship.

After two years of hard work, Imalah, *who speaks three languages,* won a scholarship, *which impressed her friends.*

Read this sentence aloud and notice the pauses you instinctively make to signal shifts in the flow of ideas.

Comma mistakes, like spelling errors, can seem like minor flaws, but they weaken your writing and make your ideas difficult to follow. Remember, when you are writing, you are taking your readers on a journey. If you use commas correctly, they will be able to follow your train of thought without getting lost. Consider how commas change the meaning of these sentences:

The doctor says the patient will die.
The doctor, says the patient, will die.

Let's visit Victoria.
Let's visit, Victoria.

We need ice cream, sugar, a lemon soda, and cups.
We need ice, cream, sugar, a lemon, soda, and cups.

Planning to leave Alberta, Blake bought a car.
Planning to leave, Alberta Blake bought a car.

The best way to master comma use is to first review all the rules, then concentrate on the ones you do not understand or find confusing.

Comma Uses

Commas have ten basic uses.

1. **Use commas with *and, or, for, nor, yet, but,* or *so* to join independent clauses to create compound sentences and avoid run-ons (see pages 244–249 and 261–262).**

   When you join two independent clauses (simple sentences), use a comma and the appropriate coordinating conjunction:

   Chinatown is a popular tourist attraction, and it serves as an important cultural centre.

   We must develop new energy sources, or we will remain dependent on foreign oil.

   We'll have to postpone the party, for nobody's RSVP'd yet. [*Note: For* as a coordinating conjunction means "because" or "since"; however, its use is considered by many to be outdated.]

   Harmeet can't go with us, nor can he meet us there.

   His movies won praise from critics, yet they failed at the box office.

   The blizzard knocked out power lines, but the hospital never lost electricity.

   Students are demanding more parking, so we expanded the lot behind the gym.

POINT TO REMEMBER

Use commas with *and, or, for, nor, yet, but,* or *so* only to join two independent clauses, not pairs of words or phrases:

Unnecessary Commas
We like cake, and ice cream.

Rising prices of fossil fuels, and environmental concerns sparked interest in solar power.

Ted worked overtime throughout the summer, and now works full-time this semester.

Correct
We like cake and ice cream.

Rising prices of fossil fuels and environmental concerns sparked interest in solar power.

Ted worked overtime throughout the summer and now works full-time this semester.

To see if you need a comma with *and, or, for, nor, yet, but,* or *so,* apply this test:

1. Place a period just before the coordinating conjunction.
2. If there is a complete sentence on the left and the right, add the comma. If placing a period creates a fragment, omit the comma.

Note: In informal writing, some writers omit commas in very short compound sentences:

    I drove but she walked.   She sings and he dances.

2. **Use a comma after a dependent clause that opens a complex sentence.**

    Because the parade was cancelled, we decided to go to the beach.
    While he waited for the bus, Raj made business calls on his cell phone.
    After she graduated from law school, Lenore moved back to Quebec City.

If the dependent clause follows the independent clause, the comma is usually deleted:

    We decided to go to the beach because the parade was cancelled.
    Raj made business calls on his cell phone while he waited for the bus.
    Lenore moved back to Quebec City after she graduated from law school.

Writers often omit commas if the opening clause is short and commas are not needed to prevent confusion:

    When he talks people listen.   Before you leave check your messages.

3. **Use a comma after a long phrase or an introductory word.**

    To prevent confusion, commas should follow long phrases that open sentences.

    There is no clear definition of a "long phrase," so use your judgment. A short opening phrase may not require a comma to prevent confusion:

After breakfast we are going to the natural history museum.

Longer phrases should be set off with commas to prevent confusion and signal the shift in ideas:

After breakfast with the new students and guest faculty, we are going to the natural history museum.

Introductory words such as interjections or transitions are set off with commas to prevent confusion and dramatize a shift in ideas:

Yes, I am cashing your cheque today.	Accordingly, we must demand more money.
No, we cannot afford a new car.	Of course, you are a welcome guest.

EXERCISE 1 Compound and Complex Sentences

Insert commas where needed in these compound and complex sentences. Note that some sentences are correct and do not need any changes.

1. The St. Lawrence Seaway is one of the world's most comprehensive inland navigation systems. Initial construction work began in 1954 and involved cooperation from the Canadian and American governments.

2. It was an impressive task to be undertaken and included moving 192.5 million cubic metres of earth adding 5.7 million cubic metres of concrete building 72 kilometres of dikes and digging 110 kilometres of channels.

3. The Seaway was officially opened April 25 1959 and linked the Atlantic Ocean to the Great Lakes.

4. The St. Lawrence Seaway generates around 40000 jobs and two billion dollars of annual personal income but its most significant contribution is related to the cargo it handles supporting a vast array of industries.

5. Pleasure boats can use the Seaway to go from the Great Lakes to the Atlantic Ocean but priority is obviously given to commercial ships at the locks.

6. The system carries bulk cargo such as grain iron ore coal and petroleum products and general cargo such as containers steel and machinery.

7. The St. Lawrence Seaway and the Great Lakes are mainly used to ship heavy raw materials and limited general cargo.

8. In spite of its success as a transportation route it is still faster to ship general cargo by railway than transporting containers through the Seaway.

9. For instance it takes a little more than 24 hours to transport a container by rail from Chicago to Montreal while this operation would take around one week through the Great Lakes and the Seaway.

10. On average though 50 million tons of freight is transported each year by the Seaway.

4. Use commas to separate words, phrases, and clauses in a series:

Words

We purchased computer paper, ink, pens, and pencils.
We sang, danced, and acted all summer.

Note: Some writers omit the final comma before the conjunction:

We purchased computer paper, ink, pens and pencils.

But most editors recommend adding the final comma to prevent confusion:

We need ice cream, sugar, chocolate and mint cookies.

[Do you need (bars of) chocolate and mint cookies or cookies made with mint and chocolate?]

Phrases

We purchased computer paper, ordered fax supplies, and photocopied the records.

We sang carefully, danced precisely, and acted flawlessly all summer.

Clauses

We purchased computer paper, Sarah ordered fax supplies, and Tim photocopied the records.

We sang opera carefully, the girls danced precisely, and the boys acted flawlessly all summer.

Note: If clauses contain commas, separate them with semicolons (see page 404).

EXERCISE 2 Commas in Series

Add commas where needed to set off elements in a series.

1. Throughout history people came across large bones fossils and teeth.

2. The word *dinosaur* did not enter the English language until 1841, when Robert Owen coined the term from Greek words meaning "terrible" and "lizard."

3. Before Owen, people thought these strange bones were evidence of extinct dragons giant birds or mythical beasts.

4. Scientists discovered more dinosaur remains in the western United States Australia and Africa.

5. At first, researchers believed all dinosaurs were cold-blooded because they resembled modern reptiles, such as alligators crocodiles and lizards.

6. In the 1950s, however, some scientists speculated that dinosaurs may have been warm-blooded because of the rich blood supply evident in their bone structure the form of their cells and their projecting plates which may have been used for cooling.

7. Dinosaurs dominated the planet for millions of years, living on grass small plants and other wildlife.

8. Although some dinosaurs weighed several tons were eighty feet long and had tremendous endurance they had very small brains.

9. The extinction of dinosaurs remains a puzzle with some scientists blaming the Ice Age others blaming changes in their food supply and some blaming a comet or asteroid.

10. Researchers think an asteroid may have struck the earth which caused massive dust clouds to blot off sunlight alter the climate and kill the plants dinosaurs depended on for survival.

5. Use commas to set off nonrestrictive or parenthetical words or phrases.

You might notice a phrase such as *who is my friend* set off with commas in one sentence, then see the same phrase without commas in another sentence. A word or phrase is or is not set off with commas depending on whether it is nonrestrictive or restrictive. When a word or words only describe or add extra information about a noun, they are **nonrestrictive** and set off with commas. Nonrestrictive words are parenthetical and can be taken out of the sentence without changing the meaning of the noun they describe. If the words limit or define the noun, they are **restrictive** and *not* set off with commas. Restrictive words tells us more about a general or abstract noun like *anyone, someone, student, person,* or *parent*:

> Anyone *who drives more than two hours a day* . . .
> Someone *who donates blood regularly* . . .
> The student *who developed the school website* . . .
> Any person *who drinks and drives* . . .
> Each parent *with a child in my class* . . .

These phrases limit or define the subject. Without them the nouns lose much of their meaning. These restrictive phrases are part of the noun and therefore are not set off with commas. These same words could be nonrestrictive and set off with commas if they followed more specific nouns:

> Nancy Sims, *who drives more than two hours a day,* . . .
> My father, *who donates blood regularly,* . . .
> Ted Greene, *who developed the school website,* . . .

In each case the phrase only adds extra information about a clearly defined noun. Removing the phrase from the sentence does not change the meaning of the noun.

Nonrestrictive	Restrictive
Adds extra information about a noun Commas needed	Defines or limits the noun No commas
My mother, who wants to lose weight, should exercise. [*My mother* can only refer to one person. *Who wants to lose weight* only adds extra information about her.]	Anyone who wants to lose weight should exercise. [*Anyone* refers to any person. *Who wants to lose weight* defines which person should exercise.]
Ted Hughes, who won an Olympic medal, will coach. [*Ted Hughes* clearly defines the noun, so his winning a medal only adds extra details about him.]	The teacher who won an Olympic medal will coach. [*Who won an Olympic medal* defines which teacher will coach.]

EXERCISE 3 Restrictive and Nonrestrictive elements

Insert commas where needed to set off nonrestrictive phrases and clauses. Remember, no commas are needed if the phrase or clause defines, or IDs, the noun.

1. In 1962 the United States which was the leading Western power during the Cold War nearly went to war with the Soviet Union.
2. Cuba which had become a communist country in 1959 was supported by the Soviet Union.
3. President Kennedy who wanted the country to take a strong stand against communism had permitted a group of Cuban exiles to attack Cuba.
4. The raid which became known as the Bay of Pigs failed.
5. Fidel Castro who feared an American invasion sought protection from the Soviet Union.
6. Cuba only ninety miles off the Florida coast gave the Soviets a valuable base to conduct surveillance against the United States.
7. The Soviets secretly shipped missiles that could carry nuclear warheads to Cuba.
8. When President Kennedy was shown photographs of missiles being installed in Cuba he and his brother who was attorney general sensed America was being threatened.
9. Although some generals suggested the United States launch a massive air strike the president who feared starting a nuclear war ordered a blockade to stop Soviet ships from bringing weapons into Cuba.
10. After days of tense negotiations Khrushchev the Soviet leader agreed to remove the nuclear missiles from Cuba ending the greatest crisis of the cold war.

POINT TO REMEMBER

To determine whether a phrase or clause is restrictive or nonrestrictive, just think of the term "ID." If the phrase or clause, identifies, or IDs, the noun, it is *restrictive* and should not be set off with commas:

Will the student who missed the test see me after class.
Which student? *the student who missed the test*
The phrase *who missed the test* IDs which student, so no commas.

If the phrase or clause does not ID the noun but only adds extra information, it is *nonrestrictive* and should be set off with commas:

Will Sam, who missed the test, see me after class.
Which student? *Sam*
The phrase *who missed the test* only adds extra information about *Sam*, who is defined by his name, so add commas.

If the phrase or clause IDs the noun—no commas.
If the phrase or clause is extra—add commas.

6. **Use commas to set off contrasted elements.**

To prevent confusion and highlight contrast, set off words and phrases with commas to signal abrupt or important shifts in a sentence:

The teachers, not the students, argue the tests are too difficult.
The company's president, unlike all his predecessors, is making employee retention a priority.

7. **Use commas after interjections, words used in direct address, and around direct quotations.**

Hey, get a life.
Iver, help Renée with the mail.
Leigh said, "Welcome to the disaster," to everyone arriving at the party.

8. **Use commas to separate city and state or city and country, items in dates, and every three numerals 1,000 and above:**

I used to work in Winnipeg, Manitoba, until I was transferred to Paris, France.

Note: A comma goes after the province or country if followed by other words.

She was born on July 7, 1986, and graduated high school in May 2004.

Note: A comma goes after the year if followed by other words. No comma is needed if only month and year are given.

The new bridge will cost the state 52,250,000 dollars.

Note: A comma separates every three numerals.

9. **Use commas to set off absolute phrases.**

Absolute phrases are groups of words that are not grammatically connected to other parts of sentences. To prevent confusion, they are attached to the main sentence with a comma:

Her car unable to operate in deep snow, Lu borrowed Andy's Jeep.
Wilson raced down the field and caught the ball on one knee, his
heart pounding.

10. Use commas where needed to prevent confusion or add emphasis.
Writers add commas to create pauses or signal shifts in the flow of words to
prevent readers from becoming confused:

Confusing
Whenever they hunted people ran for cover.
To Sally Madison was a good place to live.
To help feed the hungry Jim donated bread.

Improved
Whenever they hunted, people ran for cover.
To Sally, Madison was a good place to live.
To help feed the hungry, Jim donated bread.

Note: Reading sentences aloud can help you spot sentences that need
commas to prevent confusion.

Writers often use commas for special effect to emphasize words, phrases,
and ideas. Because readers pause when they see a comma, it forces them to
slow down and pay additional attention to a word or phrase:

Without Comma	*With Comma for Emphasis*
Today I quit smoking.	Today, I quit smoking.

EXERCISE 4 Comma Use

Insert commas where needed in each sentence.

1. Louis Pasteur a noted French chemist first discovered antibiotics.
2. He observed that certain bacteria killed anthrax a deadly disease.
3. Around 1900 Rudolf von Emmerich a German bacteriologist isolated
   pyocyanase which had the ability to kill cholera and diphtheria germs.
4. It was an interesting discovery but it worked only in the test tube.
5. In the 1920s the British scientist Sir Alexander Fleming discovered
   lysozyme a substance found in human tears that had powerful antibiotic
   properties.
6. Lysozyme however killed only harmless bacteria and it could not be
   concentrated to affect disease-producing germs.
7. In 1928 Fleming accidentally discovered penicillin and he demonstrated
   its antibiotic properties in a series of experiments against a range of germs.
8. Fleming however never conducted animal or human tests.
9. During World War II two British scientists conducted further tests on
   penicillin helping put Fleming's discovery to practical use.
10. Introduced in the last stages of the war the new drug proved effective in
    treating infected wounds saving thousands of lives.

EXERCISE 5 Comma Use

Insert commas where needed in each sentence.

1. On May 28 1934 at a farmhouse at Corbeil in northern Ontario five identical baby girls were born to a French-Canadian couple Oliva and Elzire Dionne.

2. The babies were named Yvonne Annette Cécile Émilie and Marie.

3. They were the world's first quintuplets to survive though they were tiny and very frail at first.

4. The Ontario government took the quints from their parents and placed them under the care of Dr. Allan Dafoe the doctor who had delivered them.

5. A special nursery complex was built for them together with a public observation garden for they became Canada's major tourist attraction.

6. Meanwhile their father fought a nine-year legal battle to regain them.

7. At last in 1943 the girls were returned home but they had difficulty adjusting to their new life and to their brothers and sisters. (There were twelve children in the family all told.)

8. When the quints grew up they moved to Montreal. Three of the original five are still alive.

9. According to a recent audit Ontario netted $350 million in revenues related to the quintuplets with the quints' share of the trust—once estimated at $15 million—being spent on the upkeep of Quintland leaving the surviving sisters poverty stricken.

10. On March 6 1998 the Ontario government offered the sisters an apology and $2.8 million in compensation.

Source: "Dionne Quintuplets." *The Canadian Encyclopedia*. 2005. Historica Foundation of Canada. 17 July 2006 <http://www.thecanadianencyclopedia.com>.

Avoiding Unnecessary Commas

Because commas have so many uses, we sometimes place them where they are not needed. After reviewing all the rules, you may find yourself putting commas where they don't belong.

GUIDE TO ELIMINATING UNNECESSARY COMMAS

1. Don't put a comma between a subject and verb unless setting off nonrestrictive elements or a series:

   Incorrect: The old car, was stolen.
   Correct: The car, which was old, was stolen.

2. Don't use commas to separate prepositional phrases from what they modify:

   Incorrect: The van, in the driveway, needs new tires.
   Correct: The van in the driveway needs new tires.

(continued)

3. Don't use commas to separate two items in a compound verb:

Incorrect: They sang, and danced at the party.
Correct: They sang and danced at the party.

4. Don't put commas around titles:

Incorrect: The film opens with, "Love Me Tender," and shots of Elvis.
Correct: The film opens with "Love Me Tender" and shots of Elvis.

5. Don't put commas after a series unless it ends a clause that has to be set off from the rest of the sentence:

Incorrect: They donated computers, printers, and telephones, to our office.
Correct: They donated computers, printers, and telephones, and we provided office space.

6. Don't set off a dependent clause with a comma when it ends a sentence:

Incorrect: The game was cancelled, because the referees went on strike.
Correct: The game was cancelled because the referees went on strike.

Note: A comma is needed if a dependent clause opens the sentence:

Because the referees went on strike, the game was cancelled.

EXERCISE 6 Comma Use

Correct comma use in the following passage, adding missing commas where needed and deleting unnecessary commas.

The suburbs, exploded after World War II. In 1944 only 114000 houses were built in America. By 1950 over 1700000 new houses were built. Veterans most of whom were eligible for low-interest loans through the GI Bill created a massive market for single-family homes. Developers built neighbourhoods subdivisions and entire new communities. Orchards farms wheat fields dairies and forests were bulldozed to build streets, and houses. In less than ten years many people left the cities for the new housing developments which offered young couples a chance to live in their own homes. To the parents, of the baby-boom, generation, suburbs offered security space and recreation they could not find in congested, city neighbourhoods. Anyone in the fifties who planned to stay in the city to raise a family was considered old-fashioned or eccentric.

_____

_____

_____

_____

_____

_____

_____

_____

_____

_____

_____

_____

_____

Semicolon ;

You can think of semicolons as capitalized commas. They are used to connect larger items—clauses and complex items in a list.

Semicolons have two uses:

1. **Use semicolons to join independent clauses when *and, or, for, nor, yet, but,* or *so* are not present:**

   We drove to Halifax; Jean and Bill flew.
   Charlottetown is the capital of Prince Edward Island; St. John's is the capital of Newfoundland.

   Note: Remember to use semicolons even when you use words such as *nevertheless, moreover,* and *however*:

   They barely had time to rehearse; however, opening night was a success.
   The lead has a commanding stage presence; moreover, she has a remarkable voice.

2. **Use semicolons to separate items in a series that contains commas.**

   Normally we use commas to separate items in a list:

   We need paper, pens, ink, and computer disks.

   However, if items in the list contain commas, it is difficult to tell which commas are separating items and which commas are separating elements within a single item:

   The governor will meet with Vicki Shimi, the mayor of Bayview, Jia Xiao, the new city manager, the district attorney, Trevor Plesmid, and Al Leone, an engineering consultant.

How many people will the governor meet? Is Vicki Shimi the mayor of Bayview or are Vicki Shimi and the mayor two different people? To prevent confusion, semicolons are inserted to separate items in the series:

   The governor will meet with Vicki Shimi, the mayor of Bayview; Jia Xiao, the new city manager; the district attorney; Trevor Plesmid; and Al Leone, an engineering consultant.

   The governor will meet with five people:

   1. *Vicki Shimi, the mayor of Bayview*
   2. *Jia Xiao, the new city manager*
   3. *the district attorney*
   4. *Trevor Plesmid*
   5. *Al Leone, an engineering consultant*

EXERCISE 7 Understanding Semicolons

Underline the items in each list and enter the number in the right column.

1. The clinic needs plasma, a blood product; Motrin, an analgesic; bandages; first-aid supplies; and antibiotics. # _____

2. The auto show featured a Stanley Steamer; a 1920 Model T; a Kubelwagen, a military version of the Volkswagen; a WWII jeep; a Hummer; a '57 Thunderbird; a Prism, a solar-powered car; a new Buick; and a hydrogen-powered test vehicle. # _____

3. The wedding party consisted of Cheryl, Heather's cousin; Dave Draper; Tony Prito, Dave's brother-in-law; Tony's nephew; Mindy Weiss, a fashion model; Chris, a photographer; and Heather's best friend. # _____

4. A number of campus facilities need repairs, especially Felber Hall, a science lab; the business library; Riley Hall; the math centre; Matthews Hall, the tutoring centre; and the main dorm. # _____

5. The fund-raiser attracted a former prime minister; Stephen Lewis, the former attaché to the United Nations; a Supreme Court judge; Ed Mirvish, a theatre producer; Lorne Michaels, creator of *Saturday Night Live;* and David Miller, mayor of Toronto. # _____

EXERCISE 8 Comma and Semicolon Use

Insert commas and semicolons where needed in each sentence.

1. The Marx brothers were born in New York City and were known by their stage names: Chico born Leonard Harpo born Arthur Groucho born Julius and Zeppo born Herbert.

2. The brothers studied music and they began a show business career touring vaudeville houses with their aunt and mother calling themselves the Six Musical Mascots.

3. The brothers appeared on their own as the Four Nightingales later they changed the name of their act to simply the Marx Brothers.

4. Their wild stage antics and funny sight gags made the Marx Brothers popular soon Hollywood took notice.

5. Their early films including *Animal Crackers Horse Feathers* and *Duck Soup* won praise from fans and critics.

6. Though only thirty-four Zeppo Marx decided to retire in 1935 the remaining three brothers continued making movies.

7. The late 1930s was a period of continuing success for the Marx brothers films such as *A Night at the Opera A Day at the Races* and *Room Service* became comedy classics.

8. Each brother had a distinct stage persona they hardly seemed related.

9. Groucho smoked cigars had a large false moustache and made sarcastic jokes Chico talked with an Italian accent and played the piano Harpo never spoke wore a trench coat played the harp and chased women.

10. Few Marx Brothers fans realize there was a fifth Marx brother Gummo Marx nicknamed after his rubber overshoes did not pursue a career in show business.

WORKING TOGETHER

Working with a group of students, edit this e-mail and add commas and semicolons where needed. Note how adding correct punctuation makes the message easier to read.

Dear Kali:

I read the report about the December 15 2003 and March 15 2004 power outages that affected the Pike Street Plant the Fall River Warehouse and our sales offices.

I think you are correct in assuming we will have to spend at least $1250000 to upgrade our control systems. Although all our facilities have emergency generators any power shortage causes extensive delays in data processing manufacturing and communications.

We have studied the municipal systems in Hamilton Ontario Winnipeg Manitoba and Calgary Alberta. I suggest we incorporate the control systems used by these cities. These systems are also widely used in major industries including Stelco a steel company IBM a computer firm and Nike an athletic shoe manufacturer.

Kali it's important to present your proposal in person at the budget meeting on May 12. Hope to see you there.

Maria Sanchez

_____

_____

_____

_____

_____

_____

_____

_____

_____

_____

_____

_____

_____

_____

_____

CRITICAL THINKING

GET THINKING
AND WRITING

*Write one or more paragraphs about the most challenging course you are taking
this semester. Which is your hardest course and why? Describe the problems
you face, how you try to overcome them, the way other students seem to cope,
and what you will have to do to successfully complete the course.*

WHAT HAVE YOU WRITTEN?

*Review your writing for comma and semicolon use and other errors. Read your
paragraphs aloud. Does this help you discover comma errors, misspelled words, fragments, and awkward phrases?*

GET WRITING

Do you enjoy working with other people? If you worked at home,
would you miss the social interaction?

Write a paragraph that describes past coworkers or explains the kind
of people you hope to work with in the future.

WRITING ON THE WEB

Using a search engine such as AltaVista, Yahoo!, or Google, enter terms such as *commas, semicolons, using commas, comma drills, comma rules, understanding commas,* and *punctuation* to locate current sites of interest.

WHAT HAVE YOU LEARNED?

Insert commas and semicolons where needed in the following sentences.

1. On September 1 1939 Hitler invaded Poland launching a war in Europe that would last six years and kill millions.

2. I am willing to sell my Firebird for $17500 but you must pay with cash money order or certified cheque.

3. This morning unlike most mornings I took the bus to work.

4. The teacher who gets the most votes will be placed on the school board.

5. We flew to Berlin then rented a car to tour Frankfurt Bonn Dusseldorf and Hamburg.

6. We import cocoa beans wood carvings and oil from Nigeria.

7. Because oil prices are difficult to predict trucking companies have problems guaranteeing future rate schedules.

8. Historians consider Abraham Lincoln who led the U.S. during the Civil War Franklin Roosevelt who carried the nation through the Depression and World War II and Woodrow Wilson president during World War I some of America's greatest leaders.

9. Well we will have to lower prices to compete with discount malls or we may have to close one of our downtown stores.

10. High school students report math gives them the most problems college students state writing poses the greatest challenges.

Answers appear on page 410.

POINTS TO REMEMBER

Commas are used for ten reasons:

1. Use commas with *and, or, for, nor, yet, but,* or *so* to join independent clauses to create compound sentences and avoid run-ons:

   I went to the fair, but Lisan drove to the beach.

2. Use a comma after a dependent clause that opens a complex sentence:

   Before the game began, the coach spoke to her players.

(continued)

POINTS TO REMEMBER (continued)

3. Use a comma after a long phrase or introductory word:

   Having waited in the rain for hours, I caught a cold.
   Furthermore, I caught a cold waiting in the rain.

4. Use commas to separate words, phrases, and clauses in a series:

   She bought a battered, rusted, and windowless Model A Ford.
   They dug wells, planted crops, and erected new silos.

5. Use commas to set off nonrestrictive or parenthetical words or phrases:

   Sid, who lives in Montreal, should know a lot about Quebec politics.
   Anyone who lives in Montreal should know a lot about Quebec politics.

6. Use commas to set off contrasted elements:

   Children, not parents, should make this decision.

7. Use commas after interjections, words used in direct address, and around direct quotations:

   Anna, can you work this Saturday?
   Wait, you forgot your keys.
   Shane said, "We must pay cash," every time we wanted to buy something.

8. Use commas to separate city and state or city and country, items in dates, and every three numerals 1,000 and above.

   He moved to Moncton, New Brunswick, on October 15, 2003, and bought a $125,000 house.

9. Use commas to set off absolute phrases:

   Their plane grounded by fog, the passengers became restless.

10. Use commas where needed to prevent confusion or add emphasis:

    Every time I drive, home is my final destination.
    This morning, we play to win.

Semicolons are used for two reasons:

1. Use semicolons to join independent clauses when *and, or, for, nor, yet, but,* or *so* are not present:

   We walked to school; they took a limo.

2. Use semicolons to separate items in a series that contains commas:

   I asked Frank, the field manager; Candace, the sales representative; Karla, our attorney; and Erica, the city manager, to attend the budget meeting.

410 Part 5 **Using Punctuation and Mechanics**

> **ANSWERS TO WHAT HAVE YOU LEARNED? ON PAGE 408**
>
> 1. On September 1, 1939, Hitler invaded Poland, launching a war in Europe that would last six years and kill millions.
> 2. I am willing to sell my Firebird for $17,500, but you must pay with cash, money order, or certified cheque.
> 3. This morning, unlike most mornings, I took the bus to work.
> 4. The teacher who gets the most votes will be placed on the school board.
> 5. We flew to Berlin, then rented a car to tour Frankfurt, Bonn, Dusseldorf, and Hamburg.
> 6. We import cocoa beans, wood carvings, and oil from Nigeria.
> 7. Because oil prices are difficult to predict, trucking companies have problems guaranteeing future rate schedules.
> 8. Historians consider Abraham Lincoln, who led the U.S. during the Civil War; Franklin Roosevelt, who carried the nation through the Depression and World War II; and Woodrow Wilson, president during World War I, some of America's greatest leaders.
> 9. Well, we will have to lower prices to compete with discount malls, or we may have to close one of our downtown stores.
> 10. High school students report math gives them the most problems; college students state writing poses the greatest challenges.

Using Other Marks of Punctuation

GET WRITING

Do people always have a right to protest in a democracy? Should protests ever be banned?

Write a paragraph explaining your view and support it with examples.

What Are the Other Marks of Punctuation?

Writers use punctuation to show when they are quoting other people, presenting parenthetical ideas, posing a question, or creating a contraction. Most students know when to use a question mark or an exclamation point. Other punctuation marks, however, can be confusing, so they are worth looking at in detail.

WHAT DO YOU KNOW?

Add apostrophes, quotation marks, italics, parentheses, question marks, colons, and exclamation points where needed in the following sentences.

1. Erika shouted, Run immediately to the exits now as soon as she spotted the fire.

2. The new car $32,500 with taxes was more than we could afford.

3. The team needs new equipment helmets, shoulder pads, and shoes.

4. Dont they realize that The Cask of Amontillado is one of Poes greatest short stories.

5. I saw the episode Terrorists at Our Doorstep on Sixty Minutes last Sunday.

6. Why wont they give you your money back.

7. There is a sale on mens coats, but they have only 38s and 40s left.

8. The band toured the major cities of Europe London, Berlin, Paris, Madrid, and Rome.

9. Pauls daughter took a plane, but his two boys drove the familys car.

10. The telephone is near the womens room.

   Answers appear on the following page.

GET WRITING
AND REVISING

WHAT ARE YOU TRYING TO SAY?

Many critics argue that television shows, movies, and music videos present negative images of women and minorities. Do you agree with this viewpoint? Why or why not? Write a paragraph stating your views and provide examples to support your opinion.

_____

_____

_____

_____

_____

_____

_____
_____
_____
_____
_____
_____

WHAT HAVE YOU WRITTEN?

Review the punctuation in your paragraph and circle items you think are wrong.

ANSWERS TO WHAT DO YOU KNOW? ON PAGE 412
1. Erika shouted, "Run immediately to the exits now!" as soon as she spotted the fire.
2. The new car ($32,500 with taxes) was more than we could afford.
3. The team needs new equipment: helmets, shoulder pads, and shoes.
4. Don't they realize that "The Cask of Amontillado" is one of Poe's greatest short stories?
5. I saw the episode "Terrorists at Our Doorstep" on *Sixty Minutes* last Sunday.
6. Why won't they give you your money back?
7. There is a sale on men's coats, but they have only 38's and 40's left.
8. The band toured the major cities of Europe: London, Berlin, Paris, Madrid, and Rome.
9. Paul's daughter took a plane, but his two boys drove the family's car.
10. The telephone is near the women's room.

Apostrophe '

Apostrophes are used for three reasons.

1. *Apostrophes indicate possession.* The standard way of showing possession, that someone or something owns something else, is to add an apostrophe and an -*s*:

Noun	Erica's car broke down.
Acronym	NASA's new space vehicle will launch on Monday.
Indefinite pronoun	Someone's car has its lights on.
Endings of *s, x,* or *z* sound	Phyllis's car is stalled. [or *Phyllis'*]

Note: Apostrophes are sometimes deleted from geographical names:

Rogers Pass   Seven Sisters Falls   Bobs Pond

Note: Apostrophes may or may not appear in possessive names of businesses or organizations:

Air Canada Centre   Sears   Rogers Centre   Wayne Gretzky's

Follow the spelling used on signs, stationery, and business cards.

Because we also add an -*s* to make many words plural, apostrophes have to be placed carefully to show whether the noun is singular or plural:

Singular	*Plural*
a boy's hat	the boys' hats
my girl's bicycle	my girls' bicycles
her brother's car	her brothers' car (two or more brothers own one car)
a child's toy	children's toys*
the woman's book	women's books*

*Because *children* and *women* already indicate plurals, the apostrophe is placed before the -*s*.

Compound nouns can indicate joint or individual possession. David and Juanita, for example, could own and share one car, share the use of several vehicles, or own separate cars they drive individually. The placement of apostrophes indicates what you mean:

David and Juanita's car   [David and Juanita both own one car.]
David and Juanita's cars [David and Juanita both own several vehicles.]
David's and Juanita's cars [David and Juanita individually own cars.]

2. *Apostrophes signal missing letters and numbers in contractions.* In speaking we often shorten and combine words, so that we say "don't" for "do not" and "could've" for "could have." We also shorten numbers, particularly years, so that we talk about "the Spirit of '76" or refer to a car as a "'99 Mustang." Apostrophes indicate that letters or numerals have been eliminated:

shell = an outer casing	she'll = she will
well = source of water	we'll = we will
cant = trite opinions	can't = cannot

Note: Only one apostrophe is used, even if more than one letter is omitted. Apostrophes are placed over the missing letter or letters, not where the words are joined:

do not = don't   *not*   do'nt

Deleted numbers are indicated with a single apostrophe:

The stock market crashed back in '29.
She won the gold medal in the '88 Olympics.
I am restoring his '67 VW.

3. *Apostrophes indicate plurals of letters, numbers, or symbols.* Words do not need apostrophes to indicate plurals. An added -*s* or other spelling changes indicate that a noun has been made plural. However, because adding an -*s* could lead to confusion when dealing with individual letters, numbers, or symbols, apostrophes are used to create plurals:

I got all B's last semester and A's this semester.
Do we have any size 7's or 8's left?
We can sell all the 2003's at half price.

Note: Apostrophes are optional in referring to decades, but be consistent:

> *Inconsistent*
> She went to high school in the 1990's but loved the music of the 1960s.

> *Consistent*
> She went to high school in the 1990's but loved the music of the 1960's.

> *or*

> She went to high school in the 1990s but loved the music of the 1960s.

Note: Common abbreviations such as *TV* and *UFO* do not need apostrophes to indicate plurals:

> We bought new TVs and several DVDs.

POINT TO REMEMBER

> it's = contraction of "it is"
> > It's raining.
> > I know it's going to be a long day.
> its = possessive of "it"
> > My car won't start. Its battery is dead.
> > The house lost its roof in the storm.

In editing, use this test to see if you need an apostrophe:

1. Read the sentence aloud, substituting *it is* for *its* or *it's.*
2. If the sentence sounds OK, use *it's:*
   > *It is* going to be hot.
   > It's going to be hot.
3. If the sentence sounds awkward, use *its:*
   > I like *it is* style.
   > I like its style.

EXERCISE 1 Using Apostrophes to Show Possession

Use apostrophes to create possessive forms of nouns.

1. a car belonging to one girl   _____

2. photographs belonging to the people   _____

3. the short stories of Joy Fielding   _____

4. a park operated by the city   _____

5. evidence collected by the SIU   _____

6. books owned by my mother-in-law   _____

7. pictures drawn by children   _____

8. characters created by Dickens   _____

9. a boat owned by two men   _____

10. a car owned by Steve and Fran Miller   _____

EXERCISE 2 Using Apostrophes to Show Contractions

Use apostrophes to create contractions of each pair of words.

1. you are _____
2. I am _____
3. would not _____
4. who is _____
5. should not _____
6. does not _____
7. he will _____
8. they are _____
9. could have _____
10. have not _____

EXERCISE 3 Using Apostrophes

Revise this essay, adding apostrophes where needed.

On December 17, 1917, the Halifax, Nova Scotia, harbour was very busy with troop and supply ships waiting to set sail during WWI. At 7:30 a.m. the *Mont Blanc*, one of Frances ships, arrived at the harbour mouth, its cargo hold heavily loaded with 2,300 tons of picric acid, 200 tons of TNT, and many other highly volatile mixtures. A Norwegian ship, the *Imo,* moved at the same time as the *Mont Blanc,* and an error of judgment caused the *Imo* to strike the other ships bow. The collision wasnt a major one; however, fire broke out immediately on the *Mont Blanc.* Everyone abandoned the ship, thinking that it would explode at any minute. It was almost twenty minutes before the explosion happened. Churches, houses, schools, factories, and ships in the explosions path were destroyed. There were 1,900 dead, many bodies unidentified, and many survivors left completely blind. Although the *Mont Blancs* captain and pilot were charged with manslaughter, charges couldnt be proved and, therefore, no blame was ever laid in the largest man-made explosion until the atomic age. The captain and the pilot of the *Imo* perished.

Quotation Marks " "

Quotation marks—always used in pairs—enclose direct quotations, titles of short works, and highlighted words.

- **For direct quotations**
  When you copy word for word what someone has said or written, enclose the statement in quotation marks:

  Martin Luther King said, "I have a dream."

  Note: A final question mark or exclamation point precedes the final quotation mark only if it appears in the original text:

  Did Martin Luther King say, "I have a dream"?

Remember: Set off identifying phrases with commas:

> Shelly insisted, "We cannot win unless we practise."
> "We cannot win," Shelly insisted, "unless we practise."
> "We cannot win unless we practise," Shelly insisted.

Note: Commas are not used if the quotation is blended into the sentence:

> They exploited the "cheaper by the dozen" technique to save a fortune.

Quotations within quotations are indicated by the use of single quotation marks:

> Nigel said, "I was only ten when I heard Martin Luther King proclaim, 'I have a dream.'"

Long quotations are indented and not placed in quotation marks:

> During the Depression, many cities and provinces had little or no money to pay employees:
>
> > Calgary and other cities began paying public employees with promissory notes because they did not have funds to issue standard paycheques. One town in Saskatchewan paid its police chief in chickens donated by local farmers who could not afford to feed them and could find no buyers to sell them to. A village in Prince Edward Island paid teachers with obsolete library books. (Smith 10)

Final commas are placed inside quotation marks:

> The letter stated, "The college will lower fees," but few students believed it.

Colons and semicolons are placed outside quotation marks:

> The letter stated, "The college will lower fees"; few students believed it.

Indirect quotations do not require quotation marks:

> Martin Luther King said that he had a dream.

- **For titles of short works**
  The titles of poems, short stories, chapters, essays, songs, episodes of television shows, and any named section of a longer work are placed in quotation marks. (Longer works are underlined or placed in italics.)

  > Did you read "When Are We Going to Mars?" in the *Globe and Mail* this week?

Note: Do not capitalize articles, prepositions, or coordinating conjunctions (*and, or, for, nor, yet, but, so*) unless they are the first or last words.

Quotation marks and italics (or underlining) distinguish between shorter and longer works with the same title. Many anthologies and albums have title works. Quotation marks and italics indicate whether you are referring to a song or an entire album:

> Her new CD, *Wind at My Back,* has only two good songs: "Daybreak" and "Wind at My Back."

- **To highlight words**
  Words are placed in quotation marks to draw extra attention:

> I still don't know what "traffic abatement" is supposed to mean. This is the fifth time this month Martha has "been sick" when we needed her.

EXERCISE 4 Quotation Marks and Apostrophes

Add quotation marks and apostrophes where needed.

1. Mayor Miller proclaimed during his speech, I won't raise taxes.
2. Laura Secord is famous for warning the British troops of an impending attack.
3. George Orwell began his famous novel with the sentence, It was a bright cold day in April and the clocks were striking thirteen.
4. He sang a lot of early Sinatra numbers like Ive Got You Under My Skin and Ill Never Smile Again.
5. Did you read Paul Masons article Coping with Depression?
6. Ted told us he is going to summer school.
7. Last night as we watched the news, Arras stated, This reminds me of the words of Pierre Elliott Trudeau, who said, The essential ingredient of politics is timing."
8. Forming a New Nation is the first chapter in our history book.
9. I plan to retire after next season, Terry Wilson announced to her coach, noting, CTV has offered me a job covering womens tennis.
10. Toms only eight, but he can sing O Canada in both French and English.

EXERCISE 5 Direct Quotations

Add quotation marks, commas, and apostrophes where needed to indicate direct quotations, quotations within quotations, and titles of short works.

You know Wes said I really like our English class.

I know Zoe responded. I really enjoy the stories we have been reading this semester. Which one is your favourite?

Let me think. I guess I really liked all the Poe stories Wes said, tapping his book. I really like The Pit and the Pendulum and The Tell-Tale Heart. What about you? What is your favourite so far?

Bartleby the Scrivener. I just loved that story Zoe laughed. I just love the way Bartleby keeps saying I would prefer not to every time his boss asks him to do something.

I would prefer not to Wes repeated flatly. You know there is a movie version with Crispin Glover and David Paymer?

Really? Zoe said. I'd love to see that!

_____

_____

_____

_____

_____

_____

_____

_____

_____

_____

_____

Colon :

Colons are placed after independent clauses to introduce elements and separate items in ratios, titles, and time references:

Lists	The coach demanded three things from his players: loyalty, devotion, and teamwork.

Note: Colons are placed only after independent clauses to introduce lists:

Incorrect
We need: paper, pens, pencils, and ink.

Correct
We need school supplies: paper, pens, pencils, and ink.

Phrases	The coach demanded one quality above all others: attention to detail.
Time references	The game started at 12:05 p.m.
Ratio	We have a 10:1 advantage.
Title and subtitle	Kathy Frank's new book is called *Arthur Miller: Playwright and Philosopher*.
After salutations in business letter	Dear Ms. Smith:
Scripture reference	Romans 12:1–5

Introduction of block quotations	Catherine Henley argues the loss of rain forests will have serious consequences for the planet and the quality of life in the future:

> It is obvious that the continual erosion of rain forests will increase global warming by decreasing a major producer of the planet's oxygen-generating ability. Cutting down trees will cause more mudslides, more flooding, and more water pollution.

Parentheses ( )

Parentheses set off nonessential details and explanations and enclose letters and numbers used for enumeration:

Nonessential detail	The committee on homelessness (originally headed by Olivia Chow) submitted a special report to Prime Minister Martin.
First-time use of acronym	The Greater Toronto Airport Authority (GTAA) has new security policies.
Enumeration	The report stated we must (1) improve tutoring services, (2) provide additional housing, and (3) increase funding of bilingual classes.

Brackets [ ]

Brackets set off interpolations or clarifications in quotations and replace parentheses within parentheses.

Sometimes quotations taken out of context can be confusing because readers may misunderstand a word or reference. A quotation using the word "Roosevelt" in a biography of Theodore Roosevelt would be clear in context. But if you use this quotation in a paper, readers could easily assume you're referring to Franklin, not Theodore, Roosevelt. If you have to add clarifications or corrections, place them in brackets:

Interpolations to prevent confusion	Eric Hartman observed, "I think [Theodore] Roosevelt was a great world leader."
	The *Toronto Star* noted, "Prime Minister Harper told John Harper [no relation] that he agreed with his tax policies."
	The ambassador stated, "We will give them [the Iraqi National Congress] all the help they need."
Corrections	Kaleem Hughes called 911, saying, "Come quick. We have hundreds of people [35–50 according to the radio reports] trapped in the terminal."

Parentheses within parentheses	The committee on homelessness (originally headed by Olivia Chow [to be reappointed this year]) submitted a special report to the prime minister.

Dash —

Dashes mark a break in thought, set off a parenthetical element for emphasis, and set off an introduction to a series.

Sudden break in thought	Aaron was angry after his car was stolen—who wouldn't be?
Parenthetical element	The studio—which faced bankruptcy—desperately needed a hit movie.
Introduction	They had everything needed to succeed—ideas, money, marketing, and cutting-edge technology.

Note: Create dashes by hitting your hyphen key twice. No spaces separate dashes from the words they connect.

Hyphen -

A hyphen is a short line used to separate or join words and other items.

- Use hyphens to break words:

  We saw her on tele-
  vision last night.

  Note: Only break words between syllables.

- Use hyphens to connect words to create adjectives:

  We made a last-ditch attempt to score a touchdown.

  Do *not* use hyphens with adverbs ending in *-ly:*

  We issued a quickly drafted statement to the press.

- Use hyphens to connect words forming numbers:

  The firm owes nearly thirty-eight million dollars in back taxes.

- Use hyphens after some prefixes:

  His self-diagnosis was misleading.

Ellipsis . . .

An ellipsis, composed of three spaced periods [. . .], indicates that words have been deleted from quoted material.

Original Text
The mayor said, "Our city, which is one of the country's most progressive, deserves a high-tech light-rail system."

With Ellipsis
The mayor said, "Our city . . . deserves a high-tech light-rail system."

Note: Delete only minor ideas or details—never change the basic meaning of a sentence by deleting key words. Don't eliminate a negative word like "not" to create a positive statement or remove qualifying words:

Original
We must, only as a last resort, consider legalizing drugs.

Incorrect Use of Ellipsis
He said, "We must . . . consider legalizing drugs."

Note: When deleting words at the end of a sentence, add a period before the ellipsis:

The governor said, "I agree we need a new rail system. . . ."

Note: An ellipsis is not used if words are deleted at the opening of a quotation:

The mayor said the city "deserves a high-tech light-rail system."

Note: If deleting words will create a grammar mistake, insert corrections with brackets:

Original
"Poe, Emerson, and Whitman were among our greatest writers."

With ellipsis
"Poe . . . [was] among our greatest writers."

Slash /

Slashes separate words when both apply and show line breaks when quoting poetry:

The student should study his/her lessons.
Her poem read in part, "We hope / We dream / We pray."

Question Mark ?

Question marks are placed after direct questions and to note questionable items:

Did Adrian Carsini attend the auction?
Did you read, "Can We Defeat Hunger?" in *Newsweek* last week?

Note: Question marks that appear in the original title are placed within quotation marks. If the title does not ask a question, the question mark is placed outside the quotation marks:

Did you read "The Raven"?

Question marks in parentheses are used to indicate that the writer questions the accuracy of a fact, number, idea, or quotation:

The children claimed they waited two hours (?) for help to arrive.

Exclamation Point !

Exclamation points are placed at the end of emphatic statements:

Help!
We owe over ten million dollars!

Note: Exclamation points should be used as special effects. They lose their impact if used too often.

Period .

Periods are used after sentences, in abbreviations, and as decimals:

I bought a car.
We gave the car to Ms. Chavez, who starts working for Dr. Gomez on Jan. 15.
The book sells for $29.95 in hardcover and $12.95 in paper.

When an abbreviation ends a sentence, only one period is used. Widely used abbreviations such as SIU, CBC, UofT, NAFTA, and CISC do not require periods.

EXERCISE 6 Punctuation

Add missing punctuation in each sentence.

1. The receipt is stamped Jan 5 10 05 a.m.
2. The childrens museum will close early because its going to snow.
3. The school offers students three key services tutoring, housing, and guidance.
4. The Lottery is still my favourite short story
5. Can you help me
6. I cant be in two places at the same time.
7. John Martin no relation to the former prime minister is running as an independent in the next election
8. To save money we have to accomplish three goals 1 lower travel costs, 2 cancel unnecessary magazine subscriptions and 3 cut down on cell phone use.
9. Ted and Nancy car is the only one on the island.
10. He made a lastminute effort to study for the exams.

WORKING TOGETHER

Working with a group of students, correct the punctuation in the following announcement.

```
                        New Payroll Procedure

To prevent confusion we have established a new payroll
policy. Employees pay slips must be filed by 400 every
Fri in person or sent by e-mail no later than 600 pm
Thurs in order to receive a cheque the following week.
Its too difficult for us to hand-process separate
cheques. If you want to use payroll deduction for your
childs daycare fee, just check the box at the bottom
of the form. Remember to provide your children with
insurance coverage, fill out the Provincial Insurance
form and give it to Ms Green by Mar. 30.
```

_____

_____

_____

_____

_____

_____

_____

EXERCISE 7 Cumulative Exercise for Punctuation and Coordination and Subordination

Rewrite this passage to correct errors in punctuation and reduce awkward and repetitive phrasing through coordination and subordination. You may have to reword some sentences, adding or deleting phrases. If you have difficulty revising some of the sentences, review pages 244–249.

The Group of Seven consisted of famous Canadian artists—A. Y. Jackson, Fred Varley, Lawren Harris, Franklin Carmichael, Frank Johnston, Arthur Lismer, and J. E. H. MacDonald newly formed as a group in May of 1920. Emily Carr famous for her paintings of forests and native villages was never officially one of the Group of Seven, however, they were impressed by her work and included it in a countrywide exhibition in the later 1920s. Her works were included with those of the Group of Seven, Emily Carr remained a recluse for the rest of her life. Many of the works of these artists can be seen at the McMichael Gallery in Kleinberg, Ontario.

_____

_____

_____

_____

_____

_____

_____

_____

_____

_____

_____

_____

_____

CRITICAL THINKING

GET THINKING
AND WRITING

How do you define poverty? Is an urban family with a car, TV, and VCR poor if they cannot afford vacations, new clothes, or expensive meals? Would you consider Amish farmers, who choose to live without modern conveniences or cars, poor? Is being poor a matter of income, a matter of living simply, or a matter of wanting more than you can afford? Write a paragraph explaining your definition of poverty.

WHAT HAVE YOU WRITTEN?

Review your paper for mistakes in punctuation and other errors.

KEEP IT DARK

Careless Talk costs Lives

GET WRITING

This WWII poster warned people to remain silent. Does this suggest that speech can be unpatriotic? Do you think during a war on terrorism people should be careful about what they say?

Write a paragraph stating your opinion. Can we have free speech and security?

WRITING ON THE WEB

Using a search engine such as AltaVista, Yahoo!, or Google, enter terms such as *colons, slashes, brackets, parentheses, ellipsis, question marks, exclamation points, punctuation, understanding punctuation, using punctuation,* and *punctuation rules* to locate current sites of interest.

WHAT HAVE YOU LEARNED?

Add apostrophes, quotation marks, italics, hyphens, parentheses, question marks, colons, and exclamation points where needed in the following sentences.

1. Cécile and Adrians car is an 04 BMW.

2. Its on sale for less than twenty one thousand dollars.

3. We will meet at 1030 Mon morning.

4. Tom screamed, Call 911, now.

5. Her *Globe and Mail* article Why Are We in Afghanistan makes a lot of sense.

6. The boys department has moved to the third floor.

7. The Rolls Royce $175,000 with tax was a major investment for Ms Columbo.

8. Give Rashid a call, or hell demand a refund.

9. The mens department has plenty of 38s and 40s you might like.

10. Dont let my dog scare you. Shes just scared.

Answers appear on the following page.

POINTS TO REMEMBER

1. Apostrophes show possession:

   Erica's car   NASA's rocket   someone's hat
   David and Juanita's cars.   [mutual ownership]
   David's and Juanita's cars.   [individual ownership]

   Apostrophes indicate missing letters or numbers:

   Didn't you sell the '67 Thunderbird?
   its = possessive of it   it's = it is

   Apostrophes indicate plurals of letters, numbers, or symbols:

   She got all A's this year.   Get the W-2's at the payroll office.

2. Quotation marks enclose direct quotations, titles of short works, and highlighted words:

   He said, "I'll be there."   Can you sing "Blue Eyes"?   Is he "sick" again?

   (continued)

POINTS TO REMEMBER *(continued)*

3. Colons are placed after independent clauses to introduce elements and separate items in numerals, titles, ratios, and time references:

   We need supplies: gas, oil, and spark plugs.   It is now 10:17 a.m.

4. Parentheses set off nonessential details and explanations and enclose letters and numbers used for enumeration:

   We got an apartment ($950 a month) because our provincial loan application (PLA) had not been approved for three reasons: (1) we needed more references, (2) we needed a bigger down payment, and (3) we owed too much on credit cards.

5. Brackets set off interpolations or clarifications in quotations and replace parentheses within parentheses:

   The *Globe and Mail* notes, "Frank Harper [no relation to the prime minister] will work for the legislature next fall."

6. Dashes mark breaks in thought, set off parenthetical elements, and set off introductions to series:

   She expected help— wouldn't you?

7. Hyphens separate and join words and other items:

   He wrote a fast-paced soundtrack for the action film.
   You still owe twenty-eight dollars.

8. An ellipsis indicates words have been deleted from a direct quotation:

   The MP stated, "Our country . . . needs new leadership."

9. Question marks are placed within quotation marks if they appear in the original title or quotation:

   Her article is called "Can Anyone Lose Weight?"

   Question marks are placed outside quotation marks if they are not part of the original:

   Did you read "The Gold Bug"?

ANSWERS TO WHAT HAVE YOU LEARNED? ON PAGE 426
1. Cécile and Adrian's car is an '04 BMW.
2. It's on sale for less than twenty-one thousand dollars.
3. We will meet at 10:30 Mon. morning.
4. Tom screamed, "Call 911, now!"
5. Her *Globe and Mail* article "Why Are We in Afghanistan?" makes a lot of sense.
6. The boys' department has moved to the third floor.
7. The Rolls Royce ($175,000 with tax) was a major investment for Ms. Columbo.
8. Give Rashid a call, or he'll demand a refund.
9. The men's department has plenty of 38's and 40's you might like.
10. Don't let my dog scare you. She's just scared.

Using Capitalization

Do you think smoking should be banned in all public places, including bars and restaurants? Given the cost of smoking-related illnesses, does the government have the right to restrict smoking? Do smokers have any rights?

Write a paragraph stating your views on smoking in public.

What Is Capitalization?

Capital letters are used to begin sentences, indicate special meanings, and prevent confusion.

Words are capitalized to indicate proper nouns and prevent confusion. The word *catholic* means universal; *Catholic* refers to a specific religion. The word *mosaic* describes decorations or paintings made from tiny inlaid pieces of tile or other material, but *Mosaic* refers to the Biblical figure Moses, as in *Mosaic laws*. A *mustang* is a wild horse; a *Mustang* is the brand name of a Ford car. The word *Earth* refers to the planet we live on, while *earth* means soil.

Capitalizing words changes their meaning:

Lara loves modern poetry.	[indicates an interest in current literature]
Lara loves Modern Poetry.	[indicates she likes a specific poetry class]
We flew African airlines.	[indicates several different airlines in Africa]
We flew African Airlines.	[indicates a single company called African Airlines]
Will banks cash my cheque?	[indicates financial institutions]
Will Banks cash my cheque?	[indicates someone named Banks]

WHAT DO YOU KNOW?

Underline the letters in each sentence that should be capitalized.

1. At the beginning of the civil war the south achieved its initial goal of establishing the confederate states of america.

2. Relief efforts by the united nations were hampered by floods, civil war, and poor communications.

3. Maria tucci was born in washington state but grew up in a vancouver suburb.

4. This semester i am taking english, canadian history, a music class, and professor rabinsky's introduction to abnormal psychology.

5. We took an air canada flight to lethbridge, alberta.

   Answers appear on the following page.

WHAT ARE YOU TRYING TO SAY?

Write a shopping list of common items you buy—food, clothing, office supplies, or CDs.

GET WRITING AND REVISING

_____

_____

_____

_____

_____

_____

_____

_____

_____

_____

_____

◄

WHAT HAVE YOU WRITTEN?

Review your list for capitalization. Did you capitalize proper nouns, such as names of stores or product brand names? Review the rules on the following pages, then edit your list. ◄

ANSWERS TO WHAT DO YOU KNOW? ON PAGE 429
1. At the beginning of the Civil War the South achieved its initial goal of establishing the Confederate States of America.
2. Relief efforts by the United Nations were hampered by floods, civil war, and poor communications.
3. Maria Tucci was born in Washington State but grew up in a Vancouver suburb.
4. This semester I am taking English, Canadian history, a music class, and Professor Rabinsky's Introduction to Abnormal Psychology.
5. We took an Air Canada flight to Lethbridge, Alberta.

Rules for Capitalization

There are a dozen main rules for capitalizing words. At first the list may seem overwhelming, but if you remember a simple guideline, you can avoid most problems: *Capitalize words that refer to something specific or special—proper names or specific places or things.*

1. Capitalize the first word of every sentence:

   We studied all weekend.

2. Capitalize the first word in direct quotations:

   Felix said, "The school should buy new computers."

3. Capitalize the first word and all important words in titles of articles, books, plays, movies, television shows, seminars, and courses:

"Terrorism Today"	*Gone With the Wind*	*Death of a Salesman*
The Way We Were	*Sixty Minutes*	Urban Planning II

4. Capitalize the names of nationalities, languages, races, religions, deities, and sacred terms:

> Many Germans speak English.   The Koran is the basic text in Islam.
> I bought a French poodle.   She was the city's first Italian
>   Canadian mayor.

5. Capitalize the days of the week, months of the year, and holidays:

> We celebrate Remembrance Day   The test scheduled for Monday is
> every November 11.   cancelled.
> Some people celebrate Christmas   We observed Passover with her
> in January.   parents.

> *Note:* The seasons of the year are not capitalized:

> We loved the spring fashions.   Last winter was mild.

6. Capitalize special historical events, documents, and eras:

> Battle of the Bulge   Declaration of Independence
> World War II   Middle Ages
> Magna Carta   Russian Revolution

7. Capitalize names of planets, continents, nations, states, provinces, counties, towns and cities, mountains, lakes, rivers, and other geographical features:

> Mars   North America   Canada   New Brunswick
> Toronto   Mount Everest   Lake Michigan   Mississippi
> the Badlands   Great Plains   Amazon   Kuwait

8. Capitalize *north, south, east,* and *west* when they refer to geographical regions:

> The convention will be held in the Southwest.
> He has an Eastern accent.
> He raised cattle in the West.

> *Note:* Do not capitalize *north, south, east,* and *west* when used as directions:

> We drove north for almost an hour.
> The farm is southwest of Rockford.

9. Capitalize brand names:

> Coca-Cola   Ford Thunderbird   Cross pen

10. Capitalize names of specific corporations, organizations, institutions, and buildings:

> This engine was developed by Ford.
> After high school he attended Red River College in Winnipeg, Manitoba.
> The event was sponsored by the Lions Club.
> We visited the site of Expo '67 in Montreal.

11. Capitalize abbreviations, acronyms, or shortened forms of capitalized words when used as proper nouns:

SIU	CBC	MP	ERA
SDC	NAFTA	GIC	CTV
UN	ON	NB	OPEC

12. Capitalize people's names and nicknames:

Barbara Roth   Timmy Arnold

Note: Capitalize professional titles when used with proper names:

Doctor Ryan suggested I see an eye doctor.
Three deans supported Dean Manning's proposal.
Our college president once worked for Prime Minister Chrétien.
This report must be seen by the president.
(The word *president* is often capitalized to refer to the president of the United States.)

Note: Capitalize words like *father, mother, brother, aunt, cousin,* and *uncle* only when used with or in place of proper names:

My mother and I went to see Uncle Al.
After the game, I took Mother to meet my uncle.

POINTS TO REMEMBER

The rules of capitalization sometimes vary. Some publications always capitalize *president* when it refers to the president of the United States; other publications do not. *African American* is always capitalized, but editors vary on the capitalization of *blacks.* Some writers capitalize *a.m.* and *p.m.*, while others do not.

Follow the standard used in your discipline or career and be consistent.

EXERCISE 1 Capitalization

Underline letters that should be capitalized.

1. Most cities in the world have emerged naturally, often growing up around a river, such as the nile, the rhine, or the mississippi.

2. On the other hand, brazil made a striking departure in the 1950s, creating an entirely new city in an uninhabited region.

3. The coastal city of rio de janeiro served as brazil's capital for generations.

4. Although known for its striking mountains and beaches, rio had little open land, limiting the city's potential growth.

5. As the economy expanded after wwii, government agencies and corporations needed more office space.

6. In addition, the national government wanted to exploit the rich resources of brazil's undeveloped interior.

7. During the administration of president juscelino kubitschek, planning began on the new capital, to be called brasilia.

8. To emphasize the futuristic aspect of the city, the brazilian urban planner lucio costa created a city layout that resembled a jet airliner.

9. The fuselage of the plane contains government offices, while apartment buildings form the plane's wings.

10. The plaza of the three powers and the presidential residence, called the palace of the dawn, form the nose of the airliner.

11. The famous architect oscar niemeyer designed brasilia's major buildings.

12. The city is surrounded on three sides by an artificial lake, created by damming the paraná river.

13. On april 21, 1960, brasilia was officially dedicated by the brazilian government.

14. The city is home to the university of brasilia, the national theatre, parks, a stadium, and a zoo.

15. Highways and rail lines link brasilia with rio de janeiro, são paulo, and other major brazilian cities.

16. Moving the capitol to brasilia forced thousands of civil servants to move, freeing up office and apartment space in crowded rio.

17. Although the strikingly modern city was considered an architectural marvel, many federal employees did not appreciate the actions of president kubitschek.

18. Some complained, "it's like living in a world's fair exhibit."

19. In the early years, the city was deserted on weekends as workers flew back to rio to enjoy the old city's famous beaches and nightlife.

20. Gradually brasilia developed a character of its own, and its population rapidly swelled to nearly two million by the end of the century.

EXERCISE 2 Capitalization

Underline letters that should be capitalized.

1. The aztecs took their name from azatlan, a mythical homeland in northern mexico.

2. When the toltec civilization collapsed around 1100 AD, various peoples moved into mexico's central plateau and occupied the land around lake texcoco.

3. Arriving late, the aztecs were forced into the unoccupied marshes on the western side of lake texcoco.

4. Settling on a single island of dry land in the swamp, the aztecs were dominated by powerful neighbours who forced them to pay tributes.

5. Although poor and greatly outnumbered, the aztecs gradually built a great empire.

6. Within two hundred years the aztecs developed a superior civilization and established the city of tenochtitlán on the site of modern mexico city.

7. Over the years, the aztecs built bridges to connect their island city to surrounding dry land and drained marshes to create productive gardens.

8. Causeways and canals formed a highly effective transportation system, which helped tenochtitlán become an important market city.

9. From their small island, the aztecs expanded their influence, conquering other peoples and creating an empire that reached the border of guatemala.

10. The aztecs created a highly structured society divided into three classes: slaves, commoners, and nobles.

11. They developed writing and created a calendar based on an earlier mayan date-keeping system.

12. The aztecs worshipped numerous gods, including the moon goddess coyolxauhqui, the rain god tlaloc, and the sun god uitzilopochtli.

13. The spanish explorer hernan cortés arrived in tenochtitlan in 1519.

14. Amazed by the city's architecture and network of canals, the european visitors called the city the venice of the new world.

15. At first, the aztec king montezuma ii welcomed cortés, thinking him to be the god quetzalcoatl.

16. But cortés's arrival spelled the end of the aztec empire.

17. Armed with superior weapons and aligning himself with rebellious tribes, cortés was able to defeat montezuma's army.

18. The europeans also brought smallpox and other diseases, which devastated the aztecs, who had no immunity to these foreign germs.

19. Today a million aztecs, mostly poor farmers, live on the fringes of mexico city.

20. The mexican government honours the aztecs by using many of their symbols on government emblems and paper money.

EXERCISE 3 Capitalization

Underline letters that require capitalization.

Today we are accustomed to television networks battling for ratings. During sweeps weeks, networks broadcast their most popular or controversial programs. Networks have been known to wage intense bidding wars to land a late-night tv host, news anchor, or sitcom to secure larger audiences and higher advertising revenue. In the early 1990s, nbc, for example, hoped to keep both letterman and leno after johnny carson retired from hosting the long-running *tonight show*. After a number of meetings, letterman decided to move to cbs. Such rivalry was not unknown in other media. In the pretv era, newspapers fought bitter and costly circulation wars. In chicago, newspaper distributors were often attacked and their papers burned by rival publishers. In britain the circulation battles were less violent but no less intense. Newspapers offered subscribers premium items such as free encyclopedias or special editions of dickens's most popular books. Often clever londoners would sign up with one newspaper to get a premium item, then cancel and subscribe to a rival paper to receive yet another free gift.

WORKING TOGETHER

Work with a group of students to determine the definition of each word. What difference does capitalization make? You may use a dictionary to check your answers.

1. China _____
   china _____

2. tide _____
   Tide _____

3. the Bay _____
   the bay _____

4. Corvette _____
   corvette _____

5. liberal _____
   Liberal _____

6. god _____
   God _____

7. Dodgers _____
   dodgers _____

8. cancer _____
   Cancer _____

9. Afghan _____
   afghan _____

10. mars _____
    Mars _____

CRITICAL THINKING

GET THINKING AND WRITING

Write a paragraph describing what you did on a recent weekend.

WHAT HAVE YOU WRITTEN?

Review your writing for capitalization. Did you remember to capitalize proper nouns—names of people, products, stores, movies, restaurants, or bands?

IMPROVING YOUR WRITING

Review drafts of upcoming papers, past assignments, and writing exercises in this book for capitalization. Can you find errors you have made? Note rules that apply to areas you have found confusing.

GET WRITING

Write a paragraph describing what you do to stay in shape. Do you wish you had more time to work out? Do you find dieting a challenge? If you could change anything in your lifestyle to improve your health, what would it be?

WRITING ON THE WEB

Using a search engine such as AltaVista, Yahoo!, or Google, enter terms such as *capitalization rules, using capitals,* and *proper nouns* to locate current sites of interest.

WHAT HAVE YOU LEARNED?

In each sentence underline letters that should be capitalized.

1. According to the rcmp, internet fraud is a growing problem.

2. Mayors from large cities met with prime minister harper seeking federal aid to fight crime.

3. The lecture by dr. westin was sponsored by the canadian historical society.

4. We had to ford the rock creek river to reach the boy scout camp.

5. She taught english and history in high school before getting a job at keyano college.

Answers appear on the following page.

POINTS TO REMEMBER

1. Capitalize the first word in each sentence and direct quotation.
2. Capitalize first and important words in titles of books, articles, movies, and works of art.
3. Capitalize names of nationalities, languages, races, and religions.
4. Capitalize days of the week, months, holidays, historical events, documents, and eras.
5. Capitalize proper names and nicknames of people, places, products, organizations, and institutions.
6. Capitalize abbreviations such as *CBC* and *NAACP*.
7. Capitalize titles only when they precede a name or are used in place of a name: "I took Mother to see Dr. Grant."
8. Do not capitalize seasons such as *spring* and *fall*.
9. Do not capitalize *north, south, east,* and *west* when used as directions.

ANSWERS TO WHAT HAVE YOU LEARNED? ON PAGE 436
1. According to the RCMP, Internet fraud is a growing problem.
2. Mayors from large cities met with Prime Minister Martin seeking federal aid to fight crime.
3. The lecture by Dr. Westin was sponsored by the Canadian Historical Society.
4. We had to ford the Rock Creek River to reach the Boy Scout camp.
5. She taught English and history in high school before getting a job at Keyano College.

Correcting Spelling Errors

GET WRITING

What will increase your chances of graduating? Do you need to improve your computer skills, devote more time to school, or develop better study habits?

Write three sentences that state three specific things you would like to change. Read your sentences carefully, proofreading them for errors and revising word choices to make sure they clearly express what you want to say.

Spelling influences the way readers look at your writing. Consider the impression this letter makes:

```
Dear Ms. Ling:

This semmester I will be graduting from Stanton
Community College with an assocate degree in mar-
keting. In addition to studing business law, adver-
tizing, sales management, and economics, I served as
an intern at Lockwood and Goldman. As my resumme
shows, I was a specal asistant to Grace Lockwood and
help desin websites, cataloge pages, and two radio
commercals.

Given my education and experience, I belief I would
be an asset to you're firm. I would appreciate having
the oppurtunity to meet with you at your convenince.
I can be reached at (504) 555-7878.

Sincerly,

Carlo Colfield
```

All the student's education and hard work are overshadowed by spelling errors, which make the writer appear careless and uneducated. Not every reader can detect a dangling modifier or faulty parallelism, but almost everyone can identify a misspelled word.

Some people have a photographic memory and need only see a word once to remember its exact spelling. Others, even highly educated professional writers, have difficulty with spelling. If English is your second language or if you frequently misspell words, make spelling a priority. It can be the easiest, most dramatic way to improve your writing and your grades. Make sure you reserve enough time in the writing process to edit papers to correct spelling mistakes.

WHAT DO YOU KNOW?

Underline the misspelled or misused words in each sentence.

1. The commitee reported to the Common Counsel yesterday.

2. This will cost more then the financal planner suggested.

3. I am not familar with any of the sophmores this year.

4. Her advise was quit irrevlent.

5. We are to dependant on foriegn oil.

6. This is becomming a problem.

7. I belief you are write about that.

8. This arguement has to be settled by a carring person.

9. Its tough if you don't have alot of money to loose.

10. I past the final exam.

Answers appear on the following page.

GET WRITING
AND REVISING

WHAT ARE YOU TRYING TO SAY?

Write one or more paragraphs that compare how college differs from high school. You may focus on teachers, courses, grading, or student attitudes. Include one or more examples.

_____

_____

_____

_____

_____

_____

_____

_____

_____

_____

_____

_____

WHAT HAVE YOU WRITTEN?

Review what you have written and check with a dictionary to see if you have misspelled any words.

1. Review assignments you have written in this or any other course for spelling errors. Do you see any patterns, any words you repeatedly misspell?

2. List any words you find confusing or have doubts about:

_____   _____

_____   _____

_____   _____

_____   _____

_____   _____

ANSWERS TO WHAT DO YOU KNOW? ON PAGES 439–440:
1. committee, Council; 2. than, financial; 3. familiar, sophomores; 4. advice, quite, irrelevant; 5. too, dependent, foreign; 6. becoming; 7. believe, right; 8. argument, caring; 9. It's, a lot, lose; 10. passed.

STEPS TO IMPROVING SPELLING

1. Make spelling a priority, especially in editing your papers.
2. Look up new words in a dictionary for correct spelling and meaning. Write them out a few times to help you memorize them.
3. Study the glossaries in your textbooks to master new terms.
4. Review lists of commonly misspelled words (pages 490–491) and commonly confused words (pages 487–490).
5. Create a list of words you have trouble with. Keep copies of the list next to your computer and in your notebook. Each week try to memorize three or four of these words. Update your list by adding new terms you encounter.
6. Read your writing aloud when editing. Some spelling errors are easier to hear than see.
7. Remember, *i* before *e* except after *c* or when it sounds like *a* as in *neighbour* and *weigh*:

i before *e*

achieve	field	niece	shield
brief	grievance	piece	yield

except after *c*

ceiling	deceive	perceive	receipt

or when it sounds like *a*

eight	freight	rein	vein

   Exceptions: *either, height, leisure, seize, weird*
8. Review rules for adding word endings (pages 445–447).
9. Learn to use computer spell-check programs and understand their limitations. Although such programs can easily spot typos and commonly misspelled words, not every program will alert you to confusing *there* for *their* or *affect* for *effect*. (See pages 487–490.)
10. If you are a poor speller, eliminating spelling errors is the fastest and easiest way to improve your grades.

Commonly Misspelled Words

There are many words we commonly misspell. They may be foreign words, contain silent letters, or have unusual letter combinations. Often we misspell words because in daily speech we slur and fail to pronounce every letter:

Incorrect	*Correct*
goverment	govern_ment
suppose (past tense)	suppose_d
ice tea	ice_d tea

FORTY COMMONLY MISSPELLED WORDS

absence	belief	generous	mortgage
achieve	benefit	grammar	necessary
acquire	challenge	guard	obvious
address	committee	height	opinion
among	control	heroes	parallel
analyze	decision	identity	persuade
argument	dying	label	possess
athletic	embarrass	license	privilege
beautiful	enough	marriage	separate
becoming	familiar	material	vacuum

See pages 490–491 for the complete list.

EXERCISE 1 Commonly Misspelled Words

Underline the correctly spelled word in each pair.

1. yield / yeild
2. albumn / album
3. sincerely / sincerly
4. noticable / noticeable
5. libary / library
6. fulfill / fulfil
7. equiptment / equipment
8. fourty / forty
9. surprize / surprise
10. similar / similiar

Commonly Confused Words

In addition to easily misspelled words, there are easily confused words. The word we put on the page is correctly spelled, but it is the wrong word and has a different meaning than we intend. Many words look and sound alike but have clearly different meanings:

all together	acting in unity or in the same location	"The children stood *all together.*"
altogether	totally	"The repairs will be $75 *altogether.*"
any one	a single person, idea, or item	"*Any one* of the rooms is open."
anyone	anybody	"Can *anyone* help us?"
conscious	awake or aware	"The patient is *conscious.*"

conscience	moral sensibility	"Let your *conscience* be your guide."
desert	an empty expanse of land	"There is no water in the *desert*."
dessert	an after-dinner treat	"Can we have cake for *dessert*?"

Using the wrong word not only creates a spelling error but creates confusion, often resulting in a statement that means something very different from what you intend:

Let's *adopt* the Kyoto Accord on pollution standards.	[Let's *accept* the Kyoto Accord standards.]
Let's *adapt* the Kyoto Accord on pollution standards.	[Let's *change* the Kyoto Accord standards.]
She made an *explicit* call for action.	[She made a *clear, blatant* call for action.]
She made an *implicit* call for action.	[She made an *implied, subtle* call for action.]
Personal e-mail is being examined.	[*Private or intimate* e-mail is being examined.]
Personnel e-mail is being examined.	[*Employee* e-mail or e-mail *about employees* is being examined.]

TEN MOST COMMONLY CONFUSED WORD GROUPS

accept/except

accept	to take	"Please *accept* my apology."
except	but/to exclude	"Everyone *except* Tom attended."

affect/effect

affect	to change or influence	"Will this *affect* my grade?"
effect	a result	"What *effect* did the drug have?"

farther/further

farther	geographic distance	"The farm is ten miles *farther* on."
further	in addition	"*Further* negotiations proved useless."

hear/here

hear	to listen	"Did you *hear* her new song?"
here	a place or direction	"Put it over *here*."

its/it's

its	possessive of *it*	"My car won't start. *Its* battery died."
it's	"it is"	"Looks like *it's* going to rain."

lay/lie

lay	to put or place	"*Lay* the boxes on the table."
lie	to recline	"*Lie* down. You look tired."

(continued)

principal/principle		
principal	main/school leader	"Oil is the *principal* product of Kuwait."
principle	basic law	"This violates all ethical *principles*."
than/then		
than	used in comparisons	"Nick is taller *than* Jakob."
then	refers to time	"He took the test, *then* went home."
there/their/they're		
there	direction/a place	"*There* he goes." "Put it *there*."
their	possessive of *they*	"*Their* car won't start."
they're	"they are"	"*They're* taking the bus home."
to/too/two		
to	preposition/infinitive	"Walk *to* school." "He likes *to* dance."
too	excessive/in addition	"It's *too* hot." "I want to go, *too*."
two	a number	"The dress costs *two* hundred dollars."

See pages 453–456 for a complete list.

EXERCISE 2 Commonly Confused Words

Underline and correct misspelled words in each sentence.

1. Its going to be difficult to except an out-of-province cheque.
2. The prime minister's speech made illusions to the Kyoto Accord.
3. My broker gave me advise about investing.
4. Our students don't have excess to the Internet.
5. These medications may effect your ability to drive.
6. We toured the construction sight.
7. All my school cloths are in the dryer.
8. Your welcome to use there cottage this summer.
9. Don't work to hard.
10. The evening was cool and quite.

EXERCISE 3 Commonly Misspelled and Confused Words

Underline each misspelled or misused word and write the correct spelling over it.

The Trans-Canada Highway is a fedaral–provencial highway system that joins all ten provinces of Canada. The system was aproved by the Trans-Canada Highway Act of 1948, opened in 1962, and complpleted in 1965. The longest continous stretch of highway in the Trans-Canada Highway system is reconized as the longest highway in the world, at 7,821 km, taking into acount the distance travelled on ferrys. The highway system is best known for its destinctive white-on-green maple leaf rout markers.

Unlike the American Interstate highway system, not all of the Trans-Canada Highway uses limited-acess freeways, or even four-lane roads. Canada does not have a comprehensive national highway system, as decisions about highway and freeway construction are entirely under the juresdiction of the individual provinces. In 2000 and 2001 the government of Jean Chritien considered funding an infrastruture project to have the full Trans-Canada system converted to freeway. Although freeway construction funding was made available to some provinces for portions of the system, the government ultimately decided not to pursue a comprehensive highway conversion.

Route numberring on the Trans-Canada Highway is also handled by the provinces. The Western provinces have cordinated their highway numbers so that the main Trans-Canada line is designated Highway 1 throughout the regione. However, from the Manitoba–Ontario border east, highway numbers change at each provincial boundery. As the highway is in many places composed of parts of other important highways with their own seperate identities—and the province of Quebec, in particular, is unlikly to change its geographicly-based highway numbering system to conform to a cross-Canada numbering scheme—the Trans-Canada Highway will most likely never have a uniforme designation across the whole country.

Forming Plurals

The spelling of words changes when they are plural. Most nouns simply require an -s:

Singular	Plural
book	books
car	cars
boy	boys
generator	generators
ornithologist	ornithologists

However, many nouns use different spellings to indicate plurals. In order to avoid making spelling errors, it is important to understand which words require more than an added -s to become plural:

- For words ending in s, ss, x, z, sh, or ch, add -es:

Singular	Plural
miss	misses
church	churches
wish	wishes
fox	foxes
fizz	fizzes

- For words ending in an o preceded by a vowel, add -s:

Singular	Plural
radio	radios
studio	studios

curio	curios
zoo	zoos
rodeo	rodeos

- For words ending in an *o* preceded by a consonant, add *-es:*

Singular	*Plural*
hero	heroes
zero	zeroes
echo	echoes
tomato	tomatoes
veto	vetoes

Exceptions

Singular	*Plural*
grotto	grottos
motto	mottos
photo	photos
solo	solos
piano	pianos

- For words ending in *f* or *fe,* change the *f* to *v* and add *-es:*

Singular	*Plural*
shelf	shelves
wife	wives
half	halves
wolf	wolves
thief	thieves

Exceptions

Singular	*Plural*
safe	safes
roof	roofs
proof	proofs
chief	chiefs

- For words ending in *y* preceded by a consonant, change the *y* to *i* and add *-es:*

Singular	*Plural*
city	cities
story	stories
flurry	flurries
baby	babies
celebrity	celebrities

- For some words, the plural form is irregular:

Singular	*Plural*
tooth	teeth
child	children
mouse	mice
person	people
woman	women

- For some words the singular and plural spelling are the same:

Singular	Plural
deer	deer
fish	fish
sheep	sheep
series	series

- For Greek and Latin nouns, there are special spellings:

Singular	Plural
memorandum	memoranda
datum	data
thesis	theses
alumnus	alumni
analysis	analyses

- For compound nouns—made up of two or more words—make the needed change to the main word. For compound nouns written as one word, make the ending plural:

Singular	Plural
stepchild	stepchildren
bookshelf	bookshelves
girlfriend	girlfriends

  ### Exceptions

Singular	Plural
passerby	passersby

  For compound nouns that appear as separate words or connected by hyphens, make the main word plural:

Singular	Plural
body shop	body shops
beer tap	beer taps
water tank	water tanks
brother-in-law	brothers-in-law
man-of-the-year	men-of-the-year

EXERCISE 4 Creating Plurals

Write out the correct plural form of each noun.

1. knife _____

2. fork _____

3. deer _____

4. loss _____

5. child _____

6. chapter _____

7. century _____

8. cactus _____

9. index   _____

10. stereo   _____

EXERCISE 5 Creating Plurals

Rewrite each sentence, changing all singular nouns to plurals.

1. The boy drove the new car.

   _____

2. My sister-in-law planned the wedding for the family.

   _____

3. Oil taken from grain can provide useful medicine.

   _____

4. The snow flurry made the street slippery.

   _____

5. The fox, wolf, and dog have been vaccinated.

   _____

EXERCISE 6 Plural Spellings

Correct errors in plurals in each sentence.

1. The childrens loved the rodeos, the circuss, and the zooes.

   _____

2. Today, sports heros seem more interested in money than their fans.

   _____

3. My brother-in-laws must pay taxs in two provinces because their companys do business in both Ontario and Quebec.

   _____

   _____

4. The vet examined the calfs and colts.

   _____

5. Two people lost their lifes in the accident.

   _____

Adding Endings

In most instances suffixes or word endings follow simple rules to indicate past tense or to create an adjective or adverb.

Past-Tense Spellings

Most verbs are called "regular" because one simply adds *-ed* or *-d* if the word ends with an *e:*

Regular Verbs

Present	*Past*
walk	walked
integrate	integrated
create	created
type	typed
paint	painted

- If a verb ends in *y*, change the *y* to *i* and add *-ed*:

cry	cried
spy	spied
try	tried

- If a one-syllable verb ends in a consonant preceded by a vowel, double the last letter and add *-ed*:

pin	pinned
plan	planned
drip	dripped
stop	stopped
grab	grabbed

Other verbs, called "irregular," have different spellings to indicate past tense:

Irregular Verbs

Present	*Past*
teach	taught
sing	sang
write	wrote
swim	swam
buy	bought

See pages 292–293 for a complete list.

Spelling Other Endings

Endings are added to words to create adjectives, adverbs, or nouns:

sad (adjective)	*sadly* (adverb)	*sadness* (noun)
create (verb)	*creative* (adjective)	*creatively* (adverb)
motivate (verb)	*motivation* (noun)	*motivated* (adjective)
happy (adjective)	*happily* (adverb)	*happiness* (noun)

- For words ending with a silent *e*, drop the *e* if the ending begins with a vowel:

arrive	+	-al	=	arrival
come	+	-ing	=	coming
fame	+	-ous	=	famous
create	+	-ion	=	creation

Examples of exceptions to this rule are *mileage, noticeable,* and *dyeing.*

- For words ending with a silent *e,* retain the *e* if the ending begins with a consonant:

      elope   + -ment = elopement
      safe   + -ty   = safety
      like   + -ness = likeness
      complete + -ly   = completely

- Double the last consonant of one-syllable words if the ending begins with a vowel:

      rob + -ing = robbing
      spot + -ed = spotted
      spin + -ing = spinning

- Double the last consonant of words accented on the last syllable if the ending begins with a vowel:

      refer   + -ing = referring
      admit   + -ed = admitted
      technical + -ly = technically

Note: Prefixes do not change the spelling of base words. When you add letters before a word, no letters are dropped or added:

    un- + natural = unnatural   dis- + able   = disable
    pre- + judge   = prejudge   il- + legal   = illegal
    im- + moral   = immoral   de- + mobilize = demobilize

EXERCISE 7 Past-Tense Spellings

Write the correct past-tense form of each verb.

1. drive _____
2. talk _____
3. speak _____
4. defend _____
5. negotiate _____
6. strike _____
7. wash _____
8. press _____
9. build _____
10. boil _____

EXERCISE 8 Past-Tense Spellings

Change the verbs in each sentence to past tense.

1. We take the bus to school.

_____

2. They only eat and drink what the doctor suggests.

_____

3. We meet at the library.

_____

4. We choose the courses we want.

_____

5. They sing all night.

_____

EXERCISE 9 Adding Endings

Combine the following words and endings.

1. like   +   -able   _____

2. sorrow   +   -full   _____

3. respect   +   -fully   _____

4. intensify   +   -ing   _____

5. defy   +   -ence   _____

6. force   +   -ing   _____

7. begin   +   -ing   _____

8. profit   +   -able   _____

9. notice   +   -ing   _____

10. debate   +   -able   _____

EXERCISE 10 Identifying and Correcting Misspelled Words

Underline misspelled and misused words and write the correct spelling above them.

Early on the morning of June 30, 1908, a strange light filed the sky over a remote part of Siberia. A streak of fire raced across the treetops and vanished suddenlly over the horizon, followed by a massive explosion. Seven hundred reindeer grazing in a clearing were instantlly vaporized. Over 60 million trees were flattend in a circle larger then halve of Prince Edward Island. A giant fireball rose into the sky, visible for hundreds of miles. Seismographs in America and Europe registered the impact of the blast. A grate fire swept the region for weeks, burning over 700 squre miles of forest. Thousands of tons of ash boilled into the atmosphere, creating wierd sunsets seen all over the world.

Preoccupied by revolutionarries and a recent war with Japan, the Russian government did not bother too investigate an event in an isolated part of its vast empire. In the late 1930s scientists photographed the region, still devastated from the blast. Strangeley, no crater could be found. Whatever fell to earth, weather a comet or meteor, must have broken apart before impact.

After World War II, researchers estimated that the blast was one thousand to two thousand times more powerful then the atomic bomb that destroyed Hiroshima. Further studys reveald genetic mutations in plant life and blood abnormalities in local residents. These findings led some theoriests to speculate the Earth had been hit by a nuclear weapon from another planet or visited by a UFO. Scientists, however, are convinced the event was a totaly nautral phenomonen.

EXERCISE 11 Cumulative Exercise

Rewrite these paragraphs, correcting spelling errors and eliminating fragments and run-ons.

Henry M. Robert is best remembered as the creator of *Robert's Rules of Order.* Almost every club, organization, and public meeting in the United States. Uses this nineteenth-century manual. Henry Robert was not a debator, politican, teacher, or attorny. He was an engineer working for the U.S. Army. Although his military duties carried him across the county on various construction projects, Robert was active in a number of organizations. He was once asked to head a meeting but he became frustrated because he found few guidlines for conducting an orderly discussion.

Robert studied existing manuals but he found them sketchy and incomplete. Robert began to set forth his own rules and he started to write a book. In the winter of 1874 ice in Lake Michigan delayed sheduled construction and Robert had ample time too work on his book. Robert's wife, who was active in several organizations herself. Helped him in setting forth rules and proceedures.

The first printing was only for four thousand copies but the volumn had profound influence. Professors, ministers, business leaders, and social organizations were eager to have rules that were fare and unbiased. Within a few years, Roberts revised his book, adding new sections each time. Hundreds of people rote too him, asking questions about parliamentery practices. In 1915, a thorouhly revised edition, was printed. By that time over half a million copies had been sold. Since Robert's death in 1923, his book has become the stadard book guiding how people in all walks of live conduct meetings and make decisions.

_____

_____

_____

_____

_____

_____

_____

_____

_____

_____

_____

_____

_____

_____

_____

_____

_____

_____

WORKING TOGETHER

Working with a group of students, review this résumé for spelling errors. Have each member underline misspelled words, then work as a group. Note how collaborative editing can help detect errors you may have missed on your own. Refer to a dictionary if you have questions.

ROBIN LIEBERMAN
1532 Bathurst Street
Toronto, ON M6X 2Y9
(416) 555-0909
rlieberman@aol.ca

GOAL	Editoral Assistant and Researcher
OVERVIEW	Two years experence editing both on line and hard-copy journals. Skiled at working with writers and editers. Proven ability to meet deadlines and working within bugets.

EXPERINCE
2005–

Editor, ActionDotCom
One of three editors producing online entertainment journal recieving over 75,000 hits weakly.

- Edited all movie, theater, and resturant reviews.
- Wrote and edited "Toronto on the Move" column, reprinted in *Style Now.*
- Worked as senior fact checker for investgative reports.

2003–2005

Assistant Editor, Dining Out
Edited restaurant reviews, travell articles for magazine with 50,000 circulation.

- Assisted marketing manger in developing new sales campagn.

EDUCATION	Ryerson University
	Degree in Journalism, 2004
	Completed courses in journalism, gaphic design, writing and editing, marketing, business accounting, and mass communications.

- 3.75 GPA
- Worked on student literary magazine and yearbook
- Atended Canadian Convention of Student Editors, 2003, 2004

AFFLIATIONS	Canadian Assocation of Student Journalists
REFERENCES	Aviable on request

GET THINKING AND WRITING

CRITICAL THINKING

After graduation you are offered two jobs. One pays a small salary but offers great opportunities for advancement and is in a career you enjoy. The other job pays twice as much but requires extensive overtime doing boring and repetitive tasks. Write a paragraph explaining which job you would choose and why.

WHAT HAVE YOU WRITTEN?

When you complete your writing, review it for spelling errors.

GET WRITING

What are your most important skills, experiences, or qualities that you think will impress employers when you look for a job?

Write three sentences, each providing a reason why someone should hire you. Read your sentences carefully, proofreading them for errors and revising word choices to make sure they clearly express what you want to say.

WRITING ON THE WEB

Using a search engine such as AltaVista, Yahoo!, or Google, enter terms such as *spelling, improving spelling, spelling rules,* and *using spell-check* to locate current sites of interest.

WHAT HAVE YOU LEARNED?

Underline and correct the misspelled or misused words in each sentence.

1. We had only fourty dollars when we left Moncton, New Brunswick.

2. Its never to late too start.

3. Two mens are waiting in are office.

4. He seems so hoplessy lost.

5. Her room mate wants to hold a surprize party.

6. The company was severly mismanaged.

7. We cannot start filming untill the knew camera technigue is perfected.

8. We will meat at the resturant next Teusday at three.

9. The new song has a familiar, old-fashion rythym.

10. Why can't we serve ordnary, every day coffee instead of these expensive imported blends?

   Check a dictionary to make sure you have successfully identified and corrected all twenty errors.

POINTS TO REMEMBER

1. Edit your papers carefully for commonly misspelled words such as *library, yield, opinion, opportunity,* and *separate. (See list on pages 490–491.)*

2. Edit your papers carefully for commonly confused words such as *anyone* and *any one* or *implicit* and *explicit. (See list on pages 487–490.)*

3. Remember, *i* before *e* except after *c* or when it sounds like *as* in *neighbour* and *weigh.*

   achieve   ceiling   freight
   Exceptions: *either, height, leisure, seize*

4. Follow the guidelines for creating plurals:
   For words ending in *s, ss, x, z, sh,* or *ch,* add *-es:*

   misses   boxes   churches

   For words ending in *o* preceded by a vowel, add *-s.*
   For words ending in *o* preceded by a consonant, add *-es.*

   zoos   radios   heroes   zeroes
   Exceptions: *mottos, photos, pianos, solos*

   (continued)

POINTS TO REMEMBER *(continued)*

For words ending in *f* or *fe*, change the *f* to *v* and add *-es:*

shelves	halves	thieves

Exceptions: *safes, roofs, proofs, chiefs*

For some words the plural form is irregular:

teeth	children	people

Some words have no plural spelling:

sheep	fish	series

Greek and Latin nouns have special plural spellings:

memoranda	data	theses

For compound nouns, make the needed change to the main word:

bookshelves	stepchildren	boyfriends

For compound nouns that appear as separate words, change the main word:

brothers-in-law	beer taps	water tanks

5. Follow guidelines for creating past-tense endings.

For regular verbs, add *-ed* or *-d* if the word ends in *e:*

walked	created	painted

For verbs ending in *y*, change the *y* to *i* and add *-ed:*

cried	spied	tried

For a one-syllable verb ending with a consonant preceded by a vowel, double the last letter and add *-ed:*

pinned	stopped	grabbed

Some verbs have irregular past-tense forms:

taught	sang	swam

6. Follow guidelines for adding suffixes:

For words ending with a silent *e,* drop the *e* if the ending begins with a vowel:

arrival	coming	creation

For words ending with a silent *e,* keep the *e* if the ending begins with a consonant:

safety	likeness	completely

Double the last consonant of one-syllable words if the ending begins with a vowel:

robbing	spotted	spinning

Double the last consonant of words accented on the last syllable if the ending begins with a vowel:

referring	admitted	technically

7. Make and review lists of words you commonly misspell.
8. Always budget enough time in the writing process to edit your papers for spelling errors.

IMPROVING SPELLING

Review writing exercises you have completed in this book and papers you have written in this or other courses for errors in spelling. List each word. Add words that you frequently misspell or are unsure of. Check a dictionary and carefully write out each word correctly. Add definitions to words that are easily confused, such as *conscious* and *conscience* or *then* and *than*.

1. _____ 11. _____

2. _____ 12. _____

3. _____ 13. _____

4. _____ 14. _____

5. _____ 15. _____

6. _____ 16. _____

7. _____ 17. _____

8. _____ 18. _____

9. _____ 19. _____

10. _____ 20. _____

Handbook

A Writer's Guide to Overcoming Common Errors

Basic Sentence Structure

A sentence is a group of words that contains a subject and verb and states a complete thought.

Phrases and Clauses

Phrases are groups of related words that form parts of a sentence:

After the game   Ted and Carlos   are willing to   decorations for the
                                       help distribute   party.

Clauses consist of related words that contain both a subject and a verb:

- **Independent clauses** contain a subject and verb and express a complete thought. They are sentences:

    I waited for the bus.   It began to rain.

- **Dependent clauses** contain a subject and verb but do *not* express a complete thought. They are not sentences:

    While I waited for the bus

    Dependent clauses have to be connected to an independent clause to create a sentence that expresses a complete thought:

    While I waited for the bus, it began to rain.

Types of Sentences

Sentence types are determined by the number and kind of clauses they contain. A **simple sentence** consists of a single independent clause:

Jim sings.
Jim and Nalini sing and dance at the newly renovated Second City.
Seeking to reenter show business, Jim and Nalini sing and dance at the newly renovated Second City, located next to Gretzky's.

A **compound sentence** contains two or more independent clauses but no dependent clauses:

Jim studied dance at York; Nalini studied music at Humber.
   [two independent clauses joined by a semicolon]

Jim wants to stay in Toronto, but Nalini longs to move to New York.
   [two independent clauses joined with a comma and coordinating conjunction]

A **complex sentence** contains one independent clause and one or more dependent clauses:

Jim and Nalini are studying drama because they want to act on Broadway.
Because they want to act on Broadway, *Jim and Nalini are studying drama.*
   [When a dependent clause begins a complex sentence, it is set off with a comma.]

A **compound-complex sentence** contains at least two independent clauses and one or more dependent clauses:

Jim and Nalini perform improv, and they often incorporate the audience into their skits *because the Second City draws an interactive crowd.*

Because the Second City draws an inter active crowd, Jim and Nalini perform improv, and they often incorporate the audience into their skits.

PARTS OF SPEECH

Nouns	name persons, places, things, or ideas: *teacher, attic, Italy, book, liberty*
Pronouns	take the place of nouns: *he, she, they, it, this, that, what, which, hers, their*
Verbs	express action: *buy, sell, run, walk, create, think, feel, wonder, hope, dream* link ideas: *is, are, was, were*
Adjectives	add information about nouns or pronouns: a *red* car, a *bright* idea, a *lost* cause
Adverbs	add information about verbs: drove *recklessly,* sell *quickly, angrily* denounced add information about adjectives: *very* old teacher, *sadly* dejected leader add information about other adverbs: *rather* hesitantly remarked
Prepositions	link nouns and pronouns, expressing relationships between related words: *in* the house, *around* the corner, *between* the acts, *through* the evening
Conjunctions	link related parts of a sentence: **Coordinating conjunctions** link parts of equal value: *and, or, for, nor, yet, but, so* He went to college, *and* she got a job. **Subordinating conjunctions** link dependent or less important parts: *When* he went to college, she got a job.
Interjections	express emotion or feeling that is not part of the basic sentence and are set off with commas or used with exclamation points: *Oh,* he's leaving? *Wow!*

(continued)

Words can function as different parts of speech:

> I bought more *paint* [noun].
> I am going to *paint* [verb] the bedroom.
> Those supplies are stored in the *paint* [adjective] room.

Parts of speech can be single words or phrases, groups of related words that work together:

> Trey and his entire staff [noun phrase]
> wrote and edited [verb phrase]
> throughout the night [prepositional phrase].

Sentence Errors

Fragments

Fragments are incomplete sentences. They lack a subject, a complete verb, or fail to express a complete thought:

Subject Missing
Worked all night. [Who worked *all night*?]

Revised
He worked all night.

Verb Missing
Juan the new building. [What was Juan doing?]

Revised
Juan designed the new building.

Incomplete Verb
Juan designing the new building. [*-ing* verbs cannot stand alone.]

Revised
Juan is designing the new building.

Incomplete Thought
Although Juan designed the building. [It has a subject and verb but fails to express a whole idea.]

Revised
Juan designed the building.

or

Although Juan designed the building, he did not receive any recognition.

Correcting Fragments
There are two ways of correcting fragments.

1. Turn the fragment into a complete sentence by making sure it expresses a complete thought:

   Fragments
   Simon Fraser being the centre for this research
   Based on public opinion surveys
   The mayor designated

Revised
Simon Fraser is the centre for this research. [complete verb added]
The new study is based on public opinion surveys. [subject and verb
added]
The mayor designated Sandy Gomez head of the commission.
[words added to express a complete thought]

2. Attach the fragment to a sentence to state a complete thought. (Often
    fragments occur when you write quickly and break off part of a sentence.)

    Fragments
    He bought a car. *While living in Hamilton.*
    Constructed in 1873. The old church needs major repairs.

    Revised
    He bought a car while living in Hamilton.
    Constructed in 1873, the old church needs major repairs.

POINT TO REMEMBER

Reading aloud can help identify fragments. Ask yourself, "Does this statement express a complete thought?"

Run-ons

Fused Sentences

Fused sentences lack the punctuation needed to join two independent clauses. The
two independent clauses are *fused,* or joined, without a comma or semicolon:

Travis entered the contest he won first prize

Revised
Travis entered the contest; he won first prize.

Sophie speaks Spanish but she has trouble reading it.

Revised
Sophie speaks Spanish, but she has trouble reading it.

Comma Splices

Comma splices are compound sentences where a comma is used instead of a
semicolon:

My sister lives in Victoria, my brother lives in St. John's.

Revised
My sister lives in Victoria; my brother lives in St. John's.

The lake is frozen solid, it is safe to drive on.

Revised
The lake is frozen solid; it is safe to drive on.

Identifying Run-ons

To identify run-ons, do two things:

1. Read the sentence carefully. Determine if it is a compound sentence. Ask
    yourself if you can divide the sentence into two or more independent
    clauses (simple sentences).

Sam entered college but dropped out after six months.

Sam entered college . . . [independent clause (simple sentence)]
dropped out after six months. [not a sentence]
[not a compound sentence]
Michelle graduated in May but she signed up for summer courses.
Michelle graduated in May . . .   [independent clause (simple sentence)]
she signed up for summer courses. [independent clause (simple sentence)]
[compound sentence]

2. If you have two complete sentences, determine if they should be joined. Is there a logical relationship between them? What is the best way of connecting them? Independent clauses can be joined with a comma and *and, or, for, nor, yet, but, so,* or with a semicolon.

Michelle graduated in May, but she signed up for summer courses.

But indicates a contrast between two ideas. Inserting the missing comma quickly repairs this run-on.

Repairing Run-ons: Minor Repairs

A fused sentence or comma splice may need only a minor repair. Sometimes in writing quickly we mistakenly use a comma when a semicolon is needed:

The Senate likes the finance minister's budget, the House still has questions.

Revised
The Senate likes the finance minister's budget; the House still has questions.

In other cases we may forget a comma or drop one of the coordinating conjunctions:

The Senate likes the finance minister's budget but the House still has questions.

Senators approve of the budget, they want to meet with the finance minister's staff.

Revised
The Senate likes the finance minister's budget, but the House still has questions.

Senators approve of the budget, and they want to meet with the finance minister's staff.

Repairing Run-ons: Major Repairs

Some run-ons require major repairs. Sometimes we create run-ons when our ideas are not clearly stated or fully thought out:

Pierre Trudeau was prime minister in 1980 and Jeanne Sauvé was appointed the first female Speaker of the House in Canada.

Adding the needed comma eliminates a mechanical error but leaves the sentence awkward and unclear:

Pierre Trudeau was prime minister in 1980, and Jeanne Sauvé was appointed the first female Speaker of the House in Canada.

Repairing this kind of run-on requires critical thinking. A compound sentence joins two complete thoughts, and there should be a clear relationship between them. It may be better to revise the entire sentence, changing it from a compound to a complex sentence:

Revised
Pierre Trudeau was prime minister in 1980 when he appointed Jeanne Sauvé as the first female Speaker of the House in Canada.

In some instances you may find it easier to break the run-on into two simple sentences, especially if there is no strong relationship between the main ideas:

Swansea is a port city in Wales that was severely bombed in World War II and Dylan Thomas was born there in 1914.

Revised
Swansea is a port city in Wales that was severely bombed in World War II. Dylan Thomas was born there in 1914.

POINT TO REMEMBER

A compound sentence should join independent clauses that state ideas of equal importance. Avoid using an independent clause to state a minor detail that could be contained in a dependent clause or a phrase:

Awkward

My brother lives in Halifax, and he is an architect.

Revised

My brother, who lives in Halifax, is an architect.
My brother in Halifax is an architect.

Modifiers

Dangling Modifiers

Modifiers that serve as introductions must describe what follows the comma. When they do not, they "dangle" so that it is unclear what they modify:

Grounded by fog, airport officials ordered passengers to deplane.
    [Were airport officials *grounded by fog*?]

Revised
Grounded by fog, the passengers were ordered by airport officials to deplane.
Airport officials ordered passengers to deplane the aircraft grounded by fog.

STRATEGY TO DETECT DANGLING MODIFIERS

Sentences with opening modifiers set off by commas fit this pattern:

    Modifier, main sentence

To make sure the sentence is correct, use the following test:

(continued)

1. Read the sentence, then turn the modifier into a question, asking who or what in the main sentence is performing the action:

    question, answer

2. What follows the comma forms the answer. If the answer is appropriate, the construction is correct:

    Hastily constructed, the bridge deteriorated in less than a year.
       Question: What was *hastily constructed*?
       Answer: the bridge
       This sentence is <u>correct</u>.

    Suspected of insanity, the defence attorney asked that her client be examined by psychiatrists.
       Question: Who was *suspected of insanity*?
       Answer: the defence attorney
       This sentence is <u>incorrect</u>.

    Revised: Suspecting her client to be insane, the defense attorney asked that he be examined by psychiatrists.

Misplaced Modifiers

Place modifying words, phrases, and clauses as near as possible to the words they describe:

Confusing
Scientists developed new chips for laptop computers *that cost less than fifty cents*.

   [Do laptop computers cost *less than fifty cents*?]

Revised
Scientists developed laptop computer chips that cost less than fifty cents.

Faulty Parallelism

When you create pairs or lists, the words or phrases must match—they have to be all nouns, all adjectives, all adverbs, or all verbs in the same form:

Zeinab is *bright, creative,* and *funny.* [adjectives]
Catherine writes *clearly, directly,* and *forcefully.* [adverbs]
Reading and *calculating* are critical skills for my students. [gerunds]
She should *lose* weight, *stop* smoking, and *limit* her intake of alcohol.
   [verbs matching with *should*]

The following sentences are not parallel:

The concert was loud, colourful, and many people attended.
   [*Many people attended* does not match with the adjectives *loud* and *colourful.*]
Alexander failed to take notes, refused to attend class, and his final exam is unreadable.
   [*His final exam is* does not match the verb phrases *failed to take* and *refused to attend.*]

Quitting smoking and daily exercise are important.
[*Quitting,* a gerund, does not match with *daily exercise.*]

Revised
The concert was *loud, colourful,* and *well attended.* [all adjectives]
Alexander *failed* to take notes, *refused* to attend class, and *wrote* an almost unreadable final exam. [all verbs]
Quitting smoking and *exercising* daily are important.
[both gerunds (*-ing* nouns)]

Strategies for Detecting and Revising Faulty Parallelism

Apply this simple test to any sentences that include pairs or lists of words or phrases to make sure they are parallel:

1. Read the sentence and locate the pair or list.
2. Make sure each item matches the format of the basic sentence by testing each item.

Example

Students should read directions carefully, write down assignments accurately, and take notes.

Students should read directions.
Students should write down assignments accurately.
Students should take notes.

[Each item matches *Students should* . . .]
This sentence is <u>parallel</u>.

Computer experts will have to make more precise predictions in the future to reduce waste, create more accurate budgets, and public support must be maintained.

Computer experts will have to make more precise . . .
Computer experts will have to create more accurate . . .
Computer experts will have to public support must be . . .

[The last item does not link with *will have to.*]
This sentence is <u>not parallel</u>.

A TIP ON PARALLELISM

In many cases it is difficult to revise long sentences that are not parallel:

To build her company, Shireen Naboti is a careful planner, skilled supervisor, recruits talent carefully, monitors quality control, and is a lobbyist for legal reform.

If you have trouble making all the elements match, it may be simpler to break it up into two or even three separate sentences:

To build her company, Shireen Naboti is a careful planner, skilled supervisor, and lobbyist for legal reform. In addition, she recruits talent carefully and monitors quality control.

(continued)

The first sentence contains the noun phrases; the second consists of the two verb phrases. It is easier to create two short parallel lists than one long one.

Verbs

Subject–Verb Agreement

Singular subjects require singular verbs:

The <u>boy</u> *walks* to school.
Your <u>bill</u> *is* overdue.

Plural subjects require plural verbs:

The <u>boys</u> *walk* to school.
Your <u>bills</u> *are* overdue.

Changing a verb from singular to plural changes the meaning of a sentence:

Singular
The desk and chair *is* on sale. [The desk and chair are sold as one item.]

Plural
The desk and chair *are* on sale. [The desk and chair are sold separately.]

RULES

- Not all nouns require an *s* to become plural:
    The deer run across the road.   The women play cards.

- Some nouns that end in *s* and look like plurals are singular:
    Mathematics *is* my toughest course. Economics *demands* accurate data.

- Some nouns that may refer to one item are plural:
    My scissors *are* dull.   *Are* these your gloves?

- Proper nouns that look plural are singular if they are names of companies, organizations, or titles of books, movies, television shows, or works of art:
    General Motors *is* building a new engine.   *The Da Vinci Code is* suspenseful.

- Units of time and amounts of money are generally singular:
    Twenty-five dollars *is* a lot for a T-shirt.   Two weeks *is* not enough time.

    They appear as plurals to indicate separate items:
    Three loonies *were* lying on the table.   My last weeks at camp *were* unbearable.

(continued)

- Group nouns—*audience, board, class, committee, jury, number, team,* and so on—are singular when they describe a group working together:

"Faculty Accepts School Board Offer"	[headline describing teachers acting as a group]
"Faculty Protest School Board Offer"	[headline describing teachers acting individually]

- Verbs in "either . . . or" sentences can be singular or plural. If both subjects are singular, the verb is singular:

  Either the <u>father</u> or the <u>mother</u> *is* required to appear in court.

  If both subjects are plural, the verb is plural:

  Either the <u>parents</u> or the <u>attorneys</u> *are* required to appear in court.

  If one subject is plural and one is singular, the subject closer to the verb determines whether it is singular or plural:

  Either the parent or the <u>attorneys</u> *are* required to appear in court.
  Either the parents or the <u>attorney</u> *is* required to appear in court.

- Indefinite pronouns can be singular or plural.

  Singular indefinite pronouns:

another	each	everything	nothing
anybody	either	neither	somebody
anyone	everybody	nobody	someone

  Anything is possible   *Someone* is coming.

  Plural indefinite pronouns:

both	few	many	several

  Both are here.   *Many* are missing.

  Indefinite pronouns that can be singular or plural:

all	some	more	most

Snow fell last night, but <u>most *has*</u> melted.	[*Most* refers to the singular "snow."]
Passengers were injured, but <u>most *have*</u> recovered.	[*Most* refers to the plural "passengers."]

Verb Tense

Regular Verbs

Most verbs show tense changes by adding *-ed* to words ending with consonants and *-d* to words ending with an *e:*

Present	Past	Past Participle
walk	walked	walked
create	created	created
cap	capped	capped

Irregular Verbs

Irregular verbs do not follow the *-ed* pattern.

Some irregular verbs require no spelling change to indicate shifts in tense:

Present	Past	Past Participle
cost	cost	cost
cut	cut	cut
fit	fit	fit
hit	hit	hit
hurt	hurt	hurt
put	put	put

Most irregular verbs require a spelling change rather than adding -ed:

Present	Past	Past Participle
arise	arose	arisen
awake	awoke	awoken
be	was, were	been
bear	bore	borne (not *born*)
become	became	become
break	broke	broken
bring	brought	brought
build	built	built
choose	chose	chosen
come	came	come
dive	dived (dove)	dived
do	did	done
draw	drew	drawn
eat	ate	eaten
feed	fed	fed
fly	flew	flown
forgive	forgave	forgiven
freeze	froze	frozen
get	got	gotten (got)
grow	grew	grown
hang (objects)	hung	hung
hang (people)	hanged	hanged
have	had	had
lay (place)	laid	laid
lead	led	led
leave	left	left
lie (recline)	lay	lain
lose	lost	lost
make	made	made
mean	meant	meant
meet	met	met
pay	paid	paid
ride	rode	ridden
ring	rang	rung
rise	rose	risen
run	ran	run
say	said	said

Present	Past	Past Participle
see	saw	seen
sell	sold	sold
shake	shook	shaken
shine	shone	shone
shoot	shot	shot
sing	sang	sung
sink	sank	sunk
sleep	slept	slept
sneak	sneaked	sneaked
speak	spoke	spoken
spend	spent	spent
steal	stole	stolen
sting	stung	stung
strike	struck	struck
swim	swam	swum
swing	swung	swung
take	took	taken
teach	taught	taught
think	thought	thought
throw	threw	thrown
understand	understood	understood
wake	woke	woken
write	wrote	written

Problem Verbs: Lie/Lay, Rise/Raise, Set/Sit

Lie/Lay

To lie = to rest or recline: "lie down for nap"
To lay = to put something down or place into position: "lay a book on a table"

Present	Past	Past Participle
lie	lay	lain
lay	laid	laid

Remember: *Lie* expresses action done *by* someone or something:

> Dan called 911, then *lay* on the sofa waiting for the paramedics.

Lay expresses action done *to* someone or something:

> The paramedics *laid* Dan on the floor to administer CPR.

Rise/Raise

To rise = to get up or move up on your own: "rise and shine" or "rise to the occasion."
To raise = to lift or grow something: "raise a window" or "raise children."

Present	Past	Past Participle
rise	rose	risen
raise	raised	raised

Remember: *Rise* can refer to objects as well as people:

The bread rises in the oven. Oil prices are rising.

Set/Sit

To set = to put something in position or arrange in place: "set down a glass" or "set down some notes." *Set* always takes a direct object.

To sit = to assume a sitting position: "sit in a chair" or "sit on a committee"

Present	Past	Past Participle
set	set	set
sit	sat	sat

Shifts in Tense

Avoid awkward or illogical shifts in time and write in a consistent tense:

Awkward

I *drove* to the beach and *see* Kareem working out with James.

past   present

Consistent

I *drove* to the beach and *saw* Kareem working out with James.

past   past

or

I *drive* to the beach and *see* Kareem working out with James.

present   present

Change tenses to show a logical change in time:

I *was born* in Sudbury but *live* in Newmarket. Next year I *will move* to Calgary.

past   present   future

Change tense to distinguish between past events and subjects that are permanent or still operating:

He *was born* in Sudbury, which *is* located several hours north of Toronto.

Pronouns

Reference

Pronouns should clearly refer to specific antecedents. Avoid unclear references.

- Make sure pronouns are clearly linked to **antecedents**—the nouns or other pronouns they represent. Avoid constructions in which a pronoun could refer to more than one noun or pronoun:

  Unclear

  Claire was with Charmaine when *she* got the news.
  [Who received the news—Claire or Charmaine?]

  Revised

  When Charmaine received the news, *she* was with Claire.

- Replace pronouns with nouns for clearer references:

  Unclear
  The teachers explained to the students why *they* couldn't attend the ceremony.
  [Who cannot attend the ceremony—teachers or students?]

  Revised
  The teachers explained to the students why *faculty* couldn't attend the ceremony.
  The teachers explained to the students why *children* couldn't attend the ceremony.

- State "*either . . . or*" constructions carefully.

  Either Jorge or Miguel can lend you *their* key.
  [Jorge and Miguel share one key.]

  Either Jorge or Miguel can lend you *his* key.
  [Both Jorge and Miguel have keys.]

  Either Jorge or Anna can lend you *a* key.
  [avoids need for *his or her*]

- Avoid unclear references with *this, that, it, which,* and *such:*

  Unclear
  Many people think that diets are the only way to lose weight. *This* is wrong.

  Revised
  Many people mistakenly think that diets are the only way to lose weight.

- Avoid unnecessary pronouns after nouns:

  Unnecessary
  Miriam Toews *she* wrote *A Complicated Kindness.*

  Revised
  Miriam Toews wrote *A Complicated Kindness.*

- Avoid awkward use of *you. You* is acceptable for directly addressing readers. Avoid making awkward shifts in general statements:

  Awkward
  Highway congestion can give you stress.

  Revised
  Highway congestion can be stressful.

Agreement

- Pronouns agree in number and gender with antecedents:

  Sean took *his* time.   *Gayathry* rode *her* bicycle.   The *children* called *their* mother.

- Compound nouns require plural pronouns:

  Both the *students and the teachers* argue that *their* views are not heard.
  Adriano and Miranda announced *they* plan to move to Winnipeg next year.

- Collective nouns use singular or plural pronouns:

    Singular
    The *cast* played *its* last performance.
        [The cast acts as one unit.]

    Plural
    The *cast* had trouble remembering *their* lines.
        [Cast members act independently.]

- *Either . . . or* constructions can be singular or plural. If both nouns are singular, the pronoun is singular:

    Either the city council *or* the county board will present *its* budget.
        [Only one group will present a budget.]

    If both nouns are plural, the pronoun is plural:

    The board members or *the city attorneys* will present *their* report.
        [In both instances, several individuals present a report.]

    If one noun is singular and the other is plural, the pronoun agrees with the nearer noun:

    Either the teacher or students will present *their* findings to the principal.

    Place the plural noun last to avoid awkward statements or having to represent both genders with *he and she, his or her,* or *him and her.*

- Pronouns should maintain the same person or point of view in a sentence, avoiding awkward shifts:

    Awkward Shift
    To save money, *consumers* should monitor *their* [third person] use of credit cards to avoid getting in over *your* [second person] head in debt.

    Revised
    To save money, *consumers* should monitor *their* use of credit cards to avoid getting in over *their* heads in debt.

- Indefinite pronouns. In speaking, people often use the plural pronouns *they, them,* and *their* to include both males and females. In formal writing, make sure singular indefinite pronouns agree with singular pronouns:

    Singular
anybody	everybody	nobody	somebody
anyone	everyone	no one	someone
either	neither	each	one

    Anybody can bring *his or her* tax return in for review.
    Everybody is required to do the test *himself or herself.*

    Plural
    If *many* are unable to attend the orientation, make sure to call *them.*

Indefinite pronouns like *some* may be singular or plural depending on context:

Singular
Some of the ice is losing *its* brilliance.

Plural
Some of the children are missing *their* coats.

AVOID SEXISM IN PRONOUN USE

Singular nouns and many indefinite pronouns refer to individuals who may be male or female. Trying to include both men and women, however, often creates awkward constructions:

If a student has a problem, *he or she* should contact *his or her* adviser.

In editing your writing, try these strategies to eliminate both sexism and awkward pronoun use:

- Use plurals:

  If students have problems, *they* should contact *their* advisers.

- Revise the sentence to limit or eliminate the need for pronouns:

  Students with problems should contact advisers.
  Advisers assist students with problems.

Adjectives and Adverbs

- Understand differences between adjectives and adverbs:

  She gave us *freshly sliced* peaches.
    [The adverb *freshly* modifies the adjective *sliced,* meaning that the peaches, whatever their freshness, have just been sliced.]

  She gave us *fresh sliced* peaches.
    [The adjectives *fresh* and *sliced* both describe the noun *peaches,* meaning the peaches are both fresh and sliced.]

- Review sentences to select the most effective adjectives and adverbs. Adjectives and adverbs add meaning. Avoid vague modifiers:

  Vague
  The concert hall was *totally inappropriate* for our group.

  Revised
  The concert hall was *too informal* for our group.
  The concert hall was *too large* for our group.

- Use adverbs with verbs:

  Incorrect
  Drive *careful.* [adjective]

  Revised
  Drive *carefully.*

- Avoid unnecessary adjectives and adverbs:

  Unnecessary
  We drove down the *old, winding, potholed, dirt* road.

  Revised
  We drove down the *winding, potholed* road.

- Use *good* and *well,* and *bad* and *badly* accurately. *Good* and *bad* are adjectives and modify nouns and pronouns:

  The cookies taste *good.* [*Good* modifies the noun *cookies.*]
  The wine is *bad.* [*Bad* modifies the noun *wine.*]

  Well and *badly* are adverbs and modify verbs, adjectives, and adverbs:

  She sings *well.* [*Well* modifies the verb *sings.*]
  He paid for *badly* needed repairs. [*Badly* modifies the adjective *needed.*]

Comma ,

- Use commas with *and, or, for, nor, yet, but,* or *so* to join independent clauses to create compound sentences and avoid run-ons:

  Chinatown is a popular tourist attraction, <u>and</u> it serves as an important cultural centre.

- Use a comma after a dependent clause that opens a complex sentence:

  Because the parade was cancelled, we decided to go to the shore.

  If the dependent clause follows the independent clause, the comma is usually deleted:

  We decided to go to the shore because the parade was cancelled.

- Use a comma after a long phrase or an introductory word:

  After breakfast with the new students and guest faculty, we are going to the museum.
  Yes, I am cashing your cheque today.

- Use commas to separate words, phrases, and clauses in a series:

  Words
  We purchased computer paper, ink, pens, and pencils.

  Phrases
  We purchased computer paper, ordered fax supplies, and photocopied the records.

  Clauses
  We purchased computer paper, Sarah ordered fax supplies, and Ji Ying photocopied the records.

  If clauses contain commas, separate them with semicolons (see page 404).

- Use commas to set off nonrestrictive or parenthetical words or phrases. *Nonrestrictive* words or phrases describe or add extra information about a noun and are set off with commas:

  George Gzosky, who loves soccer, can't wait for the World Cup.

  Restrictive words or phrases limit or restrict the meaning of abstract nouns and are not set off with commas:

  Anyone who loves soccer can't wait for the World Cup.

- Use commas to set off contrasted elements:

  The teachers, not the students, argue the tests are too difficult.

- Use commas after interjections, words used in direct address, and around direct quotations:

  Hey, get a life.
  Tomoko, help Cecile with the mail.
  George said, "Welcome to the disaster," to everyone arriving at the party.

- Use commas to separate city and province or city and country, items in dates, and every three numerals 1,000 and above:

  I used to work in Summerside, P.E.I., until I was transferred to Paris, France.
    [A comma goes after the province or country if followed by other words.]
  She was born on July 7, 1986, and graduated high school in May 2004.
    [A comma goes after the date if followed by other words. No comma needed if only month and year are given.]
  The new bridge will cost the province 52,250,000 dollars.

- Use commas to set off absolute phrases:

  Her car unable to operate in deep snow, Sarah borrowed Jaden's Jeep.
  Wilson raced down the field and caught the ball on one knee, his heart pounding.

- Use commas where needed to prevent confusion or add emphasis:

  Confusing
  Whenever they hunted people ran for cover.
  To Sally Kleinburg was a good place to live.
  To help feed the hungry Robel donated bread.

  Improved
  Whenever they hunted, people ran for cover.
  To Sally, Kleinburg was a good place to live.
  To help feed the hungry, Robel donated bread.

  Reading sentences aloud can help you spot sentences that need commas to prevent confusion.

1. Don't put a comma between a subject and verb unless setting off nonrestrictive elements or a series:

   Incorrect
   The old car, was stolen.

   Correct
   The car, which was old, was stolen.

2. Don't use commas to separate prepositional phrases from what they modify:

   Incorrect
   The van, in the driveway, needs new tires.

   Correct
   The van in the driveway needs new tires.

3. Don't use commas to separate two items in a compound verb:

   Incorrect
   They sang, and danced at the party.

   Correct
   They sang and danced at the party.

4. Don't put commas around titles:

   Incorrect
   The film opens with, "Love Me Tender," and shots of Elvis.

   Correct
   The film opens with "Love Me Tender" and shots of Elvis.

5. Don't put commas after a series unless it ends a clause that has to be set off from the rest of the sentence:

   Incorrect
   They donated computers, printers, and telephones, to our office.

   Correct
   They donated computers, printers, and telephones, and we provided office space.

6. Don't set off a dependent clause with a comma when it ends a sentence:

   Incorrect
   The game was cancelled, because the referees went on strike.

   Correct
   The game was cancelled because the referees went on strike.

   A comma is needed if a dependent clause opens the sentence:

   Because the referees went on strike, the game was cancelled.

Semicolon ;

Semicolons have two uses.

1. Use semicolons to join independent clauses when *and, or, for, nor, yet, but,* or *so* are not present:

   > Charlottetown is the capital of P.E.I.; St. John's is the capital of Newfoundland.

   Remember to use semicolons when you use words such as *nevertheless, moreover,* and *however:*

   > They barely had time to rehearse; however, opening night was a success.

2. Use semicolons to separate items in a series that contain commas:

   > The premier will meet with Michael Di Biase, the mayor of Vaughan; Sandy Bert, the new city manager; the district attorney; Peter Plesmid; and Al Leone, an engineering consultant.

Apostrophe '

Apostrophes are used for three reasons:

1. Apostrophes indicate possession:

Noun	Erica's car broke down.
Acronym	NASA's new space vehicle will launch on Monday.
Indefinite pronoun	Someone's car has its lights on.
Endings of *s, x,* or *z* sound	Phyllis' car is stalled. [or *Phyllis's*]

   Apostrophes are deleted from some geographical names:

Smiths Falls	Holls Gate	Jones Falls

   Apostrophes may or may not appear in possessive names of businesses or organizations:

Eaton's	Rogers Centre Sears	Allan's Pub

   Follow the spelling used on signs, stationery, and business cards.

2. Apostrophes signal missing letters and numbers in contractions:

   > Ted can't restore my '67 VW.

3. Apostrophes indicate plurals of letters, numbers, or symbols:

   > I got all B's last semester and A's this semester.
   > Do we have any size 7's or 8's left?
   > We can sell all the 2003's at half price.

Apostrophes are optional in referring to decades, but be consistent:

> She went to high school in the 1990's but loved the music
> of the 1960's.

or

> She went to high school in the 1990s but loved the music
> of the 1960s.

Common abbreviations such as *TV* and *UFO* do not need apostrophes to indicate plurals:

> We bought new TVs and several DVDs.

POINT TO REMEMBER

it's = contraction of "it is"

> It's raining.

its = possessive of "it"

> My car won't start. Its battery is dead.

Quotation Marks " "

Quotation marks—always used in pairs—enclose direct quotations, titles of short works, and highlighted words:

- For direct quotations:

  > Martin Luther King said, "I have a dream."

  The final mark of punctuation precedes the final quotation mark, unless it does not appear in the original text:

  > Did Martin Luther King say, "I have a dream"?

  Set off identifying phrases with commas:

  > Stephanie insisted, "We cannot win unless we practise."
  > "We cannot win," Stephanie insisted, "unless we practise."
  > "We cannot win unless we practise," Stephanie insisted.

  Commas are not used if the quotation is blended into the sentence:

  > They exploited the "cheaper by the dozen" technique to save a fortune.

  Quotations within quotations are indicated by the use of single quotation marks:

  > Stephanie said, "I was only ten when I heard Martin Luther King proclaim, 'I have a dream.'"

  Final commas are placed inside quotation marks:

  > The letter stated, "The college will lower fees," but few students believed it.

Colons and semicolons are placed outside quotation marks:

> The letter stated, "The college will lower fees"; few students
> believed it.

Indirect quotations do not require quotation marks:

> Martin Luther King said that he had a dream.

- **For titles of short works**
  Titles of short works—poems, stories, articles, and songs—are placed in quotation marks:

  > Did you read "When Are We Going to Mars?" in *Madean's* this week?

  Do not capitalize articles, prepositions, or coordinating conjunctions (*and, or, for, nor, yet, but, so*) unless they are the first or last words. (Longer works—books, films, magazines, and albums—are underlined or placed in italics.)

- **To highlight words**
  Highlighted words are placed in quotation marks to draw extra attention:

  > I still don't know what "traffic abatement" is supposed to mean.
  > This is the fifth time this month Martha has "been sick" when we
  > needed her.

Colon :

Colons are placed after independent clauses to introduce elements and separate items in numerals, ratios, titles, and time references:

> The coach demanded three things from his players: loyalty, devotion, and teamwork.
> The coach demanded one quality above all others: attention to detail.
> The coach says the team has a 3:1 advantage.
> I am reading *Arthur Miller: Playwright of the Century*.
> The play started at 8:15.

Parentheses ( )

Parentheses set off nonessential details and explanations and enclose letters and numbers used for enumeration:

> The labour task force (originally headed by Knudson) will submit a report to the premier's office.
> The Greater Toronto Airport Authority (GTAA) has new security policies.
> The report stated we must (1) improve services, (2) provide housing, and (3) increase funding.

Brackets [ ]

Brackets set off interpolations or clarifications in quotations and replace parentheses within parentheses:

Leah Mintz observed, "I think [Lester] Pearson was the greatest prime minister."
The premier noted, "Stephen Harper told Francis Harper [no relation] that he agreed with her ideas for tax incentives."
The ambassador stated, "We will give them [the Iraqi National Congress] all the help they need."

Dash —

Dashes mark a break in thought, set off a parenthetical element for emphasis, and set off an introduction to a series:

Ted was angry after his car was stolen—who wouldn't be?
The movie studio—which faced bankruptcy—desperately needed a hit.
They had everything needed to succeed—ideas, money, marketing, and cutting edge technology.

Hyphen -

A hyphen is a short line used to separate or join words and other items.

- Use hyphens to break words:

    We saw her on tele-
    vision last night.

    Only break words between syllables.

- Use hyphens to connect words to create adjectives:

    We made a last-ditch attempt to score a touchdown.

    Do *not* use hyphens with adverbs ending in *-ly:*

    We issued a quickly drafted statement to the press.

- Use hyphens to connect words forming numbers:

    The firm owes nearly thirty-eight million dollars in back taxes.

- Use hyphens after some prefixes:

    His self-diagnosis was misleading.

Ellipsis . . .

An ellipsis, three spaced periods [. . .], indicates words are deleted from quoted material:

Original Text
The mayor said, "Our city, which is one of the country's most progressive, deserves a high-tech light-rail system."

With Ellipsis
The mayor said, "Our city . . . deserves a high-tech light-rail system."

Delete only minor ideas or details—never change the basic meaning of a sentence by deleting key words. Don't eliminate a negative word like "not" to create a positive statement or remove qualifying words:

Original
We must, only as a last resort, consider legalizing drugs.

Incorrect
He said, "We must . . . consider legalizing drugs."

When deleting words at the end of a sentence, add a period before the ellipsis:

The premier said, "I agree we need a new rail system. . . ."

An ellipsis is not used if words are deleted at the opening of a quotation:

The mayor said the city "deserves a high-tech light-rail system."

If deleting words will create a grammar mistake, insert corrections with brackets:

Original
"Atwood, Ondaatje, and Laurence were among our greatest writers."

With Ellipsis
"Atwood . . . [was] among our greatest writers."

Slash /

Slashes separate words when both apply and show line breaks when quoting poetry:

The student should study his/her lessons.
Her poem read in part, "We hope / We dream / We pray."

Question Mark ?

Question marks are placed after direct questions and to note questionable items:

Did Adrian Carsini attend the auction?
Did you read "Can We Defeat Hunger?" in *Madean's* last week?

Question marks that appear in the original title are placed within quotation marks. If the title does not ask a question, the question mark is placed outside the quotation marks:

Did you read "The Raven"?

Question marks in parentheses are used to indicate that the writer questions the accuracy of a fact, number, idea, or quotation:

The children claimed they waited two hours (?) for help to arrive.

Exclamation Point !

Exclamation points are placed at the end of emphatic statements:

Help!
We owe her over ten million dollars!

Exclamation points should be used as special effects. They lose their impact if overused.

Period .

Periods are used after sentences, in abbreviations, and as decimals:

I bought a car.
We gave the car to Ms. Chavez who starts working for Dr. Gomez on Jan. 15.
The book sells for $29.95 in hardcover and $12.95 in paper.

When an abbreviation ends a sentence, only one period is used.

Common abbreviations such as RCMP, CIA, ABC, BBC, and UNB do not require periods.

Capitalization

- Capitalize the first word of every sentence:

    We studied all weekend.

- Capitalize the first word in direct quotations:

    Felix said, "The school should buy new computers."

- Capitalize the first word and all important words in titles of articles, books, plays, movies, television shows, seminars, and courses:

    "Terrorism Today"   *Gone with the Wind*   *Lord of the Rings*

- Capitalize the names of nationalities, languages, races, religions, deities, and sacred terms:

    Many Germans speak English.
    The Koran is the basic text in Islam.

- Capitalize the days of the week, months of the year, and holidays:

    We celebrate Victoria Day every May.
    The test scheduled for Monday is cancelled.
    Some people celebrate Christmas in January.
    We observed Passover with her parents.

    The seasons of the year are not capitalized:

    We loved the spring fashions.   Last winter was mild.

- Capitalize special historical events, documents, and eras:

    Battle of the Bulge   Confederation

- Capitalize names of planets, continents, nations, states, provinces, counties, towns and cities, mountains, lakes, rivers, and other geographic features:

  Mars   North America   Rocky Mountains   Ontario

- Capitalize *north, south, east,* and *west* when they refer to geographic regions:

  The convention will be held in the Southwest.

  Do not capitalize *north, south, east,* and *west* when used as directions:

  The farm is southwest of Rockford.

- Capitalize brand names:

  Coca-Cola   Ford Thunderbird   Cross pen

- Capitalize names of specific corporations, organizations, institutions, and buildings:

  This engine was developed by General Motors.
  After high school he attended George Brown College.
  We visited the site of the former World Trade Center.

- Capitalize abbreviations, acronyms, or shortened forms of capitalized words when used as proper nouns:

  RCMP   CIA   MP   ERA
  NOP   JFK   LAX   CBC

- Capitalize people's names and nicknames:

  Barbara Roth   Timmy Arnold

Capitalize professional titles when used with proper names:

  Last week Doctor Ryan suggested I see an eye doctor.
  Our college president once worked with Prime Minister Harper.
  This report must be seen by the prime minister.
  [The words prime minister and *president* are often capitalized to refer to the prime minister of Canada and the president of the United States.]

Capitalize words like *father, mother, brother, aunt, cousin,* and *uncle* only when used with or in place of proper names:

  My mother and I went to see Uncle Ali.
  After the game, I took Mother to meet my uncle.

POINT TO REMEMBER

A few capitalization rules vary. *African American* is always capitalized, but editors vary on the capitalization of *blacks.* Some writers capitalize *a.m.* and *p.m.,* while others do not. Follow the standard used in your discipline or career and be consistent.

Spelling

Commonly Confused Words

accept	to take	Do you *accept* checks?
except	but/to exclude	Everyone *except* Joe went home.
adapt	to change	We will *adapt* the army helicopter for civilian use.
adopt	to take possession of	They want to *adopt* a child.
adverse	unfavourable	*Adverse* publicity ruined his reputation.
averse	opposed to	I was *averse* to buying a new car.
advice	a noun	Take my *advice*.
advise	a verb	Let me *advise* you.
affect	to influence	Will this *affect* my grade?
effect	a result	What is the *effect* of the drug?
all ready	prepared	We were *all ready* for the trip.
already	by a certain time	You are *already* approved.
allusion	a reference	She made a biblical *allusion*.
illusion	imaginary vision	The mirage was an optical *illusion*.
all together	unity	The teachers stood *all together*.
altogether	totally	*Altogether*, that will cost $50.
among	relationship of three or more	This outfit is popular *among* college students.
between	relationship of two	This was a dispute *between* Mohit and Lina.
amount	for items that are measured	A small *amount* of oil has leaked.
number	for items that are counted	A large *number* of cars are stalled.
any one	a person, idea, item	*Any one* of the books will do.
anyone	anybody	Can *anyone* help me?
brake	to halt/a stopping mechanism	Can you fix the *brakes?*
break	an interruption to destroy	Take a coffee *break*. Don't *break* the window.
capital	money	She needs venture *capital*.
	government centre	Trenton is the *capital* of New Jersey.
capitol	legislative building	He toured the nation's *capitol*.

cite	to note or refer to	He *cited* several figures in his speech.
site	a location	We inspected the *site* of the crash.
sight	a view, ability to see	The *sight* from the hill was tremendous.
complement	to complete	The jet had a full *complement* of spare parts.
compliment	express praise, a gift	The host paid us a nice *compliment*.
conscience	moral sensibility	He was a prisoner of *conscience*.
conscious	aware of awake	Is he *conscious* of these debts? Is the patient *conscious?*
continual	now and again	We have *continual* financial problems.
continuous	uninterrupted	The brain needs a *continuous* supply of blood.
council	a group	A student *council* will meet Tuesday.
counsel	to advise/adviser	He sought legal *counsel*.
discreet	tactful	He made a *discreet* hint.
discrete	separate/distinct	The war had three *discrete* phases.
elicit	evoke/persuade	His hateful remarks will *elicit* protest.
illicit	illegal	Her use of *illicit* drugs ruined her career.
emigrate	to leave a country	They tried to *emigrate* from Costa Rica.
immigrate	to enter a country	They were allowed to *immigrate* to Canada.
eminent	famous	She was an *eminent* eye specialist.
imminent	impending	Disaster was *imminent*.
everyday	ordinary	Wear *everyday* clothes to the party.
every day	daily	We exercise *every day*.
farther	distance	How much *farther* is it?
further	in addition	He demanded *further* investigation.
fewer	for items counted	There are *fewer* security guards this year.
less	for items measured	There is *less* security this year.
good	an adjective	She has *good* eyesight.
well	an adverb	She sees *well*.

hear	to listen	Can you *hear* the music?
here	a place/direction	Put the table *here*.
imply	to suggest	The prime minister *implied* he might raise taxes.
infer	to interpret	The reporters *inferred* from his comments that the prime minister might raise taxes.
its	possessive of *it*	The car won't start because *its* battery is dead.
it's	contraction of *it is*	*It's* snowing.
lay	to put/to place	*Lay* the books on my desk.
lie	to rest	*Lie* down for a nap.
licence	a noun	May I see your driver's *licence*?
license	a verb	We have to *license* our dog.
loose	not tight	He has a *loose* belt or *loose* change.
lose	to misplace	Don't *lose* your keys.
moral	dealing with values	She made a *moral* decision to report the crime.
morale	mood	After the loss, the team's *morale* fell.
passed	successfully completed	She *passed* the test.
past	history	That was in my *past*.
personal	private/intimate	She left a *personal* note.
personnel	employees	Send your resume to the *personnel* office.
plain	simple/open space	She wore a *plain* dress.
plane	airplane/geometric form	They took a *plane* to Saskatoon.
practice	a noun	Marina missed baseball *practice* yesterday.
practise	a verb	Marina will *practise* today.
precede	to go before	A film will *precede* the lecture.
proceed	go forward	Let the parade *proceed*.
principal	main/school leader	Oil is the *principal* product of Kuwait.
principle	basic law	I understand the *principle* of law.
raise	to lift	*Raise* the window!
rise	to get up	*Rise* and shine!

right	direction/correct	Turn *right*. That's *right*.
rite	a ritual	She was given last *rites*.
write	to inscribe	They *write* essays every week.
stationary	unmoving	The disabled train remained *stationary*.
stationery	writing paper	The hotel *stationery* was edged in gold.
than	used to compare	I am taller *than* Helen.
then	concerning time	We *then* headed to class.
their	possessive of *they*	*Their* car is stalled.
there	direction/place	Put the chair over *there*.
they're	contraction of *they are*	*They're* coming to dinner.
there're	contraction of *there are*	*There're* two seats left.
to	preposition/infinitive	I went *to* school *to* study law.
too	in excess/also	It was *too* cold to swim.
two	a number	We bought *two* computers.
wear	concerns clothes/ damage	We *wear* our shoes until they *wear* out.
where	a place in question	*Where* is the post office?
weather	climatic conditions	*Weather* forecasts predict rain.
whether	alternatives/no matter what	You must register, *whether* or not you want to audit the class.
who's	contraction of *who is*	*Who's* on first?
whose	possessive of *who*	*Whose* book is that?

Commonly Misspelled Words

absence	amateur	attention	career	consistent
accept	analysis	attitude	carrying	continually
accident	analyze	basically	celebrate	control
accommodate	annual	basis	cemetery	controversial
accumulate	anonymous	beautiful	challenge	criticism
achieve	apparent	becoming	characteristic	curious
achievement	appreciate	beginning	column	dealt
acquaint	approach	belief	coming	decision
acquire	arctic	believe	commitment	definite
across	argument	benefit	committee	deliberate
address	article	breakfast	competition	dependent
advertisement	assassination	business	completely	description
adolescence	assistance	calendar	complexion	difficult
a lot	athletic	candidate	conceive	disappear

disappoint
discipline
discuss
dominant
dying
efficient
eighth
eligible
embarrass
enough
environment
equipment
essential
exaggerate
excellent
existence
experience
explanation
extremely
fallacy
familiar
fantasy
fascination
favourite
February
feminine
field
finally
foreign
forgotten
forty
fourth
frequent
friend
frighten
fulfill
fundamental
further
generally
generous
government
gradually
grammar
grateful
guarantee

guard
guidance
happiness
height
heroes
holocaust
huge
humorous
hypocrite
identity
identically
immediately
importance
incidental
independence
influence
intelligence
interest
interpret
interrupt
involvement
irrelevant
irresistible
irresponsible
judgment
judicial
judicious
knowledge
label
laboratory
language
leisure
libel
library
lightning
loneliness
luxury
lying
magazine
maintenance
manoeuvre
marriage
martial
material
mathematics

meant
mechanical
medieval
mere
miniature
mischief
misspell
mortgage
necessary
ninety
noticeable
obligation
obvious
occasionally
occupation
occurred
omit
operate
opinion
opportunity
oppose
optimism
ordinarily
original
paid
pamphlet
parallel
particularly
perform
permanent
permission
persistent
persuade
persuasion
philosophy
physical
playwright
politician
positive
possession
possible
precede
preference
prejudice
presence

primitive
probably
procedure
prominent
psychic
psychology
publicly
qualify
quality
quantity
query
quiet
quizzes
realize
recede
receive
reception
recognition
recommend
refer
regulation
relation
religious
remember
repetition
responsible
restaurant
rhythm
ridicule
roommate
sacrifice
safety
scene
schedule
seize
separate
sergeant
severely
significance
significant
similar
simplify
sincerely
situation
skillfully

sociology
sophisticated
sophomore
special
specimen
stereotype
straight
strict
studying
success
summary
surprise
synonymous
technique
temperament
tenable
tendency
thorough
thought
throughout
tomorrow
tragedy
tremendous
truly
unfortunate
uniform
unique
until
unusual
useful
using
usually
vacillate
vacillation
vacuum
valuable
various
vengeance
villain
violence
vulnerable
weird
whole
writing
yield

Add other words you often misspell:

_____

_____

_____

_____

_____

_____

_____

_____

_____

_____

_____

_____

_____

_____

Two Hundred Topics for College Writing

best friends
gangs
fad diets
job interviews
athletes as role
    models
bad habits
child support
NHL salaries
doctors
terrorism
fair trade
solar power
right to die
best teacher
car insurance
health clubs
shopping malls
fashion models
hobbies
foreign aid
airport security
cruise ships
blind dates
exploring Mars
being "in"
used cars
Stephen
    Lewis
democracy
being religious
highways
televised trials
sitcoms
cheating
today's comics
drug prevention
ethnic
    stereotypes
lotteries
euthanasia
goal for this year
oil sands in
    Alberta
daycare
taxes

AIDS
cults
lawsuits
sweatshops
chat rooms
drunk drivers
out sourcing
commercials
student housing
wearing fur
work ethic
eating disorders
insanity defence
Internet
voting
adoption
celebrity justice
favourite movie
teen eating
    habits
cable TV bills
minimum wage
the prime
    minister
health insurance
images of
    women
taking the bus
discrimination
TV moms
the World Cup
pensions
welfare reform
the UN
being downsized
favourite singer
prenatal care
workaholics
cable news
parties
reality TV
school loans
women in
    combat
secondhand
    smoke

working while in
    school
drinking age
coffee bars
subsidized
    housing
labour unions
married priests
night clubs
gas prices
car repairs
plea bargaining
banks
lying
fast food
cable TV
fatherhood
racism
study skills
immigration
the Olympics
cell phones
property taxes
bilingual
    education
world hunger
slavery
reparations
worst boss
binge drinking
the pope
college
    instructors
cyberspace
best restaurant
profanity in
    public
reporters
your mayor
the CN Tower
shopping till you
    drop
overcoming
    depression
alternative energy
    sources

racial profiling
casinos
prisons
family values
online dating
steroids
binge drinking
single parents
summer jobs
animal testing
life after death
Hollywood
school choice
hate speech
suburbs
public schools
birth control
credit cards
funerals
toughest course
working out
globalization
talk shows
heating bills
drug testing
aging population
summer jobs
stereotypes
car prices
affirmative action
moving
animal rights
living wills
marriage vows
reading
grandparents
plastic surgery
passion
dreams
family values
hospitals
best jobs
stalking
gay marriage
NHL
pets

divorce
domestic
   violence
war zones
gay bashing
MuchMusic
Islam
sex ontelevision
hip-hop
glass ceiling
remembering the
   2004 tsunami

gun control
the homeless
soap operas
learning
   English
being in debt
relationships
roommates
person you
   admire
surveillance
   cameras

sexual
   harassment
workplace stress
rape shield laws
world hunger
right to privacy
Internet
   pornography
biological
   weapons
downloading
   music

teaching methods
coping with
   illness
sexist or racist
   jokes
definition of
   success
drug busts
final exams
raising boys
   and girls

What's The Difference?

Journal, Magazine, Trade, and Newspaper Articles

When selecting articles for research, it is important to distinguish between journal, magazine, newspaper, and trade articles. The chart below is meant to help you in this process. Journal articles are often referred to as "academic" or "scholarly."

	Journal Article (Scholarly)	Magazine Article (Popular)	Newspaper Article	Trade Magazine Article
Description/ Content	• Main purpose is to report results of original research. • Articles usually have narrow subject focus. • Articles critically evaluated by panel of experts in the field of research (peer-reviewed).	• Main purpose is to entertain, sell products, or promote a viewpoint. • Information provided is usually of current or general interest. • Often heavily illustrated with many advertisements.	• Main purpose is to provide readers with a good account of current events locally, nationally, or internationally. • Can be published daily, semiweekly, or weekly. • Can provide introduction to current topics.	• Main purpose is to update and inform readers on current trends in a specific industry or trade. • May have photos and numerous advertisements but still assume understanding of specific jargon of the profession.
Author	• Author is an expert or specialist in the field. • Author's position and affiliation will be provided.	• Usually a staff writer or a journalist. • May or may not have subject expertise. • Name and credentials often NOT provided.	• Articles are usually written by journalists. • May or may not have subject expertise.	• Professionals working in the specific trade or industry • Usually published by an association.
Audience	• Researchers, scientists, students, professionals.	• Appeal to the general public. • Articles tend to be short—fewer than five pages. • No consistent format.	• General public.	• Members of a specific industry or trade. • Professionals, professors, students.

(continued)

495

	Journal Article (Scholarly)	Magazine Article (Popular)	Newspaper Article	Trade Magazine Article
Bibliography or Works Cited List	• Sources always cited in detail and at length. • Consistent formatting includes an abstract (brief summary), discussion, results, and conclusion. • Articles usually longer than five pages.	• Little, if any, information about sources is provided.	• Little, if any, information about sources is provided.	• May or may not provide information about sources.
Examples	• *Journal of Abnormal Psychology* • *Business and Education Research*	• *Oprah* • *Maclean's*	• *Toronto Star* • *Globe and Mail*	• *Speechwriter's Newsletter* • *Advertising Age*

Do I Trust This Information?

Evaluating Information Sources

A research assignment can be only as good as the information used to create it. The following set of criteria and list of questions should be used when evaluating various resources, including books, magazine, journal, and newspaper articles, and Internet websites.

RELEVANCE?	• Does the information address some aspect of your research question? • Does the information provide evidence for your argument? • Is the information well suited to your needs as a college student or is it too advanced or elementary?
BIAS, OBJECTIVITY?	• What is the author's purpose? To inform? To persuade? To entertain? • Is more than one side of the issue or topic presented? • To what extent does the site present opinions versus facts?
CURRENCY?	• Is the information up-to-date? When was it published or last revised? • Do I need the most current information for this topic or issue? • Can I find information from the time period?
AUTHORITY? RELIABILITY?	• Is the author or source qualified to provide information on the topic? • Who are the authors and what are their credentials? Institutional affiliation, educational background, expertise? • Is the information fact, opinion, or propaganda? • Do the authors give credit for information provided? Is there a bibliography or Works Cited list? • Has anyone verified or reviewed the information for accuracy?

Why Evaluate Websites? Because:

- The *quality* of information varies tremendously.
- *Anyone* can publish and post a website on the Internet.
- Most websites *don't* employ editors or fact checkers.
- You need *reliable* resources for your assignments.

Plagiarism and Copyright: What Are They?

When writing a report, essay, or presentation, it is important to cite sources to avoid plagiarizing and respect copyright. Some cultures do not treat plagiarism as a problem, but there are serious consequences in Canada and at college.

Plagiarism can involve many things, including:

- Copying all or part of websites, essays, pictures, music, charts or other materials without giving credit
- Buying or taking and submitting papers written by others as your own
- Replacing only some words in another's passage without giving credit
- Using the ideas of others without giving credit
- Using your own paper in more than one course

In other words, plagiarism is when you use works or ideas that are not your own but you do not give credit to the person whose idea it is. Remember, *plagiarism is stealing and cheating*. When you plagiarize, not only are you not giving credit to the creator or writer but you may also face serious repercussions.

Are There Exceptions?

You do not need to give credit for common knowledge found in many sources. For example:

- Paul Martin succeeded Jean Chrétien as the Canadian Prime Minister on December 12, 2003.
- Earth has a diameter of 12,742 km and is the third planet closest to the Sun.
- Water is composed of two hydrogen atoms combined with one oxygen atom.

How Do I Avoid Plagiarizing?

To avoid plagiarizing, carefully document all information sources. This involves:

- Keeping good research notes on where the information comes from
- Organizing your paper carefully
- Citing your sources using the appropriate format, both in the body of the paper and in the bibliography or Works Cited list at the end.

Quick Guide to MLA Style

Use this quick guide to organize in-text citations and the works cited list according to guidelines from the *MLA (Modern Languages Association) Handbook* http://library.senecacollege.ca/Research_Help/Citing_Sources/mla_guide.html.

Works Cited Page

Works Cited lists all of the sources that you have paraphrased, quoted, or otherwise used in your research paper. All of the listed sources should also be cited within your paper (see "In-Text Citations" below).

GENERAL RULES FOR THE WORKS CITED PAGE

- On a separate page at the end of the research paper, list all the sources cited within the text of your paper.
- Arrange sources alphabetically by author's surname or by title if no author exists.
- Start the first line of each citation at the left margin. Indent each subsequent line one-half inch.
- Double-space the *entire* list, both between and within entries.

Sample Works Cited Page

Works Cited

"Armed Forces 'Discriminated' Against Older Men." *Toronto Star* 2 Jan. 2001: A2. Lexis Nexis. 30 Oct. 2005.

"Economic Survey of the United States 2005" *OECD* 27 Oct. 2005. Organization for Economic Co-operation and Development. 2 Nov. 2005 <http://www.oecd.org>.

"Europeans for the U.S." *U.S. News & World Report* 8 Apr. 2004:27. ProQuest. Seneca Lib. 20 Sept. 2005.

Martin, John L. and Ray Eldon Hiebert. *Current Issues in Communication.* New York: Longman, 2001.

Ontario Provincial Police. 23 Sept. 2004. Govt. of Ontario. 27 Sept. 2005 <www.gov.on.ca>.

Pery, Robert. "Emerging Markets: Doing Business in Latin America." *Paper, Film & Foil CONVERTER (PFFC)* 2 Feb. 2004. Primedia Business Magazines & Media. 24 Aug. 2005 <http://pffc-online.com>.

In-Text Citations

When writing your paper, use "in-text citations" to indicate the source of your information. The in-text citation points to a matching full citation in your Works Cited.

An in-text citation includes the author's last name and the page number (if available) or if you do not know the author, the citation will include the first word of a title, omitting initial articles (*a, an, the*). Put quotation marks around words from an article title, and underline words from a book or website title just as you would in the works cited list.

Note: Your in-text citation usually includes the first word or words from a matching full citation in your Works Cited.

The following examples of in-text citations match citations in the works cited list above.

Latin America has some of the "world's most important" emerging markets (Pery).

In the early 1970s, age discrimination was apparent in the recruiting practices of the Canadian Forces ("Armed").

Impaired driving is the leading cause of death in Canada (*Ontario*).

RULE

If it's in your paper, it's on the Works Cited list. If it's on the works cited list, it's in your paper.

Print Sources

Follow examples in the tables to create citations in your Works Cited and matching in-text citations within your research paper.

Type of Document	Works Cited Entry	In-Text Citations
Magazines, Journals, and Newspapers		
One Author	Author Last Name, First Name *Book Title* Publication year Brown, Dan *The Da Vinci Code: A Novel.* New York: Doubleday, 2003 City of Publication: Publisher, often shortened	(Brown 252) *or* Brown states "Quoted passage" (252)
Two Authors	Last Name, First Name, Second and Subsequent Authors: First Name Last Name Martin, John L., and Ray Hiebert *Current Issues in International Communications.* New York: Longman, 2001.	(Martin and Hiebert 145) *or* as reported by Martin and Hiebert (145)

(continued)

Type of Document	Works Cited Entry	In-Text Citations
Magazines, Journals, and Newspapers		
Three Authors	Cuthbertson, Keith, Stephen G. Hall, and Mark Taylor *Introduction to Psychology.* New York: Harcourt, 2004	(Cuthbertson, Hall, and Taylor 33)
More than Three Authors	Blum, John M., et al. *The National Experience.* 5th ed., New York: Harcourt, 2001.	(Blum et al., 387)
Unknown Author	*Résumés for Nursing Careers.* Chicago: VGM, 2002.	(<u>Résumés</u> 52)
Corporate Author	Calgary Educational Partnership Foundation, *Employable Skills: Creating My Future.* Scarborough: Nelson, 1996.	(*Calgary Educational*) Partnership Foundation 17-18
Selection from an Edited Book or Anthology	Hoag, Kevin. "Communicating the Information" *skills Development for Engineers: An Innovative Model for Advanced Learning in the Workplace.* Ed David Larmour London: Institution of Electrical Engineers, 2001 149-170.	(*Hoag 149*)
Edited Book (Editor as Author)	Holbrook, M.C., ed., *Children with Visual Impairments.* Bethesda: Woodbine, 1996.	(*Holbrook 34*)
Encyclopedia or Dictionary Article (Unsigned)	"Croatia" *The New Encyclopaedia Britannica: Micropaedia* 15th ed. 1995.	("Croatia" 133)
Government Document	Canada Canadian Judicial Council. *One Trial Court: Possibilities and Limitations.* Ottawa: Ministry of Supply and Services, 1985.	(Canadian Judicial Council 17-18)

Print Sources

Type of Document	Works Cited Entry	In-Text Citations
Magazines, Journals, and Newspapers		
Magazine Articles	Author (if available): Last Name, First Name. Richler, Kevin. "Slouching Towards Israel." *Time* 11 July 2003: 24+. "Article Title" *Magazine Title*. Publication Date: Page (*use + when page numbers are not consecutive*)	(Richler 29)
Journal Article	Barlow, Andrew. "The Student Movement of the 1960's and the Politics of Race." *Journal of Ethnic Studies* 19.3 (2003): 22-30. Volume.Issue	(Barlow 22)
Newspaper Article (Unknown Author)	"Talks on Bosnia Bog Down Over Borders." *Toronto Star* 18 Aug. 2004: B6.	("Talks")
Book Review (In Magazine)	Bemrose, John. "Hockey's Raging Bull." Rev. of *Gross Misconduct: The Life of Brian Spencer*, by Martin O'Malley. *Maclean's* 9 Jan. 2001: 22-30. Abbreviation of the word review.	(Bemrose 24)

Electronic Sources

Library Databases from a Subscription Service

Type of Document	Works Cited Entry	In-Text Citations
Library Databases		
To cite newspaper, journal, and magazine articles from a library database: • Cite the article first as you would an article from a print journal, magazine, or newspaper. Follow formats provided in the "Print Sources" table under Magazines, Journals, and Newspapers. • Add the database name (underlined), the service name, the name of the library subscribing to the service, and your access date. • It is not necessary to add a URL (web address) to a citation for a database from a subscription service. URLs are not useful in relocating information in a subscription database.*		
Newspaper Articles from a Library	"Canada's Public Schools Attract Foreign Families Willing to Pay Dearly." *Globe & Mail* 7 Sept. 2004: A-1. *CPI.Q.* Gale. Seneca Lib. 21 Sept. 2005.	("Canada's")
Database (Unknown Author)	Access Date Publication Title Publication Date Database name Database Services Library Subscribing to the Service	
*The *MLA Handbook* allows the option of "simply [ending] the citation with the date of access" (Gibaldi 5.9.7).		

Library Databases

Type of Document	Works Cited Entry	In-Text Citations
Magazine Articles from a Library Database	Newman, Peter, C. "Our Policy: Made in America." *Maclean's* 14 Mar., 2005: 42-43 *Academic Search Premier,* EBSCO Seneca Lib. 30 June 2005.	(Newman 42-43)
Journal Article from a Library Database	Falvey, Rod "Globalization and Factor Returns in Competitive Markets." *Journal of International Economics* 66.2(2004): 33-38, ProQuest. Seneca Lib. 12 Dec. 2003. **Database Service** *If you have searched multiple databases at the same time, you may not know the name of the source database. In that case, name the service you used, but omit the database name.*	(Falvey 33-38)
Article/Document from a Library Reference Database	"Company Snapshot: Sears Canada Inc." FP Corporate Profiler and Reports. 2005 *FPinfomart.ca* Seneca Lib. 12 Sept. 2005. Last Modified or Copyright Date *A last modified or copyright date can often be found at the foot of the web page.*	"Company"
Online Book (E-book) from a Library Database	Allen, Carolyn, and John Williamson *Dreamweaver MX for Beginners* New York: Bantam, 2004. NetLibrary.SenecaLib. 3 Oct. 2004. Database Service	(Allen and Williamson)

Electronic Sources: Websites, E-mail

Type of Document	Works Cited Entry	In-Text Citations
Websites		

To cite a website, include the name of author or editor (if given), the title of the site (underlined), a last modified or copyright date, and the name of the sponsoring organization or institution. If you cannot find some of this information, cite what is available (Gibaldi 5.9.2). However, keep in mind that "authoritative" information (information that you can trust) most often comes from websites that:

- include a "last update" or "last modified" date
- have a sponsoring organization or institution.
- provide an author or editor name or explain where the information came from

NOTE: When the URL for a document is impractically long and complicated, give instead the URL for the site's home page (Gibaldi 5.9.1).

Type of Document	Works Cited Entry	In-Text Citations
Newspaper Article from a Website	Stewart, Sinclair. "Flashy Bay St. Trader Faces Probe" *Globe and Mail* 29 June 2005 30 June 2005 <http://www.theglobeandmail.com> Publication Date Access Date When an online source does not provide page numbers, page numbers are omitted.)	(Stewart)
Magazine Article from a Website	Shachtman, Noah "Attack of the Drones." *Wired Magazine* June 2005: 1-4 29 June 2005 <http://www.wired.com/wired/archive/>	(Shachtman 3)

Type of Document	Works Cited Entry	In-Text Citations
Websites		
Professional or Business Website	*Canadian Tire.* 2004. Canadian Tire Corporation. 5 July 2005 <http://www2.canadiantire.ca>. Name of Website. Name of the Sponsoring Organization or Institution. Access Date	(*Canadian*)
Article/Document from a Professional or Business Website	"Company Profile: Vision, Purpose, & Team Values." *Canadian Tire.* 2004. Canadian Tire Corporation. 5 July 2005 <http://www2.canadiantire.ca>. Last modified or copyright date.	("Company")
Article/Document from a Government Website	"Weight Loss Claims." *Competition Bureau.* 28 June 2005. Competition Bureau Canada. 4 July 2005 <http://www.competitionbureau.gc.ca>.	("Weight")

(continued)

Type of Document	Works Cited Entry	In-Text Citations
Websites		
Home Page, Personal Site	Miller, Peter C. Home page. 17 Aug. 2004. Seneca College. 14 Aug. 2005 <http://people.senecac on ca/peter.miller>. Last modified or copyright date. Access date.	(Miller)
E-mail Messages		
E-mail	Anderson, Robert. "Re: Collecting Marketing Data." E-mail to author. 20 Aug. 2005. Name of Writer. Message Date. Title of Message (Taken from the subject line) Name of Writer: Type "E-mail to the author" if the e-mail was written to you or type the name of the recipient if you are quoting an e-mail written to someone else.	(Anderson)

Non-print

Type of Document	Works Cited Entry	In-Text Citations
Media, Interviews		
Videos & DVDs	*Mandela: The Man & His Country*. Narr. Morton Dean. Videocassette. ABC News, 1990.	(*Mandela*)
Television Program	"The Cop, the Kid, and the Knife." *60 Minutes*. Prod. Norm Gorin. CBS. WIVB, Buffalo, NY. 16 Nov. 2005.	("The Cop")
Interview (Personal or Telephone)	Copps, Sheila. Personal interview. 20 Sept. 2005.	(Copps)

Consult the following resources to cite materials not included in this "quick" MLA style guide:

Gibaldi, Joseph. *MLA Handbook for Writers of Research Papers*. 6th ed. New York: MLA, 2003.

"Seneca Libraries MLA Style Guide." *Seneca Libraries*. 2005. Seneca College. 7 Nov. 2005 <http://library.senecacollege.ca/Research_Help/Citing_Source/mla_guide.html>.

Quick Guide to APA Style

In-Text Citation

Author, publication year citations, for example (Smith, 2006), are inserted in the body of your research paper to indicate the source of your information. (Within a paragraph, it is not necessary to include the year after the first citation.)

In-text Citations: Work by Known Author(s)

Paraphrasing Information from a Source

- When the author's name is used in the sentence, include only the year of publication in the parentheses.

Mother–infant attachment became a leading topic of development research following the publication of John Bowlby's studies (Hunt, 1993).

or

Hunt (1993) describes how mother–infant attachment became a leading topic of developmental research after the publication of John Bowlby's studies.

Direct Quotation

- When using a direct quotation, always add the page, chapter, figure or paragraph number, for example, (Smith, 2006, p. 15).

Mother–infant attachment has been a leading topic of development research since John Bowlby found that "children raised in institutions were deficient in emotional and personality development" (Hunt, 1993, p. 358).

Quotation from an Internet Document

- For electronic sources that do not provide page numbers, cite the heading and the paragraph number following it.

Bowlby described "three phases of the separation response: protest, despair, and detachment" (Garelli, 2001, Bowlby's initial stance section, para. 3).

Reference list that would accompany these in-text citations

References

Hunt, M. (1993). *The story of psychology*. New York: Doubleday.

Garelli, J. C. (2001, July 22). Controversial aspects of Bowlby's attachment theory. In *A critical approach to attachment theory*. Retrieved April 2, 2004, from http://www.geocities.com/Athens/Acropolis/3041/.

Work by More than One Author

- When there are two authors, cite both every time the reference appears in the text.

- For one to five authors, cite all the authors the first time the reference appears, and after that include only the last name of the first author followed by et al. (*et al.* means "and others").

Source	**In-Text Citation**
2 authors (direct quote)	(Smith & Jones, 1998, pp. 12-15)
3 to 5 authors	(Smith, Jones, & James, 2000)
	next citation: (Smith et al., 2000)
6 or more authors	(Miller et al., 2001)

In-text Citation: Work by an Unknown Author

- When the author is unknown, include the first few words of the title and the year of publication.
- Use double quotation marks around words from the title of an article or chapter: for example, "Brief title".
- Italicize words from the title of a periodical, book, brochure, report, or Web document; for example, *Brief title.*
- Capitalize important words in all titles within your research paper, including brief titles in in-text citations.

QUICK RULES FOR A REFERENCE LIST

Your research paper ends with a reference list. The list includes all of the sources that you have cited in the text of the paper. Here are nine quick rules for your reference list.

1. Start a new page for your reference list. Centre the title, References, at the top of the page.
2. Double-space the list.
3. Start the first line of each reference at the left margin; indent each subsequent line 1/2 inch (a hanging indent).
4. Put your list in alphabetical order. Alphabetize the list by the first word in the reference. In most cases, the first word will be the author's last name. Where the author is unknown, alphabetize by the first word in the title, ignoring the words *a, an, the.*
5. For each author, give the last name followed by a comma and the first (and middle, if listed) initials followed by periods.
6. Put a period after the author, publication date, the title, and the facts of publication.
7. Italicize the titles of works: books, audiovisual material, Internet documents and newspapers, and the title and volume number of journals and magazines.
8. Do not italicize titles of parts of works, for example: titles of articles from newspapers, magazines, or journals/essays, poems, short stories or chapter titles from a book/chapters or sections of an Internet document.
9. In titles of nonperiodicals (books, videotapes, websites, reports, poems, essays, chapters, etc.), capitalize only the first letter of the first word of a title and subtitle, and all proper nouns (names of people, places, organizations, nationalities).

Sample Reference List

References

Dworkin, R. W. (2001). Science, faith and alternative medicine. *Policy Review, 108*, 3-19. Retrieved April 14, 2003, from Academic Search Premier database.

Medicine. (1991). In *The new encyclopaedia Britannica* (Vol. 16, p. 2). Chicago: Encyclopaedia Britannica.

Naturopathic medicine network. (2006, April). Retrieved April 14, 2006, from http://www.pandamedicine.com/

Pelletier, K. R. (2000). *The best alternative medicine: What works? What does not?* New York: Simon.

Storring, V. (Producer) & Zaritsky, J. (Writer/Director). (1992). *Choosing death.* [Motion picture]. Washington, DC: PBS Video.

Journals and Magazines in Print

- Italicize the name and volume number of the journal or magazine.
- Consider titles of magazines and journals to be proper nouns and capitalize all important words.

Article in a Journal Paginated by Issue

A journal paginated by issue has page numbers that begin at page one for every issue. For these journals, include volume and issue numbers.

Format

Author, A.A., Author, B.B., & Author, C.C. (year). Title of article. *Title of Journal, volume* (issue), pages.

Example

Doern, G. B. & Kinder, J. S. (2001). One size does not fit all: Canadian government laboratories. *Journal of Canadian Studies*, 37(3), 33-55.

Article in a Journal Paginated by Volume

A journal paginated by volume has page numbers that run continuously from the first issue to the last for each volume. For these journals, include only the volume number (not the issue number).

Format

Author, A.A., Author, B.B., & Author, C.C. (year). Title of article. *Title of Journal, volume*, pages.

Example

Bigras, M. & Dessen, M. (2002). Social competence and behavior evaluation in Brazilian preschoolers. *Early Education and Development, 13*, 139-151.

Article in a Weekly Magazine

Marshall, R. (2003, October 27). Five ways to make the Canadian healthier. *Maclean's, 116*, 53.

Article in a Monthly Magazine

Anderson, N. & Anderson, P. E. (2003, April). Secrets & lies: Why they make us sick. *Psychology Today, 2*, 60-64.

Article in a Magazine (Unknown Author)

Atkins cheaters beware. (2003, November 10). *Newsweek, 142*, 67.

Newspapers: In Print

Article in a Newspaper

- For newspaper articles, precede pages by "p." for a single page or "pp." for more than one page.
- Italicize the newspaper title and capitalize all important words in the title.

Format

Author, A.A., Author, B.B., & Author, C.C. (year, Month day). Title of article. *Title of Newspaper*, page(s).

Example

Woods, A. & Greenberg, L. (2003, November 20). Ontario, Manitoba order infection control audits. *National Post*, pp. A8, A12.

Article in a Newspaper— Unknown Author

Ontario has enough power to handle cold snap. (2004, January 13). *Daily Press*, p. 16.

Journal, Magazine, and Newspaper Articles From a Library Database

Databases from a library website provide electronic versions of articles originally published in print.

1. Cite the article first as you would an article from a print journal, magazine, or newspaper. Follow formats provided under "Journal and Magazines: In Print" and under "Newspapers: In Print."
2. Add **Retrieved Month day, year, from _____ database.**

Example (Journal paginated by volume)

Elliott, A. (2003). Government faces pressure to tackle obesity. *British Medical Journal, 327*, 1125. Retrieved December 15, 2003, from ProQuest Nursing Journals database.

Journals, Magazines, and Newspapers From the Internet

Newspaper, magazines or journal articles published on the Internet are cited differently from articles retrieved from a database. If you have retrieved the article from a database, refer to the section of this guide titled Journals, Magazines, and Newspapers From a Library Database.

Internet Articles Based on a Print Source

1. If the article is from a magazine, journal or newspaper based on a print source, cite the article first as you would a print article. Follow examples provided in the sections titled "Journals and Magazines: in Print" and "Newspapers: in Print."
2. Add: **Retrieved Month day, year, from http://_____**
3. If it is necessary to break the URL, break it after a slash or before a period.

Example (Newspaper Article)
Shanker, T. (22 March, 2006). *New York Times*. Retrieved March 26, 2006, from http://www.nytimes.com/2006/03/22/politics/22lincoln.html

Articles in Internet-Only Magazines, Journals, or Newspapers

1. Include available publication information. If volume and issue numbers are not given, the name of the periodical is all that can be provided in the reference. For Internet-only publications, there are no page numbers given.
2. Add a retrieval statement that includes the date of retrieval and the URL (web address).
3. The URL should link directly to the article; use cut and paste to make sure that the URL is correct.

General Format
Author, A.A., Author, B.B., & Author, C.C. (date). Title of article. *Title of Periodical, volume* (issue), if applicable. Retrieved Month day, year, from http://_____

Example
Seleim, R.S., Sahar, R.M., Nover, M.H., & Gobran, R.A. (2004). Salmonella infection in calves: Virulence proteins. *International Journal of Veterinary Medicine*. Retrieved April 6, 2006, from http://www.priority.com/vet.htm

Books: In Print

The information is taken from the title page and the copyright page. For most books give: (1) the author's last name followed by a comma and the first (and middle) initials (2) the date of publication in parentheses (3) the title and subtitle italicized (4) the place of publication and the publisher. Each unit is followed by a period and one space.

One Author

Livingston, J. A. (1994). *Rogue primate: An exploration of human domestication*. London: Hogarth.

Two to Six Authors/Editors

McPhee, S.J., Vishwanath, L.R., & Ganong, W.F. (Eds.) (2003). *Pathophysiology of disease: An introduction to clinical medicine.* New York: Lange Medical/ McGraw-Hill.

More than Six Authors/Editors

Name the first six authors or editors and then add the phrase *et al.* which means *and others.*

Harris, M., Karper, E., Stacks, G., Hoffman, D., DeNiro, R., Cruz, P., et al. (2001). *Writing labs.* Washington, DC: American Psychological Association.

Unknown Author/Editor

If the author is unknown, place the title in the author position.

The career directory. (1999). Toronto: Encore.

Corporate Author

International Conference on Fire Research and Engineering. (1999). *Proceedings: Third international conference on fire research and engineering.* Bethesda, MD: Society of Fire Protection Engineers.

Author as Publisher/Second or Subsequent Edition

When the author is also the publisher, use the word Author as the name of the publisher.

American Psychological Association. (2001). *Publication manual of the American Psychological Association* (5th ed.). Washington, DC: Author.

Multi-Volume Work

Ettinger, S. J. & Feldman, E. C. (Eds.). (2000). *Textbook of veterinary internal medicine: diseases of the dog and cat* (Vol. 2). Toronto, ON: W.B. Saunders.

Article/Chapter from an Edited Work

Stallard, R. F. (2000). Erosion. In P. L. Hancock & B. J. Skinner (Eds.), *The Oxford companion to the earth* (pp. 314-318). Oxford: Oxford University Press.

Article/Chapter from a Multi-Volume Edited Work

Roediger, H. L. (1988). Sir Frederick Charles Bartlett: Experimental and applied psychologist. In G.A. Kimble & M. Wertheimer (Eds.), *Portraits of pioneers in psychology* (Vol. 4, pp. 149-161). Washington, DC: American Psychological Association.

Encyclopedia/Dictionary— Signed Article

King, P. N. & Wester, L. (1998). Hawaii. In *The world book encyclopaedia* (Vol. 9, pp. 88-110). Chicago: World Book.

Encyclopedia/Dictionary — Unsigned Article

- If the author is unknown, place the title in the author position.

Croatia. (2002). In *The new encyclopaedia Britannica* (Vol. 4, pp. 14-18). Chicago: Encyclopaedia Britannica.

Government Document

Canada. Advisory Committee on Radiological Protection. (2001). *Guidelines on hospital emergency plans for the management of minor radiation accidents.* Ottawa: Canadian Nuclear Safety Commission.

Other Sources: Reference Material from a Library Database

- Libraries purchase access for students to several reference databases.
- Include the publication date, copyright date, or the date of last revision. The copyright date can usually be found at the bottom of the web page.
- Add a retrieval statement that provides the date of retrieval and the database name in place of the URL (Web address).
- The following are a few examples of reference databases:
  - Britannica Online
  - Financial Post Corporate Profiler and Corporate Reports
  - Oxford Reference Online
  - Canadian Encyclopedia Online
  - Dictionary of Canadian Biography Online

Page/Article from a Reference Database.

Format

Author, A.A. (date of last revision/publication date). *Title of document.* Retrieved Month day, year, from _____ database.

Example

Gannon, P. (2003, November 21). *Brain evolution.* Retrieved April 6, 2006, from, Access Science: McGraw-Hill Encyclopedia of Science and Technology database.

Page/Article from a Source within a Reference Database

Some databases include more than one source. If a source or a work within the database is named, then give the name in your citation.

Format

Author, A.A. (date of last revision/publication date). Title of page/article. In *Title of collection within the database.* Retrieved Month day, year, from _____ database.

Example

Scheub, H. (2000). Juok and the dog that preserved mankind. In *A dictionary of African mythology.* Retrieved February 24, 2004 from Oxford Reference Online database.

Other Sources: Material from the Internet

- Use n.d. (no date) when a publication date or date of latest revision is not provided.
- Add a retrieval statement that includes the date of retrieval and the URL (Web address).
- If necessary, break the URL after a slash or before a period.
- For **multipage documents,** provide the URL for the home (entry) page of the document.
- To cite part of a document, provide the URL that leads directly to that part.

Internet Document. Author/Editor Named.

Format

Author [Author, A.A. or Corporate Author Name]. (year, Month day). or (n.d.) *Title of document.* Retrieved Month day, year, from http://_____

Example

Secretariat, World Health Organization. (2003, November 27). *Severe acute respiratory syndrome (SARS).* Retrieved February 2, 2004, from http://www. who.int/gb/EB_WHA/PDF/EB113/eeb11333.pdf

Internet Document. Unknown Author/Editor

Format

Title of document. (year, Month day). or (n.d.). Retrieved Month day, year, from http://_____

Example

Thomson/CCBN. (n.d.). Retrieved March 1, 2006, from http://www.thomson. com/common/view_brand_overview.jsp?section=financial&body_include=/ financial/brand_overviews/

Chapter or Section from an Internet Document

Format

Author, A.A. (year, Month day). Title of chapter/section. In *Title of document* (chap. xx or section xx). Retrieved Month day, year, from http://

_____

Example

Norris, S., Nixon, A., & Murray, W. Epidemiology of HIV/AIDS. (2001, December 18). In *AIDS: Medical and scientific aspects* (section A). Retrieved April 2, 2004, from http://dsp-psd.pwgsc.gc.ca/Collection-R/LoPBdP/ CIR/935-e.htm

Other Sources: Videorecordings

Format

Motion picture is the media type for both videorecordings and DVDs.

Director, B.B. (Director) & Producer, A.A. (Producer). (year). *Title of film*
[Motion picture]. Place of publication: Publisher.

Example

Ziegler, A. (Director) & Cameron, D. (Producer). (1998). *Facing the Demons*
[Motion picture]. New York: First Run/Icarus Films.

Odd-Numbered and Partial-Paragraph Answers to the Exercises in Chapters 3–28

CHAPTER 3

Exercise 1

1. Home is where the heart is.

3. The word *trade* was first recorded in 1546 to distinguish a "skilled handicraft" from a profession, business, or unskilled occupation.

Exercise 2

1. d

3. a

5. d

Exercise 3

Answers vary.

Exercise 4

Answers vary.

Exercise 5

I loved East Bay, Nova Scotia. We lived only a few miles from the shore, and I often spent summer afternoons sailing on the lake or walking on the beach. I enjoyed my high school because I had a lot of friends and participated in a lot of activities. I played softball and football.

My father was transferred to Toronto when I was in grade eleven. I hated leaving my school and friends but thought I would be able to adjust. I found the move harder to deal with than I thought. Instead of living in a colonial house on a half-acre lot, we moved into a downtown loft. It was spacious, offered a wonderful view, and had both a swimming pool and a health club. As big as our two-floor loft was, it began to feel like a submarine. I missed the feel of wind and fresh air. . . .

Exercise 6

I love my sister, but often Sharon drives me crazy. Just last week I faced a crisis. I had to

```
drive to school to take a makeup exam before my
math teacher had to file her midterm grades. I got
dressed, packed up my books, and raced downstairs to
my car only to discover I had a flat tire. I raced
upstairs and woke Sharon, who was still sleeping.
    "Sharon, I need to borrow your car," I blurted
out.
    "Why," she asked, upset that I disturbed her.
    "My car has a flat."
    "So, this is your day off."
    "I know, but I have to make up an exam today."
    "Go tomorrow after work," she said. . . .
```

CHAPTER 4

Exercise 1
Answers vary.

Exercise 2
1. b, c, e
3. a, b, e
5. a, c, d

Exercise 3
Answers vary.

Exercise 4
Answers vary.

Exercise 5
Answers vary.

CHAPTER 5

Exercise 1
The prairies are desolate and depressing.

Exercise 2
Answers vary.

Exercise 3
Answers vary.

Exercise 4
Answers vary.

Exercise 5
Answers vary.

CHAPTER 6

Exercise 1

Answers vary.

Exercise 2

When I first arrived in Moncton . . .
After checking in . . .
It was not until after . . .

Exercise 3

Answers vary.

Exercise 4

Answers vary.

CHAPTER 7

Exercise 1

1. Politicians—Party
2. Music—Genre
3. Artists—Country

Exercise 2

Answers vary.

Exercise 3

Answers vary.

Exercise 4

Answers vary.

CHAPTER 8

Exercise 1

Answers vary.

Exercise 2

Answers vary.

Exercise 3

Answers vary.

CHAPTER 9

Exercise 1

1. X
3. C
5. P

7. P
9. P

<u>Exercise 2</u>
1. Why do celebrities become social activists?

<u>Exercise 3</u>
Oil kills birds in many ways.

<u>Exercise 4</u>
Answers vary.

CHAPTER 10

<u>Exercise 1</u>
Answers vary.

CHAPTER 11

<u>Exercise 1</u>

introduction
description of the mother's Woodbridge

According to my mother, <u>Woodbridge was a great place to grow up.</u> There were no shopping malls or big box stores nearby. Chapters, Starbucks, and HMV did not exist. My mother and her brothers didn't mind: the open fields and meadows surrounding her childhood home provided all the entertainment that they needed.

transition and topic sentence
description of the old neighbourhood

<u>Woodbridge was still a small town 40 years ago.</u> When the weather was fine, my mother walked to school with her brothers and the other children on the street, and afterward took a shortcut home through open fields. On warm autumn days, they often stopped to fish in the Humber River. In the winter, they skated on the pond in the meadow across from their house, and built elaborate snow forts. After my grandfather bought the family

details

a snowmobile for Christmas one year, the area surrounding the pond became a crisscross of snowmobile tracks. In the summer, they ventured a few fields over to a neighbour's 200 acre farm, where my mother experienced two memorable firsts: she rode her first horse

transition

and kissed her first boy.

contrast

<u>It was during her first year of high school that the bulldozers appeared.</u> From that time until now, the meadows and fields of Woodbridge have been steadily filled with houses, shopping plazas, schools, libraries, and, most recently, big box

details

stores. The shortcut from her house to school is now a busy thoroughfare; houses cover the meadow where my mother and her brothers skated, and where there were skidoo tracks, there are now neatly paved driveways dotted with SUVs. Of course the farm disappeared long ago. The fences holding back the horses have been replaced by the walls of an exclusive gated community, and the vast fields that were once overrun with wild-flowers are now overrun with subdivisions. Any grass that does remain is enclosed by cement, and the wild-flowers that once sprawled across the acres of land don't stand a chance against modern-day pesticides and ride-on lawn mowers.

My grandparents left Woodbridge many years ago. At first they loved driving by their house whenever they returned to visit friends; however, they stopped when the changes became too painful to see. When I drove my grandmother through Woodbridge last year, she had trouble finding any familiar landmarks. Finally, she sighed deeply and said, "This can't possibly be Woodbridge. Where is my little town?"

Exercise 2
Answers vary.

Exercise 3
Answers vary.

CHAPTER 12

Exercise 1
Answers vary.

Exercise 2
Answers vary.

Exercise 3
Answers vary.

Exercise 4
Answers vary.

Exercise 5
Answers vary.

Exercise 6
Answers vary.

CHAPTER 13

Exercise 1
1. principal
3. Whether
5. who's

7. emigrated
9. allusions

Exercise 2

archaic	old	*lucrative*	profitable
discriminate	differentiate	*patron*	customer or donor
homicide	killing of one person by another	*topical*	current

Exercise 3

Answers vary.

Exercise 4

1. In July 1976 an employee of a cotton warehouse in Nzara, Sudan, suddenly suffered shock and died from uncontrollable hemorrhages.
3. The disease raced through the village, infecting and killing the people of Nzara.
5. Not understanding the deadly nature of the disease, hospital doctors and nurses contracted the disease as they examined patients.
7. Suddenly the epidemic ended when the virus ran out of healthy people it could infect.
9. Medical experts saw the outbreak as greatly significant because it suggested that science had not conquered infectious disease.

Exercise 5

1. During the war on Iraq, the opposition party pressured Jean Chrétien to agree to send Canadian troops to Iraq.
3. Affirmative action policies that once energized the administration to employ more minorities have been ignored to reduce costs.
5. Until our insurance problem is fixed, don't let anyone from the sales department use company cars.

Exercise 6

Answers vary.

CHAPTER 14

Exercise 1

1. forest fires (plural)
3. the Kelowna area
5. more than 800 wildfires
7. thousands
9. Gordon Campbell

Exercise 2

1. Stephen Leacock
3. Leacock
5. Leacock
7. focus *and* he (pronoun) [compound sentence]
9. He (pronoun)

Exercise 3

1. guesswork
3. experts
5. calculations
7. studies
9. oil deposits

Exercise 4

1. people (subject) in the country, of thieves, in black masks, into houses
3. About five years ago, group (subject), of criminals, in California
5. ATMs (subject), to any banking network
7. customers (subject)
9. After a month, of complaints, criminals (subject), to the mall owners

Exercise 5

Answers vary.

Exercise 6

1. discovered
3. gripped
5. mounted
7. discovered
9. closed

Exercise 7

1. are
3. could (helping verb) carry
5. was
7. could (helping verb) operate
9. would (helping verb) change

Exercise 8

Answers vary.

Exercise 9

1. laser (subject), stands (verb)
3. beam (subject), diffuses (verb)
5. geographers and mapmakers (subject), use (verb)
7. weapons (subject), could (helping verb), disable (verb), disrupt (verb)
9. loss (subject), could (helping verb), ruin (verb)

CHAPTER 15

Exercise 1

1. OK
3. OK
5. F
7. F
9. F

Exercise 2

1. Throngs of people visit Ottawa every year to celebrate the tulip festival.

3. OK

5. OK

7. OK

9. A special parliamentary law making her rooms at the Ottawa Civic Hospital "extraterritorial" allowed her daughter to be born on temporarily declared Dutch soil.

Exercise 3

1. Although computers have revolutionized writing and publishing, some historians are concerned about the effect technology will have on written records.

3. In addition, literary scholars have been able to view various drafts of a play or poem, allowing them to see how a writer like Ibsen or Poe worked.

5. Journalists also wonder if computers will make it easier for political and business leaders to alter records.

7. OK

9. On the other hand, computers and the Internet allow today's researchers to examine documents held by libraries around the world.

Exercise 4

Jim Carrey was born in Newmarket, Ontario, in 1962, the son of a frequently out-of-work performer. At fifteen, Carrey began doing standup comedy routines at Yuk-Yuk's in Toronto and discovered his talent for celebrity impressions. In 1979, at the age of 19, Carrey moved to Los Angeles. He started out doing standup comedy but soon landed a role in the trendy TV show *In Living Color*. This was followed by his first starring role in a movie, *Ace Ventura: Pet Detective*. Carrey was a hit. He went on to make *Mask, Dumb and Dumber,* and *The Cable Guy*. Although he became famous for his ability to mould his face into cartoonish expressions, Carrey wanted to prove that he was more than a comedic actor. In 1998 he starred in his first dramatic film; he portrayed the deluded main character in *The Truman Show*. However, it was for a comedic role in *Liar Liar* that he received a Golden Globe Best Actor nomination. . . .

Exercise 5

Long before people could communicate using the Internet, telephones, or the telegraph, they saw the need to relay information quickly. Without electricity all messages had to be delivered by coach or runner. During the French Revolution, a young engineer proposed a signalling system to connect Paris and Lille using semaphores. Claude Chappe, who received backing from the government, worked with his brother to construct a series of towers five to ten miles apart. The towers were equipped with two telescopes and two long wooden arms that could be set in forty-nine different positions, each signalling a letter or symbol. Letter by letter, the operator in one tower set the wooden arms to send a message to the operator in the next tower who watched through a telescope. . . .

CHAPTER 16

Exercise 1

Answers vary.

Exercise 2

1. Lee De Forest developed the sound-on-film technique, and it revolutionized the film industry.
3. Immigrant stars with heavy accents seemed laughable playing cowboys and cops, and their careers were ruined.
5. Hollywood's English-language films lost foreign markets, and dubbing techniques had to be created.

Exercise 3

Answers vary.

Exercise 4

Answers vary.

Exercise 5

Answers vary.

Exercise 6

1. I loved skating on the canal when I lived in Ottawa. When I lived in Ottawa, I loved skating on the canal.
3. Many children still delight in old-fashioned puppet shows although people are accustomed to watching television.
   Although people are accustomed to watching television, many children still delight in old-fashioned puppet shows.
5. Although he completed only four major plays, Chekhov is considered one of the world's greatest dramatists.
   Chekhov is considered one of the world's greatest dramatists although he completed only four major plays.

Exercise 7

1. Donovan Bailey, who was born in Manchester, Jamaica, became one of the most inspiring sprinters in Canadian history.
3. After graduating from high school, Bailey went to Sheridan College, where he earned a degree in economics.
5. Bailey won his first major event, the men's 100-metre race, in Sweden, becoming a Canadian world champion in 1995.

7. The following year, he challenged U.S. sprint champion Michael Johnson to a 150-metre sprint race at the Skydome in Toronto to determine who the faster runner was.
9. Having experienced a series of injuries and a serious car accident, Bailey retired from running in 2001.

Exercise 8
Answers vary.

CHAPTER 17

Exercise 1
1. OK
3. CS
5. F
7. CS
9. F

Exercise 2
Today's college students are accustomed to using notebook computers they are smaller and lighter than the portable typewriters of earlier generations. These slim models bear no relation to their ancestors. The first generation of computers were massive contraptions they filled entire rooms. They used thousands of vacuum tubes, which tended to burn out quickly. To keep the computers running, people had to run up and down aisles, they pushed shopping carts full of replacement tubes. Because of their size, computers had limited military value. . . .

Exercise 3
Answers vary.

Exercise 4
Answers vary.

Exercise 5
1. Recovering alcoholics sometimes call themselves Friends of Bill W.; he was a founder of Alcoholics Anonymous.
3. He tried to remain sober and focus on rebuilding his career, but the temptation to drink often overwhelmed him.
5. To keep himself from drinking he knew he needed to talk to someone, and he began calling churches listed in a hotel directory.
7. Wilson was put in touch with Dr. Robert Smith; he was a prominent physician whose life and career had been nearly destroyed by drinking.
9. They shared the guilt about broken promises to their wives; they knew how alcohol affected their judgment, their character, and their health.

Exercise 6

"Kanadian Korner," also known as "The Great White North" was one of the strangest series of skits ever made, but it served a purpose. On September 19, 1980, the first skit aired in the final minutes of the CBC series *SCTV*, featuring Rick Moranis and Dave Thomas as beer guzzling Canadian brothers Bob and Doug McKenzie. It was an instant success.

Many people don't know the reason behind the development of this offbeat yet cultishly successful part of the *SCTV* series. CBC demanded that *SCTV* include more Canadian content on the show. Moranis and Thomas balked at being told what to include in the show, so in an attempt to illuminate what they considered the ridiculousness of the request, they asked if they should wear toques and parkas and lounge in front of a map of Canada while guzzling beer. To their surprise, CBC loved the idea, and Bob and Doug McKenzie were born. . . .

CHAPTER 18

Exercise 1

1. MM
3. OK
5. MM
7. MM
9. MM
11. OK
13. OK
15. MM
17. MM
19. OK

Exercise 2

1. The mayor, speaking on television, tried to calm the anxious crowd.
3. The tourists, unfamiliar with French law, requested Paris attorneys.
5. We served lamb chops covered in mint sauce to our guests.

Exercise 3

1. DM
3. OK
5. OK
7. DM
9. OK
11. DM
13. DM
15. DM

17. DM
19. OK

Exercise 4

1. DM
3. OK
5. OK
7. DM
9. OK
11. OK
13. DM
15. DM
17. OK
19. DM

Exercise 5

Answers vary.

Exercise 6

Answers vary.

Exercise 7

1. The landlord demanded police protection from angry tenants facing eviction.
3. Having won eight games in a row, the coach was cheered by fans when he appeared.
5. Having been translated into dozens of languages, *Harry Potter* has enthralled readers all over the world.

Exercise 8

No other radio program had more impact on the American public than Orson Welles's famous "War of the Worlds" broadcast. <u>Only twenty-three at the time</u>, Welles's newly formed Mercury Theatre aired weekly radio productions of original and classic dramas. On October 30, 1938, an Americanized version of H. G. Wells's science fiction novel *The War of the Worlds* was aired by the Mercury Theatre, <u>which described a Martian invasion</u>.

Regular listeners understood the broadcast was fiction and sat back to enjoy the popular program. The play opened with the sounds of a dance band. Suddenly, the music was interrupted by a news report that astronomers <u>on the surface of Mars</u> had detected strange explosions. The broadcast returned to dance music. But soon the music was interrupted again with reports of a meteor crash in Grovers Mills, New Jersey. The broadcast then dispensed with music, and a dramatic stream of reports covered the rapidly unfolding events.

> Equipped with eerie special effects, the strange
> scene in the New Jersey countryside was described by
> anxious reporters. The crater, listeners were told,
> was not caused by a meteor but by some strange space-
> craft. A large, octopuslike creature emerged from the
> crater, presumably coming from Mars, and blasted
> onlookers with powerful death rays. . . .

Exercise 9

1. Caroline, who was born in Charlottetown, took Monika to Prince Edward Island this summer.
3. The television show, which suffered low ratings, cost the network millions in lost advertising revenue.
5. The missing girl, who is only three years old, was last seen by her mother.

Exercise 10

Answers vary.

CHAPTER 19

Exercise 1

1. NP
3. OK
5. NP
7. NP
9. OK
11. NP
13. NP
15. OK
17. NP
19. OK

Exercise 2

1. In the 1990s the Internet revolutionized business, education, the media, even family life.
3. A small entrepreneur can participate in the global economy without the cost of maintaining branch offices, mailing catalogues, or airing television commercials.
5. No single person invented the Internet, but Robert E. Taylor played a role in designing the first networks and overcoming numerous obstacles.
7. At that time computers were like paper notebooks, so that whatever was entered into one could not be transferred to another without reentering the data, which was costly and time consuming.
9. The government provided grants to corporations and universities to stimulate research into connecting computers, overcoming incompatibility, and developing standards.

Exercise 3

1. The system is large, convenient, and inexpensive.
3. The log is a record of problems and services.

5. In our first list we inadvertently omitted the seven lathes in room B-101, four milling machines in Room B-117, and sixteen shapers in room B-118.
7. The manual gives instructions for operating and adjusting the machine.
9. To analyze the data, carry out the following steps: Examine the details, eliminate the unnecessary details, and create a flow chart.

Exercise 4
Answers vary.

CHAPTER 20

Exercise 1
1. stock market/attracts
3. Investors/plan
5. Investors/buy
7. Speculators/rely
9. person/needs

Exercise 2
1. is
3. sponsors
5. declares
7. are
9. plan

Exercise 3
1. have
3. is
5. buys
7. were
9. are

Exercise 4
1. is
3. is
5. were
7. were
9. believe

Exercise 5
1. were
3. are
5. meets
7. was
9. are

Exercise 6
1. are
3. were
5. were

7. were
9. were
11. was
13. was
15. was

Exercise 7

Answers vary.

Exercise 8

Today many colleges offer courses through the Internet. The idea of broadcasting classes is not new. For decades, universities, colleges, and technical institutions have used television to teach classes. Unlike educational television programs, Internet courses are interactive. Professors can use chat rooms to hold virtual office hours and class discussions so that a student feels less isolated. . . .

CHAPTER 21

Exercise 1

1. Present   I speak to youth groups.
     Past   I <u>spoke</u> to youth groups.
     Past participle   I have <u>spoken</u> to youth groups.
3. Present   They buy silk from China.
     Past   They <u>bought</u> silk from China.
     Past participle   They have <u>bought</u> silk from China.
5. Present   Hope springs eternal.
     Past   Hope <u>sprang</u> eternal.
     Past participle   Hope has <u>sprung</u> eternal.

Exercise 2

1. was
3. ate
5. began, faced
7. designed
9. created

Exercise 3

     The summer of 1961 <u>saw</u> a great season for the New York Yankees. Two players, Roger Maris and Mickey Mantle, <u>challenged</u> Babe Ruth's record of hitting sixty home runs in a season. The 1927 record <u>seemed</u> unbreakable. Despite a slow start that season, Maris soon <u>began</u> hitting one home run after another, keeping pace with Mickey Mantle. <u>Called</u> the "M&M boys" by sportswriters, Maris and Mantle <u>became</u> national heroes.

As the summer <u>wore</u> on, and both players had <u>hit</u> over forty home runs, attention grew. Even President Kennedy <u>stopped</u> the nation's business to follow their progress. Not everyone <u>was</u> enthusiastic about their hitting. Many Ruth fans, including the baseball commissioner, <u>did</u> not want to <u>see</u> the classic record <u>broken</u>. . . .

Exercise 4

1. laid

3. sit

5. raise

7. had lain

9. Set

Exercise 5

1. A

3. P

5. P

7. P

9. A

Exercise 6

1. Jason Andrews signed the contract.

3. Paramedics rushed the children to the hospital.

5. The county repaired the bridge.

Exercise 7

1. We should have taken a cab to the airport.

3. You should have never paid them in cash.

5. They should have been sued for breach of contract.

Exercise 8

1. She didn't have any car insurance.

3. The patients were so weak they could hardly take any steps.

5. Mary scarcely had time to play sports.

CHAPTER 22

Exercise 1

1. Sara went to her favourite Winnipeg restaurant, taking Carla as her guest.

3. Until he moved to Regina, my cousin worked with Fred.

5. Armando's nephew told Mr. Mendoza, "My car needs new tires."

Exercise 2

1. The classrooms are dusty. The halls are marked by graffiti. The lockers are smashed. Students just don't care about their school.

3. You would think a museum would take better care of fragile artwork.

5. When are manufacturers going to build cars with better engines?

Exercise 3

1. their
3. their
5. their
7. their
9. their

Exercise 4

1. When he moved to Vancouver, a nice apartment cost three hundred dollars a month.
3. We always thought he would be a star—we could tell by watching him rehearse.
5. We went to the beach to swim, but it was so cold we had to stay inside.

Exercise 5

1. I
3. us
5. him
7. us
9. her

Exercise 6

1. them/us
3. this
5. These/they
7. him
9. he

Exercise 7

1. Jim or I am working on the July 1.
3. The teachers and they discussed the new textbook; it comes with free CDs.
5. They gave the job to us students, but they never provided the supplies we needed.

CHAPTER 23

Exercise 1

1. powerful, wartime
3. clear, sunny, historic
5. wood
7. unattractive, serviced, outmoded
9. hard

Exercise 2

Answers vary.

Exercise 3

1. iced
3. mashed
5. borrowed

7. dated

9. boiled

Exercise 4

1. undeniably

3. largely, quick, fast

5. increasingly

7. carefully, just

9. actually, carefully

Exercise 5

Answers vary.

Exercise 6

1. good

3. better

5. better

7. good

9. badly

Exercise 7

1. frequently/particularly

3. readily

5. vast

7. quickly

9. newly

Exercise 8

1. more effective

3. rustier

5. happier

7. colder

9. more fragile

Exercise 9

1. Born to former slaves, Sarah Walker was orphaned at seven, married at fourteen, and widowed at twenty, enduring one of the worst upbringings possible.

3. Her life radically changed when she invented a remarkable line of hair-care products for black women.

5. Soon Sarah Walker's company was employing hundreds of new workers.

7. Walker's rapidly expanding enterprise also trained women to become sales agents and salon operators, allowing many black women to form independent businesses.

9. She became a respected figure in black society and was actively involved in the civil rights movement.

CHAPTER 24

Exercise 1

1. except

3. in

5. through

7. at

9. to

Exercise 2

1. During the night, by the storm

3. Against his doctor's advice, to Europe, through the mountains

5. In the morning, from Calgary, with textbooks, for the public schools

7. between the mayor and the city council, from a long argument, over property taxes

9. along the beach, in the rain

Exercise 3

1. <u>Benito Juarez</u> is one <u>of the most important figures</u> <u>in Mexican history</u>.

3. <u>Despite many obstacles</u>, <u>Juarez</u> graduated <u>from a seminary</u>.

5. <u>During his term</u> <u>as governor</u> <u>Juarez</u> initiated policies that brought him <u>into conflict</u> <u>with powerful forces</u> that began to align <u>against him</u>.

7. After liberals assumed power, <u>they</u> recalled Juarez <u>from exile</u> to become the Minister <u>of Justice</u>.

9. <u>In 1857</u> <u>he</u> was elected chief justice <u>of the Mexican Supreme Court</u>.

Exercise 4

1. Tim was exhausted by the marathon and passed out in the locker room.

3. I want a sandwich without mustard for lunch.

5. From the window we watched the children skating on the lake.

7. The hikers took shelter in a cave from the sudden blizzard.

9. Tickets for the midnight game will be available at noon.

Exercise 5

```
     Expecting veterans to be tall, battle-scarred
warriors, the American public found Audie Murphy an
unlikely hero. Standing only five feet five inches
and weighing only 112 pounds, the boyish twenty-year-
old Texan had been thought unfit for combat. But
having killed 241 enemy soldiers in seven bitter cam-
paigns, Murphy emerged in 1945 as the most decorated
soldier in American history. He appeared on the cover
of Life magazine, and his smiling good looks fasci-
nated the public. Impressed by the young man's charm,
Jimmy Cagney invited Audie Murphy to Hollywood. Still
recovering from war wounds, Murphy studied acting
and worked to soften his Texas accent. Murphy began
appearing in movies, and he wrote an autobiography of
his war experiences. . . .
```

CHAPTER 25

Exercise 1

1. The St. Lawrence Seaway is one of the world's most comprehensive inland navigation systems. Initial construction work began in 1954 and involved cooperation from the Canadian and American governments.

3. The Seaway was officially opened April 25, 1959, and linked the Atlantic Ocean to the Great Lakes.
5. Pleasure boats can use the Seaway to go from the Great Lakes to the Atlantic Ocean, but priority is obviously given to commercial ships at the locks.
7. The St. Lawrence Seaway and the Great Lakes are mainly used to ship heavy raw materials and limited general cargo.
9. For instance, it takes a little more than 24 hours to transport a container by rail from Chicago to Montreal, while this operation would take around one week through the Great Lakes and the Seaway.

Exercise 2

1. Throughout history people came across large bones, fossils, and teeth.
3. Before Owen, people thought these strange bones were evidence of extinct dragons, giant birds, or mythical beasts.
5. At first, researchers believed all dinosaurs were cold-blooded because they resembled modern reptiles, such as alligators, crocodiles, and lizards.
7. Dinosaurs dominated the planet for millions of years, living on grass, small plants, and other wildlife.
9. The extinction of dinosaurs remains a puzzle, with some scientists blaming the Ice Age, others blaming changes in their food supply, and some blaming a comet or asteroid.

Exercise 3

1. In 1962 the United States, which was the leading Western power during the Cold War, nearly went to war with the Soviet Union.
3. President Kennedy, who wanted the country to take a strong stand against communism, had permitted a group of Cuban exiles to attack Cuba.
5. Fidel Castro, who feared an American invasion, sought protection from the Soviet Union.
7. The Soviets secretly shipped missiles that could carry nuclear warheads to Cuba.
9. Although some generals suggested the United States launch a massive air strike, the president, who feared starting a nuclear war, ordered a blockade to stop Soviet ships from bringing weapons into Cuba.

Exercise 4

1. Louis Pasteur, a noted French chemist, first discovered antibiotics.
3. Around 1900 Rudolf von Emmerich, a German bacteriologist, isolated pyocyanase, which had the ability to kill cholera and diphtheria germs.
5. In the 1920s the British scientist Sir Alexander Fleming discovered lysozyme, a substance found in human tears that had powerful antibiotic properties.
7. In 1928 Fleming accidentally discovered penicillin, and he demonstrated its antibiotic properties in a series of experiments against a range of germs.
9. During World War II, two British scientists conducted further tests on penicillin, helping put Fleming's discovery to practical use.

Exercise 5

1. On May 28, 1934, at a farmhouse at Corbeil in northern Ontario, five identical baby girls were born to a French-Canadian couple, Oliva and Elzire Dionne.
3. They were the world's first quintuplets to survive, though they were tiny and very frail at first.

5. A special nursery complex was built for them, together with a public observation garden, for they became Canada's major tourist attraction.

7. At last in 1943, the girls were returned home, but they had difficulty adjusting to their new life and to their brothers and sisters. (There were twelve children in the family all told.)

9. According to a recent audit, Ontario netted $350 million in revenues related to the quintuplets, with the quints' share of the trust—once estimated at $15 million—being spent on the upkeep of Quintland, leaving the surviving sisters poverty stricken.

Exercise 6

```
     The suburbs exploded after World War II. In 1944
only 114,000 houses were built in America. By 1950
over 1,700,000 new houses were built. Veterans, most
of whom were eligible for low-interest loans through
the GI Bill, created a massive market for single-
family homes. Developers built neighbourhoods, subdi-
visions, and entire new communities. Orchards, farms,
wheat fields, orange groves, dairies, and forests
were bulldozed to build streets and houses. . . .
```

Exercise 7

1. plasma, Motrin, bandages, first-aid supplies, antibiotics   5

3. Cheryl, Dave Draper, Tony Prito, Tony's nephew, Mindy Weiss, Chris, Heather's best friend   7

5. a former prime minister, Stephen Lewis, a Supreme Court judge, Ed Mirvish, Lorne Michaels, David Miller   6

Exercise 8

1. The Marx brothers were born in New York City and were known by their stage names: Chico, born Leonard; Harpo, born Arthur; Groucho, born Julius; and Zeppo, born Herbert.

3. The brothers appeared on their own as the Four Nightingales; later, they changed the name of their act to simply the "Marx Brothers."

5. Their early films, including *Animal Crackers, Horse Feathers,* and *Duck Soup,* won praise from fans and critics.

7. The late 1930s was a period of continuing success for the Marx brothers; films such as *A Night at the Opera, A Day at the Races,* and *Room Service* became comedy classics.

9. Groucho smoked cigars, had a large false moustache, and made sarcastic jokes; Chico talked with an Italian accent and played the piano; Harpo never spoke, wore a trench coat, played the harp, and chased women.

CHAPTER 26

Exercise 1

1. a girl's car

3. Joy Fielding's short stories

5. the SIU's evidence

7. children's pictures

9. two men's boat

Exercise 2

1. you're

3. wouldn't

5. shouldn't

7. he'll

9. could've

Exercise 3

On December 17, 1917, the Halifax, Nova Scotia, harbour was very busy with troop and supply ships waiting to set sail during WWI. At 7:30 a.m. the *Mont Blanc*, one of France's ships, arrived at the harbour mouth, its cargo hold heavily loaded with 2,300 tons of picric acid, 200 tons of TNT, and many other highly volatile mixtures. A Norwegian ship, the *Imo*, moved at the same time as the *Mont Blanc*, and an error of judgment caused the *Imo* to strike the other ship's bow. The collision wasn't a major one; however, fire broke out immediately on the *Mont Blanc*. Everyone abandoned the ship, thinking that it would explode at any minute. It was almost twenty minutes before the explosion happened. Churches, houses, schools, factories, and ships in the explosion's path were destroyed. There were 1,900 dead, many bodies unidentified, and many survivors left completely blind. . . .

Exercise 4

1. Mayor Miller proclaimed during his speech, "I won't raise taxes."

3. George Orwell began his famous novel with the sentence, "It was a bright cold day in April and the clocks were striking thirteen."

5. Did you read Paul Mason's article "Coping with Depression"?

7. Last night as we watched the news, Arras stated, "This reminds me of the words of Pierre Elliott Trudeau, who said, 'The essential ingredient of politics is timing.'"

9. "I plan to retire after next season," Terry Wilson announced to her coach, noting, "NBC has offered me a job covering women's tennis."

Exercise 5

"You know," Wes said, "I really like our English class."

"I know," Zoe responded. "I really enjoy the stories we have been reading this semester. Which one is your favourite?"

"Let me think. I guess I really liked all the Poe stories," Wes said, tapping his book. "I really like

```
'The Pit and the Pendulum' and 'The Tell-Tale Heart.'
What about you? What is your favourite so far?" . . .
```

Exercise 6

1. The receipt is stamped Jan. 15, 10:05 a.m.
3. The school offers students three key services: tutoring, housing, and guidance.
5. Can you help me?
7. John Martin [no relation to the former prime minister] is running as an independent in the next election.
9. Ted and Nancy's car is the only one on the island.

Exercise 7

```
    The Group of Seven consisted of famous Canadian
artists. A. Y. Jackson, Fred Varley, Lawren Harris,
Franklin Carmichael, Frank Johnston, Arthur Lismer,
and J. E. H. MacDonald comprised the newly formed
group in May of 1920. Emily Carr, famous for her
paintings of forests and native villages, was never
officially one of the Group of Seven; however, they
were impressed by her work and included it in a coun-
trywide exhibition of their work in the later 1920s.
Emily Carr remained a recluse for the rest of her
life. Many of the works of these artists can be seen
at the McMichael Gallery in Kleinberg, Ontario.
```

CHAPTER 27

Exercise 1

1. Most cities in the world have emerged naturally, often growing up around a river, such as the Nile, the Rhine, or the Mississippi.
3. The coastal city of Rio de Janeiro served as Brazil's capital for generations.
5. As the economy expanded after WWII, government agencies and corporations needed more office space.
7. During the administration of President Juscelino Kubitschek, planning began on the new capital, to be called Brasilia.
9. The fuselage of the plane contains government offices, while apartment buildings form the plane's wings.
11. The famous architect Oscar Niemeyer designed Brasilia's major buildings.
13. On April 21, 1960, Brasilia was officially dedicated by the Brazilian government.
15. Highways and rail lines link Brasilia with Rio de Janeiro, São Paulo, and other major Brazilian cities.
17. Although the strikingly modern city was considered an architectural marvel, many federal employees did not appreciate the actions of President Kubitschek.
19. In the early years, the city was deserted on weekends as workers flew back to Rio to enjoy the old city's famous beaches and nightlife.

Exercise 2

1. The Aztecs took their name from Azatlan, a mythical homeland in northern Mexico.
3. Arriving late, the Aztecs were forced into the unoccupied marshes on the western side of Lake Texcoco.
5. Although poor and greatly outnumbered, the Aztecs gradually built a great empire.
7. Over the years, the Aztecs built bridges to connect their island city to surrounding dry land and drained marshes to create productive gardens.
9. From their small island, the Aztecs expanded their influence, conquering other peoples and creating an empire that reached the border of Guatemala.
11. They developed writing and created a calendar based on an earlier Mayan date-keeping system.
13. The Spanish explorer Hernan Cortés arrived in Tenochtitlan in 1519.
15. At first, the Aztec king Montezuma II welcomed Cortés, thinking him to be the god Quetzalcoatl.
17. Armed with superior weapons and aligning himself with rebellious tribes, Cortés was able to defeat Montezuma's army.
19. Today a million Aztecs, mostly poor farmers, live on the fringes of Mexico City.

Exercise 3

```
     Today we are accustomed to television networks
battling for ratings. During sweeps weeks, networks
broadcast their most popular or controversial pro-
grams. Networks have been known to wage intense bid-
ding wars to land a late-night TV host, news anchor,
or sitcom to secure larger audiences and higher
advertising revenue. In the early 1990s, NBC, for
example, hoped to keep both Letterman and Leno after
Johnny Carson retired from hosting the long-running
Tonight Show. After a number of meetings, Letterman
decided to move to CBS. . . .
```

CHAPTER 28

Exercise 1

1. yield
3. sincerely
5. library
7. equipment
9. surprise

Exercise 2

1. Its [It's] going to be difficult to except [accept] an out-of-state cheque.
3. My broker gave me advise [advice] about investing.
5. These medications may effect [affect] your ability to drive.
7. All my school cloths [clothes] are in the dryer.
9. Don't work to [too] hard.

Exercise 3

The Trans-Canada Highway is a federal-provincial highway system that joins all ten provinces of Canada. The system was approved by the Trans-Canada Highway Act of 1948, opened in 1962, and completed in 1965. The longest continuous stretch of highway in the Trans-Canada Highway system is recognized as the longest highway in the world, at 7,821 km, taking into account the distance travelled on ferries. The highway system is best known for its distinctive white-on-green maple leaf route markers.

Unlike the American Interstate highway system, not all of the Trans-Canada Highway uses limited-access freeways, or even four-lane roads, making it more similar to the U.S. highway system. Canada does not have a comprehensive national highway system, as decisions about highway and freeway construction are entirely under the jurisdiction of the individual provinces. In 2000 and 2001 the government of Jean Chrétien considered funding an infrastructure project to have the full Trans-Canada system converted to freeway. Although freeway construction funding was made available to some provinces for portions of the system, the government ultimately decided not to pursue a comprehensive highway conversion. . . .

Exercise 4

1. knives
3. deer
5. children
7. centuries
9. indexes (indices)

Exercise 5

1. The boys drove the new cars.
3. Oils taken from grain can provide useful medicines.
5. The foxes, wolves, and dogs have been vaccinated.

Exercise 6

1. The children loved the rodeos, the circuses, and the zoos.
3. My brothers-in-law must pay taxes in two states because their companies do business in both New York and New Jersey.
5. Two people lost their lives in the accident.

Exercise 7

1. drove
3. spoke
5. negotiated
7. washed
9. built

Exercise 8

1. We took the bus to school.
3. We met at the library.
5. They sang all night.

Exercise 9

1. likeable (likable)
3. respectfully
5. defiance
7. beginning
9. noticing

Exercise 10

Early on the morning of June 30, 1908, a strange light <u>filed</u> [filled] the sky over a remote part of Siberia. A streak of fire raced across the treetops and vanished <u>suddenlly</u> [suddenly] over the horizon, followed by a massive explosion. Seven hundred reindeer grazing in a clearing were <u>instantlly</u> [instantly] vaporized. Over 60 million trees were <u>flattend</u> [flattened] in a circle larger <u>then</u> [than] <u>halve</u> [half] of Prince Edward Island. A giant fireball rose into the sky, visible for hundreds of miles. Seismographs in America and Europe registered the impact of the blast. A <u>grate</u> [great] fire swept the region for weeks, burning over 700 <u>squre</u> [square] miles of forest. Thousands of tons of ash <u>boilled</u> [boiled] into the atmosphere, creating <u>wierd</u> [weird] sunsets seen all over the world.

Preoccupied by <u>revolutionarries</u> [revolutionaries] and a recent war with Japan, the Russian government did not bother <u>too</u> [to] investigate an event in an isolated part of its vast empire. In the late 1930s scientists photographed the region, still devastated from the blast. <u>Strangeley</u> [Strangely], no crater could be found. Whatever fell to earth, <u>weather</u> [whether] a comet or meteor, must have broken apart before impact. . . .

Exercise 11

Henry M. Robert is best remembered as the creator of *Robert's Rules of Order*. Almost every club, organization, and public meeting in the United States uses this nineteenth-century manual. Henry Robert was not a debater, politician, teacher, or attorney. He was an engineer working for the U.S. Army. Although his military duties carried him across the country on various construction projects, Robert was active in a number of organizations. He was once asked to head a meeting, but he became frustrated because he found few guidelines for conducting an orderly discussion.

Robert studied existing manuals, but he found them sketchy and incomplete. Robert began to set forth his own rules, and he started to write a book. In the winter of 1874 ice in Lake Michigan delayed scheduled construction, and Robert had ample time to work on his book. . . .

Credits

Photo Credits

3: Yuri Arcurs/Shutterstock; **9:** Marianne Venegoni/Shutterstock; **11:** Jeff Metzger/Shutterstock; **24:** Howard Sandler/Shutterstock; **29:** Michael G. Smith/Shutterstock; **43:** David MacFarlane/Shutterstock; **45:** Rommel/Masterfile; **59:** Lee Morris/Shutterstock; **61:** First Light: Kent Dannen/Photoresearchers; **76:** J. McPhail/Shutterstock; **77:** Stephen Rudolph/Shutterstock; **95:** Nir Levy/Shutterstock; **96:** PhotoCreate/Shutterstock; **107:** Photos.com; **109:** Cate Frost/Shutterstock; **125:** Karl Naundorf/Shutterstock; **127:** Anita Patterson Peppers/Shutterstock; **145:** First Light/digitalvision; **147:** Andres Rodriguez/Shutterstock; **159:** Phil Date/Shutterstock; **160:** Arrow Studio/Shutterstock; **168:** Karen Roach/Shutterstock; **170:** Yuri Arcurs/Shutterstock; **193:** Graham Prentice/Shutterstock; **197:** Photos.com; **210:** Rui Vale de Sousa/Shutterstock; **212:** Tan Kian Khoon/Shutterstock; **227:** Photos.com; **229:** Dimitrii Sherman/Shutterstock; **240:** Milos Luzanin/Shutterstock; **242:** TAOLMOR/Shutterstock; **258:** Microsoft clip art; **260:** Microsoft clip art; **274:** GeoM/Shutterstock; **276:** Kevin Britland/Shutterstock; **289:** First Light: Toronto Star/Rick Madonik; **291:** CP(Jonathan Hayward); **300:** CP(Frank Gunn); **305:** Kippy Lanker/Shutterstock; **318:** ChipPix/Shutterstock; **321:** PhotoCreate/Shutterstock; **337:** Gudelia Marmion/Shutterstock; **340:** Jacom Stephens/Shutterstock; **357:** Adam Tinney/Shutterstock; **359:** Eric Martinez/Shutterstock; **374:** Gilles DeCruyenaere/Shutterstock; **376:** BL Photo Corp/Shutterstock; **386:** Elena Elisseeva/Shutterstock; **391:** Karen Roach/Shutterstock; **407:** Marcin Balcerzak/Shutterstock; **411:** First Light: Toronto Star/Colin McConnell; **425:** First Light/Heritage Image Partnership; **428:** Tavrov Konstantin/Shutterstock; **436:** Phil Date/Shutterstock; **438:** Jason Stitt/Shutterstock; **454:** Marcin Balcerzak/Shutterstock; ***Working Together*** icon: ©Photodisc/Getty Images

Text Credits

34: "A Please for the Physical," by Kate Braid; **37:** "Yukon" from *Souvenir of Canada* by Douglas Coupland, © 2002. Published by Douglas & McIntyre Ltd. Reprinted by permission of the publisher; **37:** "Caught in the Net" excerpt, by Eva Tihanyi. Used with permission; **41:** Excerpt from "The Fender Bender" is reprinted with permission from the publisher of *Diary of an Undocumented Immigrant* by Ramón T. Pérez (Houston: Arte Público Press—University of Houston, 1991); **51:** "Growing up Native," by Carol Geddes. Used with permission; **53:** Montreal Symphony Orchestra, *Famous Musicians,* Canadian Portraits series, Louise G. McCready. Clarke Irwin, Toronto, 1971, p. 91; **54–55:** "The Law of the Curb: Garbage is, well, junk," by Matthew McClearn. *Canadian Business* magazine, January 31-February 13, 2005. Rogers Media; **68–70:** "Prospects grim for Davis Inlet's gas-sniffing children, residents say," by Michael MacDonald, January

Index

that, 314–315
that; who; which, 314–315
there; their; they're, 199, 444
Thesis, 16–17
they, 346–347
through; throughout, 382
"Tickets to Nowhere" (Rooney), 86
Tihanyi, Eva, "Caught in the Net," 37
"'Tis the Season to be Kissing" (Katz), 101
Titles of short works, 417
to; too; two, 199, 444
Topic development, 13–16
Topic sentence, 33–38
   developing, 35–36, 37–38
   identifying, 33–34
   improving, 47–48
   restating, 48
   when not needed, 36
   writing, 34–36
toward; towards, 382
Transitions/transitional expressions
   narration paragraph, 81–82
   persuasive paragraph, 149

Verb, 221, 321–339
   action, 221–222
   could have, 335
   double negative, 336
   helping, 222, 323
   irregular, 325–327
   lie; lay, 329–330
   linking, 222
   must have, 335
   phrasal, 223–224
   points to remember, 338–399
   regular, 325
   rise; raise, 330
   set; sit, 330
   shifts in tense, 331–332
   should have, 335
   strong/weak, 202
   subject, and. *See* Subject-verb agreement
   tense, 323–324
   voice, 333–335
   would have, 335
Verb tense, 323–324
Voice, 333–335

well; good, 367
which, 314–315
who, 314–315
who; which;, that, 314–315
"Who Uses Blogs?", (Coggins), 103
"Why We Crave Horror Movies" (King), 136
Word choice, 197–211
   appropriate words, 204–205
   clichés, 202–203
   concrete nouns, 202
   connotation, 207–208
   correct words, 199–200
   effective words, 202–203
   idioms, 206
   levels of diction, 204–205
   points to remember, 201, 211
   strong verbs, 202
Work, writing at. *See* Writing at work
"World View of the Computer Hacker, The" (Ritter), 34
would have, 335
Writing
   context, 6
   good, 5–6
   hints/tips, 8. *See also* Strategies
   importance, 4
   practice, 8, 10
   process. *See* Writing process
   questions to ask, 12
Writing at work, 170–194
   basic principles, 171
   cover letter, 188–191
   e-mail, 171–175. *See also* E-mail
   letter, 179–185. *See also* Letter
   memo, 175–178
   points to remember, 194
   résumé, 185–188
Writing process, 11–25
   cool (put your work aside), 19
   editing, 21
   first draft, 19
   planning, 16–18
   prewriting, 13–16
   revising, 19–20
   steps in process, 12
   write, 19

"Yukon, The" (Coupland), 37